After many years leading tourist groups all over the world, from Albania to Zimbabwe, **Christopher Knowles** is now a full-time writer.

His first introduction to Italy was in Genoa where he taught English and learned the language. He went on to take a degree in Italian at University College, London, during which time he spent a year in Rome. Since then he has returned to Italy as often as practicable.

This is his third book, following *Shanghai Rediscovered* and a guidebook on *Moscow and St Petersburg*. He is now working on a book in Istanbul.

Dedication

To my mother

Acknowledgements

The Italian State Tourist Office, London; Sig. Lando Gonnelli of the Associazione Provinciale di Turismo in Florence; to Marcella Randall for friendly and helpful editing; to Roger and Heidi Lascelles for their hospitality; to Paula Thompson for coming on holiday with us; to Ann Frost for her help in any number of ways; and to my son Daniel who insisted with reckless frequency that I abandon this book to play with him

Front Cover: *The Cathedral (Duomo), with Brunelleschi's dome and Giotto's campanile, dominating Florence's skyline.*

Lascelles City Guides

FLORENCE AND TUSCANY

Christopher Knowles

Roger Lascelles, Cartographic and Travel Publisher
47 York Road, Brentford, (Middx) TW8 0QP. Tel: 081 847 0935 Fax: 081 568 3886

Publication Data

Title	Florence and Tuscany
Photographs	By the Author
Maps	By kind courtesy of Litografia Artistica Cartografica, (LAC), Florence.
Printing	Phototypeset in Times and printed by Kelso Graphics, Kelso, Scotland
ISBN	1 872815 23 5
Edition	First November 1992
Publisher	Roger Lascelles
	47 York Road, Brentford, Middlesex, TW8 0QP
Copyright	Christopher Knowles

Distribution

Africa:	South Africa	Faradawn, Box 17161, Hillbrow 2038
Americas:	Canada	International Travel Maps & Books, P.O. Box 2290, Vancouver BC V6B 3W5.
	U.S.A.	Available through major booksellers with good foreign travel sections
Asia:	India	English Book Store, 17-L Connaught Circus,P.O. Box 328, New Delhi 110 001
Australasia:	Australia	Rex Publications, 15 Huntingdon Street, Crows Nest, N.S.W.
Europe:	Belgium	Brussels – Peuples et Continents
	Germany	Available through major booksellers with good foreign travel sections
	GB/Ireland	Available through all booksellers with good foreign travel sections.
	Italy	Libreria dell'Automobile, Milano
	Netherlands	Nilsson & Lamm BV, Weesp
	Denmark	Copenhagen – Arnold Busck, G.E.C. Gad, Boghallen
	Finland	Helsinki – Akateeminen Kirjakauppa
	Norway	Oslo – Arne Gimnes/J.G. Tanum
	Sweden	Stockholm/Esselte, Akademi Bokhandel, Fritzes, Hedengrens.Gothenburg/Gumperts, Esselte. Lund/Gleerupska
	Switzerland	Basel/Bider: Berne/Atlas; Geneve/Artou; Lausanne/Artou: Zurich/Travel Bookshop

Contents

Part III: Background

Part IV: Sightseeing in Florence

Part V: Sightseeing beyond Florence

17 Northern Tuscany

18 To the West of Florence

19 Southern Tuscany and the Coast

ONE

Planning Your Trip

Independent travel

You are recommended to travel to Italy under your own steam if feasible – it is my opinion that individual travel is in general more satisfying. Ignorance of the language is not really a major handicap. Certainly, life is easier when you know something of the language and few Italians speak much English (although more than English who speak Italian). But Italians are enormously friendly – they will encourage you if you are trying to speak Italian and will do their utmost to help if you are not. Of course many aspects of life are different in Italy (otherwise this book would in some respects be redundant) but not impossibly different. If you are patient and do not panic at moments of incomprehension, you will not find a visit to Italy very difficult. Women travelling alone may have to learn to develop ways of deflecting unwelcome attention but the bark of the average Italian male, though insistent, is worse than his bite. More information is given under 'Getting there' about train, plane and car travel to Italy.

Of course, for those who wish or who find it easier, there are plenty of companies offering packages of all types and some are listed here.

Tour operators offering inclusive air holidays

Abercrombie and Kent, Sloane Square House, Holbein Place, London SW1. Tel: 071-730 9600

Amathus, 51 Tottenhan Court Road, London W1. Tel: 071-636 9873

Arena, Hamilton House, Cambridge Road, Felixtowe, Suffolk. Tel: 0394 273262

British Airways Leisure, Atlantic House, Hazelwick Avenue, Three Bridges, Crawley, West Sussex. Tel: 0533 461000

Introduction

Tuscany has everything. Mountains, sea, sunshine, courteous people, excellent food, exquisite and varied countryside, unspoilt medieval towns and a sense of history and culture unmatched almost anywhere in the world. It is not possible to suffer from boredom, unless it be through an excess of good things; for although there is undoubtedly a tendency to associate Tuscany only with art, it is more than possible to have a memorable holiday there without entering a single museum.

One of Tuscany's most winning virtues is that the past and present blend in a generally unselfconscious manner and are simply a part of everyday life. Yet a knowledge of the history of the area is vital to appreciate the whys and wherefores of its extraordinary beauty; and more so if your intention is to do more than idle away the days in restful contemplation. It is therefore worthwhile to read the reasonably extensive history section of this book.

The history section, it is true, concentrates on Florence which is to be expected. Tuscany, in the centuries of her greatest influence, depended much upon Florence; and when she did not, then the history of Florence is typical of the rest of the region. Where there are omissions in the history section, the author has tried to make up for it in the course of the book.

Tuscany is not merely about the past. Italy is a prosperous, sophisticated country, rich in the comforts and conveniences offered by modern life. Where she differs is that she has not allowed modern life to take over; time passes slowly, the midday siesta remains important, people prefer, in general, to prepare food with fresh ingredients. Despite the mercurial character of Italians, life is tranquil.

Caprice, Market Place Chambers, 1 Market Place, Stevenage, Herts..
Tel: 0438 316622

Citalia, Marco Polo House, 3-5 Lansdowne Road, Croydon, Surrey.
Tel: 081-686 0677

Club Mediterranee, 106-108 Brompton Road, London SW3. Tel:
071- 581 1161

Cosmos, Tourama House, 17 Homesdale Road, Bromley, Kent. Tel:
081-464 3444

Cresta, Cresta House, Victoria Street, Altrincham, Cheshire. Tel:
0345 056511

Edwards and Hargreaves, 10 The Square, Market Harborough,
Leicestershire. Tel: 0858 32123

Enterprise Holidays, Groundstar House, London Road, Crawley,
W. Sussex. Tel: 0293 519151

Enterprise Travel, PO Box 1, Bradford, W. Yorks.. Tel: 0274 488116

Hamilton, 3 Heddon Street, London W1. Tel: 071-437 4627

Hayes and Jarvis, 152 King Street, London W6. Tel: 071-748 5050

Italian Escapades, 227 Shepherds Bush Road, London W6. Tel:
081-748 2661

Italian Interlude, 91 Regent Street, London W1. Tel: 071-494 2031

Italian Options, 26 Tottenham Street, London W1. Tel: 071-631 4632

Italiatour, 241 Euston Road, London NW1. Tel: 071-383 3886

Italviaggi, High Street, Gillingham, Dorset. Tel: 0747 825353

Kirker, 3 New Concordia Wharf, Mill Street, London SE1. Tel:
071-231 3333

Magic of Italy, 227 Shepherds Bush Road, London W6. Tel:
081-748 7575

Martin Rooks, Groundstar House, London Road, Crawley,
W. Sussex. Tel: 0293 560777

Mays A. T., 21 Royal Crescent, Glasgow. Tel: 041-331 1121

Osprey, 110a StreetStephen Street, Edinburgh. Tel: 031-226 2467

Page and Moy, 136-140 London Road, Leicester. Tel: 0533 552521

Quo Vadis, 243 Euston Road, London NW1. Tel: 071-387 6122

Saga, The Saga Building, Middelburg Square, Folkestone, Kent. Tel:
0303 47000.

Schools Travel Service, 24 Cullodon Road, Enfield, Middx.. Tel:
081-367 9090

Sunvil, Sunvil House, 7/8 Upper Square, Old Isleworth, Middx.. Tel:
081-568 4499.

Taber, 126 Sunbridge Road, Bradford, W. Yorks.. Tel: 0274 735611

Thomson, Greater London House, Hampstead Road, London NW1.
Tel: 071-387 8484

Time Off, Chester Close, Chester Street, London SW1.
Tel: 071- 235 8070.
Travelscene, Travelscene House, 11-15 St. Ann's Road, Harrow,
Middx.. Tel: 081-427 4445
Ultimate, 3rd Floor, Redstone House, Crown Gate, Harlow, Essex.
Tel: 0279 454478
Weekender, 35 Eyre Street Hill, London EC1. Tel: 071-278 5319.

All the major **coach tour operators** (Angela, Chequers, Contiki,
Continental, Crusader, Cotswold, Da, Epsom, Eurobout, Excelsior,
Facet, Frames, Highways, Insight, Land, Leger, Link Up, Mancunia,
Piero, Robinson, Shearings, Success, Thomas Cook, Titan, Top
Deck, Trafalgar, Wallace Arnold, Wrysdale and others mentioned
above) sell tours to Italy which include Tuscany.

Special interest holidays

Companies specialising in art, history, food and wine

Art in Europe, Ladywell Cottage, Wilcote Lane, Ramsden, Oxon..
Tel: 0993 868864
British Museum Tours, 46 Bloomsbury Street, London WC1. Tel:
071-323 8895
C.H.A. – see 'Adventure, Walking' below.
Citalia – see 'Inclusive air holidays'
Inter-Church, PO Box 58, Folkestone, Kent. Tel: 0800 300444
Italian House Parties, 10 St. Marks Crescent, London NW1. Tel:
071-267 2423
Italiatour, see 'Inclusive air holidays'
Nadfas, Hermes House, 80-98 Beckenham Road, Beckenham, Kent.
Tel: 081-658 2308
Prospect, 454-458 Chiswick High Road, London W4. Tel:
081-742 2323
Quest, Oliver House, 18 Marine Parade, Brighton, Sussex.
Tel: 0273 606688
Quo Vadis, see 'Inclusive air holidays'
Renaissance, The Saga Building, Middelburg Square, Folkestone,
Kent. Tel: 0303 857931
Serenissima, 21 Dorset Square, London NW1. Tel: 071-723 6556
Sunvil, see 'Inclusive air holidays'
Schools Journey Association, 48 Cavendish Road, London SW12.
Tel: 081-673 4849

Swan Hellenic, 77 New Oxford Street, London WC1. Tel:
071-831 1616

The Plantagenet Tours, 85 The Grove, Moordown, Bournemouth,
Dorset. Tel: 0202 521895

Voyages Jules Verne, 21 Dorset Square, London NW1. Tel:
071- 730 9841

World Wine Tours, 4 Dorcester Road, Drayton St. Leonard, Oxon..
Tel: 0865 891919.

Adventure and walking holidays

Walking holidays, with the problems of luggage transportation and
hotel bookings taken out of your hands, are a splendid way of getting
to know a small area well.

Alternative Travel Group, 1-3 George Street, Oxford. Tel:
0865 251195

C.H.A., Birch Heys, Cromwell Range, Manchester. Tel:
061 224 2855

Explore, 1 Frederick Street, Aldershot, Hants.. Tel: 0252 319448

Ramblers, Box 43, Welwyn Garden City, Herts.. Tel: 0707 331133

Renaissance, see 'Art tours'

Sherpa, 131a Heston Road, Hounslow, Middx.. Tel: 081-577 2717

Waymark, 44 Windsor Road, Slough, Middx.. Tel: 0753 516477.

Cycling

Fresco, 3 Woodberry Crescent, London N10. Tel: 081-365 2870.

Self-catering

In many ways this is one of the best ways of enjoying a holiday in
Tuscany. Some companies offer flats in the centre of towns such as
Florence – but in general the houses and villas are in the countryside
which means you will need a car unless you are after rural peace in
one spot only.

The author has personal experience of one only (Tuscany – from
Cottages to Castles) who provided an excellent service, but there are
many others in the same field.

Eurovillas, 36 East Street, Coggeshall, Essex. Tel: 0376 561156

Hoseasons, Sunway House, Lowestoft, Suffolk. Tel: 0502 500555

Lunigiana, 71 Bushridge Lane, Godalming, Surrey. Tel:
04868 21218

Magic of Italy, see 'Inclusive air holidays'

Sojourn in Italia, 30 Chestnut Avenue, Staplehurst, Kent. Tel: 0580 893578

Solemar/Continental Villas, 3 Caxton Walk, Phoenix Street, London WC2H 8PW. Tel: 071-497 0444

Tuscany – from Cottages to Castles, Tuscany House, 351 Tonbridge Road, Maidstone, Kent. Tel: 0622 726883.

Vacanze in Italia, Bignor, Nr. Pulborough, W. Sussex. Tel: 07987 426

Villas Italia, Hillgate House, 13 Hillgate Street, London W8. Tel: 071-221 4432.

Newspapers and periodicals (eg, the *Spectator*) are often filled with private offers for villas in Tuscany.

Pilgrimages

Inter-Church, see 'Art tours'

Leahys, 116 Harpenden Road, St. Albans, Herts. Tel: 0727 52394

Orientours, Kent House, 87 Regent Street, London W1. Tel: 071- 434 1551.

Special events

For the Torre del Lago, Maggio Musicale:

Blair, 117 Regents Park Road, London NW1. Tel: 071-483 2297

Henebery, Kareol, Islip, Oxon.. Tel: 08675 6341

JMB, Rushwick, Worcester. Tel: 0905 425628

Lirica, 9 Burgess Road, Sutton, Surrey. Tel: 0273 304910.

For the Siena Palio:

Airtrack, 5 Lees Parade, Uxbridge Road, Hillingdon, Uxbridge. Tel: 0895 70921.

Passports and visas

Citizens of Ireland, the UK, the USA, Canada, Australia, New Zealand and holders of a British passport whose national status is specified as 'British Subject and Citizen of the United Kingdom and Colonies' do not require visas for a stay of up to three months but must be in possession of a valid passport (or 'Visitors Passport'). Any uncertainty may be reassured by application to the Italian Consulate in the following cities:

London – 38 Eaton Place, London SW1. Tel: 071-259 6322/ 071-235 9371.

Manchester – 111 Piccadilly
Bedford – 23 Allhallows
Edinburgh – 6 Melville Crescent
Belfast – 2 Kincraig Park, Newtownabbey BT36 7QA. Tel: 232-778353
Dublin – 63 Northumberland Road, Dublin 4. Tel: 601744
Canberra – 12 Grey Street, Deakin, ACT 2000. Tel: 6-733333
Melbourne – 34 Anderson Street, South Yarra, VIC 3141. Tel: 3-2675744
Sydney – 100 William Street, NSW 2000 (PO Box 295). Tel: 2-3582955
Wellington – 34 Grant Road. Tel: 4-736667
Hong Kong – 801 Hutchison House, 10 Harcourt Road. Tel: 5-220033
Johannesburg – 196, Louis Botha Avenue, Houghton Estate. Tel: 728 1309
Ottawa – 275 Slater Street. Tel: 613-232 2401
Montreal – 3489 Drummond Street. Tel: 514-849 8351
Toronto – 136 Beverly Street. Tel: 416-977 1566
Vancouver – Suite 505-1200, Burrard Street. Tel: 604-684 7288
Boston – 101 Tremont Street, MA 02108. Tel: 617-542 0483
New York – 690 Park Avenue, NY 10021. Tel: 212-737 9100
Los Angeles – 11661 San Vicente Blvd., Suite 911, CA 90049. Tel: 213-826 5998
San Francisco - 2590 Webster Street, CA 94115. Tel: 415-931 4929.

Visitors wishing to stay longer than three months are supposed either to obtain a visa before leaving or, in Italy, to apply to a 'questura' (police headquarters) for a 'Permesso di Soggiorno' for which you will have to demonstrate your economic independence.

Other useful addresses

The **Italian State Tourist Office,** 1 Princes Street, London W1. Tel: 071-408 1254. Fax: 071-493 6695. The staff here are very helpful and friendly. There are, however, sometimes difficulties in obtaining pertinent leaflets and brochures. In that case you may either contact the various provincial tourist offices directly in Tuscany (see relevant sections for addresses) or wait until you arrive when you will be able to obtain all the literature you desire.

The Italian Institute, 39 Belgrave Square, London SW1X 8NX. Tel: 071-235 1461

The Italian Chamber of Commerce for Great Britain, 296 Regent Street, London W1. Tel: 071-637 3153

Italian Trade Centre, 37 Sackville Street, London W1. Tel: 071-734 2412

British Italian Society, 24 Rutland Gate, London SW7. Tel: 071-823 9204

Banca d'Italia, 39 King Street, London EC2. Tel: 071-606 4201.

Customs regulations

Duty-free allowances for UK citizens going to or returning from Italy:

Goods obtained in the EC – 300 cigarettes or 150 cigarillos, 75 cigars or 400 grams of tobacco. Alcohol over 22% volume – 1¹/₂ litres. Less than 22% volume – 3 litres. Fortified, sparkling or table wines – 4 litres. Perfume: 75g, 3 fl.oz., 90cc. Other goods – £250. The corresponding quantities for goods bought outside the EC are: 200 cigarettes, 100 cigarillos, 50 cigars, 250 grams tobacco. 1 litre, 2 litres, 2 litres. 50g, 2 fl.oz., 60cc, £32.

There is no limit for items of personal use.

Health and vaccinations

Citizens of the above countries do not need any vaccinations, although it is never a bad idea to be innoculated against tetanus. Italy is no dirtier than Britain – in many ways it is cleaner – but summer heat can be intense and you must be prepared for it. Save yourself expense and trouble by taking a hat, suncream, insect repellant, electrolite powders (against dehydration which is one of the main causes of diarrhoea), tablets for diarrhoea, and a water bottle. Natural fibre clothes are far more comfortable in the heat. Sandals are cool but not comfortable for much walking.

Minor ailments may be treated free of charge in an ambulatorio (clinic or surgery) or at the pronto soccorso (casualty) division of a hospital. Citizens of EC countries have the right to claim the health service available to Italians but must be in possession of a Form E111 available before you leave home from the Department of Health and Social Security. Citizens of other countries will find that private medicine is good but quite expensive. In any case it is as well to check your insurance policy to see what it covers.

Italian pharmacists are usually sufficiently educated and qualified to diagnose a problem or decide whether further treatment is required. In towns of any size there is nearly always one chemist (Farmacia) open at night or on a Sunday. All chemists display a list of them. You will find that it is possible to buy many medicines across the counter in Italy that would require a prescription at home.

Emergencies: dial 113 for all services (police = polizia, ambulance = ambulanza, fire brigade = vigili del fuoco). English-speaking doctors may be discovered on application to the nearest consulate.

Water

Italians tend to drink mineral water, which is readily available everywhere. Nonetheless, tap water is generally drinkable. If you wish to check ask, 'L'aqua e potabile?' Fruit will not suffer from being thoroughly washed before eating.

Climate and when to go

Overall, the climate of Tuscany may be considered mild. However, in some respects this description gives a false impression because summers are generally very hot and winters can be cold. The best seasons for a visit are late spring to June and late summer/early autumn to the end of September when the temperature is comfortable and the light clear. Early October is chancy but can be rewarding. July and August are particularly hot and when Italians themselves take their holidays which means that the cities lose their animation. In winter you can ski, visit museums in comfort and walk the streets with little trouble. In late April and May the countryside is covered with flowers.

A temperatature and rainfall chart for Florence, Viareggio and some other towns of Italy is included on the next page.

Annual holidays, festivities and cultural events

It is as well to take these into consideration, either because you may wish to be there for them or avoid them. Remember that many shops close altogether for part or for the whole of August. National

Temperature tables

		JAN.	FEB.	MAR.	APR.	MAY.	JUN.	JUL.	AUG.	SEP.	OCT.	NOV.	DEC.
FLORENCE	AV. TEMP F.	42	43	50	56	63	71	77	77	70	61	52	43
	AV. TEMP C.	5.6	5.8	9.9	13.3	17.4	22.1	25	24.8	21.2	15.8	11.2	6.0
	RAINFALL MM.	61	68	65	74	62	49	23	38	54	96	107	72
VIAREGGIO	AV. TEMP F.	48	49	50	56	62	69	73	72	70	62	54	48
	AV. TEMP C.	9.1	9.4	10.3	13.4	17.1	20.5	23.1	22.8	21.2	16.8	12.5	9.1
	RAINFALL MM.	96	96	87	90	86	32	20	28	70	84	125	92
BOLOGNA	AV. TEMP F.	36	38	47	57	64	73	79	78	70	59	49	39
	AV. TEMP C.	2.5	3.4	8.6	13.8	18.1	23.3	26	25.4	21.3	15.2	9.7	3.9
	RAINFALL MM.	44	52	48	57	40	35	18	22	61	47	67	61
CAGLIARI	AV. TEMP F.	50	51	55	60	65	73	79	78	73	67	60	53
	AV. TEMP C.	9.9	10.3	12.9	15.3	18.6	22.8	25.8	25.7	23.3	19.5	15.6	11.8
	RAINFALL MM.	54	59	50	43	39	5	3	10	32	53	57	74
GENOA	AV. TEMP F.	47	47	53	58	64	71	76	77	70	64	55	49
	AV. TEMP C.	8.4	8.7	11.5	14.5	17.8	21.9	24.6	25.0	21.8	18.1	13.3	9.5
	RAINFALL MM.	109	105	101	82	61	42	35	62	63	135	206	112
MILAN	AV. TEMP F.	35	39	47	55	62	71	77	75	68	56	47	37
	AV. TEMP C.	1.9	3.8	8.6	13.2	17.3	22.2	24.8	23.9	20.3	13.7	8.5	3.0
	RAINFALL MM.	62	54	72	82	70	68	47	57	66	75	90	71
NAPLES	AV. TEMP F.	47	47	53	57	64	71	77	77	71	64	58	50
	AV. TEMP C.	8.7	8.7	11.4	14.3	18	22.3	24.8	24.8	22.3	18.1	14.5	10.3
	RAINFALL MM.	87	77	76	55	37	33	14	16	56	102	135	105
PALERMO	AV. TEMP F.	50	51	55	61	65	73	77	77	73	68	62	54
	AV. TEMP C.	10.3	10.4	13	16.2	18.7	23	25.3	25.1	23.2	19.9	16.8	12.6
	RAINFALL MM.	141	129	89	65	32	16	6	29	54	123	99	179
ROME	AV. TEMP F.	45	46	52	58	65	73	78	78	72	63	56	48
	AV. TEMP C.	7.4	8	11.5	14.4	18.4	22.9	25.7	25.5	22.4	17.7	13.4	8.9
	RAINFALL MM.	74	87	79	62	57	38	6	23	66	123	121	92
VENICE	AV. TEMP F.	38	39	46	54	62	70	74	73	69	59	51	41
	AV. TEMP C.	3.8	4.1	8.2	12.6	17.1	21.2	23.6	23.3	20.4	15.1	10.5	5.0
	RAINFALL MM.	58	39	74	77	72	73	37	48	71	66	75	54

holidays, during which you may expect to find everything closed and public transport at best limited and very crowded, are:

Jan	01	(New Year's Day or Capodanno)
Jan	06	(Epiphany or La Beffana)
Easter Monday		(Pasqua)
Apr	25	(Liberation Day or Festa della Liberazione)
May	01	(Labour Day or Festa di Lavoro)
Aug	15	(Assumption of the Blessed Virgin Mary or Ferragosto)
Nov	01	(All Saints or Ognissanti)
Dec	08	(Immaculate Conception of the Blessed Virgin Mary or Concezione Immacolata)
Dec	25, 26	(Christmas Day or Natale, Boxing Day or San Stefano).

Festivals have for long been part of Tuscan life and are a reflection of the exuberant Italian nature. In the Florence of Lorenzo il Magnifico, due to certain guild-backed statutes, there were only 275 working days a year, and festivities were commomplace – dances in the Mercato Vecchio, mock battles in the Piazza Santa Croce. During Calendimaggio (May Day) young swains rose early to place flowering shrubs decorated with ribbon and sugared nuts on the doors of their sweethearts who would dance in Piazza Santa Trinita to the music of lutes. On St. John the Baptist day riderless horses raced from Porta al Prato, along Via della Vigna, through the Mercato Vecchio to Porta alla Croce. Life was hard but not that hard.

Many towns and villages have wine (vino) festivals at the end of September or during the first week of October; or sometimes at other times. Every village, commune and town has a variety of festivals throughout the year, either religious, historical, commercial or in celebration of harvests (raccolto or, for wine, vendemmia). Several words are used in connection with them – mostra, sagra, festa, fiera and mercato.

A 'mostra' indicates a fair designed to promote something new; a 'sagra' is used in connection usually with food and wine; a 'festa' is a general word for a celebration of one sort or another; a 'fiera' is a fair that is commercial in some way; 'mercato' is a market. Of course these definitions can overlap. Something is bound to be happening somewhere – ask at an information office to see a booklet called 'Sagre e Fiere Ambulanti della Toscana' published by the Giunta Regionale Toscana.

Look out for celebrations of strawberries (fragole) in May; of cherries (ciliegi) in June; of peaches (pesca); of grapes (uva) in September; of chestnuts (castagne) in October; fried potatoes (patate fritte), maccheroni; cucumber (cocomero), crostino, bruschetta, ice cream (gelato), chocolate (cioccolato), fig (fico), hazel-nuts (nocciola) in March/April, plums (prugnolo) in May, olive oil (olio d'ulivo), cinghiale (boar), snail (lumaca), beer (birra) in August, fish (pesce), artichokes (carciofo), pine nuts (pinolo), antiques (antiquario), and so on.

Furthermore, all towns have weekly markets (mercati ambulanti) selling fresh produce, clothes and crafts. These are an attraction in themselves and a source of good food at good prices, particularly for picnics or self-catering. A comprehensive list of these markets is given under 'Shopping'.

Other holidays and celebrations peculiar to towns in Tuscany, which may well involve closure of shops as well as public festivities are:

Arezzo: 15-30 August – choir competition; first Sunday in September - Saracen Joust.

Cerreto Guidi, near Empoli: first Sunday in September - Palio dei Cerri.

Florence and locale: the Scoppio del Carro (Expulsion of the Cart) on Easter Day; Festa di San Giovanni on 24 June; exhibition of craft work in Fortezza da Basso, flower show in the Piazza della Signoria in April and May; Festa del Grillo ('cricket') in Casine Park on Ascension Day; from May to July there is the Maggio Musicale Fiorentino; from June to September there is the summer festival in Fiesole; 24 June (S. Giovanni, patron saint of Florence) there is in Florence the game of Calcio Storico Fiorentino; 7 September, the Rificolona; 28 September, the bird market in Porta Romana; September to October (biannually in odd-numbered years) in Palazzo Strozzi is the Antiques Show; winter Opera season. Also Amici della Musica in winter.

Grassina, near Florence: Good Friday candlelight procession.

Siena: San Giuseppe (19 March); the Palio (2 July and 16 August); August music festival; 22 November – Musical festival of Santa Cecilia; 13 December – pottery fair of Santa Lucia.

Lucca: second Sunday after Easter in Querceta (near Lucca) – Donkey Palio (also in early June); 10 April – Liberty Festival; April/ June – sacred music festival in the town churches; early June in Camaiore – procession; 1 July in Querceta – Versilian celebration

The distinctive medieval skyline of San Gimignano.

with flag throwing; 1-15 July in Camaiore – opera season; third Sunday in July – festa of San Paolino with parade and crossbow joust; July to August in Barga (province of Lucca) is the Opera Barga; in August in Torre del Lago Puccini (province of Lucca) – festival of Puccini operas in open-air theatre; 13 September – Luminaria di Santa Croce on eve of the Holy Cross with illuminated buildings and torchlight procession.

Bagni di Lucca: 8 December – Festa of the Immaculate Conception.

Bibbiena: last day of Carnevale with dance and bonfire.

Camporgiano, near Lucca: 24 December – bonfire.

Carmignano, near Poggio a Caino: third Sunday in September – donkey palio.

Elba (Le Ghiaie): last week in July – wine festival.

Fivizzano (Massa): second Sunday in July – archery contest

Greve: second Sunday in September – festival of food and dance.

Impruneta: third Sunday in September – wine festival.

Livorno: 17 August – Palio Marinaro, boat races.

Massa Marittima: third week of May – Parade and Crossbow tournament; second Sunday in August – crossbow joust

Montecatini Terme: First Sunday of June - bruschetta (garlic toast) festival.

Montepulciano: second Sunday in August – Bruscello festival of food and wine.

Pietrasanta: June – concerts in the town's churches, 'Estate Musicale Pietrasantese'.

Marina di Pietrasanta: July to mid-August – Drama and Ballet in open-air theatre.

Pistoia: 25 July – Joust of the Bear, medieval tournament

Porto San Stefano: second Sunday in August – regatta.

Prato: Easter Day and 25-26 December, the showing of Mary's girdle from Donatello's pulpit.

San Donato in Poggio: last Sunday in June – La Bruscellata dance and song festival.

San Gimignano: July and August – cultural festival.

In **San Miniato** (near Empoli): first Sunday after Easter, kite Festival.

San Polo in Robbiana: May – Iris festival.

San Quirico d'Orcia (not far from Pienza): 18 June – Festa del Barbarossa in which meeting of Pope and the Holy Roman Emperor is honoured with archery, dance and feasting.

Viareggio: February – Carnevale

Arezzo: first Sunday of September - Giostra del Saracino.

Sansepolcro (province of Arezzo): second Sunday of September – Palio Balestrieri, crossbow contest between Sansepolcro and Gubbio.

Pisa: 16/17 June – San Ranieri, illumination of buildings and historical regatta; 25 June – Gioco del Ponte (Bridge Game), a tug of war; first weekend of August – festa di San Sisto; every four years Pisa hosts the maritime states celebration (the maritime states being Pisa, Amalfi, Genoa and Venice).

Time

Italian Summer Time starts from the last weekend of March until the final weekend of September. In general it is one hour behind Britain.

TWO

Travel and Preparation

Getting there

By aeroplane

The principal airport for Tuscany is that of Pisa to which there are a number of scheduled flights available with British Airways, Alitalia and other airlines as well as an array of charter flights. Florence does have its own airport – currently comparatively little used – and efforts are being made to increase its appeal. A new airline, Meridiana, offers flights to Florence.

Pisa airport is well located for visiting much of Tuscany but it is small and sometimes chaotic (see 'Arrival and Departure'). It may sometimes be worthwhile to think of flights to Milan, Genoa, Bologna or Rome which are not far from the motorway system and which may be convenient for certain parts of Tuscany (although Milan is subject to delays in winter because of fog). In general charter flights are cheaper than scheduled flights and many are now very good; but they are more often subject to delay than scheduled flights – sometimes it is worth paying more to avoid hassle and to give yourself more flexibility. Furthermore, some airlines have arrangements with car hire companies that may include reduced prices. Bargains are sometimes possible by booking long in advance or at the last minute. There is no reduction for children on APEX fares.

Luggage allowance: 44lb (20kg) in economy class and 66lb (30kg) in first. Flying time is about 90 to 100 minutes.

Florence is 40 miles (64kms) from Pisa airport.

By train

It is possible to go by train to Florence from London, Victoria and will take just over 24 hours. It is not necessary to change trains once you board a train on the Continent; from 1993 it may well be possible to travel directly from London via the Channel Tunnel. Tickets issued by British Rail are valid for two months. Don't forget that concessionary cards are available to people under 26 and over 60 (women) and 65 (men) and may be used on Italian railways. Children under four years travel free in Italy; between four and 12 they pay only 50 per cent.

Travellers under 26 may also buy discount tickets from Eurotrain (on 071-730 3402) or from their kiosk at Victoria Station.

Tickets for travel in Italy may be bought in advance from:

Italian State Railways, CIT, Marco Polo House, 3-5 Lansdowne Road, Croydon, Surrey. Tel: 081-686 0677

Ultima Travel, 424 Chester Road, Little Sutton, South Wirral L66 3RB. Tel: 051-3396171

Wasteels Travel, 121 Wilton Road, London SW1. Tel: 071-834 7066.

For passengers travelling extensively on Italian railways it is possible to buy a discounted ticket in advance that will allow unlimited travel on any train over a certain period of time. These are worthwhile only if you plan to use Italian trains a great deal since domestic train fares are already low. They may be bought at the above addresses or at the main stations in Italy (Florence, Santa Maria Novella). Similar tickets (Inter-Rail or EurRail) can be bought for travel throughout Europe.

It is essential to make bookings for seats/sleepers on international journeys well in advance. Second class sleepers on international trains are for three people (sometimes two); first class for one or two people. Couchettes (seats turned into couches at night, four people in first, six in second) are sometimes available.

There will be a restaurant car on most services or some form of snack available (from the platform if not on the train); it is sensible to bring a supply of food however, because restaurant cars can be expensive or crowded.

By coach
The cheapest way but also the most uncomfortable. Services run between London Victoria (Tel: 071-730 0202) and Florence (arriving at Via Santa Caterina da Siena).

By car and motorbike
There is a lot to be said for taking your car if you have the time (you will need to allow 30 hours of non-stop driving from London to Florence). Firstly, you have mobility and secondly you avoid car hire

about which you need to be careful (see 'Arrival and Departure'). Driving in Italy is not as difficult as you might think – it is true that Italians drive fast but generally speaking they drive very well and since many towns do not allow cars in the town centre the problem of parking is made generally easier. Furthermore, the Italian/Tuscan countryside is extremely beautiful.

Foreign registered cars are entitled to a 15 per cent discount on supergrade petrol and a reduction on motorway toll prices. Coupons are available in advance from Wasteels Travel at 121 Wilton Road, London SW1 (Tel: 071-834 7066), from the AA, the RAC and from the Italian Automobile Club (ACI) at frontier posts. You will also be given a Carta Carburante (Fuel Card) which entitles you to a free breakdown service by the ACI. These coupons are available on personal application by the driver with passport and vehicle registration document. Unused coupons may be refunded from the issuing office. Petrol coupons are available for car-hire vehicles only at Milan Linate and Rome Fiumicino airports.

Make sure you are correctly insured and that you have a green card and that you obtain a translation of your driving license from CIT, Wasteel, ACI, frontier posts or your home information centre. Make sure you are in possession of all your car documents.

There are a few car transporter trains to Italy but this may be expensive – check with British Rail or Italian Railways (address above).

Your route to Italy is a personal matter and you are advised to consult the AA or RAC or equivalent for the most recent information about road conditions and general recommendations. Obviously motorways are faster but in France and Italy involve tolls. Whatever you do you must cross the Alps (unless you follow the south coast of France). The passes are open in the summer, offer beautiful if winding driving and are free. The tunnels (San Bernardino, Mont Blanc, Frejus) are always open but are rather expensive, in the region of £20 for a car.

Drivers of right-hand drive cars should remember to alter the beam of their headlights so that they do not dazzle oncoming drivers on the continent. Remember to attach your country identification sticker and to purchase a breakdown triangle (or hire one at frontier post).

AA Motoring Holidays, PO Box 100, Halesowen, W. Midlands. Tel: 021 550 7401

RAC Motoring Services, RAC House, PO Box 100, South Road, Croydon. Tel: 081 686 2525.

Driving in Italy

As has been stated above, Italians drive quickly but well. I should add that this is not a view shared by everyone – many people think they drive like lunatics. As in all countries there are some mad drivers and some bad drivers but no more than anywhere else. Lunatic driving tends to be judged according to known criteria. Italians tend to ignore rules in a rather cavalier way but do so with considerable skill. Driving fast, for many Italians, is an art and an obligation. You are advised to drive within your own capabilities and not to allow yourself to be intimidated.

The worst habit is the tendency for drivers to sit on your tail, especially in the fast lane on motorways. There is little to be done about this – when you overtake double check the speed of approaching vehicles (likely to be faster than you are used to) and return to a slower lane as soon as possible.

The official speed limit on motorways is 130 kph/81 mph, on other roads 90/56, in town 50/31. Tolls are payable only on motorways (autostrade), indicated with green signs and prefixed with the letter A eg A1. On all other roads, including 'superstrade' (SS + number), tolls are not payable.

Remember that petrol stations often close for lunch and that you cannot always rely on being able to use credit cards (except on motorways). Some, however, have machines that accept 10,000 lire notes. The Italian for unleaded is 'senza piombo'; for diesel is 'nafta'. Fill it up is 'il pieno per favore'.

Signposting is generally comprehensive – in fact there are sometimes too many signs. After a time you will come to know what the various types, colours and sizes correspond to enabling you to pick out the ones you want.

It is compulsory to wear seatbelts and for motorcyclists to wear helmets.

Should you breakdown then call 116 from the nearest telephone. Inform the operator of your location, registration number and car type whereupon the nearest ACI office will be informed. If you have a carta carburante (see above) and if the repair time is to be longer than 12 hours, ACI will try to provide a car free for up to ten days' use. This does not apply to coaches or motorcycles.

The ACI can be found at the following addresses in Tuscany and in airport cities:

Arezzo – Viale Luca Signorelli 24a. Tel: (0575) 23253
Bergamo – Via A. Maj.16. Tel: (035) 247621
Bologna – Via Marzabotto 2. Tel: (051) 389908

Genova (Genoa) – Viale Brig. Partigiane 1. Tel: (010) 567001
Florence – Viale Amendola 36. Tel: (055) 24861
Grosseto – Via Mazzini 105. Tel: (0564) 21071
Livorno (Leghorn) – Via G. Verdi 32. Tel: (0586) 34651
Lucca – Via Catalani 1. Tel: (0583) 582626
Massa Carrara – Via Europa 9. Tel: (0585) 42122
Milano (Milan) – Corso Venezia 43. Tel: (02) 7745
Roma (Rome) – Viale C. Colombo 261. Tel: (06) 5106
Pisa – Via S. Martino 1. Tel: (050) 47333
Pistoia – Via Racciardetto 2. Tel: (0573) 32101
Siena – Viale Vittorio Veneto 47. Tel: (0577) 49001.

Parking (Parcheggio)

It is now not possible to park in many city centres (often the area within the old city walls). In general this is not a problem because most Tuscan towns are small and can be seen easily on foot. Parking is usually provided on the outskirts of a town. In larger towns (eg Florence) regular buses take people from carpark to city centre. Do not think that you can easily get away with illegal parking – not so long ago this was possible but Italian police are stricter than of old.

Traffic lights

You need to get used to looking for lights suspended above the centre of junctions.

Pedestrians

Theoretically pedestrians take precedence at uncontrolled zebra crossings. Drivers are inclined to overlook this.

Road terminology

Senso vietato, ingresso vietato/entrata vietata – no entry
Sosta vietata – no parking
Sosta autorizzata – parking permitted
Parcheggio – carpark
Vietato Transito Autocarri – closed to heavy vehicles
Rallentare – slow down
Lavori in corso – roadworks ahead
Senso unico – one way street.
Ingresso, entrata – entrance
Uscita – exit
Passaggio a livello – level crossing
Velocita – speed.

Car Hire (Autonoleggio)

Almost as straightforward as anywhere else although it is more expensive than in Britain. Payment with credit cards obviates having to leave a large deposit. All the major hire companies have offices in the main towns and at airports. There is an assortment of smaller, local companies who may be cheaper but who do not offer the same level of service.

You must beware, however, of a tendency for hidden charges to appear when it comes to settling the bill. Check carefully what is included and that it corresponds to the agreement you sign. If your car hire is part of a pre-paid package with a holiday company you should have only to pay for petrol used but it may not include the collision damage waiver. This is where the use of a credit card may be a problem – the car hire company is in a position to charge you for extras without your knowledge. If the company is dishonest enough to do this it is likely to be a fairly trifling amount, enough to irritate but not enough, you may feel, to warrant pursuit because of the costs involved. It may be worth having a word with your credit card company before leaving. Remember to ask if the car uses leaded or unleaded petrol.

It is also possible to hire scooters, bicycles, caravans and campers.

Some Italian car hire companies are represented in London:

Maggiore is represented by Transhire, Unit 16, 88 Clapham Park Road, London SW4 7BX. Tel: 071-978 1922

Quo Vadis, 243 Euston Road, London NW1. Tel: 071-387 6122

Italy by Car, is represented by Pilgrim Air, 227 Shepherds Bush Road, London W6. Tel: 071-748 1333

Autotravel, is represented by Eurodollar, Swan National House, 3 Warwick Place, Uxbridge, Middx.. Tel: 0895 56565.

What to take

If you are travelling in your own car the question of weight or portability is obviously less important than if going by air or by rail. Travelling light is an art that is well worth cultivating. It is all too easy to fill a suitcase with essentials that will not be used. Of course, if you want to wear a different set of clothes every day, and don't object to carrying them or the expense of having them carried, so be it. If not, then why take more than two changes of casual clothes for touring and something different for the evening? Thus all you need is one small suitcase and a piece of handluggage for cameras and other bits.

What sort of clothes is covered in this section under 'Clothing' (below). In a big town like Florence you will be able to find all you need. Of course, many of these things have different names or at least unfamiliar brand names – take a small dictionary or phrase book. Bring your own reading matter although it is possible to buy a limited range of books in English (see bibliography and shopping). And if you have very particular tastes (for Gentleman's Relish, say) don't rely on being able to find it. Bring a good supply of prescribed medicine, an extra pair of glasses, a penknife, a torch, specialist film requirements, a corkscrew, alarm clock, plug adaptor (220AC, twin round pin) and washing powder or equivalent.

Clothing

Casual clothes are fine in general. Italians are fond of good clothes and in general are very conscious of their appearance. It is not essential to imitate them although you will look out of place without something presentable for an occasion like the opera.

Shorts are acceptable, though designer versions find more favour. Bare flesh is not appreciated in places of worship. In addition to daily clothes bring an umbrella or light raincoat; walking shoes; beach shoes; sunglasses; sun hat; beach towel. Air-conditioning is not widespread.

Tuscan winters can be cold, wet and snowy in the hills – pack accordingly.

Money and budget

Try and obtain some lire before you leave – it can sometimes be surprisingly difficult to obtain lire at certain hours once you arrive in Italy.

Travellers cheques and Eurocheques are widely used and of course are the best proof against robbery. Some cash is always useful, however, particularly American dollars (although in general you will need to change them into lire first). The pound sterling coin is a nuisance.

Credit cards are fairly widely used (and can be used to obtain cash in some banks – see 'banks') but not as widely as in some countries – an ordinary restaurant of the trattoria type, for example, will prefer cash. Petrol stations do not generally accept credit cards except on motorways.

Money can be wired from abroad to a bank but this can be a surprisingly problematic process and best avoided. If you have to do it ensure that your identification details are given by the sender.

Electricity and plugs
The current is 220 AC. Plugs are twin round pin.

Photography
Film is a little more expensive in Italy than in Britain and the USA – so is developing. You will find that glare is something of a problem in the summer. This can be minimised with a polarising filter. A wide angle lens is useful too – towns are small with small squares and tall buildings.

Cigarettes
Italian and American cigarettes are widely available; British cigarettes less so.

Books to read

Some of the following may be out of print but may be found in your library.

The Italians by Luigi Barzini – a penetrating analysis of the Italian mind.

Italia! Italia! by Peter Nichols – a look at modern Italy through the eyes of a journalist from *The Times*.

The Decameron by Boccaccio – a surprisingly readable Italian classic.

The Divine Comedy by Dante Alighieri – less accessible but worth the effort.

The Prince by Machiavelli – an insight into the Renaissance mind.

Pictures from Italy by Charles Dickens – an idiosyncratic look at 19th century Italy.

Where Angels Fear to Tread and *Room With a View* by E.M. Forster – two novels with Tuscan links.

The Divine Country by Olive Hamilton – British connections with Tuscany.

The Spedale degli Innôcenti on Piazza Santissima Annunziata – Andrea della Robbia's delightful infants appeal from Brunelleschi's elegant Portico.

The Companion Guide to Florence by Eve Borsook – a scholarly view of Florence.

Tradition and Innovation in Renaissance Italy by Peter Burke – details of the art and social structure of the Renaissance

Daily Life in Florence in the Time of the Medici by J. Lucas-Dubreton – as the title suggests.

History of the Italian People by Giuliano Procacci – a short and readable history of Italy.

The Rise and Fall of the House of Medici by Christopher Hibbert – the Florence of the Medici from first to last.

Florence in the Forgotten Centuries 1527-1800 by Eric Cochrane – a detailed look at Florence after her greatest days.

The Italian Renaissance in its Historical Background by Denis Hay – a readable analysis of an extraordinary era.

Culture and Society in Italy 1290-1420 by John Larner – thorough but straightforward account.

A Short History of Italian Literature by J.H. Whitfield – as the name suggests.

The Rise of Rome to 264 BC by Jacques Heurgon – despite the title this book contains a good introduction to the Etruscans.

Siena by Judith Hook – an insight into Tuscany's second illustrious city.

The Michelin Red Guide to Hotels and Restaurants in Italy – accurate and worth every penny.

Eating Out in Florence by Christopher Cowie – describes many of the city's eating places and their menus.

Chianti Handbook – a guide to the region and its famous wines.

Maps

Reasonably good maps of Tuscany can be had from any information office. However, these will fall into the touring category which is usually inadequate for driving purposes. A larger scale (1:250,000) is indispensable for car travel and the best available is Toscana, Carta Stradale (Tuscany, Road Map) published by Litografia Artistica Cartografica (L.A.C.), available in Britain under the imprint of Roger Lascelles.

For visitors to Tuscany who are interested in exploring small areas of Tuscany, self-cover provincial maps (1:150,000) of each of the nine Tuscan provinces are available from L.A.C. who also publish good 'all streets' town plans of Florence, Siena and Pisa (for Siena, see inside back cover). Town plans may also be obtained from the information offices of every Tuscan town.

For walkers the Italian equivalent of OS maps might be found in specialist bookshops abroad (eg Stanford's in London) or good bookshops in Italy. Otherwise, apply to the Istituto Geografico Militare; or Edizioni Multigraphic of Florence; or perhaps Geographica, Via Cimatori 16, Florence (Tel: 055 296637).

THREE

Arrival and Getting About

Passport and Customs control

Passport control is usually perfunctory. So is customs control although it is rigorous if a traveller is suspected – customs regulations are given in 'Before you go', as are visa requirements.

It is customary for hotels to hold on to your passport for registration when you check in.

Airports

The smaller airports can be chaotic – Pisa airport, for example, has a small baggage hall and departure lounge. You may need patience.

Arrival at Pisa Airport

As you emerge from the baggage hall, you will find car hire offices round the corner to the right. If there is more than one person in the party, it is suggested that the driver goes ahead with passport, voucher and credit card/money to deal with paperwork while others deal with the luggage. Once documentation has been dealt with you will find a shuttle-bus stop outside which will take you and the luggage to the car pound. You return the car to the same place. Facilities for changing money (cambio) are available in the same area.

Pisa airport is linked to Florence by fast, clean, comfortable and reasonably priced trains (the station is adjacent to the terminal). Buses will take you to Pisa city centre.

Departure from Pisa

There is an airport terminal at Florence railway station where you can check in your luggage (but not less than 20 minutes before the departure of the train).

You are advised not to pass through passport control at Pisa airport until you are sure that your flight home is departing on time. The departure lounge is small, crowded and hot. The duty free shop is small.

Arrival at Florence airport (Peretola)

Peretola is not linked by train to the centre. There is a bus service (23C) and a taxi will not prove too expensive since the airport is just on the edge of the city.

Arrival at Rome Airport

Rome Fiumicino is a modern international airport and is linked to the city by bus and by train. Car-hire offices are situated in the car pounds – shuttle buses leave from outside the terminal.

Departure from Rome

Leave sufficient time to get there – Fiumicino is linked to motorways by the Rome ring road (Raccordo Annulare) which sometimes becomes very congested.

There are a large number of duty free shops in the departure area.

Arrival at Florence railway station

Florence Santa Maria Novella is not too far from the city centre – a 15-20 minute walk. It is a terminal-type station, and on the concourse at the exits from the platforms are most of the various available services – ticket offices, newspaper kiosks selling bus tickets, and hotel reservation office. The left-luggage office is to the left of the platforms as you emerge from them.

Note that the hotel reservation office will make a small charge for the service. Please note too that the hotel reservation office is altogether separate from the Tourist Information Office which is outside.

Bus stops are outside the station on both sides. Just outside (turning left as you emerge from the platforms), across the road, you will see a thin, low level metal pillar giving you directions. The Tourist Information Office is 100 yards to the right as you leave the station on this side in a new building. It closes for lunch and does not make hotel reservations.

Buses 1, 7, 13, 14, 17, 23 go to the Duomo.

International Departure from Florence railway station

Purchase international tickets well in advance. There are two linked areas for these and it may be you need to go to both – one for the ticket, another for reservations. Check carefully.

Getting about

Buses

There is a good network of inter-city bus routes. In general buses depart from the area of the railway station and often tickets need to be bought in advance. Buses might be more expensive than trains but they are very useful when the nearest train station is far away. Routes tend to revolve around the provincial capitals. Different companies serve different areas. An inter-city bus is called a 'pullman' pronounced 'poolman'.

Town/city buses (autobus, pronounced 'outobooss') are generally excellent – reliable and frequent. Tickets need to be bought in advance from tobacconists and some newspaper kiosks. You pay a flat fee for a single journey of any length and offer it for punching to a machine on the bus. It is possible to buy tickets which can be used for any number of journeys within a specified time, usually one hour. Some cities offer 24-hour tourist tickets.

Buses to and from Florence

There are several bus companies operating services all over Tuscany with which it is possible to reach the remotest corners. The easiest way to determine which company to use and where to board the bus is to find out from one of the information offices. It is necessary to buy a ticket from the company office before boarding. Here are the companies with their addresses and some of their destinations:

CAP (Via Nazionale 13) Borgo San Lorenzo, Impruneta, Prato.
CAT (Via Fiume 2r) Arezzo, Citta di Castello, Valdarno.
CLAP (Piazza Stazione 15r) Lucca direction.
COPIT (Piazza Santa Maria Novella) Pistoia, Poggio a Caiano, Vinci.
LAZZI (Piazza Stazione 4) Cerreto Guidi, Empoli, Livorno, Lucca, Massa-Carrara, Montecatini, Pisa, Signa, Viareggio.
RAMA (Piazza Stazione) Grosseto.
SITA (Via Santa Caterina da Siena) Val d'Elsa, Chianti, Mugello, Casentino, Bibbiena, Certaldo, Poggibonsi, Siena.

Buses around Florence

Florence is small enough to enjoy on foot. However, there will be times when some other means of transport may be necessary eg in the heat. There is a very good urban bus service (details of how to use them are given in the Arrival and Departure section) by orange buses marked ATAF; a route map ('pianta dei percorsi d'autobus') may be obtained from tourist information offices. Some main routes are:

1: Stazione-Duomo-Via Cavour-Piazza Liberta
4: Piazza Stazione-Via Vitt. Emanuele (Museo Stibbert)
6: Rondinella-Duomo-San Frediano/Santo Spirito
7: Stazione-Duomo-San Marco-San Domenico-Fiesole
10: Piazza San Marco-Ponte a Mensola-Settignano
11: Cento Stelle-Universita-Duomo-Porta Romana-Poggio Imperiale
13: Stazione-Duomo-Ponte alle Grazie-Piazzale Michelangelo
14: Girone-Duomo-Stazione-Careggi
15: Porta Romana-Ponte San Trinita-Tornabuoni-Duomo-Fortezza da
Basso
16: Le Pavoniere-Teatro Communale-Stazione-Ognissanti-Vitt. Veneto (holidays only)
17B: Salviatino-San Marco-Duomo-Stazione-Porta al Prato-Boito.
The 17C goes to Cascine.
23C: Piazza Stazione-Peretola Airport.

Trains

Train travel is very popular, with a comprehensive network and is, on the whole very comfortable. It is also somewhat cheaper than in Britain.

Trains in Italy may be classified in the following way:

Accelerato/Locale – local stopping train.
Diretto – train stopping at most stations.
Espresso/Direttissimo – express stopping only at main stations.
Rapido – fast non-stop trains which are sometimes only first class and for which a supplement is payable. Sometimes seat reservation is compulsory.
Super Rapido Inter City – luxury first class trains where seat reservation is compulsory and where supplements are charged.

Timetables clearly indicate the service in question. For further information about Florence station, see 'Arrival and Departure.

Trains can be very crowded at certain times and theft can be a problem. It is, for a small fee, possible to reserve seats on many

An antique face with a modern purpose – a post box in Florence.

services. Tickets are usually valid only for the day of purchase. They may be bought on board but with a penal charge. Foreigners can buy a fixed price unlimited travel ticket (Biglietto turistico libera circolazione – good for 'rapidos' too) if you are intending to do a lot of travelling. other similar tickets are available for various periods of time.

Stations usually have left-luggage service (deposito bagagli), good snack bars and waiting rooms. Snack service on trains is often via a trolley or you can buy through the window from vendors on the platform. Larger stations have an 'albergo diurno' where you can have a bath and so on.

By car

You are not allowed to park in the centre of Florence unless staying in a hotel (which may require documentary proof). The city centre is broadly defined by the old walls and gates and which, for parking purposes, is called the ZTL (Zona Traffico Limitato). Note that if you are able to park in the city, each street has to be cleared of cars once a week for cleaning purposes. However, the city is well provided with **car parks** (with custodians), which are not too expensive and are generally placed on the edge of the old city (centro storico). The main and cheaper ones, run by SCAF, are at:

Porta Romana, Piazza Liberta, Piazza Beccaria, Viale Mazzini, Viale Segni, Piazza Savonarola, Il Prato, Piazza Vespucci, Piazza

Ognissanti, Lungarno La Zecca, Lungarno Torrigiani, Santa Maria Nuova, Via Veneto, Fortezza da Basso.

The more expensive are: Piazza Ghiberti and Piazza Mercato Centrale. The parking place for caravans is at the Fortezza da Basso. A large car park is being built beneath the station.

If your car is towed away call 351562.

By Taxi

Taxis are usually found outside stations on ranks and are not particularly cheap. They are metered. Tipping is not necessary.

Taxis in Florence are to be found at the station and at ranks on the main squares. or call 47.98 or 43.90.

Bicycles and motorbikes

It is possible to hire bicycles and they may also be transported by train. Bicycles can sometimes be rented free in Florence at the Fortezza da Basso, for a limited period for people parking there – take your parking ticket to the Bici-Citta booth. This system sometimes operates at some other car parks. Bikes may be rented at Ciao & Basta, Via Alamanni (Tel: 293357). Motorbikes/scooters are available from Free Motor, Via Santa Monica 6/8r (Tel:295102) and Motorent, Via San Zanobi 9r. (Tel:490113). The general word for rent is 'noleggio'. A bicycle is 'bicicletta' pronounced 'beecheecletta'. For scooter say 'Vespa' and for motorbike, 'motocicletta'.

Walking

A pleasant way of getting to know a small area of Tuscany is to walk, if you are prepared to travel lightly. It is quite easy to find a suitable route – hotels can be arranged in advance – and since the concept of private property is less rigid than in the Anglo-Saxon or Gallic world, you will have no problem in making your way across the country. There are companies that specialise in organised walking holidays – they will transport your luggage and ensure your safe journey from town to town. Addresses of companies are given in the 'before you go' section.

The Italian equivalent of OS maps are available, if a little hard to find (see maps in the 'before you go' section).

FOUR

Accommodation

The following is a comprehensive list of hotels of all types in Florence, which is likely to prove the most difficult place in which to find a room at certain times of year. You are advised to book in advance. For the rest of Tuscany the problem is less acute and although it is always as well to make arrangements in advance if at all possible, lists of hotels may be obtained from the Italian Information Office in your country or in the town when you arrive. Note that in Florence there is an office devoted to helping with accommodation at the station.

Hotels within the city of Florence

These hotels appear in alphabetical order within each star category. The locations are given as follows:-

Central: the immediate are of the Duomo.

Near central: no further than a short bus ride from the Duomo.

Suburban: beyond 'near central'.

Station: right by the station.

Oltrarno and central: south bank but within walking distance of the centre.

Oltrarno and beyond: south bank but not easy walking distance of centre.

These are followed by references to the Florence map (inside back cover) which are given in brackets.

Prices can vary within a category. All four- and five-star hotels have rooms with bathroom. However, even within the three-star category some of the older hotels have some rooms without private bathroom. Further down the scale rooms without private bathroom are more common and there are some hotels which do not offer any rooms with private bathroom.

Also please note that hotels – especially one- and two-star are often apartments occupying one floor of a house. Therefore some hotels in this list share the same address.

Prices must be displayed in each room and cannot exceed the registered price. All prices include VAT which is charged at 19% for five-star hotels and 9% for hotels in other categories. The following breakdown of prices is offered as a guideline and represents the cost of rooms offered for the 1991 season. (Source: Tourist office of Florence.)

Five-star hotels: 370,000 to 420,000 lira for a single room
550,000 to 630,000 lira for a double room

Four-star hotels: 130,000 - 260,000 lira for a single room
140,000 - 310,000 lira for a double room

Three-star hotels: 44,000 - 63,000 lira for single room without bath
78,000 - 93,500 lira for double room without bath
60,000 - 80,500 lira single room with bath
85,000 - 120,000 lira double room with bath

Two-star hotels: 35,000 - 38,500 lira single room without bath
53,000 - 56,000 lira double room without bath
46,000 - 49,000 lira single room with bath
65,000 - 72,000 lira double room with bath

One-star hotels: 26,000 - 30,000 lira single room without bath
37,000 - 43,000 lira double room without bath
35,000 - 40,000 lira single room with bath
44,000 - 55,000 lira double room with bath.

Five-star hotels (VAT charged at 19%)

EXCELSIOR, Piazza Ognissanti 3. Tel: 264 201 Telex: 570022 Fax: 210278. Near central (6F)

GRAND HOTEL, Piazza Ognissanti 1. Tel: 288 781 Telex: 570055 Fax: 217400. Near central (6F)

HELVETIA & BRISTOL, Via Dei Pescioni 2. Tel: 287 814 Telex: 572696 Fax: 288353. Central (6I)

REGENCY, Piazza D'Azegelio 3. Tel: 245 246 Telex: 571058 Fax: 245247. Near central (5N)

SAVOY, Piazza della Republica 7. Tel: 283 313 Telex: 570220 Fax: 284840. Central (6I)

VILLA CORA, Viale Machiavelli 18. Tel: 229 8451 Telex: 570604
Fax: 229086.   Oltrarno-beyond (9M)
VILLA MEDICI, Via Il Prato 42. Tel: 238 1331 Telex: 570179 Fax:
2381336.   Station (4E)

Four-star hotels (VAT charged at 9%)

ADRIATICO, Via Maso Finiguerra 9. Tel: 238 1881 Telex: 572265
Fax: 289661.   Central (5F)
ALEXANDER, Viale Guidoni 101. Tel: 437 8951 Telex: 574026
Fax: 416818.   Suburban (AB)
ANGLO AMERICAN, Via Garibaldi 9. Tel: 282 114 Telex: 570289
Fax: 268513.   Nearcentral (5E)
ASTORIA PULLMAN, Via del Giglio 9. Tel: 239 8095 Telex:
571070 Fax: 214632.   Central (5H)
ATLANTIC PALACE, Via Nazionale 12. Tel: 294 234 Telex:
571183 Fax: 268 353.   Near central (4H)
AUGUSTUS & DEI CONGRESSI, Vicolo dell'Oro 5. Tel: 283 054
Telex: 570110 Fax: 268557.   Central (7H)
BAGLIONI, Piazza Unita Italiana 6. Tel: 218 441 Telex: 570225
Fax: 215695.   Central (5H)
BERCHIELLI, Lungarno Acciaiuoli 14. Tel: 264061 Telex: 575582
Fax: 218636.   Central (7H)
BERNINI PALACE, Piazza S. Firenze 29. Tel: 288 621 Telex:
573616 Fax: 268272.   Central (7I)
BRUNELLESCHI, Piazza S. Elisabetta 3. Tel: 562 068 Telex:
575805 Fax: 219653.   Central (6I)
CONTINENTAL, Lugarno Acciaiuoli 2. Tel: 282 392 Telex: 580525
Fax: 283139.   Central (7H)
CROCE DI MALTA, Via della Scala 7. Tel: 218 351 Telex: 570540
Fax: 283139.   Near central (5G)
DE LA VILLE, Piazza Antinori 1. Tel: 238 1805 Telex: 570518 Fax:
2381809.   Central (6H)
DELLA SIGNORIA, Via delle Terme 1. Tel: 214 530 Telex: 571561
Fax: 216101.   Central (7H)
EXECUTIVE, Via Curtatone 5. Tel: 217 451 Telex: 574522 Fax:
268346.   Near central (5E)
FENICE PALACE, Via Martelli 10. Tel: 289 941 Telex: 575580
Fax:210087.   Central (5I)
HOLIDAY INN, Via Europa 205. Tel: 653 1841 Telex: 570376 Fax:
6531806.   Suburban (11T)
J AND J, Via di Mezzo 20. Tel: 240 951 Telex: 570554 Fax: 240282.
                                                 Near central (6M)

JOLLY CARLTON, Piazza V. Veneto 4-A. Tel: 2770 Telex: 570191 Fax: 294794. Near central (4D)

KRAFT, Via Solferino 2. Tel: 284 273 Telex 571523 Fax: 298267. Near central (5E)

LAURUS, Via Cerretani 8. Tel: 238 1752 Telex: 571580 Fax: 268308. Central (5H)

LONDRA, Via Jacobo da Diacceto 18/20. Tel: 238 2791 Telex: 571152 Fax: 210682. Station (4F)

LUNGARNO, Borgo San Jacobo 14. Tel: 264 211 Telex: 570129 Fax: 268437. Central (5H)

MAJESTIC, Via del Melarancio 1. Tel: 264 021 Telex: 570628 Fax: 268428. Central (5H)

MARTELLI, Viale Fratelli Rosselli 2. Tel: 217 151 Telex: 573137 Fax: 268504. Central (5H)

MICHELANGELO, Viale Fratelli Roselli 2. Tel: 28 84 Telex: 571113 Fax: 2382232. Station (3E)

MINERVA, Piazza Santa Maria Novella 16. Tel: 284 555 Telex: 5704124. Station (5G)

MIRAGE, Via Baracca 231 int 18. Tel: 352 011 Telex: 571469 Fax: 374096. Suburban (AB)

MONTINEVRO, Via di Novoli. Tel: 431 441 Telex: 571469 fax: 4378257. Suburban (AB)

MONNA LISA, Borgo Pinti 27. Tel: 247 9751 Telex: 573300 Fax: 2479755. Near central (5M)

MONTEBELLO SPLENDID, Via Montebello 60. Tel: 2398 051 Telex: 574009 Fax: 211867. Near central (5E)

NORD FLORENCE, Via Baracca 199-A. Tel: 431 151 Telex: 574586 Fax: 431202. Suburban (AB)

PARK PALACE, Piazzale Galileo 5. Tel: 222 431 Telex: 573075 Fax: 220517. Suburban (11M)

PIERRE, Via Lamberti 5. Tel: 217 512 Telex: 573175 Fax: 296573. Near central (6H)

PLAZA HOTEL LUCCHESI, Lungarno della Zecca Vecchia 38. Tel: 264 141 Telex: 570302 Fax: 2480921. Near central (8M)

PRESIDENT, Via della Piazzola 36 bis. Tel: 587 603 Telex: 575690 Fax: 500471. Suburban (1P)

PRINCIPE, Lungarno Vespucci 34. Tel: 284 848 Telex: 571400 Fax: 283458. Near central (5G)

QUEEN PALACE HOTEL, Via Solferino 5. Tel: 239 6818 Telex: 575691 Fax: 213143. Near central (5E)

RAFFAELLO, Viale Morgagni 19. Tel: 439 871 Telex: 580035 Fax: 434374. Suburban (FG)

RELAIS CERTOSA, Via di Colle Ramole. Tel: 2047 171 Telex: 574332 Fax: 268575.   Oltrarno-beyond (DE11)

RITZ, Lungarno Zecca Vecchia 24. Tel: 2340 650 Telex: 573170 Fax: 240863.   Near central (8M)

RIVOLI, Via della Scala 33. Tel: 282 853 Telex: 571004 Fax: 294041.   Station (5G)

ROMA, Piazza S. Maria Novella 8. Tel: 210 366 Telex: 575831 Fax: 215306.   Central (5G)

SHERATON, Via G. Agnelli. Tel: 64 901 Telex: 575860 Fax: 680747.   Suburban

TORRE DI BELLOSGUARDO, Via Roti Michelozzi.
                                                                                                                Suburban (9L)

VILLA BELVEDERE, Via Castelli 3. Tel: 222 501 Telex: 575648 Fax: 223163.   Suburban (EF11)

VILLA CARLOTTA, Via Michele di Lando. Tel: 220 530 Telex: 573485 Fax: 2336147.   Suburban (EF11)

VILLA SULL'ARNO, Lungarno C. Colombo 1. Tel: 670 971 Telex: 678244 Fax: 573297.   Suburban (8R)

Three-Star Hotels (VAT charged at 9%)

ALBA, Via della Scala 22. Tel: 282 610 Telex: 571004 Fax: 294041.
                                                                                                                Station (5G)

ALBION, Via il Prato 22r. Tel: 214 171 Telex: 580522 Fax: 283391.
                                                                                                                Near central (5F)

AMBASCIATORI, Via Alamanni 3. Tel: 287 421 Telex: 571390 Fax: 212360.   Station (4F)

ANDREA, P.za Indipendenza 19. Tel: 483 890.   Near central (3I)

ANNALENA, Via Romana 34. Tel: 222 402 Fax: 222403.
                                                                                                                Oltrarno central (9G)

APRILE, Via della Scala 6. Tel: 216 237 Telex: 575840. Station (5G)

ARGENTINA, Via Curtatone 12. Tel: 215 408 Telex: 580323 Fax: 216731.   Near central (5E)

ARIELE, Via Magenta 11. Tel: 211 509 Telex: 570093 Fax: 216731.
                                                                                                                Near central (5D)

ARIZONA, Via Farini 2. Tel: 245 321 Telex: 575572. Near central (5N)

ASTOR, Viale Milton 41. Tel:573 155 Telex: 573155. Suburban (1I)

AUTO PARK HOTEL, Via Valdegola 1. Tel: 431 771 Telex: 570674 Fax: 4221557.   Suburban (AB)

BALESTRI, Piazza Mentana 7. Tel: 214 743.   Near central (8L)

BASILEA, Via Guelfa 41. Tel: 214 587 Telex: 571689 Fax: 268350.
                                                                                                                Near central (4H)

BEACCI TORNABUONI, Via Tornabuoni 3. Tel: 212 615 Telex: 570215.   Central (6H)

BONCIANI, Via Panzani 17. Tel: 238 2341 Telex: 572426 Fax: 268512.   Central (5H)
BOSTON, Via Guelfa 68. Tel: 496 747 Fax: 470934.   Near central (3H)
BYRON, Via della Scala 49. Tel: 216 700 Telex: 570278 Fax: 213273.   Near central (5F)
CALIFORNIA, Via Ricasoli 30. Tel: 282 753 Fax: 216268.
                                                                                Near central (4I)
CALZAIUOLI, Via de'Calzaiuoli 6. Tel: 212 456 Telex: 580589 Fax: 268310.   Central (5I)
CAPITOL, Viale Amendola 34. Tel: 234 3210 Telex: 575853 Fax: 2682394.   Near central (7O)
CARAVEL, Via Alamanni 9. Tel: 217 651.   Station (4F)
CASTRI, Piazza Indipendenza 7. Tel: 496 412 Telex: 575582 Fax: 475602.   Near central (3I)
CAVOUR, Via del Proconsolo 3. Tel: 210 907 Telex: 580318 Fax: 218955.   Central (6I)
CELLAI, Via XXVII Aprile 14. Tel: 489 291 Telex: 580578 Fax: 268370.   Central (6I)
CITY, Via S. Antonino 18. Tel: 211 543 Telex: 573389 Fax: 295451.
                                                                               Near central (4H)
CLARIDGE, Piazza Piave 3. Tel: 268 533 Telex: 580527 Fax: 2341199.   Near central (8N)
CLASSIC, Viale Machiavelli 25. Tel: 229 351.   Oltramo-beyond (11MN)
CLUB HOTEL, Via S. Caterina da Sienna. Tel: 213 635 Telex: 588566 Fax: 284872.   Near central (5F)
COLUMBUS, Lungarno C. Colombo 22-A. Tel: 677 251 Telex: 570273.   Suburban (8R)
CONCORDE, Viale Luigi Gori 10. Tel: 373 551 Telex: 573362 Fax: 373555.   Suburban (AB)
CONSIGLI, Lungarno Vespucci 50. Tel: 214 172 Fax: 219367.
                                                                                Near central (5E)
CORALLO, Via Nazionale 22a. Tel: 496 645 Telex: 573221.
                                                                                Near central (4H)
COROLLE, Via G. Caccini 24. Tel: 4221 991 Fax: 4221993.
                                                                                      Suburban (4H)
CORONA, Via Nazionale 14. Tel: 288 631 Telex: 580354 Fax: 288639.   Near central (4H)
DANTE, Via San Cristofano 2. Tel: 241 772 Fax: 2345819.   Central (7M)
DA VERRAZZANO, Via di Bellariva 18. Tel: 679 766. Suburban (8S)
DAVID, Viale Michelangelo 1. Tel: 681 1695 Telex: 574553 Fax: 680602.   Oltrarno-central (9O)
DE LA PACE, Via Lamarmora 28. Tel: 577 343 Telex: 573087 Fax: 577576.   Near central (2M)

DUOMO, Piazza Duomo 1. Tel: 219 922 Telex: 580252. Central (5I)
EMBASSY HOUSE, Via Nazionale 23. Tel: 238 2266 Telex:
580445 Fax:268245. Near central (4H)
EURHOTEL, Via Pistoiese 30. Tel: 319 234 Telex: 588655 Fax:
288043. Suburban
FIORINO, Via Osteria del Guanto 6. Tel: 210 579. Central (7I)
FIRENZA NOVA, Via Panciatichi 51. Tel: 477 851 Telex: 572559
Fax: 4376645. Suburban (AB)
FLEMING, Viale Guidoni 87. Tel: 437 6773 Telex: 574027 Fax:
435894. Suburban (AB)
FRANCHI, Via Sgambati 28. Tel: 315 425 Telex: 580425 Fax:
315563. Suburban (AB)
GIOIA, Via Cavour 25. Tel: 282 804 Telex: 575645 Fax: 2398997.
Near central (4I)
GOLDONI, Via Borgognissanti 8. Tel: 284 080. Near central (5G)
GOLF, Viale Fratelli Rosselli 56, Tel: 293 088 Telex: 571630 Fax:
268432. Station (3E)
GRIFONE, Via G. Pilati 20-22. Tel: 677 474 Telex: 570624 Fax:
677628. New central (7R)
IL GUELFO BIANCO, Via Cavour 57R. Tel: 288 330 Telex: 570596
Fax: 295203. New central (4I)
HERMITAGE, Vicolo Marzio. Tel: 287 216 Fax: 212208. Central (7H)
JANE, Via Orcagna 56. Tel: 677 382 Fax: 677383. Near central (7P)
JENNINGS RICCIOLI, Corso Tintori 7. Tel: 244 751 Telex:
575849. Central (8L)
LA GIOCONDA, Via Panzani 2. Tel: 213 150 Fax: 213 136.
Central (5H)
LA RESIDENZA, Via La Tornabuoni 8. Tel: 284 197 Telex:
570093. Central (6H)
LA DUE FONTANE, Piazza SS Annunziata 14. Tel: 280 086 Telex:
575550 Fax: 294461. Near central (4L)
LEONARDO DA VINCI, Via G. Monaco 12. Tel: 357 751 Fax:
357752. Station (3F)
LIDO, Via del Ghirlandaio. Tel: 677 864. Near central (8P)
LOGGIATO DEI SERVITI, Piazza SS Annunziata 3. Tel: 289 592
Telex: 575808 Fax: 289595. Near central (4L)
LOMBARIDA, Via Panzani 19. Tel: 215 276. Central (5H)
MACHIAVELLI PALACE, Via Nazionale 10. Tel: 216 622 Telex:
570568. Near central (4H)
MARIOS, Via Fraenza 89. Tel: 216 801 Fax: 212039. Near central (4H)
MEDITERRANEO, Lungarno del Tempio 44. Tel: 660 241 Telex:
571195 Fax: 679560. Near central (8O)

MORANDI ALLA CROCETTA, Via Laura 50. Tel: 234 4747 Fax: 2480954. Near central (4M)

OLIMPIA, Piazza della Repubblica 2. Tel: 238 2860 Telex: 588655 Fax: 2382860. Central (6I)

PAGNINI, Via Montebello 40. Tel: 2381 238 Fax: 216685.
Near central (5F)

PALAZZO BENCI, Via Faenza 6/R. Tel: 217 049 Telex: 575851 Fax: 288308. Near central (4H)

PARIS, Via dei Banchi`2. Tel: 280 281 Telex: 572281 Fax: 268505.
Central (5H)

PENDINI, Via Strozzi 2. Tel: 211 170 Telex: 580278. Central (6H)

PITTI PALACE, Via Barbadori 2. Tel: 282 257. Oltrarno-central (8H)

PORTA ROSSA, Via Porta Rossa 19. Tel: 287 7551 Telex: 570007 Fax: 282174. Central (7H)

PRIVILEGE, Lungarno della Zecca Vecchia 26. Tel: 234 1221 Fax: 243287. Near central (8N)

QUISISANA - PONTE VECCHIO, Lungarno Arhcibusieri 4. Tel: 216 692 Fax: 268303. Central (7I)

RAPALLO, Via Santa Caterina d'Alessandria 7, Tel: 472 412 Telex: 574251 Fax: 268364. Near central (2I)

REX, Via Faenza 6, Tel: 215 872 Telex: 573606 Fax: 2382390.
Near central (4H)

RIVER, Lungarno della Zecca Vecchia 18, Tel: 233 4529 Telex: 580584 Fax: 2343531. Near central (8N)

ROYAL, Via delle Ruote. Tel: 490 648 Fax: 490976 Near central (2I)

SAN GIORGIO & OLIMPIC, Via Sant'Antonino 3. Tel: 284 344 Telex: 573606 Fax: 262390. Central 5H)

SAN REMO, Lungarno Serristori 13. Tel: 234 2823 Fax: 2342269.
Oltrarno-central (9M)

SELECT, Via Galliano 24. Tel: 330 342 Telex: 572626 Fax: 351506.
Suburban

SILLA, Via dei Renai 5. Tel: 234 2888 Fax: 2341437.
Oltrarno-central (9L)

UNICORNO, Via de'Fossi 27. Tel: 287 313 Fax: 268332.
Near central (6G)

VICTORIA, Via Nazionale 102r. Tel:287 019 Telex: 575836 Fax: 2398806. Near central (4H)

VILLA AZZALEE, Viale Fratelli Rosselli 44. Tel: 214 242 Fax: 268264. Station (3E)

VILLA BETANIA, V.le Poggio Imperiale 23. Tel: 222 234.
Oltrarno-central (E11)

VILLA LE RONDINI, Via Bolognese Vecchia 224. Tel: 400 081 Telex: 575679 Fax: 268212. Suburban (LM)

VILLA LIBERTY, Viale Michelangelo 40. Tel: 681 0581 Telex: 573389 Fax: 6812595.   Oltrarno-central (10N)

Two Star Hotels (VAT charged at 9%)

ADAM, Via Monalda 1. Tel: 210 369.   Central (6H)
ALESSANDRA, Borgo SS. Apostoli 17. Tel: 283 348 Fax: 210619.
                    Central (7H)
ALFA, Via Alfieri 9. Tel: 245 825.   Near central (4N)
APOLLO, Via Faenza 77. Tel: 284 119 Fax: 210101.   Central (5H)
ARIANNA, Via di Barbano 12r. Tel: 496 742.   Near central (3H)
ARISTON, Via Fiesolana 40. Tel: 247 6693 Telex: 571603.
                    Near central (3M)
ARNO, Lungarno del Tiempio 16. Tel: 666 342.   Near central (8P)
ASCOT, Via Nazionale 8-A, Tel: 284 171.   Near central (4H)
AURORA, Via L. Alamanni 5. Tel: 210 283.   Station (3F)
AUTOSTRADA, Via L. Gori 31. Tel: 316 856 Fax: 375277.
                    Suburban (AB)
BEATRICE, Via Fiume 11. Tel: 216 790.   Station (4G)
BELLETTINI, Via dei Conti 7. Tel: 213 561 Fax: 283551.
                    Central (5H)
BENVENUTI, Via Cavour 112. Tel: 572 141 Fax: 586727.
                    Near central (2M)
BERKLEYS, Via Fiume 11. Tel: 212302.   Near central (3I)
BOBOLI, Via Romana 63. Tel: 233 7169.   Oltrarno-central (9G)
BODONI, Via Martiri del Popolo 27. Tel: 240 741 Fax: 244432.
                    Near central (6M)
BOLOGNA, Via Orcagna 50. Tel: 678 359 Fax: 661241.
                    Near central (7P)
BRETAGNA, Lungarno Corsini 6. Tel: 289 618.   Central (7G)
CAPRI, Via XXVII Aprile 3. Tel: 215 441 Telex: 580652.
                    Near central (3I)
CAREGGI, Via T. Alderotti 43. Tel: 436 0262.   Suburban (FE)
CASA DEL LAGO, Lungarno Vespucci 58. Tel: 216 141.
                    Near central (SE)
CENTRALE, Via dei Conti 3. Tel: 215 215.   Central (5H)
CENTRO, Via Ginori 17. Tel: 230 2901.   Near central (4I)
CHIARI-BIGALLO, Via Adimari 26. Tel: 216 086.   Central (6I)
CHIAZZA, Borgo Pinti 5. Tel: 248 0363.   Near central (5M)
CIMABUE, Via Bonifacio Lupi 7. Tel: 471 989 Telex: 573155.
                    Near central (2I)
CORDOVA, Via Cavour 96. Tel: 587 948 Fax: 582850.
                    Near central (4I)

COSTANTINI, Via Calzaiuoli 13. Tel: 215 128. Central (6L)
CRISTALLO, Via Cavour 27. Tel: 215 375. Near central (3H)
CROCINI, Corso Italia 28. Tel: 212 905 Fax: 573137.

Near central (5D)
DE LANZI, Via delle Oche 11. Tel: 239 6377 Telex: 588655 Fax: 268354. Central (6I)
DELLE CAMELIE, Via di Barbano 10. Tel: 490 467.

Near central (3H)
DELLE NAZIONI, Via Alamanni 15. Tel: 283 575 Telex: 574451 Fax: 283579. Station (4F)
DERBY, Via Nazionale 35. Tel: 219 308. Near central (4H)
DESIREE, Via Fiume 20. Tel: 238 2382 Fax: 2382382. Station (4G)
EDEN, Via Nazionale 55. Tel: 483 722. Near central (4H)
ELITE, Via della Scala 12. Tel: 215 395. Station (4F)
ERINA, Via Fiume 17. Tel: 284 343. Near central (4I)
EUROPA, Via Cavour 14. Tel: 210 361. Near central (4L)
FEDORA, Viale S. Lavagnini 45. Tel: 480 013. Near central (2H)
GENESIO, Via XXVII Aprile 9. Tel: 496 208. Near central (3I)
GIADA, Canto dei Nelli 2. Tel: 215 317. Central (5H)
GIGLIO, Via Cavour 85. Tel: 486 621 Fax: 296377.

Near station (2L)
GIOTTO, Via del Giglion 13. Tel: 289 864 Fax: 296377. Central (5H)
GISELDA, Via L. Alamanni 5. Tel: 211 145. Station (4F)
HERMES, Via L. Alamanni 11. Tel: 293 420. Station (4F)
JOLY, Via Fiume 8. Tel: 292 079. Station (4G)
LA NOCE, Borgo La Noce 8. Tel: 213 519. Near central (4H)
LA PERGOLA, Via A. del Pollaiolo 16. Tel: 702 152.

Suburban (A5/6)
LA SCALETTA, Via Guicciardini 13. Tel: 283 028.

Oltrarno-central (8H)
LA TERAZZA, Via Taddea 8. Tel: 294 322 Fax: 572430.

Near central (4I)
LE CASCINE, Largo F.lli. Alinari 15. Tel: 211 066. Near central (4H)
LE VIGNE, Piazza S. Maria Novella 24. Tel: 294 449 Fax: 2302263.

Central (5G)
LIANA, Via Vittorio Alfieri 18, Tel: 245 303 Fax: 2344596.

Near central (4N)
LORENA, Via Faenza 1. Tel: 282 785. Central (5H)
MADRID, Via della Scala 59. Tel: 282 776. Station (5F)
MAGGIORE SOVRANA, Largo F.lli. Alinari 15. Tel: 210 309.

Station (4H)
MEARINI, Via Guelfa 110. Tel: 471 177. Near central (4I)

MEDICI, Via de'Medici 6. Tel: 284 818 Telex: 571530 Fax: 216202.
Near central (6I)

NIZZA, Via del Giglio 5. Tel: 239 6897. Central (5H)

NORD OVEST, Via Cennini 11. Tel: 212 753. Station (4G)

NORMA, Borgo SS. Apostoli 8. Tel: 239 8577. Central (7H)

NUOVO ITALIA, Via Faenza 26. Tel: 268 430. Station (4H)

ORCAGNA, Via Orcagna 57. Tel: 670 500. Near central (7P)

PALAZZO VECCHIO, Via Cennini 4. Tel: 212 182. Station (4G)

PATRIZIA, Via Montebello 7. Tel: 282 314 Fax: 287856. Station (5F)

PETRARCA, Via Fiume 20. Tel: 261 209. Station (4G)

PICCADILLY, Via XXVII Aprile 18. Tel: 483 238. Near central (3J)

PRIMAVERA, Via Maso Finiguerra 12r. Tel: 287 072 Fax: 213021.
Station (3F)

RIGATTI, Lungarno Diaz 2. Tel: 213 022. Oltrarno-central (8L)

RITA MAJOR, Via della Mattonaia 43. Tel: 247 7990 Fax: 2478358.
Near central (5O)

ROMAGNA, Via Panzani. Tel: 211 005. Central (5H)

SAN LORENZO, Via Rosina 4. Tel: 284 925. Near central (4I)

SANTA CROCE, Via Bentaccordi 3. Tel: 217 000. Central (7L)

SEMPIONE, Via Nazionale 15. Tel: 212 463. Near central (4H)

SPAGNA, Via Panzani 9. Tel: 211 860. Central (5H)

SPLENDOR, Via San Gallo 30. Tel: 483 427 Fax: 461276.
Near central (3I)

STAZIONE, Via dei Banchi 3. Tel: 283 133 Fax: 289590. Central (5H)

STELLA MARY, Via Fiume 17. Tel: 215 694. Station (4G)

TIRRENO, Via Lupi 21. Tel: 490 695. Near central (2L)

VENETO, Via Santa Reparata 33. Tel: 294 816 Telex: 574532 Fax:
283132. Near central (3I)

VERSAILLES, Via Martelli 3. Tel: 287 575. Central (5I)

VIENNA, Via XXVII Aprile 14. Tel: 483 256. Near central (3I)

VILLANI, Via delle Oche 11. Tel: 239 6451 Fax: 215348.
Central (6I)

One Star Hotels (VAT charged at 9%)

A.B.C., Borgognissanti 67. Tel: 218 882. Near central (5F)

ACCADEMIA, Via Faenza 7. Tel: 293 451. Central (5H)

ADRIA 2, Via Montebello 49. Tel: 215 029. Near central (4E)

ADUA, Via Fiume 20. Tel: 287 506. Station (4G)

ALDINI, Via Calzaiuoli 13. Tel: 214 752. Central (6I)

ALEX, Via Baccio da Montelupo 20. Tel: 732 1059.
Oltrarno-central (4A)

ALINE, Via XXVII Aprile 20. Tel: 483 256. Near central (3I)

ANNA, Via Faenza 56. Tel: 239 8322. Station (4H)
ANTICA, Via Pandolfini 17. Tel: 239 6644. Central (6L)
ARCHIBUSIERI, Vicolo Marzio 1. Tel: 282 480. Central (7H)
ARMONIA, Via Faenza 56. Tel: 211 146. Station (4H)
ASSO, Via Lamarmora 27. Tel: 576 729. Near central (3L)
AUSONIA E RIMINI, Via Nazionale 24. Tel: 496 547.
Near central (4H)
AZZI, Via Faenza 56. Tel: 213 806 Fax: 213806. Station (4H)
BANDINI, Piazza Santo Spirito 9. Tel: 215 308. Oltrarno-central (8G)
BAVARIA, Borgo degli Albizi 26. Tel: 234 0313. Central (6L)
BELLAVISTA, Largo F.illi. Alinari 15. Tel: 284 528. Station (4H)
BERNA, Largo F.illi. Alinari 11. Tel: 287 701. Station (4H)
BIJOU, Via Fiume 6. Tel: 214 156. Station (4E)
BRUNETTA, Borgo Pinti 5. Tel: 247 8134. Near central (5M)
BRUNORI, Via del Proconsolo 5. Tel: 289 648. Central (6I)
BURCHIANTI, Via del Giglio 6. Tel: 212 796. Central (5H)
CANADA, Borgo San Lorenzo 14. Tel: 210 074. Central (5I)
CASA CRISTINA, Via B. Lupi 14. Tel: 496 730. Near central (2L)
CASCI, Via Cavour 13. Tel: 211 686 Fax: 296461. Near central (4I)
CELY, Piazza Santa Maria Novella 24. Tel: 218 755. Central (5G)
CESTELLI, Borgo SS. Apostoli 25. Tel: 214 213. Central (7H)
COLOMBA, Via Cavour 21. Tel: 289 139. Near central (4I)
COLORADO, Via Cavour 66. Tel: 217 310 Fax: 582850.
Near central (4I)
COLORE, Via Calzaiuoli 13. Tel: 210 301. Central (6I)
CONCORDIA, Via dell'Amorino 14. Tel: 213 233. Central (5H)
CRISTINA, Via Condotta 4. Tel: 214 484. Central (6I)
DAVANZATI, Via Porta Rossa 15. Tel: 283 414. Central (7H)
DELLE ROSE, Canto de Nelli 2. Tel: 239 6373. Central (5H)
D'ERRICO, Via Faenzo 69. Tel: 214 059. Station (4H)
DONATELLO, Via Alfieri 9. Tel: 245 870. Near central (4N)
DUILIO, Corso Italia 13. Tel: 287 331. Near central (5E)
ENZA, Via S. Zanobi 45. Tel: 490 990. Near central (3I)
ESPERANZA, Via dell'Inferno 3. Tel: 213 773. Central (6H)
ESPLANADE, Via Tornabuoni 13. Tel: 287 078. Central (6H)
ESTER, Largo F.lli. Alinari 15. Tel: 212 741. Station (4H)
ESTRUSCA, Via Nazionale 35. Tel: 213 100. Near central (4H)
FANI, Via Guelfa 28. Tel: 283 731 Telex: 574532 Fax: 283132.
Near central (4I)
FERDY, Via S. Gallo. Tel: 475 302. Near central (3L)
FERRETTI, Via delle Belle Donne 17. Tel: 238 1328. Central (6G)
FIORENTINA, Via dei Fossi 12. Tel: 219 530. Central (6G)

FIORENTINO, Via Degli Avelli 8. Tel: 212 692.   Central (5G)
FIORITA, Via Fiume 20. Tel: 283 693.   Station (4G)
FIRENZE, Piazza Donati 4. Tel: 214 203.   Central (6I)
FLORA, Via Buonvicini 50. Tel: 578 612.   Near central (2O)
FLORISE, Viale S. Lavagnini 8. Tel: 489 056.   Near central (2I)
GARDEN, Piazza Vittorio Veneto 8. Tel: 212 669. Near central (4D)
GENEVE, Via della Mattonaia 43. Tel: 247 7923. Near central (5O)
GENZIANELLA, Via Cavour 112. Tel: 573 909. Near central (2M)
GIAPPONE, Via dei Banchi 1. Tel: 210 090.   Central (5H)
GIGLIOLA, Via della Scala 40. Tel: 287 981.   Station (4F)
GINORI, Via Ginori 24. Tel: 218 615.   Near central (4I)
GIOVANNA, Via Faenza 69. Tel: 238 1353.   Station (4H)
GLOBUS, Via Sant'Antononino 24. Tel: 211 062. Near central (4H)
GRAZIA, Via L. Alamanni 5. Tel: 211 145.   Station (4F)
GRAZIELLA, Via P. Capponi 87. Tel: 572 807.   Near central (2M)
GUELFA, Via Guelfa 28. Tel: 215 882 Telex: 574532 Fax: 283132.
                                                                          Near central (4I)
HOUSE FOR TOURISTS – AGLIETTI, Via Cavour 29. Tel: 287
824.   Near central (4I)
IL BARGELLINO, Via Guelfa 87. Tel: 238 2658.   Near central (4I)
IL GRANDUCA, Via Pier Capponi 13. Tel: 572 803.
                                                                          Near central (3N)
IL PERSEO, Via Cerretani 1. Tel: 212 504 Fax: 2883377.
                                                                                  Central (5H)
INDIPENDENZA, Piazza Indipendenza 8. Tel: 496 630.
                                                                          Near central (3H)
IRIS, Piazza S.Maria Novella 22. Tel: 239 6735.   Central (5G)
KURSAAL, Via Nazionale 24. Tel: 496 324.   Near central (4H)
LA LOCANDINA, Via dei Pepi 7. Tel: 240 880.   Central (7M)
LA MIA CASA, Piazza S. Maria Novella 20. Tel: 213 061.
                                                                                  Central (5G)
LA ROMAGNOLA, Via della Scala 40. Tel: 211 597.   Station (4F)
LA SCALA, Via della Scala 21. Tel: 212 629.   Station (5G)
LOMBARDI, Via Fiume 8. Tel: 283 151.   Station (4G)
L'OROLOGIO, Via dell'Oriuolo 17. Tel: 234 0706. Near central (4L)
LOSANNA, Via Alfieri 9. Tel: 245 840.   Near central (4N)
MAGLIANI, Via S. Raparata 1. Tel: 287 378.   Near central (4I)
MARCELLA, Via Faenza 58. Tel: 213 232.   Station (4H)
MARGARETH, Via della Scala 25. Tel: 210 138.   Station (5G)
MARIA LUISA DE'MEDICI, Via del Corso 1. Tel: 280 048.
                                                                                  Central (6I)

MARILENA TOURIST HOUSE, Via Fiume 20. Tel: 238 1705.

	Station (4G)
MARINI, Via Faenza 56. Tel: 284 824.	Station (4H)
MARY, Piazza Indipendenza 5. Tel: 496 310.	Near central (3H)
MASACCIO, Via Masaccio 228. Tel: 578 153.	Near central (3O)
MAXIM, Via de'Medici 4. Tel: 217 474.	Central (6I)
MERLINI, Via Faenza 56. Tel: 212 848.	Station (4H)
MIA CARA, Via Faenza 58. Tel: 216 053.	Station (4H)
MIRELLA, Via degli Alfani 36. Tel: 247 8170.	Central (5M)
MONICA, Via Faenza 66. Tel: 283 804.	Station (3H)
MONTREAL, Via della Scala 43. Tel: 238 2331.	Station (5G)
NAZIONALE, Via Nazionale 22. Tel: 238 2203.	Near central (4H)
NELLA, Via Faenza 69. Tel: 284 256.	Station (4H)
ORCHIDEA, Borgo degli Albizi 11. Tel: 248 0346.	Central (6L)
OTTAVIANI, Piazza degli Ottaviani 1. Tel: 239 6223.	Central (6G)
PALAZZUOLO, Via Palazzuolo 71. Tel: 284 883.	Near central (5F)
PALMER, Via degli Avelli 2. Tel: 238 2391.	Near central (5G)
PAOLA, Via Faenza 56. Tel: 213 682.	Station (4H)

PARODI, Piazza Madonna degli Aldobrandini 8. Tel: 211 866.

	Central (5H)
PINA, Via Faenza 69. Tel: 212 231.	Station (4H)
POLO NORD, Via Panzani 7. Tel: 287 952.	Central (5H)
POR SANTA MARIA, Via Calimaruzza 3. Tel: 216 370.	Central (7I)
RINA, Via Dante Alighieri 12. Tel: 213 209.	Central (6I)
SAN GIOVANNI , Via Cerretani 2. Tel: 213 580.	Central (5H)
S.EGIDIO, Via S. Egidio. Tel: 248 0330.	Central (6L)
SAVONAROLA, Viale Matteotti 27. Tel: 587 824.	Near central (2M)
SCOTI, Via Tornabuoni 7. Tel: 292 128.	Central (6H)
SERENA TOURIST HOUSE, Via Fiume 20. Tel: 213 643.	Station (4G)
SOFIA, Via Cavour 21. Tel: 283 930	Near central (4I)
SOLE, Via del Sole 8. Tel: 239 6094.	Central (6G)
TE-TI PRESTIGE, Via Porta Rossa 5. Tel: 239 8248.	Central (7H)
TONY'S INN, Via Faenza 77. Tel: 217 975.	Station (4H)
TOSCANA, Via del Sole 8. Tel: 213 156.	Central (6G)

UNIVERSO, Piazza Santa Maria Novella 20. Tel: 211 484 Fax: 292335.

	Central (5G)
VARSAVIA, Via Panzani 5. Tel: 215 615.	Central (5H)
VIGNA NUOVA, Vigna Nuova 17. Tel: 211 119.	Central (6G)
VISCONTI, Piazza degli Ottaviani 1. Tel: 213 877.	Central (6G)
ZURIGO, Via dell'Oriuolo 17.	Central (6L)

FIVE

Food and wine

Italy is a marvellous place for lovers of food. You are surrounded by the fruits of nature at their most abundant and by a people who for the most part still prefer, even insist on, the freshest of ingredients. Italian cooking, therefore, remains essentially regional so that by and large you can expect to eat Tuscan food whilst in Tuscany (although these days more and more dishes from other regions will also appear on the menu). The virtue of Tuscan food is that in many ways it is rather straightforward: 'The Florentine, careful and calculating, is a man who knows the measure of all things, and his cooking is an austerely composed play upon essential and unadorned themes.' Another factor is the lie of the land. The area's hilliness means that it is easier to cultivate olives than to raise cows – thus Tuscan cooking is based on oil, not butter.

Italian cooking is very much a domestic affair. The best food is traditionally found in the bosom of the family. Restaurant food has been, until recently, either rather unsophisticated or rather pretentious so that the best places for eating were, and often still are, family run 'trattorie', which are restaurants of the simplest kind. It is probably fair to say that there are changes taking place. Although real trattorie still abound, the word is sometimes misapplied to what are really full-scale restaurants with professional staff. This does not mean that the food will be bad – just a little more expensive. The other thing is that attempts are being made to turn Italian cooking into an art form. This meets with mixed success, although the best thing is that more care is taken in general and the chances of having a bad meal become fewer. But on the whole, the essence of Italian food has changed but little – wholesome, fresh, delicious and convivial.

The main meals are: prima colazione (breakfast), pranzo (lunch), cena (dinner).

Bars

Bars are convivial places used in the main for quick visits for breakfast (cappuccino and 'brioche', cake), snacks ('panini', which are filled rolls), and similar items, as well as cakes and pastries, (paste), ice cream, coffee and aperitifs. They may close for lunch.

Italian bars are generally splendid institutions with agreeable but polished service. If you sit down to eat or drink you must pay more, often twice the standing price. All bars should have a price-list visible near the till. In many bars you must pay first at the till, obtain a receipt and hand it to the barman. Don't worry about explaining in Italian – simply point and the cashier will sort it out. Most bars have lavatories and telephones.

Eating in Tuscany

In general you must follow your nose. A list of restaurants is given further on but try and trust your own judgement. You should experiment; it is difficult to have a really bad meal – although in Florence there are too many restaurants interested only in foreign money. Look at the menu outside and see what's available and how much it costs. Once you are inside look around and see what people are eating. Find out what is in season. Ask if there is anything not on the menu.

Sometimes there is no menu – the waiter or owner will come to the table and recite a list. If your knowledge of Italian is nil then try and use the glossary at the end of this section. Often the most unlikely looking places produce the best meal – simple, perhaps, but robust and satisfying. Perhaps the bread will be a little stale, the wine rustic – but you will eat well. In general a 'trattoria' provides the best value.

The types of restaurant are:

Ristorante – tend to be more expensive and more formal, less local in character.
Osteria – a simple, family-run country restaurant, perhaps serving a small selection of 'minestra'.
Trattoria – a town osteria, perhaps with more choice, often excellent. Some trattorie are closer to a 'ristorante'.
Buco – it means 'hole' but is often used in Tuscany for a trattoria.
Locanda – an inn, a little up from osteria.
Pizzeria – specialises in pizza but serves other dishes as well.

Tavola calda – snack bar, often self-service.
Rosticceria – another type of snack-bar, perhaps with take-away service.

The meal

Whilst Tuscan cooking has its own characteristics, the pattern of the meal remains the same throughout Italy. There is not really a main course but several courses, each defined by certain choices. In a full meal it is possible to have as many as six courses but many people are quite likely to have only two – pasta or soup or risotto, and a meat dish.

A full meal might consist of the following courses: antipasto, minestra (pasta), carne, formaggio, dolce or frutta. These are as follows:

Antipasto: literally 'before the meal'. These are appetisers outside the main body of the meal and, whilst frequently delicious, are superfluous to needs unless you are very hungry or you eat them instead of another course. They might consist of cold meats or anchovies, fish mousse or stuffed tomatoes and so on.

Minestra (primo): this word really means soup, although it is often used as a general word for first course (il primo) which may therefore be either a soup, pasta or risotto. If soup it may be a broth with pasta in it, or any of a vast array of other soups. If a pasta then it may be spaghetti or another type of pasta – and there are many of them – with a sauce.

Carne (secondo): carne is meat. Generally the second course is a meat or fish dish, usually grilled or roasted, austerely prepared in contrast to the comparative sophistication of the pasta sauces. Tuscan beef is some of the best in the world. The second course will be accompanied, if desired, by a 'contorno' (salad or vegetables) in a separate dish.

Formaggio: cheese

Dolce, frutta: pudding, fruit. Puddings do not feature much in Italian cooking. The best sweet things are found in shops or bars to be eaten with coffee at breakfast. However, there will usually be something on the menu and it can be very good indeed. A few names of dishes are given at the end of this section in the glossary. Italians prefer to round off the meal with fresh fruit.

Caffe: coffee.

Menu terms
Fresco – fresh
Il conto – the bill
Il coperto – cover charge
Crudo – raw
Pane – bread
Panna – cream
Piccante – spicy
Pizzaiola – tomato sauce with oregano or basil and garlic
Ragu – meat sauce
Servizio compreso – service included.

Tuscan dishes

Ingredients are the essence of Tuscan cooking – it is the cuisine of the farmer/peasant, the hunter and the fisherman.

Antipasti
Some of these can appear as other courses.

Bruschetta – toasted garlic bread wet with oil
Crostini – toasted bread with different toppings
Fagioli toscani col tonno – white beans with oil and tuna fish
Fave con pecorino – broad beans with sheep's cheese
Fettunta – as Bruschetta
Frittata – a sort of omelette – may also be served as a main course
Funghi – a general word for mushrooms of which there are many. Porcini are the finest and most expensive. Seasonal, they are found at the end of the summer. Cremini are found all year round. Morchelle are morels. Funghi Trifolati means sliced mushrooms sauteed in olive oil, garlic and parsley
Insalata di Fagioli – bean salad
Pasticcio – a 'fine mess or trouble'. A mixture of unlikely ingredients that tastes good
Peperonata – sweet peppers, onions, tomatoes in oil, garlic, served cold
Prosciutto e Fichi – Ham and figs.

Minestre (soups – zuppe)

Minestre covers both soup and pasta but in Tuscany soups are particularly important.

Zuppa di Pane – bread soup
Acquacotta – onion soup, Maremma style
Acquacotta dei Logaioli – gardener's soup (bread soup with vegetables)
Zuppa di Cavolo e Pane – cauliflower and bread soup
Cacciucco alla Livornese – fish stew, Livorno/Leghorn style This is Tuscany's most famous soup containing squid, shrimps,cod, scallops, halibut, sage, garlic and tomatoes.
Ribollita – very well cooked bread and vegetable soup
Pappa al Pomodoro – tomato and bread soup
Zuppa di Ceci – chick-pea soup
Zuppa di Lenticchie – lentil soup
Pasta e Fagioli – pasta and bean soup
Cacciucco ai funghetti – mushroom soup
Il Buglione – boiled bits of different meats with herbs
Polenta – cornmeal mash with salt and pepper.

Pasta

There are basically two types of pasta – soft and fresh with eggs, or brittle hard wheat. The latter is more common in Tuscany. The following is as comprehensive as possible but there are many variations using local names; other types of pasta may be used for each recipe.

Farfalle alla caprese – butterfly pasta with tomatoes, basil and mozzarella
Farfalle con pumate v as above, with sun-dried tomatoes
Frittata di pasta – omelette with pasta
Pasta con fiori di zucca v with marrow flowers
Lasagnette del lucchese – lasagna with rippled edges and a sauce of spinach, ricotta, liver, mushrooms and nutmeg
Pappardelle con la lepre – thick, flat, long pasta with hare sauce
Penne con salsa rossa al funghetto – nib-shaped pasta with tomato and mushroom sauce
Penne ai funghi e salsiccia – as above, baked with mushroom sauce and sausage
Penne alla salvia v as above, with sage (and sometimes veal)
Penne alla rozza – as above, with mushroom, onion, celery, herbs and ham

Penne al sugo di porcini – as above, with red porcini sauce

Rigatoni alla buttera – tubular pasta peasant style (sausage, peas, cream)

Rotelle con ricotta e noce moscata – round pasta with ricotta cheese and nutmeg

Rotelle al pomodoro e parmigiano – as above with tomato and parmesan

Spaghetti alla cavalleggera – with eggs, walnuts, cream

Spaghetti con salsa di noci – with walnut sauce

Spaghetti con broccoletti e radicchio – with broccoli rabe and chicory

Spaghetti al sugo di spigola – with sea bass sauce

Spaghetti con aglio, olio e peperoncino – with garlic, oil and hot pepper

Spaghetti alla Maremma – style of the Maremma region, strong taste with mushrooms, peas, aubergine, cheese and sausage.

Spaghetti alla rustica – 'rustic' spaghetti (tomatoes, onion)

Spaghetti al filetto di pomodoro – with fresh tomato sauce

Spaghetti alla pirata – 'pirate' style, with shrimp, mussels etc.

Spaghettini al cacio e pepe – thin spaghetti with goat cheese and pepper

Tagliatelle al sugo d'agnello – strips of pasta with lamb sauce

Tagliatelle all' ortolana – as above, with seasonal garden vegetables

Tagliatelle con porcini al funghetto – as above, in white mushroom sauce

Tagliatelle al sugo di caccia – as above, with game sauce

Tagliatelle con porcini mantecati – as above, with porcini and butter

Tagliolini al tartufo – thin pasta strips with truffles.

Risotto

Risotto alla Toscana – with minced beef, veal kidney and liver, tomatoes and cheese

Risotto nero alle seppie/alla fiorentina – black rice with cuttlefish

Risotto alla pescatora – fisherman's style with mussels, shrimp

Risotto alla contadina – peasant style with sausage, peas, onion.

Eggs (uova)

Uova affogate – poached eggs

Uova al guscio – soft boiled

Uova in tegame – fried

Uova sode – hard – boiled egg

Uove stracciate – scrambled eggs.

Fish (pesce)

Acciughe – anchovies
Alici all' olio – anchovies in olive oil
Anguilla alla fiorentina – eel florentine style, with oil, garlic and sage
Baccala alla Livornese – dried salt cod Livorno/Leghorn style with oil and white wine, vegetables and tripe
Bianchetti – whitebait
Cacciucco – Tuscan fish stew
Calamari ripieni alla Fiorentina – squid Florentine style, stuffed with spinach
Capitone – conger eel
Cefalo alla diavola – devilled mullet
Cozze – mussels
Dentice al guazzetto – baby grouper or red snapper poached in tomato sauce
Dorata – gilt-head
Gamberi alla Pescatora – shrimp fisherman style
Granchio – crab
Insalata di mare alla Toscana – cold Tuscan-style seafood salad
Insalata di Pesce con vegetali – cold fish, vegetable salad
Lo Scaveccio – Maremma dish of marinated eel
Luccio – pike
Lumache – snails
Merluzzo – cod
Minestra di Granchi – crab soup
Ostriche – oysters
Pesce spada – swordfish
Polipetti in umido – baby octopus stew
Sarde fritte – fried sardines
Seppie nere in umido – black cuttlefish stew
Sogliola arrosto – roast sole
Sogliola con capperi – sole with capers
Spigola – sea bass
Tonno alla Livornese – Tuna steak Livorno/Leghorn style
Trota Salmonata all'aceto balsamico – salmon trout with balsamic vinegar
Vongole alla marinara in bianco – clams steamed in garlic/wine.

Game (cacciagione) and Poultry (pollame)

Anitra all'arancia – duck with orange, originally from Tuscany
Beccaccia – woodcock
Cappone al forno - roast stuffed capon

Capriolo – roe-deer
Cervo al Marsala – venison with marsala wine
Cinghiale – wild boar
Coniglio alla cacciatora – rabbit, hunter's style
Fagiano alla cacciatora – pheasant, hunter's style
Faraona – guinea fowl
Lepre – hare
Oca – goose
Pernice – partridge
Petti di pollo al funghetto – stuffed chicken breast in mushroom sauce
Petti di pollo alla fiorentina – boned chicken breasts fried in butter
Pollo al limone – chicken with lemon
Pollo alla cacciatora – chicken, hunter's style
Pollo in fricassea alla fiorentina – poached chicken with egg and
    lemon sauce
Piccione in salmi – wild pigeon with giblets and sage
Quaglie arrosto al Tarragone – roast quail with tarragon
Quaglie e salsiccia con polenta – quail, sausage with polenta
Selvaggina – game, particularly venison
Tacchino – turkey.

Meat (carne)

Agnello di Pasqua – Easter lamb (roast with rosemary, garlic)
Animelle al burro nero e salvia – sweetbreads in black butter and sage
Arista alla fiorentina – loin of porkroasted in water or little oil with
    garlic, rosemary and cloves
Arrosto – roast
Bistecco alla fiorentina – Tuscan steak, from Chianina cattle, is
    among the best in the world. 'Florence takes a T-bone steak of
    noble size and grills it quickly over a blazing fire, adding nothing
    but the aroma of freshly ground pepper and olive oil. It is a
    triumph'.
Bollito misto – mixed boiled meats, often with salsa verde or green
    sauce
Braciola di maiale – pork chop
Calzone – hollow half pizza stuffed with ham and mozzarella cheese
Capra – goat
Carpaccio – thin slices of raw, lean beef with mustard sauce or olive
    oil and lemon juice
Cervello – brain
Coda alla vaccinara – oxtail stew
Cotechino e lenticchie – pork sausage and lentils

Cuore – heart

Fegato alla salvia/Toscana – calf liver fried with oil, sage

Fritte alla fiorentina – brains Florentine style, marinaded in oil and vinegar, breadcrumbed, fried with anchovies and spinach

Fritto misto alla fiorentina – mixed fry of chicken breast, brain, sweetbreads, artichoke hearts

Lesso – boiled meat

Maiale – pork

Manzo – beef

Ossobuco – veal knuckle with bone marrow, tomatoes, white wine

Paillard – grilled steak (veal or beef)

Piccata – escalope of veal

Polpette – meatballs

Porchetta – roast sucking pig with garlic and rosemary

Prosciutto – ham

Rognone di maiale – grilled pork kidney

Rostinciana – grilled spare-ribs

Salsicce – pork sausages

Saltimbocca – veal covered in sage and ham, cooked in butter

Scaloppina – escalope of veal

Spezzatino di agnello e carciofi – lamb and artichoke stew

Stracotto alla Fiorentina – pot roast, Florentine style

Testina alla toscana – calf's head, boiled then sauteed

Trippa alla fiorentina – braised tripe in tomato with marjoram and Parmesan

Vitello – veal.

Contorno (side dishes): vegetables (verdura or vegetali), and salads (insalata)

Aceto – vinegar

Aglio – garlic

Asparagi – asparagus

Broccoletti saltati – sauteed broccoli rabe

Carciofi alla Giudea – fried baby artichokes

Cavolofiore – cauliflower

Ceci – chick peas

Cetriolo – cucumber

Cipolla – onion

Condimento – dressing

Fagioli – white haricot beans

Fagiolini – french beans

Fave – broad beans

Finocchio – fennel
Lattuga – lettuce
Melanzane – aubergines
Olio di oliva – olive oil
Panzanella – bread salad with cucumber, scallions, tomato
Patate – potato
Patatine fritte – chips
Peperoncini – small hot chilli peppers
Peperoni – sweet peppers
Piselli – peas
Pomodori – tomatoes
Puntarelle in salsa di alici – chicory salad with anchovy dressing
Radicchio – chicory, endive
Radice – radish
Rape – turnip
Segato di carciofi con carote - salad of artichokes and carrots
Spinaci – spinach
Vegetali alla griglia – grilled vegetables
Zucchini – courgettes.

Cheese

The famous Italian cheeses (gorgonzola etc.) are usually available but Tuscany specialises in sheep's cheese – a younger one is called caciotta (di pecora), an older, tangier one is 'pecorino stagionato'. 'Ricotta' is fresh cottage cheese.

Olive oil

This is considered a very healthy food and a basic ingredient of Italian, and particularly Tuscan, cooking. The olive family goes back 40 million years and the olive branch has been a symbol from almost the beginning of recorded history. Its oil is considered an indispensable element of life itself among Mediterranean peoples.

According to definition, extra-vergine olive oil is the processing of the Olea Europea (the olive) without the addition of other oils, or anything else. Altogether, there are some 300 varieties of olive grown in the Mediterranean. Some are grown specifically to be eaten raw, others, notably in the Chianti region, are grown to be turned into oil.

(Opposite) *Cortona – a classic view of the Piazza della Repubblica.*

Between 18 and 26 per cent of an olive is oil, found both in the flesh and the nut. Once the olives have been harvested they need to be pressed as soon as possible to prevent fermentation, superfluous flavours and acidity. Modern techniques first turn the flesh and nut into a paste which is then pressed, separating the oil and vegetable water from the flesh. The oil and water is separated by means of a centrifuge and the oil is filtered.

The best oil should be used within a year as the flavour begins to diminish after that. It is rich in vitamins and easily digested, and is excellent with raw salads and vegetables but also, according to scientific tests, as a frying oil.

In Chianti the Chianti Classico Extra-Vergine Olive Oil Consortium has recently been formed, to control and guarantee the nature of the local oil. More information can be obtained from their headquarters at Sant' Andrea in Percussina, Via degli Scopeti 155-158 (Tel: 055/822102).

Pudding (il dolce) and fruit (frutta)

There are few if any true puddings peculiar to Tuscany – Tuscans prefer fruit and cheese – but there will always be something on the menu, either which utilises fresh fruit or something that is generally Italian.

Albicocche – apricots
Amaretti – macaroons
Ananas – pineapple
Arancia – orange
Biscotti/Cantucci di Prato – hazelnut biscuits from Prato, to be dipped in Vin Santo
Brutti ma Buoni – 'ugly but good', biscuits similar to the preceding
Budino – pudding
Buonissima – walnut and honey tart
Castagne/Marroni arrosti – roast chestnuts
Cenci – light, crunchy biscuits
Ciliege – cherries
Cocomero – watermelon
Fichi secchi e noci – dried figs and walnuts

(**Opposite**) **Top:** *The Ponte Vecchio in Florence – a bridge that is lived in.*
(**Opposite**) **Bottom:** *A jewellery shop on the Ponte Vecchio.*

Fragole all'aceto – strawberries in vinegar

Gelato – ice cream

Granita – flavoured water ice

Lamponi – raspberries

Macedonia – fruit salad

Mandorle – almond

Mela – apple

Mirtilli – bilberries

Monte Bianco – chestnut puree with whipped cream

Nocciole – hazlenuts

Panforte di Siena – hard rich cake of spices and candied peel

Pere o mele cotte – baked pears or apples

Pesche al vino rosso – peaches in red wine

Pesche con noci al forno – baked peaches stuffed with nuts and chocolate

Polenta dolce – sweet mixture of chestnut flour, with whipped cream and ricotta cheese.

Pompelmo – grapefruit

Prugna – plum

Schiacciata con l'uva – grape tart

Tiramisu – 'Pick me up', one of the most original and delicious of Italian puddings. A rich combination of egg, sugar, rum and espresso

Torta – flan or tart

Uva – grapes

Zabaglione – whipped egg yoke, sugar, Marsala.

Zuccotto – ice-cream cake with whipped cream, chocolate, liqueur

Zuppa inglese – so called 'English soup or custard'; something like a trifle, it is supposed, in fact, to have its origins in Fiesole.

Wine and drink

Tuscany is filled with good local wines. A short section below tells you more about the changes that have taken place in bottled wines in the region; but it is often possible to find a good, rustic, locally-made wine in small trattorie, in which case it might well come in a carafe. You drink your fill from it and a rough estimate of the cost will be made on the bill. In general, trattorie err on the side of generosity. Otherwise you can ask for 'una bottiglia di vino del posto/di qua' (locally produced wine) or 'vino vostrano' (your house wine). However, it has been said that you should experiment with the oldest available red and aim for the youngest available white.

Italians love wine but they drink it mostly with food and not in large quantities. There is always mineral water on the table (acqua minerale), either sparkling (frizzante or con gas/gassata) or still (naturale) and it is not unusual for people to add it to their wine particularly at lunch time.

Of the good bottled wines, the following is a selection of the main ones, all of which (except the last) are DOC (denominazione di origine controllata), and some DOCG (the additional 'g' meaning garantita or guaranteed):

Bianco della Valdinievole – white from Montecatini
Bianco di Pitigliano – dry white
Bianco Vergine Valdichiana v white from Cortona
Bolgheri – coastal white
Brunello di Montalcino – dry red
Candia dei Colli Apuani – white from northern Tuscany
Carmignano – dry red
Chianti – dry red
Chianti Classico – dry red
Montecarlo – dry white from Lucca
Montescudaio Rosso – dry red
Morellino di Scansano – dry red from Grosseto
Parrina Rosso – red from Orbetello
Pomino Rosso – dry red
Rosso delle Colline Lucchesi – dry red
Vino Nobile di Montepulciano – dry red
Vernaccia di S. Gimignano – dry white
Vinsanto – sweet dessert wine.

Useful words

Aperitivo – aperitif
Digestivo – digestive drink
Rosso – red
Bianco – white
Vecchio – old
Giovane – young
Secco – dry
Abboccato – semi-sweet
Dolce – sweet
Frizzante – lightly sparkling or slightly fizzy
Spumante – sparkling
Freddo – cold

Ghiaccio – ice
Birra – beer
Sfuso – draught
Una caraffa – carafe
Un litro – litre
Un mezzo litro – half-litre
Una bottiglia – bottle
Una mezza bottiglia – half-bottle
Un bicchiere – glass
Liquore – liqueur.

Chianti wine

The wines of Chianti started to develop a reputation beyond that of a solid country wine in the 17th century culminating in the edict of 1716. It gained a mark of distinction by the technique of refermentation brought about by the addition of musts of semi-dried grapes to make it fuller and smoother. Chianti wine is essentially a blend of Sangiovese and Canaiolo grapes with Malvasia and Trebbiano.

Baron Bettino Ricasoli, the 19th century politician who did much research into wine production, described this blend in the following way:

'the wine receives from Sangioveto the principal dose of its aroma ... and a certain vigour of sensations; from Canaiolo the light sweetness that tempers the coarseness of the first while taking away nothing of the aroma, with which it itself is endowed; Malvasia, which should be used less in wines destined for ageing, tends to dilute the product of the first two grapes, while amplifying the flavour and making it lighter and more readily adaptable to daily use at table'.

As we have seen, the Chianti wine is grown in a vast area of Tuscany, beyond the limits of Chianti Classico. This area is bottled as Chianti DOCG (denominazione di origine controllata e garantita), in other words, guaranteed Chianti wine, a method of control introduced in 1984.

Within this area there are many variations of style, some depending still on traditional peasant methods and instinct but more and more adopting modern scientific methods. Among the most famous are Brunello di Montalcino, Vino Nobile di Montepulciano, Vernaccia di S. Gimignano, Carmignano, Pomino and Galestro. DOCG was introduced as a way of controlling quality which tended to be highly variable in the 1960s and 1970s as production increased. This has certainly helped, although it is felt in some quarters that some of the good, unique aspects of Chianti wine have been thrown out with the bad. Some things had to change, however, effective though it might have been. It became impractical to seal in the freshness with a layer of olive oil, and the old straw flask suffered, in the main, the same fate. DOCG was preceded in 1967 by DOC (controllata but not garantita) in expectation of a boom in production. This came about but the decline in quality, or at least the decline in distinctive Chianti character, needed to be rectified, hence the addition of the guarantee.

The introduction of DOCG meant that grape yields had to be reduced and the use of concentrates, particularly from outside the region, was curtailed. The resulting decline in production of traditional Chianti has led to an increase in the production of white wines and new red wines (vini novelli, in the Beaujolais Nouveau vein), as well as new types of red wines for ageing. Now that the cultivation of wine has become not only organised on a large scale but also with an eye to quality, the future is being considered carefully in view of the fact that many thousands of acres need to be planted with new vines. Experiments are being conducted on the grape varieties, particularly the Sangiovese and Canaiolo, as well as the best techniques for cultivation and the possibilities of mechanical harvesting.

Young Chianti goes well with antipasti, soups, pastas, tripe and salt cod (baccala). When older (2-5 years) it goes with poultry, veal and grills and mild cheeses. Older wines go with roasts, game, stews and old cheeses.

Vinsanto

'Holy wine' is not only used at the church altar, although that is no doubt where it obtained its name. It is much appreciated and widely drunk by all Tuscans. It is a strong, sweet dessert wine, vaguely sherry like, and often used as a sort of pudding by dipping hard almond biscuits into it.

The recipe is as follows: grapes are placed in clean, dry, tubs, and pressed to extract the must (grape juice) which is then passed through a sieve and then placed in caratelli (small wooden casks). The must is left to ferment with the bung hole open and refilled twice daily with more must. After 10-15 days the cask should be sealed with chalk or pitch and placed in an airy upstairs room out of the sunlight. The wine should then be decanted to demijohns to clear before bottling.

Coffee

At the end of dinner or lunch it is customary to take an espresso (small, strong, black) coffee. A cappuccino is diluted with frothy milk, and perhaps with a sprinkling of cocoa, and is taken in the morning. Caffelatte is milky coffee. Caffe macchiato is an espresso with a dash of milk, whilst latte macchiato is the opposite. Caffe lungo is a weak espresso, ristretto is strong. Caffe corretto is with the addition of a liqueur (grappa or brandy). Caffe Hag is decaffeinated.

Picnics

If you don't want to sit in a bar or restaurant at lunchtime, then have a picnic. In Italy this is easy to do and cheap: buy some rolls (rosette), wine, water or beer from an alimentari shop (grocer) and some cheese and salami either there or from a local market (see under 'shopping'). Cheese etc. is bought by the 'etto' (100 grams).

Selected Restaurants in Tuscany

Here follows a list of some restaurants in the region. It is impossible to be exhaustive so the list merely gives some ideas based on personal experience and on reputation. For those with a real interest in eating well the *Michelin Red Hotel* and *Restaurant Guide* to Italy is excellent and gives a very accurate idea of quality and price.

For the restaurants listed below, prices vary from between 20,000 lira to 60,000 lire per head. Restaurants which are more expensive are marked as are restaurants which offer menus at exceptional value.

Florence

Acquerello, Via Ghibellina 156. Tel: 2340554.
Il Biribisso, Via dell'Albero 28. Tel: 293180.
Baldini Trattoria, Via Il Prato 96. Tel: 287663.
Buca Lapi, Via del Trebbio 1. Tel: 213768.
Il Barone, Via Romano 123. Tel: 220585.
Cantinone Gallo Nero, Via Santo Spirito 6. Tel: 218898. (Inexpensive.)
La Capannina Di Sante, Ponte da Verrazzano/Piazza Ravenna. Tel: 688345.
Cantinetta Antinori, Piazza Antonori 3. Tel: 292234.
Camillo, Borgo San Jacopo 57. Tel: 212427.
Cavallino, Piazza della Signoria. Tel: 215818.
Cibreo, Via de'Macci 118. Tel: 2341100.

Da Noi, Via Fiesolana 40. Tel: 242917.
Dino, Via Ghibellina 51. Tel: 241452, Fax: 241378.
Don Chisciotte, Via Ridolfi 4. Tel: 475430.
Enoteca Pinchiorri, Via Ghibellina 87. Tel: 242777, Fax: 244983.
    (Expensive but recommended.)
Del Fagioli, Corso Tintori 47. Tel: 2480170.
La Fonticine, Via Nazionale 9. Tel: 82106.
13 Gobbi, Via del Porcellana 9. Tel: 2398769.
Harry's Bar, Lungarno Vespucci 27. Tel: 2396700.
Leo in Santa Croce, Via Torta 7. Tel: 210829.
La Loggia, Piazzale Michelangelo 1. Tel: 2342832
Mamma Gina, Borgo Sant'Jacopo 37. Tel: 2396009.
Martinicca, Via Del Sole 27. Tel: 218928.
Marione, Via della Spada 27. Tel: 214756.
Osteria Numero Uno, Via del Moro 20. Tel: 284897.
Ottorino, Via delle Oche 12-16. Tel: 218747.
La Posta, Via de'Lamberti 20. Tel: 212701.
Il Profeta, Borgo Ognissanti 93, Tel: 212265.
Quattro Stagioni, Via Maggio 61. Tel: 218906.
La Rucola, Via del Leone 50. Tel: 224002.
Sabatini, Via de'Panzani 9/a. Tel: 211559, Fax: 210293.
Trattoria Casalinga, Via del Michelozzi 9. Tel: 218624.
    (Reasonable.)
Traverna Del Bronzino, Via delle Ruote 25. Tel: 495220.

South of Florence
Antico Crespino, Largo Enrico Fermi 15. Tel: 221155.

Florence province
Da Nello, San Casciano Val di Pesa. (Excellent food at very
    reasonable prices.)
Da Archimede, Reggello. Tel: 868182.
Il Pirana, Via Tobia Bertini via Valentini, Prato. Tel: 25746.
    (Expensive)
Trattoria Bruno, Via Verdi 12, Prato. Tel: 0574 23810.
Da Verrazzano, Piazzo Matteotti 28, Greve in Chianti. Tel: 853189.

Arezzo
Buca di San Francisco, Piazza San Francisco 1. Tel: 23271.
Antica Trattoria al Principe, Via Giovi 25. Tel: 362046.
Le Tastevin, Via de'Cenci 9. Tel: 28304.

Province of Arezzo
Fonte dei Frati, Localita'Case Sparse 294, Cortona. Tel: 601370.
Castellucci, San Giovanni Valdarno. Tel: 941679.

Grosseto
Buca di San Lorenzo, Via Manetti 1. Tel: 25142.
La Maremma, Via Fulcheri Paolucci de'Calboli 5. Tel: 21177.

Province of Grosseto
Taverna del Vecchio Borgo, Via Parenti 12, Massa Marittima.
   Tel: 93950. (Very reasonable.)

Livorno (Leghorn)
Gran Duca, Piazza Micheli 16. Tel: 891024.

Province of Livorno
L'Arco Vecchio, Via Pacinotti 55/57, Ardenza. Tel: 505193.
Da Oscar, Via Franchini 78. Ardenza. Tel: 501258.
Rossi-La Torre di Calafuria, Calafuria. Tel: 580547.

Elba (Isola d')
Il Chiasso, Via Nazario Sauro 20. Capoliveri. Tel: 968709.
Publius, Piazza XX Settembre 13, Poggio. Marciana. Tel: 99208.
Perseo, Chiessi. Tel: 906010.
Rendez-Vous da Marcello, Marciana Marina. Tel: 99251.
Longone Inn, Porto Azzurro. Tel: 957995.

Lucca
Buca di Sant'Antonio, Via della Cervia. Tel: 55881 Fax: 55881.
   (Recommended.)
Da Giulio, Via San Tommaso 29. Tel: 55948.
   (Very reasonably priced: recommended.)
Il Giglio, Piazza del Giglio. Tel: 44058.

Outside Lucca
La Mora, Via Sesto da Moriano, Ponte a Moriano. Tel: 57109
Vipore, Pieve S. Stefano, Tel: 59245.
Solferino, San Macario in Piano. Tel: 59118.

Province of Lucca

Il Patriarca, Viale Carducci 79, Viareggio. Tel: 53126, Fax: 55181.
(Expensive: recommended.)
Romano, Via Mazzini 120, Viareggio. Tel: 31382. (Recommended.)

Pisa

Ristorante Sergio, Lungarno Pacinotti 1. Tel: 48245, Fax: 850334.
(Recommended.)
Al Ristoro dei Vecchi Macelli, Via Volturno 49. Tel: 20424.
(Recommended.)
Da Bruno, Via Bianchi 12. Tel: 560818 Fax: 550607.

Province of Pisa

Da Beppino, Via delle Prigioni 15, Volterra. Tel: 86051.
Etruria, Piazza dei Priori, Volterra. Tel: 86064.
Osteria dei Poeti, Via Matteotti 55, Volterra. Tel: 86029.

Province of Pistoia

Cugna, Via Bolognese 236, La Cugna. Tel: 475000.
Rafanelli, Via Sant'Agostino 47, San Agostino. Tel: 23046.
Trattoria da Fagiolino, Via Carega 1, Cutigliano. Tel: 60814.
(Very good value.)
La Capannina, Abetone. Tel: 60562.
Da Pierone, Abetone. Tel: 60068.

Siena

Al Marsili, Via del Castoro 3. Tel: 47154, Fax: 280970.
Guido, Vicolo Pier Pettinaio 7. Tel: 280042.
Medio Evo. Via dei Rossi 40. Tel: 280315.
Tullio ai Tre Cristi, Vicolo dei Rossi 40. Tel: 280608.

Province of Siena

Arnolfo, Piazza Santa Caterina, Colle Val d'Elsa. Tel: 920549.
(Expensive.)
Il Pozzo, Piazza Roma, Monteriggioni. Tel: 304127.
Le Terrazze, Piazza della Cisterna 24, San Gimignano. Tel: 940328.
I Cinque Gigli, San Gimignano. Tel: 940186.

SIX

Shopping and Markets

Whilst Italy is no longer particularly cheap, quality is generally high and value for money is good. It is probably the best place for what are known in Britain vulgarly as 'fancy goods' – marvellous writing paper and notebooks, for example, and picture frames. Another good buy is glass and crystal – particularly in Colle di Val d'Elsa.

There are antique markets each month in Arezzo (first Sunday), Pistoia (second Sunday), Lucca (third Sunday) and Florence (last Sunday). Ceramics are widely sold; Sesto Fiorentino is famous for its porcelain and Volterra is well known for alabaster. Wrought ironwork and copperware are also widely sold.

Designer clothes shops abound and bargains are to be had with careful looking, although in general clothes are cheaper at home. There is a great deal of good kitchenware and charming designer toys for children, but they can be expensive and are not always suitable for robust youngsters. If you have come by car, you will be able to take home a goodly supply of wine; but even if you haven't, the best olive oil is cheaper than at home, as is good cheese and Vinsanto with Pratesi biscuits to dip in it.

Shopping in Florence

The main shopping areas are along Via Tornabuoni, Via Calzaiuoli and in the general area of the Duomo. Florence is particularly noted for leather goods (in the Santa Croce area and in the cloister of Santa Croce itself) and work in gold, and jewellery in general (the Ponte Vecchio is famous for this but there are plenty of small shops dealing in it throughout the town). Books (libri pronounced 'leebree') are expensive, particularly in a foreign language. Books in English are to be found at Feltrinelli at Via Cavour 2, the Paperback Exchange at Via Fiesolana 31r, the BM Bookshop at Borgo Ognissanti 4r. Cloth (tessuti) at the Casa dei Tessuti, Via de' Pecori 20-24r; high quality paper (including marbled) at Giulio Giannini e Figlio, Piazza Pitti 37r. Food shops abound but vegetarians may like to try Sugar Blues,

Via XXVII Aprile 16/48r; whilst medieval remedies are to be found still at the Farmaceutica di Santa Maria Novella, Via della Scala 16n and at Bizzarri, Via Condotta 32r.

Markets

Markets are an attraction in themselves. They are still an important part of daily life, where people expect to shop for fresh food, household items and bargain clothes. As well as being good places for picnic shopping, they are a glimpse into Italian life.

Here are some of the main ones by province and commune; where used, 'frazione' refers to a particular hamlet within the commune). Remember too that the capital, after which the province is named, is also a commune and therefore figures in the list along with all the other communes in the province, e.g. the city of Florence in the province of Florence:

Province of Massa
Aulla – Saturday am
Avenza Carrara – Wednesday am
Bagnone – Monday am
Carrara – Monday am
Fivizzano – Tuesday am and Thursday am
Licciana Nardi – Sunday am
Marina di Carrara – Thursday am
Massa – Tuesday am, Friday am; Frazione Partaccia – daily from mid-June to mid-September
Montignoso – Friday am; and Tuesday am from mid-June to mid-September
Pontremoli – Wednesday am and Saturday am
Villafranca in Lunigiana – Friday am.

Province of Lucca
Altopascio – Thursday am
Bagni di Lucca – Tuesday am, Friday am at Piazza A. Moro; Wednesday am, Saturday am at Piazza Via Veneto
Barga – Saturday am, Friday am
Camaiore – Monday am on Viale Pistelli; on Viale Colombo, in Secco, June-September, on Wednesday am, Thursday am, and Saturday and Sunday; Tuesday am on Piazza degli Alpini; Friday am on Viale Oberdan
Capannori – Friday am

Castelnuovo di Garfagnana – Thursday am, Tuesday am, Thursday am, Saturday am

Coreglia Antelminelli – Wednesday am, Saturday am

Forte dei Marmi – Wednesday am on P.Marconi and Via V.Veneto

Gallicano – Wednesday am

Lucca – daily (except Sunday and Wednesday am) on Piazza del Carmine; Wednesday am, Saturday am on Via dei Bacchettoni; monthly antique market on Piazza Antelminelli, Saturday, Sunday

Massarosa – Tuesday am

Piazza al Serchio – Tuesday am

Pietrasanta – daily (except Sunday, Wednesday am) on Piazza Oberdan; Saturday am on Piazza Villeparisis; Thursday am on Via Oberdan.

Pieve Fosciana - Saturday am

Porcari – Saturday am

Seravezza – Monday am and Saturday am

Viareggio – Thursday am on Piazza Cavour; daily (except Sunday) on Piazza Santa Maria.

Province of Pistoia

Abetone – Thursdays.

Agliana – Saturday am on Via Matteotti; Thursday am on Piazza Gramsci

Buggiano – Tuesday am

Chiesina Uzzanese – Wednesday am

Cutigliano – Tuesday am

Lamporecchio – Saturday am

Larciano – Saturday am

Monsummano Terme – Monday am

Montale – Friday am

Montecatini Terme – Thursday am

Pescia – Saturday am

Pieve a Nievole – Saturday pm

Pistoia – Wednesday am, Saturday am

Ponte Buggianese – Monday am, Friday am

Quarrata – Saturday am

S. Marcello Pistoiese – Monday am, Thursday am

Serravalle Pistoiese – Friday am.

City of Florence

Markets may be found all over the city every day except Sunday. The main markets (mercati) are as follows:-

San Lorenzo, Via dell'Ariento, Piazza Mercato Centrale for bags etc. (Open 0900-1930 except Sunday/Monday am in winter November to March.)

Mercato del Porcellino, Piazza del Mercato Nuovo for straw goods, bags, gifts. (Hours as San Lorenzo.)

Mercato di San Ambrogio, Piazza Ghiberti for food and various goods. (Open 0800-1330, closed Sunday.)

Mercato delle Cascine, Viale A. Lincoln, Parco delle Cascine for various items. (Every Tuesday 0800-1400.)

Mercato delle Pulci (Flea Market), Piazza dei Ciompi for antiques. (Open 0900-1300 and 1500-1930, closed Sunday and Monday. On the last Sunday of each month it is open all day and is larger than usual. Between 15 April and 15 September it is open also on Mondays.)

Province of Florence

Bagno a Ripoli – Thursday am, Tuesday am, Friday am
Barberino del Mugello – Saturday am
Barberino di Val d'Elsa – Saturday am
Borgo S.Lorenzo – Tuesday am, Friday pm
Calenzano – Wednesday am, Friday am
Campi Bisenzio – Saturday am
Cantagallo – Wednesday am
Capraia e Limite – Monday am and Wednesday am
Carmignano – Tuesday am, Wednesday am
Castelfiorentino – Saturday am
Cerreto Guidi – Saturday am, Tuesday am, Wednesday am
Certaldo – Wednesday am, Saturday am
Dicomano – Saturday am
Empoli – Thursday am and others each day except Sunday and Monday
Fiesole – Saturday am
Figline Valdarno – Tuesday am
Firenzuola – Monday (all day), Sunday am
Fucecchio – Wednesday am
Gambassi Terme – Tuesday am
Greve in Chianti – Saturday am; in Panzano, Sunday am; in San Polo, Thursday am; in Strada in Chianti, Tuesday am;
Impruneta – Saturday am; in Tavarnuzze, Wednesday am
Incisa Val d' Arno – Friday am
Lastra a Signa – Saturday am, Wednesday am
Marradi – Monday am
Montaione – Friday am

Montelupo Fiorentino – Saturday am
Montemurlo – Friday am, Tuesday am
Montespertoli – Tuesday am
Palazzuolo sul Senio – Tuesday am , Saturday am
Pelago – Thursday am
Poggio a Caino – Thursday am; Friday am
Pontassieve - Wednesday am
Prato – daily (except Sunday) on Piazza Duomo; Monday am on
   Piazza Mercato Nuovo; Saturday am, Via G.Braga.
Reggello – Saturday am
Rignano sull'Arno – Thursday am
Rufina – Monday pm
San Casciano Val di Pesa – Monday am; Thursday am
San Godenzo – Sunday am
San Piero a Sieve – Saturday pm
Scandicci – all day Saturday and daily am except Sunday on Piazza
   Togliatti
Scarperia – Friday am, all day Tuesday on Via Santa Croce
Sesto Fiorentino v all day Saturday
Signa – Monday pm, Friday am
Tavarnelle Val di Pesa – Thursday am; San Donato in Poggio, Friday am
Vaiano – Saturday am
Vernio – S. Quirico market, Friday am; Mercatale market, Thursday am
Vicchio – Thursday am
Vinci – Wednesday am.

Province of Livorno
Bibbona – Thursday am
Campo nell' Elba – Wednesday am
Capoliveri – Thursday am
Castagneto Carducci – Thursday am
Cecina – Tuesday am
Collesalvetti – Thursday am; in Stagno on Tuesday am
Livorno – Friday am on Via Trieste; daily on Piazza Cavallotti,
   Piazza Garibaldi, Piazza XX Settembre, Via Buontalenti (except
   Sunday)
Marciana – Thursday am
Marciana Marina – Tuesday am
Piombino – Wednesday am
Port Azzurro – Saturday am
Portferraio – Friday am
Rio Marina – Monday am

Rio nell' Elba v Tuesday am
Rosignano Marittimo v Monday am
San Vincenzo – Saturday am
Suvereto – Monday am.

Province of Pisa

Bientina – Tuesday am; monthly antiques market on Saturday, Sunday
Buti – Monday am
Calci – Wednesday am
Calcinaia – Thursday am
Capannoli – Tuesday am
Casale Marittimo – Friday am
Casciana Terme – Thursday am
Cascina – Thursday am
Castelfranco di Sotto – Monday am on Piazza XX Settembre; Monday am on Piazza Beato Gherardo; daily (except Sunday, Monday) on Piazza Ferretti
Castellina Marittima – Saturday am
Castelnuovo Val di Cecina – Wednesday am
Crespina v Thursday am
Fauglia – Tuesday am
Guardistallo – Thursday am
Lajatico v Wednesday all day
Lari – Monday am
Montecatini Val di Cecina v Monday am, Wednesday am, Friday am
Montescudaio – Friday am
Montopoli in Val d' Arno – Saturday am
Palaia – Thursday am
Peccioli – Tuesday am
Pisa – daily food market (except Sunday) on Piazza Vettovaglie; daily market on Piazza Duomo; Wednesday am, Saturday am on Piazza Guerrazzi and Via Buonarroti.
Pomarance – Thursday am
Ponsacco – Wednesday am
Pontedera – Friday am and the Sundays either side of Christmas.
San Giuliano Terme – Tuesday am
San Miniato – Tuesday am, Thursday am
San Croce sull'Arno – Saturday am, Tuesday am
San Maria a Monte – Thursday am
Vecchiano – Friday am
Vicopisano – Saturday am
Volterra – Saturday am.

Province of Arezzo

Anghiari – Wednesday am
Arezzo – daily (except Sunday) on Piazza Sant'Agostino
Bibbiena – Thursday am
Bucine – Wednesday am
Capolona – Friday am
Castel Focognano – in Rassina on Wednesday am
Castelfranco di Sopra – Friday am
Castel San Niccolo – in Strada in Casentino on Monday PM
Castiglion Fibocchi v Thursday am
Castiglion Fiorentino v Friday am
Chitignano – Tuesday am
Chiusi della Verna – Sunday am
Civitella in Val di Chiana – Wednesday am
Cortona – Saturday am, Tuesday am
Foiano della Chiana – Monday am
Laterina – Monday am
Loro Ciuffenna – Monday am
Lucignano – Thursday am
Montemignaio – Sunday am
Monterchi – Sunday am
Monte San Savino – Wednesday am
Montevarchi – Thursday am
Pergine Valdarno – Friday am
Pian di Sco – Saturday pm
Pieve San Stefano – Monday am
Poppi – at Ponte a Poppi on Tuesday am; on Piazza Amerighi Saturday am
Pratovecchio – Friday am
San Giovanni Valdarno – Saturday am
Sansepolcro – at Porta del Ponte-Porta Tunisi on Tuesday am and Saturday am; on V.XX Settembre on Saturday am
Sestino – Thursday am
Stia – Tuesday pm

(Opposite) Top: *A panel from the (East) doors of the baptistry of the Duomo in Florence. Ghiberti's masterpiece, they were described by Michaelangelo as the Gates of Paradise.*
(Opposite) Bottom: *The Tee-shirt of the Painting – the Mona Lisa, among others, finds immortality on the streets of Florence.*

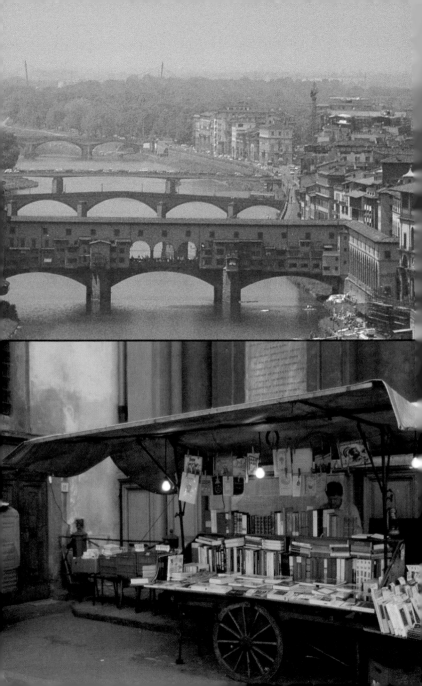

Subbiano – Monday am
Talla – Sunday am
Terranuova Bracciolini – Friday am.

Province of Siena

Abbadia San Salvatore – bi-weekly Thursday am on V.della Pace; daily (except Sunday) on Via Italia.

Asciano – daily food market (except Sunday) on V.Mameli; bi-weekly markets on Saturday am on V.Trento and V.Arbia

Buonconvento – Saturday am

Casole d' Elsa – bi-weekly on Monday am

Castellina in Chianti – Saturday am

Castelnuovo Berardenga – Thursday am

Cetona – Saturday am; Thursday am

Chianciano Terme – Wednesday am

Chiusdino – Thursday am

Chiusi – in Chiusi Scalo Monday am; in Chiusi Citta Tuesday am

Colle di Val d' Elsa – Friday am

Gaiole in Chianti – monthly on Monday pm

Montalcino – Friday am

Montepulciano – Thursday am and others in area on Saturday am

Monteriggioni – Thursday am

Monteroni d' Arbia – Tuesday am

Monticiano – Friday am

Murlo – bi-weekly on Tuesday am; bi-weekly Thursday am

Piancastagnaio – bi-weekly Saturday am

Pienza – Friday am

Poggibonsi – Tuesday am

Radda in Chianti – monthly on Monday pm

Radicofani – Thursday am

Radicondoli – Monday am

Rapolano Terme – Thursday am

San Casciano dei Bagni – bi-weekly on Thursday am

San Gimignano – Thursday am

San Giovanni d' Asso – monthly on Monday pm

San Quirico d' Orcia – bi-weekly on Tuesday am

(Opposite) Top: *A view of the Arno, Florence, with the Ponte Vecchio in the foreground.*
(Opposite) Bottom: *An open-air bookseller in Florence.*

Sarteano – Friday am
Siena – Wednesday am
Sinalunga – Tuesday am and Saturday am
Sovicille – bi-weekly on Piazza del Cirolo; in Rosia; in San Rocco
Torrita di Siena – Friday am
Trequanda – monthly on Thursday pm.

Province of Grosseto

Arcidosso – Tuesday am
Campagnatico – Monday am, Friday am
Capalbio – Monday am; Wednesday am
Castel del Piano – monthly on Wednesday all day.
Castell' Azzara – Thursday am
Castiglion della Pescaia – Saturday am; in Vetulonia on Friday am
Cinigiano – Tuesday am
Follonica – Friday am on V.Amendola; daily covered food market
    (except Saturday and Sunday) on Piazza XXIV Maggio.
Gavorrano – daily food market (except Sunday) on Piazza del
Montaccio; daily food market on Piazza XXIV Maggio (except
    Wednesday, Sunday) and other products Tuesday
Grosseto – daily (except Sunday) food market on Piazza Tripoli,
Piazza Saleli and Piazza de Maria; weekly market on Piazza
    Esperanto, Thursday am
Isola del Giglio – Wednesday am, Thursday am
Magliano in Toscana – Wednesday am
Manciano – Saturday am
Massa Marittima – Wednesday am; food on Saturday am
Monte Argentario – Porto San Stefano Tuesday am and daily (except
    Sunday) food market on V.IV Novembre; Porto Ercole on Monday am
Montieri – Friday am
Monterotondo Marittimo – bi-weekly on Saturday am
Orbetello – Saturday am; in Talamone Monday am
Pitigliano – Wednesday am
Roccalbenga – monthly market Thursday am
Roccastrada – Wednesday am
Santa Fiora – bi-weekly on Thursday am
Scansano – Friday am
Scarlino – Tuesday am
Seggiano – bi-weekly on Thursday am
Sorano – Tuesday am
Semproniano – Thursday am.

SEVEN

Practical Information A-Z

Addresses
In Florence private residences have their numbers written in blue, commercial premises in red. In Italy the house number always follows the street name.

Airline Offices – Florence
Air France, Borgo SS Apostoli 9. Tel: 289208.
Alitalia, Lungarno Acciaiuoli 10r. Tel: 27889.
British Airways, Via Vigna Nuova 36r. Tel: 218655.
Iberia, Piazza Antinori 2. Tel: 289758.
KLM, Viale Lavagnini 14. Tel: 474489.
Lufthansa, Via Pellicceria 6. Tel: 262890.
Sabena, Via Tornabuoni 1. Tel: 211001.
SAS, Lungarno Acciaiuoli 8. Tel: 262701
Swissair, Via Parione 1. Tel: 295055.
TWA, Piazza Santa Trinita 1r. Tel: 296856.

Airports

Peretola Airport Via del Termine 1. Tel: 373498.

Pisa Air Terminal Santa Maria Novella station Tel: 216073.

Banks and changing money
Banks are open from 0830 in the morning to 1315. Afternoon hours vary but are usually from 1500 to 1600. They are not open at weekends.

Despite their high-tech look, Italian banks are not particularly efficient. Paper work is heavy, queues are long. Make sure you go to the right queue and make it plain at the outset that you are a foreigner. 'Cambio' (change) is the word you want – not all banks deal in foreign transactions. If you are not sure, show someone this phrase – 'Qual'e la coda per fare il cambio?' (Which is the right queue for changing money?) and if they don't know they will probably ask on your behalf. Even banks with a 'cambio' will not always provide cash on a credit card.

To get into a modern Italian bank, press the button of the first door until you see a green light; enter, wait until the door shuts behind you and you see a green light at the next door.

In the larger towns, especially Florence, many banks have introduced multi-currency change machines, built into the wall outside. These will accept notes of any major currency and convert them into lire. Of course this service is available 24 hours a day.

American Express Bank Via Guiccardini 49, Florence, near the Pitti Palace.

British Council
Via Tornabuoni, 2, Florence.

Churches and places of worship
Services in the principal Roman Catholic churches in Florence take place up to midday and from 1800-1900. Confession may be heard in English on Sundays in the Duomo, San Miniato, Santa Croce, San Marco, San Lorenzo, Orsanmichele and Santa Trinita.

Anglican: Via Maggio 16.
American Episcopalian: Via Bernardo Rucellai 9.
Greek Orthodox: Viale Mattioli 76.
Jewish Synagogue: Via Farini 4.
Lutheran: Lungarno Torrigiani 11.
Russian Orthodox: Via Leone X 8.

Consulates (Consolati)
Great Britain (Gran Bretagna), Lungarno Corsini 2, Florence. Tel: 212594/284133.
USA (Stati Uniti), Lungarno Vespucci 38, Florence. Tel: 298276.

Currency
There are notes of 500, 1,000, 2,000, 5,000, 10,000, 20,000, 50,000 and 100,000 lire. The notes of 2,000 and 5,000 are similar – always check your change carefully. There are coins of 5, 10, 20, 50, 100, 200, and 500 lire. Sometimes you will be given a gettone (telephone

token), worth 200 lire at the moment, as change; or sometimes, for an even smaller sum, a sweet.

Language and art courses

There are plenty of courses available for people interested in learning Italian either in Italy or before you go, and there are also courses about the history of Italian art. Information can be obtained from the Italian Institute (see 'useful addresses'). It is possible to do courses which combine both. The main centres for such courses are Siena and Florence but you will find them in Viareggio, Cortona and most of the towns of historical or artistic significance. The British Institute in Florence also offers courses. There are many companies offering packages which specialise in a particular or several aspects of Tuscan life and history – see 'Before you go'.

Lavatories

Public lavatories are few and far between, although you will of course find them in public institutions like museums. All bars have one but quite reasonably it is preferred that you do not use them without at least having a coffee or a mineral water.

In some public lavatories you will be expected to pay the attendant a couple of hundred lire and sometimes to buy paper.

Il bagno/la toiletta – lavatory	Signore – ladies
Carta igienica – paper	Signori – gentlemen

Lost Property (Oggetti ritrovati)

Via Circondaria 19, Florence. Tel: 367943. Mornings only, closed Thursday and Sunday.

Medical – Florence

The Tourist Medical Service, 24 hours. Tel: 475411.

Ambulance or First Aid: Misericordia, Piazza del Duomo 20. Tel: 212222.

Hospital (ospedale): General Hospital, Piazza Santa Maria Nuova. Tel: 27581.

Chemist (farmacia): 24-hour chemists are at the station and near the Baptistry at Piazza San Giovanni 20r and on Via Calzaiuoli 7r.

For emergency, call 113.

Newspapers

Foreign newspapers are sold at street kiosks. Italian newspapers have a noticeably regional emphasis, although the major newspapers – the

Corriere della Sera, La Stampa, La Repubblica – have large international sections. The Florence newspaper is *La Nazione*.

Opening hours for shops, museums and churches

The midday rest remains an important part of the day; so, whilst there is some variation, the basic hours for shops are 0900-1300 and 1600-1900/2000. Many shops close on Saturday afternoons, on Sunday and on Monday.

Museums tend to follow the same pattern as far as times are concerned (except that they close earlier in the afternoons or are open only in the morning) and usually close only one day in the week, often Sunday or Monday. Churches generally close for the midday period.

You must expect to pay, sometimes quite steeply, in order to see the Tuscan artistic heritage. In churches there are often facilities for lighting gloomy chapels for which you may need to pay – go armed with change.

Where the hours are given in the text, Sunday hours will also apply on holidays, if the monument in question is open at all. Sunday (Domenica) is a 'festa' in Italy.

Police

Emergency call 113, (police is polizia).
The Foreigners Office (Ufficio Stranieri) is on Via Zara 2, Florence.
    Tel: 49771.

Post and telephone

Post is slow. Stamps can be obtained from post offices or tobacconists, none of whom seem to know the correct postal rates. At the time of writing a postcard stamp for Britain costs 650 lire; letters up to 20 grams cost 750. If you need to use a Poste Restante service ask your correspondent to add Fermo Posta to the name of the locality. They can be picked up from the local main post office on production of proof of identity.

Main post offices can be used for making telephone calls, consulting telephone directories, sending telegrams etc.

Telephones accept either 'gettoni' (tokens, currently worth 200 lire, with which you feed the phone before dialling), or change. Most bars have a phone. Some have a 'telefono a scatti' (metered – ask the barman to switch it on), which can be used for local or international calls.

Intercity and international calls may also be made from post offices or offices run by SIP which have private booths.

The code for Britain is 0044 plus city code minus the 0.

Stamp of 650 lire – francobollo da 650 lire
Postcard – carta postale
Letter – lettera
Main Post Office – ufficio postale centrale
Registered – raccomandata
Swiftair – espresso
Intercity – interurbano.

The main post office in Florence is on Via Pellicceria, off Piazza della Repubblica, from where you may make long distance calls (and pay after) and consult the 'Yellow Pages' (Pagine gialle), if you need a particular service.

Security

Whilst violent crime is rarer than in the UK, pickpocketing is more common – but take sensible precautions and you will have no trouble. Use hotel safes; have photocopies of the first few pages of your passport; carry only a little cash on your person.

The emergency number for the polizia is 113.

Sightseeing

Tuscany is vast in terms of what there is to see. Everything depends on your interests and how you are moving around. Florence is likely to be on the itinerary whatever your motive for going to Tuscany; Siena follows close behind (for some it is the other way around). But there are plenty of smaller places worth spending time in, Lucca and San Gimignano to name but two. And one of the joys of Tuscany (and Italy in general) is that history is preserved in the stones and ways of life of the smallest unsung town or village, nestling in or overlooking captivating countryside.

Spending time away from the major centres is recommended. In this book an attempt has been made to include almost everywhere of any interest but if you see a pretty hill-top village not mentioned here, go and have a look. If you find something of particular interest, let the author know.

However, Tuscany can be broadly cut into two – Florence and the north and Florence and the south, with a certain overlap in the Florence area itself. The countryside in each differs considerably from the other. Your itinerary will much depend on: where you landed if coming by aeroplane, where you entered if arriving by car, and particularly how much time you have. If you arrive at Pisa airport, then it would make sense to visit Lucca and Pistoia, for example, as well as Pisa and Florence. If on the other hand you arrive at Rome airport, there is plenty to see in the southern part of Tuscany and the likes of Lucca may be too far out of the way.

Arrival at Pisa – an itinerary might include the following:
Pisa, Viareggio, Lucca, Pistoia, smaller places of that area mentioned in the text, Florence, Chianti, and the Certaldo/Empoli route back to Pisa.

Arrival at Rome: Florence, San Gimignano, Volterra, Siena, Arezzo, Cortona and any of the smaller places in the area.

Of course it is possible to base your itinerary on a theme. This, however, may mean racing from one part of the province to another. Still, if it is wine you are after, then you need look no further than the Chianti area. Scenery is attractive almost everywhere but especially splendid in the hilly regions of North Tuscany including the Apuan Alps, Lunigiana, Garfagnana; the coastal area of Maremma with Monte Argentario and Monti dell'Uccellina; Monte Amiata; the area between Siena and Massa Marittima; and the Casentino area east of Florence. Etruscan relics are to be found in Fiesole, Volterra, Chiusi, Orbetello, Ansedonia, Populonia, Vetulonia, Roselle and Cortona. Gardens and villas may be seen or visited in Florence (Villa Stibbert, Arcetri, Boboli); Fiesole; the Medici villas of Mugello and at Careggi, La Petraia, Poggio a Caino, Cerreto Guidi; and near Lucca (Castello Garzoni).

Following directions as you walk around towns and cities of narrow streets is not always easy. When you remember that you are never far from a church and that the high altar is always at the east end, this may be of use when trying to find your bearings.

Sports and recreation
There are opportunities to do almost all sports. Most towns are equipped with a swimming pool (piscina, pronounced 'pisheena'), football pitch (campo sportivo), tennis courts and basketball is popular.

Swimming on the coasts is variable but efforts have been made to clean up the beaches and they are much improved – the best water is

The ubiquitous black and white 'T' sign – the tobacconists where you buy stamps and postcards.

found on the islands. Sailing and fishing on the coast are available (the information offices will help you with tuition). It is also possible to go rowing on the Arno in Florence.

Trotting (racing of light horse-drawn carts) is popular. There are golf courses in Florence, Orbetello, Montecatini Terme, Punta Ala and Portoferraio, although the game is not yet very popular in Italy. It is easy to go riding and walking. Hunting has long been popular in Italy, at the expense of the wildlife, but this is now better regulated. Indeed it is possible to go bird-watching in the Maremma. Potholers may find their heart's desire in the areas of Sarteano, Monsummano and Montecatini Alta. You may ski on Monte Amiata and Abetone. Precise and up-to-date information may be obtained from local Tourist information offices.

EIGHT

Pre-Renaissance Tuscany

Ancient History

The region of Tuscany, and the cities within it, are rich in history - its people and their achievements have had a lasting influence on the outlook of Europe and the world. Machiavelli was a Tuscan; so was Dante, so was Galileo and Da Vinci, and hundreds more of lesser or greater importance in all fields of human endeavour. Some were not Tuscan by blood but by adoption, finding there, in the period known as the Renaissance, the conditions for fulfilment and advancement. Much of what is visible now, and the reason why the area is cherished by visitors, dates back to that period.

The Florentine Renaissance (for the history of Tuscany at that time in many ways mirrors events in Florence) is considered by many to have been the apogee of Italian and European civilisation. But of course the Renaissance did not burst into life in a night or a season - its seeds had been sown in the preceding centuries. Moreover, Tuscany had known a great civilisation some 2,000 years before.

The Etruscans

The name Tuscany comes from the Latin word for a people, the Etruscans, who ruled the area and indeed much of the Italian peninsula at the time of the rise of Rome. Because their origins are obscure and because theirs was a civilisation of greatness but about which tantalisingly little is known, the Etruscan world has acquired the elements of myth and legend.

The Tuscany of today corresponds roughly to what was northern Etruria. The Etruscan civilisation lasted, it is thought, from 700 BC to 300 BC. Before their rise, Italy had been home to a variety of tribes and peoples of varying degrees of sophistication, none of whom had succeeded in establishing overall dominion. The most successful was the Villanovan culture which dates back to 1000 BC and which seems to have thrived on a highly developed knowledge of metallurgy. They, possibly connected with people from the Aegean whose destiny had depended on the outward drive of Balkan tribes, have left considerable evidence of their existence and may be regarded as proto-Etruscans. Certainly every known Etruscan city is preceded by a Villanovan settlement.

It is thought by some that the Etruscans, too, came from further east, from somewhere in Greece. That the Etruscans had substantial contact with the ancient Greeks is in no doubt - there is much evidence of this from archaeological investigation. Yet there are too many unanswered questions to rest content with this explanation and it is perhaps wiser to assume that the Etruscan civilisation was a furtherance of a direction already taking place in Italy and which was much influenced by the Greeks. 'The Etruscans, whatever may have been the various racial elements in their composition as a people, had no true historical existence except in Etruria' (Jacques Heurgon, *The Rise of Rome to 264 BC*).

Whatever their origins, so it is that in about 700 BC the Etruscans begin to figure prominently with a unique civilisation that is strikingly oriental and which, in its sophistication, differs from anything that preceded it in Italy.

The Etruscsan meteor

It seems that the rise of Etruscan power depended on the discovery of deposits of copper and iron on the island of Elba and on the Tuscan coast opposite. As a result, a people who had barely stood out from their neighbours began to prosper quickly; they developed an urban civilisation, building in stone rather than wood, as well as sophisticated farming techniques which depended on skilled hydraulic engineering methods. Politically it is known that the Etruscans were a federation of 12 tribes, although it is thought that the federation was rather a loose one and that their gradual expansion throughout the peninsula was probably not a concerted effort. It is more likely that when one of the members made a conquest the others would follow in his wake. At first they were ruled by kings, although by the fifth century this system gave way to annually elected magistrates. It remained a highly patrician society, based on nobles and peasants or domestics, with nothing in between, although there was some mobility between the classes; and women seem to have enjoyed a privileged position.

It is clear that the Etruscan civilisation had its own character, although it was considerably influenced by Greek culture (although just how this came about is much debated) and others like that of the Phoenicians. Such influences are clear from the tombs which have been discovered in number and which are the principal relics that have come down to us. They are often decorated in Greek style painting and filled with the terracotta and bronze statues at which they excelled. For the Etruscans, religion and death were of enormous importance – they believed in an immutable fate, which had been revealed through semi-divine prophets and which had been codified in the 'disciplina Etrusca'. Livy, the Roman writer, said 'No people was ever more devoted to religious observances', although secular life was of course important too.

The Etruscans and Rome

As their power grew, the Etruscans' influence spread some way south, as far as Magna Graecia (Greek settlements in the south of Italy), and including the Latin tribes of central Italy, among whom were the Romans. For a time the Romans and the Etruscans merged – the Etruscans had an alphabet (based on the Greek one which the Romans adapted for their own language) and a sense of their own history, and indeed the first Roman annalists took their accounts of the Roman monarchy in its Etruscan period from Etruscan sources. It seems that early Rome owed a lot to the Etruscan civilisation which taught the Romans to be literate and passed on their own achievements in organisation of the army and in civil life. The main thing was that 'Etruscan rule opened up new horizons for Rome; those who ruled her in the sixth century made her a sharer in their vast enterprises, and aroused a spirit of imperialism which survived their going' (Jacques Heurgon, *The Rise of Rome to 264 BC*). Thus it was that the first Roman kings were in fact Etruscan.

However, the Romans grew powerful in their turn at the expense of the Etruscans. From 300 BC the Etruscans lost ground to their former pupils, to the extent that astonishingly little of Etruscan civilisation has survived, although it is known that northern Etruria (today's Tuscany) was not absorbed into the Roman empire until 91 BC, after which inscriptions are in both Etruscan and Latin. Within the lifetime of Cicero the Etruscans and their language had disappeared.

The Romans and after in Tuscany

Etruria, known as Tuscia, became Rome's seventh province. The Romans did the same here as they did all over their empire – they constructed roads and villas to build up an efficient communications network and to provide a sound base for strong rule. Sometimes, as in Volterra and Fiesole, they built on or with the Etruscan construction that preceded them. Pisa was developed as a naval base and Florentia (Florence) was founded by Julius Caesar at the easiest crossing point of the Arno, soon surpassing Fiesole in importance, which had been founded by the Etruscans. Lucca still retains, in part, its Roman layout; and according to legend Siena was founded through the rivalries of Roman factions. Christianity quickly took root in Tuscany, Lucca claiming to be the first city to be converted, and Volterra providing the first bishop of Rome.

Tuscany and its cities were not to establish a separate identity, however, for several hundred years, during which time the Italian peninsula, and indeed Europe, were continually rocked by events most telling for their future – the decline of the Roman Empire, the coming of the 'barbarians' and the establishment of the Papacy and the Holy Roman Empire. In order to understand the rise of the Tuscan city states from the eleventh century it is important to know something of what took place in the intervening centuries.

The coming of the barbarian

The Germanic tribes proved to be a thorn in the side of the Romans right from the start. Their migrations southwards were the gradual expansion of land-hungry peasantry, driven on by the pressures of climatic change and population shifts. They came up against the Romans who defeated them but who never succeeded in assimilating them into Roman life. They remained subject to Rome but in their own tribes, not as citizens. The size of their population continued to grow over the centuries – the resulting restlessness was a constant source of irritation to the empire; yet without the Germans, who paradoxically were a substantial element in the ranks of the Roman army, Rome would not have survived for as long as it did. In the service of the Empire many 'barbarians' became powerful in their own right, maintaining large followings of retainers. Yet only the tribe called Ostrogoth succeeded in organising themselves under one leader; and only timely reforms prevented usurpation of the empire by them. Then came the Huns – the Romans had lost the strength to repel them, but managed to absorb them into the empire, which was taking on an increasingly 'barbarian' hue.

In 395 the Empire was divided into an eastern and a western empire – real power now lay in Constantinople. The Emperors there tried to deflect the threatening Germanic tribes away towards the west, so that Rome was temporarily occupied by the Visigoths in 410 AD. By 476, however, the 'barbarians' had succeeded in taking over the whole of Italy, with Odoacer proclaimed King, and the Roman Empire in the west effectively at an end, although Justinian did briefly reconquer Italy from Constantinople in the mid-sixth century. He was overwhelmed in 568 by another tribe from the Danube plains who, although they failed to take either Rome or Ravenna, were to play the most important role in the peninsula during the coming centuries. In fact the simpler Germanic approach to the administration of basic Roman law and political knowhow enabled Europe to hold together; and 'through their conversion to Christianity they became members of the Roman Church, which had most fully inherited the culture of antiquity'. Thus, although these years are traditionally thought of as a low point in European history, it is clear that the 'barbarians' as well as bringing their own artistic heritage, which was by no means to be sneered at, knew to adapt Roman civilisation to their needs and indeed to a certain extent preserved it for future generations. 'The heritage of Rome was fused with the Germanic and Christian elements to provide the medieval foundation of Western civilisation'.

While all this was going on another character, destined to play a major role in European civilisation, entered the scene – the Pope.

The growth of the church

The Pope had come to be recognised as pre-eminent by the fourth century emperors and with the absence of imperial government in Rome, their power grew, and with it the theory of the Petrine succession. As the empire disintegrated into barbarian states, the church assumed more secular powers, becoming a lone symbol of western unity. With Papal power threatened by the Lombards and the heresy of iconoclasm, the Pope appealed to the Franks, on the northern borders of Italy, for help. Here was the origin of the Papal states, given authority by the forged Donation of Constantine, which purported to be a grant of supreme authority in the West from the Emperor in Constantinople to the Pope and his successors. The greatest of the Frankish kings from whom the Pope had asked help was Charlemagne, who conquered the Lombards and who in 800 was crowned Holy Roman Emperor by the Pope, thus creating a myth that served as a grail for aspiring leaders for centuries to come; and which confirmed the authority of the popes.

Nonetheless, Charlemagne's successors squabbled incessantly to the point where the empire was broken up – here are the real Dark Ages. Italy was briefly ravaged by the Magyars at the end of the ninth century, only finally repulsed by Otto I, who in 962 assumed the mantle of Holy Roman Emperor, which had lain unworn for almost 40 years.

Throughout the eleventh century the church was reformed through the influence of the French monasteries. This was at first resisted by the Popes, until the Holy Roman Emperor imposed it on the Roman church, after which Papal influence spread once again beyond the Alps. Nonetheless, there were frequent battles between the Emperors and Popes over how much influence one should have over the other, until Frederic I Barbarossa set out to restore his imperial authority in Italy in the twelfth century. He met resistance from the northern communes, the so-called Lombard League, those cities like Florence which, caught between Emperor and Pope, were beginning to grow in independence; and the Papacy. In the end a compromise was reached whereby the communes maintained their self-government, while recognising the Emperor's suzerainty; and the Pope kept his independence. Papal influence became wide ranging, the church becoming the focal point for all aspects of life from the law to education. Naturally, such all-encompassing powers provoked heresy, so that orders like the Dominicans and the Franciscans grew up to combat it. As Papal power grew, the Holy Roman Emperors, like Frederic II, tried to check it, but failed.

This, then, was the situation prevailing in Italy – echoes of a glorious lost age of antiquity vying for power with the forces of Christianity – as the era of the city states approached.

The ports

Whilst the inland cities of the north were beginning to find their feet, it was the coastal cities like Pisa that first developed their potential. The Crusades provided the impetus for greater trade with the Levant and as the city grew more prosperous, so she gained control over most of the western Mediterranean. Ports also acted as cultural conduits – indeed it was the Pisan, Fibonacci, who introduced Arabic numerals to the west. Here too communal government took shape – the first mention of a magistracy of consuls came in 1080, indicating a decline in both the authority of the bishops and the feudal nobility.

Inland

Of course the hinterland cities gained from all this too, sustaining ever-increasing economic activity. They could do this because the

Lombard dukes and officials chose to settle in towns rather than in castles. Economic growth was phenomenal, many towns being forced to rebuild their city walls in order to cope (e.g. Florence between 1050 and 1100). Unlike the south of Italy, and the rest of Europe, agricultural and urban development were interdependent

'what is less obvious, and represents a new trait in the evolution of Italian society, is the fact that in much of Italy the economic interdependence allowed a fusion of city and country also on the territorial, political and human level' (Giuliano Procacci, *History of the Italian People*).

The communes

'The Italian commune was a composite, dual organism that had from its beginnings two spirits and two vocations: the one bourgeois and enterprising, the other landowning and deriving profit from the land' (Giuliano Procacci, *History of the Italian People*).

On the whole, the rise of the so-called commune can be understood as conquest of countryside living by urban living. For example, Florence took over the feudal town of Fiesole, castles were pulled down and feudal lords were forced to spend at least part of each year in town. Many nobles chose to live in town permanently, building towers to demonstrate their standing. The most famous example of this is San Gimignano, but Florence probably looked similar at one time. Nonetheless, lords remained landlords and in fact land ownership was often a prerequisite for citizenship – for example, in San Gimignano 84 per cent of the land was owned by citizens. At first it was the bourgeois enterprising spirit, particularly in the form of banking, that prevailed in the rise of these cities – the day of the landowner was to return later. Nonetheless, despite the scrapping and feuding that accompanied the growth of cities like Florence, there was a sense of kinship between all the classes, a sense of belonging to your city – at this stage, perhaps, your city was more important than your class.

Guelf and Ghibelline

In the wider world, the ambitions of Emperor and Pope continued to dictate events. Those who supported the Emperor were called

Ghibellines, those who supported the Pope, Guelfs. The origin of these words is obscure, although a story told by the fourteenth century writer Ser Giovanni Fiorentino illustrates, fancifully, their provenance.

Two German nobles, one named Guelf, the other Gibelin, quarrelled over a bitch dog as they returned from the hunt. Their quarrel was taken up by the other lords and barons – those siding with Gibelin felt themselves the weaker party and appealed to the Emperor; compelling Guelf and his followers to appeal to the Pope, who was inimical to the Emperor. That is why the Papacy is Guelf and the Empire Ghibelline – all because of a wretched bitch.

Fiorentino goes further:

'The strife entered Italy in a different way. A wealthy and brave knight of the house of Buondelmonti in Florence became betrothed to a daughter of the Amidei. When, however, he met Ciulla, daughter of the Donati, who was fairer still, he changed his mind and pledged his troth to her instead. The Amidei were unhappy, and murdered Buondelmonti by the Ponte Vecchio. The city exploded, causing the nobility to split in two – the Buondelmonti became leaders of the Guelfs and the Amidei leaders of Ghibellines. Soon, the whole of Italy was cleft in two. Thus the Guelf and Ghibelline factions arose in Germany on account of a bitch and in Italy on account of a woman.'

The story perhaps seems quintessentially Italian – it does however highlight the factional nature of the seemingly endless battle between Guelf and Ghibelline.

At any rate, the Ghibelline Emperor was able to depend on the feudal lords (who were violently anti-commune) for support, as well as some communes like Pisa and Siena who feared the expansionist policies of Florence. The Guelfs seemed the more vulnerable of the two parties since the only thing that held them together was a common enemy, whilst rivalries prevented a solid alliance. As the story above illustrates, the strife extended into the commune cities themselves, exploiting feuds that had nothing to do with the Empire or the Papacy (e.g. in Florence, a Guelf city, which itself became divided into Black and White factions).

Nonetheless, the Guelf states were by far the richer and when Charles d' Anjou was called into the battle by Pope Clement IV, it was Florentine money which enabled him to defeat Frederic II. The empire was finished.

The rise of the commune

And yet peace was still not to be, for the former Guelf states feared that Charles would take advantage of his victory. When the war of the Sicilian Vespers broke out the northern communes saw it as a chance to settle old scores and consolidate their growing strength. Thus Pisa was destroyed by Genoa, and Florence, having defeated Arezzo, Prato and Pistoia, threatened Lucca. The end of the thirteenth century was a tempestuous time, as reflected in Dante's *Divine Comedy*.

The church was heavily involved in all this – it was a time of millenial prophecies and of instability, when it was felt that the end of the world was nigh. In the end the Papacy was transferred to Avignon. Suddenly Italy was without Pope or Emperor and the communes awoke to their own worth, ushering in the age of Dante and Giotto. The walls of the main towns were extended still further to accommodate their expansion, town chronicles were written, and communal palaces (e.g. in Florence and Siena) were built. Deep rivalries between cities were not all negative, for a deep sense of civic pride was reflected in art that varied in style from city to city.

Unlike most of the communes, which in the end fell back on the old families to look after their interests, Florence evolved institutions that wholly corresponded to its economic organisation. Florence was comparatively new to the world of superpowers but quickly made her presence felt. She introduced the gold 'florin' for use by her own bankers and merchants. Siena was the only city able to compete, because their bankers happened to be the lease-holders and debt-collectors for the Papal Curia. However, Siena was soundly beaten by Florence in 1269.

Florentine industry was intensive and organised along market economy lines. Her merchants, who in the process of trading learnt a great deal about the world at large, became so successful that they wished for a say in how their city was run. Thus in 1282 the system of commune government was overhauled to entrust rule to 'Priori' and later, in 1293, to the Gonfaloniere di Giustizia, who ruled the city on behalf of the guilds. The power of the guilds reflected the growing importance of Florence's main industry – the business of dressing and dyeing woollen fabrics. The new ruling class, the merchants, were certain eventually to clash with the old noble families, but for the time being they had the upper hand. In fact in 1293 every citizen was compelled to register with a guild. So if Florence became home to high culture this was owing to the

Florence, Santa Maria del Fiore – Brunelleschi's miraculous dome and Giotto's elegant campanile.

Republican spirit and to the merchant ruling class. 'In Florence the democracy aimed at disparaging the old nobility and at the same time absorbing it'.

NINE

The Renaissance and the Medici

The rise of an intellectual and artistic Tuscany

With the approach of the fourteenth century it will be as well to mention something about two concepts that play an important role in Tuscan history during the next 200 years – the Renaissance and Humanism – for although neither can be said to truly take hold until the end of the fourteenth century, the seeds are sown somewhat earlier.

Visiting Florence and the other cities of Tuscany is a pleasure in itself – in fact much of their appeal lies in an openness to simple visual pleasure and there is no greater pleasure than to idle through the towns and countryside of Tuscany. There is no compulsion to do more. It is not necessary to enter a single palace or to leave the sunlight for the cool gloom of an art gallery. Yet the chances are that at least once you will find yourself confronted with the culture of the area, be it Etruscan or Renaissance. Again, much of it speaks for itself, but simple appreciation is not always easy amid the welter of terms and discussion that is its accompaniment. On the one hand the phenomonen of the Renaissance 'just happened', on the other hand there were reasons for it. Much of it corresponds, as a sort of by-product, to historical events – hence the extensive historical section included in this guide which aims to provide a general background against which the details of Tuscan life become clearer. On the other hand the period known as the Renaissance, certainly the most important period of Tuscan history from the point of view of its effect on the rest of Europe, and the part which will confront you at every corner, seems somehow distinct from history, with a life of its own. So what do people mean by the Renaissance and what is this Humanism so often mentioned in connection with it?

Renaissance or 'rebirth', (the term continues to be a subject of endless debate among academics) is usually associated with Italy of the fourteenth and fifteenth centuries. On the one hand it refers to a rough period of time; on the other it refers to an artistic and philosophical revival of lasting influence. A combination of events at a certain time brought about a new consciousness, a new attitude to life as expressed in art, politics and religion. It transformed society from medieval to modern. To speak thus makes it sound as if a conscious effort on the part of a few clever people changed society. In fact it was a gradual recognition of other possibilities in a society that was beginning to change as it emerged from the so-called Dark Ages. Much of it took place in Tuscany and particularly in Florence. Inseparable from the notion of the 'Renaissance' is the term 'Humanism'.

Humanism and the Renaissance

Humanism describes a new approach to thinking. The word itself gives a clue, for it implies a new emphasis on man and his role in the order of things; it implies a shift away from God and theology (as something immutable) towards man as a creature to a certain extent in control of his own destiny (though still ultimately answerable to God). The researches of the humanists extended in several directions – ethics, politics, economics, aesthetics, logic and rhetoric, as well as the natural sciences. It assumed, for example, that the logic of Aristotle is not the word of God, but a product of history. This brings us to another point, for much humanist thinking was based on the works of the thinkers of Ancient Rome and Greece. Of course these texts, or many of them, had been available for study in the preceding centuries, though mostly within the confines of monasteries; but the point was that the method of study had been one-dimensional, based on the hierarchical certainties of Aristotle which uneasily coexisted with, or complemented, the equally fixed certainties of contemporary theology. In other words medieval interest in the ancient texts was really limited to the extent to which they demonstrated the truth of an unchanging order of things. The Humanists, on the other hand, were more interested in the shape of the human city and the nature of human customs and rituals and of understanding them in a historical light, as part of particular experiences, with all their contradictions and differences. This is why the Platonic school of thought, sensitive to the problems and contradictions of humanity, yet still concerned with the divine, was generally favoured at the expense of the Aristotlean.

'In the enthusiastic classicism of the Florentine humanists are to be found the origins of Donatello's imitation of classical forms and Brunellechi's search to revive the ancient way of building' (John Larner, *Culture and Society in Italy 1290-1420*).

Three wise men

Three precursors of the Tuscan Renaissance, though not strictly speaking part of it, are in fact the three most famous men of Italian letters: Dante, Petrarch and Bocaccio. Their prominence reflects changes in Italian society, but it should be remembered that until about 1370, generally considered the rough beginning of the Renaissance, the fourteenth century was influenced by ideas beyond the Alps (e.g. Gothic) : 'As in literature . . . so in art, early fourteenth-century Italy was not quite ready for a fresh style'.

Dante, politics and language

The earliest of these, and in a sense separate from the others, is Dante Alighieri. He was born in Florence in 1265, staying there until 1301, during which time he was actively involved in politics and held public office. The political rivalry within the city (black versus white, as we have seen) led to Dante's exile, since he had backed the losing white faction. He spent the last years of his life until his death in 1321 in Ravenna, wandering from princely court to princely court. In those years he wrote the work for which he is most famous, *The Divine Comedy* (La Divina Commedia), which 'is one of the few works of world literature, like Tolstoy's *War and Peace* or Joyce's *Ulysses*, that can be said to contain everything, the whole sense of an age, with all its contradictions and doubts' (*History of the Italian People*, Giuliano Procacci).

Furthermore he wrote it not in Latin, as most literature of the period, but in the 'vernacular', Italian, and Tuscan Italian at that. The Italian language plays an interesting role at this time, for as 'learning', with the creation of the first universities, moved from the confines of the church, so the need for a common, easily understood language became more urgent. With this need came the comprehension of a place that was Italy which, though divided into myriad small states, nonetheless shared a common heritage.

The growing number of intellectuals in the prosperous northern communes realised that a link between the old learning and the newly educated classes had to be found. After all, Florence's Via del Proconsolo was in 1290 already known as a street of booksellers.

Italy was filled with many dialects – which to choose? Towards the end of the thirteenth century the poets of Florence, and particularly Dante, initiated the 'dolce stil novo' ('beautiful new style') school of poetry, a refinement of older forms of poetry based on the Tuscan dialect. Dante went further, writing, in Latin, ardent defences of vernacular Italian. Thus language played an important role in the realisation of a national consciousness, that Petrarch would refine still farther ('sumus non graeci, non barbari, sed itali et latini') and in the spread of a humanist approach.

As for Dante, the greatest proof of his belief in the vernacular as a literary language as well as for ordinary communion, was *The Divine Comedy*. It is the story of his journey, in the company of the Roman poet Virgil, through Hell, Purgatory and Heaven. It is far from being a didactic piece of religious propaganda – on the contrary it is a personal, highly opinionated vision of his times and a insight into the Italy of the late thirteenth century, written in an Italian quite comprehensible to the modern reader both in the Italian used and in the vividness of metaphor.

Dante stands on his own as the great original; but testifies, even before the Renaissance gets into its stride, to the huge mental changes taking place in Italy, particularly in Florence.

Petrarch (1304-74)

Petrarch is usually thought of as the father of Italian Humanism. He was born, in Arezzo, into a Florentine family of notaries. Like Dante, his father was exiled and he grew up to wander from court to court. First he trained as a lawyer, for which he needed to know Latin, and he grew to love its literature. He wrote extensively in Latin, though in his own time he was famed more for his Italian verse. Since he held several benefices he was able to live off them (though he would never have accepted any post that involved the care of souls). One of his most interesting Latin works is the *Secretum*, a dialogue on Christian virtues in which he debates with St. Augustine. He also, in Latin, answered the criticism of his studies by adherents of Aristotle, by exalting the importance of eloquence as a reflection of the soul. His followers were to be of two types – those who emulated his vernacular poetry and those who emulated his Latin defences of the importance of the cultivation of wisdom.

Although he was noted in his own day for Italian verse, most of which was dedicated to his hopeless love for one Laura, Petrarch seemed to think Latin a nobler language, for his works on the nature of morality are in Latin. The importance of his prose lies in his emphasis on the moral value of literature and the fundamental role to be played in that by the notion of antiquity (ie Latin and Greek). In any case vernacular Italian was not suited to the sort of prose he was writing; but his basic and most influential position was that he found more in the ancients to guide modern problems. He debated the virtues of a reclusive or an active life. His bequest to his contemporaries was the identification of Humanism with life, although this did not follow at once – it needed to be formalised in teaching. Thus, in the mercantile world of the communes, schools arose that could cope with the new ideas and delighting in literature in a fresh way. Although Petrarch refused to return to Florence, his teachings took root faster there than anywhere else, for people were literate there and developing a taste for literature.

Boccaccio (1313-75)

Because of the level of education in Florence, acceptance of the first great writer of prose in Italian, Giovanni Boccaccio, was rather easier. An admirer of Dante, admirer of and friend to Petrarch, he too had a legal training but, unlike them, he spent a good deal of time in Florence (as well as elsewhere). He too was conscious of his role in the stimulation of interest in the literary field, in both Latin and vernacular Italian. Latin he reserved for treatises, Italian for his prose masterpiece, the *Decameron*.

The *Decameron* consists of one hundred stories told by a group of ladies and gentleman over a period of ten days in an idyllic rural setting outside plague-ravaged Florence. Some of the stories are bawdy, others are tinged with the poignancy of the human condition. All are told in vibrant Italian and filled with the characters of the streets of the Florence and other cities of his day.

In his Latin works he tried to help in the understanding of classical literature, as Petrarch had done, but with less brilliance and more enthusiasm. He was more accessible than Petrarch to the ordinary reader, in fact bringing Petrarch to the Florentine readers' attention. Both played a huge role in the process of changing a whole generation's outlook on the world, an outlook reflected in politics since both had strong views, as Dante had done before them, on republicanism, monarchism, the Papacy and the Roman Empire.

Changes in art – from Byzantine to Baroque

With the reburgeoning of an urban culture, citizens became more prosperous and more enterprising; this was also reflected in art. The first changes took place in France in about 1150, and came to be known as Gothic. First, art was no longer confined to the monasteries. Secondly, there was a tendency to portray the past with trappings of the present. There were significant developments: attempts to enliven pictures with shading, to give greater depth; the beginning of the era of stained glass; and the construction of the great northern cathedrals.

In Italy, however, it was different. Mural painting continued to flourish and the urban outlook was already stronger than elsewhere. Nonetheless, Italian painting was very much tied to the frozen Byzantine style which had prevailed for 700 years. In Siena and in Florence, however, changes were afoot.

Giotto and the pre-Renaissance painters

The date of Giotto di Bondone's birth, in the village of Vespignano near Florence, is uncertain (c. 1270) although we know he died in 1337. His first documented appearance in Florence is in 1301, although it is likely that his reputation was already made. He was the supreme artist of his time. Cennino Cennini, from the next generation of artists, said that 'he had translated the art of painting from Greek into Latin'; and Ghiberti said he had cut away the 'rozzezza dei Greci' or the crudeness of the Byzantine style. According to Dante 'Cimabue thought that he had the field of painting to himself, but Giotto gets the vote now, so that the fame of the other is already eclipsed'. It is clear that painting, like literature, was going through a period of direct, intellectual reassessment. These appreciations are seen in the light of the Renaissance – he should also be judged on his own merits.

The evolution of style and material

It is difficult, and anyway the subject of much debate, to place styles of painting in strict chronological sequence. It is clear that the Renaissance produced distinctive changes in the field of art, culminating in the perception of a painter as an artist rather than artisan. Before the fifteenth century art seems not to have played the same role – certainly the skills of the artist were appreciated but his personality barely extruded from the conventions that bound his work. Nonetheless the years preceding the Renaissance show evidence of change and have been categorised in the following way. The first stage during the twelfth century marked the beginnings of a distinctively Italian school of painting in Tuscany. It was evinced particularly in Lucca, Pisa, Siena and Florence, reaching its apogee with Cimabue's Byzantine style. In Siena the principal master was Guido da Siena, in Florence Coppa di Marcovaldo. The second stage was evinced by the classicism of Cavallini, which culminates in Giotto in Florence, foreshadowing Fra Angelico and Masaccio, and Duccio in Siena (who acts as a bridge between the first two stages). Giotto shows mastery of spatial elements whilst the Sienese school, Simone Martini for example, who foreshadows Pisanello and Gentile da Fabriano, clung still to decorativeness and mysticism. Tempera (colours mixed with egg yolk and water to make a thin, smooth paint that dries to an enamel film) was widely used for miniatures and predella panels.

The third stage, the middle and end of the fourteenth century, was a reaction to the new styles, reverting somewhat to pre-Giotto traditions, as exemplified by Orcagna and Andrea Vanni. This change is sometimes attributed to a reassessment of values due to the appalling outbreak of the Black Death but this does not tell the whole story. At this time the styles of Italian and northern European painters were remarkably similar, using a style sometimes called 'International Gothic'.

Rebirth

The final stage reverted to the new realism of Giotto and so to the Renaissance. Through it all religion played the main role – secular paintings, even when not lost, were a rarity. The development of naturalism took place within the limitations imposed by the orderly medieval picture of the Universe. Most commissions, controlled by guilds, were altarpieces on panel in tempera, usually of the Virgin or Crucifixion. The early fourteenth century saw the Gothic influence in narrative in predella panels at the base of the altarpiece but the preoccupation of the period was the revival of fresco and the gradual disappearance of mosaic, for fresco was cheaper and faster. The pure fresco method was where the colours were painted into a thin plaster layer, while still wet, known as the intonaco. This was applied to the smoothed wall surface on which the the design had been sketched. The fresco became part of the wall and proved very durable.

One of the important changes in art at this time was the change in the artist's perception of light and how it affects the subject of a picture. Changes like this began to affect the direction of art at the beginning of the fifteenth century.

From the early Renaissance to Baroque

The changes evolved into the late Gothic styles of northern Europe and early Renaissance of Italy, which really began in Florence. Masaccio reverted to the outlook of Giotto but employed a more natural style where figures were more real, the emotions more delicate and the pictures had a life of their own.

Meanwhile, international Gothic continued to be influential until the middle of the fifteenth century in the work of Fra Angelico, for example. Others, like Piero della Francesca, followed Masaccio. The Humanistic influence is clear – whereas the older styles showed scenes where the hand of God guided events, the new style, with Classical influences, extols the virtue of man's free will, although in tune with God.

The high Renaissance of the early fifteenth century was marked by an interest in harmony, as evinced in the work of Leonardo, and the extremes of human emotion and the beauty of the human body, as evinced by Michelangelo.

After the beginning of the sixteenth century, the faith in the rebirth of the human spirit began to dwindle and, perhaps in the spirit of the Reformation, the belief in the power of forces outside human control began to reassert itself in art. This style is known as Mannerism and is a more anarchic world of distortion and dream. Pontormo, Rosso Fiorentino are exponents of this 'anti-Classical' style.

Baroque is the art of the seventeenth century and in some ways sums up the lessons of the previous 200 years. It is more decorative, for now the world was beginning to be expressed scientifically - the age of Newton and Galileo. Whilst Florence and Tuscany have their fair share of Baroque art, Rome was its real home.

The tempestuous fourteenth century

Although a 'civilisation' was developing, as life became sweeter and better organised, many old problems continued to bedevil society. The old battle between bourgeois and noble dragged on. There were the irreconcilable differences between the poorer members of the population, for whom war was a tragedy, and those richer members for whom war spelt profit. These problems manifested themselves in different ways – the rivalry between the aristcratic Donati family (as mentioned in the story earlier) and the wealthy merchant family Cerchi became a feud between the so-called 'blacks' and 'whites' which spread all over Tuscany and which ultimately led to the exile of figures like Dante. During this period dictators came and went, interspersed with short-lived oligarchical constitutions; and the country was afflicted with a series of plagues, which decimated the population.

Although Florence continued to prosper overall, there were periods of severe recession. Banks lent vast sums to the kings of Naples and England; when the King of England reneged on his debts, it precipitated a financial crisis. At the same time Lucca, bought by the Florentines for 150,000 gold florins in 1341, was captured by Pisa.

The plague was at its worst in 1348 and war was never far away; 1351 against Milan, Pisa in 1362-4 and the Pope 1375-78. Popular discontent finally spilt over following the war with the papacy between 1375 and 1378. Resentment against high taxes culminated in the Ciompi uprising of 1378 (Ciompi being a word covering all the lowest artisanal guilds who were excluded from government). They succeeded in making some gains for themselves but the newly found cohesion of the lower classes lasted only until 1382 when the usual factional problems allowed government to favour the major guilds once again, after which there followed a period of comparative stability.

Yet Florence and the other cities of Tuscany prospered through it all. In 1338 there were 200 cloth factories, 110 churches, 30 hospitals and 40 banks in Florence. The big banking families employed representatives all over Europe; and the vast majority of children in the city were reasonably literate. Clearly politics failed to interfere with the business of prospering, although patriotism did not extend to arms and it was usual to rely on mercenaries for security, a weakness that Machiavelli was to attend to in the future. In the meantime military defeats were the order of the day, by the Pisans in 1315 and by Lucca in 1325.

Florence blossoms

Despite some military setbacks, Florence's expansion was ineluctable. Arezzo was taken in 1384, Pisa won for good in 1406, Cortona in 1411 and Livorno in 1421 – the outline of what was later to be the Grand Duchy of Tuscany.

At the beginning of the fifteenth century, three classes prevailed in middle class, and the artisans. Government was in the hands of both aristocracy and guild, democracy of a highly specialised, oligarchical kind. It amounted to dictatorship by the few, rather than by one. In Florence itself the most telling domestic event was in creation, between 1427-29, of a land-register providing the basis for a more equable and more productive distribution of taxation. The wealthiest family was the Medici with a taxable capital of 79,472 florins – a hint of things to come.

The Constitution

In order to understand the history of Florence and the rise of the Medici it is necessary to know something of the apparatus of government. The theory behind the constitution of Florence was as follows: The city was divided into four quarters: Santo Spirito (Oltrarno), Santa Croce, Santa Maria Novella and San Giovanni. Each quarter was in turn divided into four 'gonfaloni' (banners), each with a distinctive name, e.g. the Dragon.

The Signoria was made up of eight Priori (two from each quarter), then 12 Buonomini (three 'good men and true' from each quarter) who acted as counsellors, and then a number of Gonfalonieri della Giustizia, representing the guilds. To become a member of the Signoria was a profitable business and much sought after; nevertheless, because the rules of elegibility for such a position were strict, corruption tended to dictate who ruled. There were other officers and committees of government too, like the Capitano del Popolo who appears to have been a sort of public watchdog. Bureaucracy was as much an obstacle then as it is now.

The guilds were divided in the following manner. The oldest and most powerful was the Calimala (from the Via Mala, of ill repute), which imported raw or undressed cloth from Flanders, England and France. It governed itself, electing its own officials (who had to be Guelf and devout with it) who were responsible for enforcing very strict regulations e.g. that cloth only from the aforementioned countries was to be used, ensuring that the streets remained open thoroughfares and so on. All the major guilds at first were connected with the rag trade – the Guild of Manufacturers of Woollens and the Silk Manufacturers' Guild to name but two. Then, as trade grew, so did the importance of a proper financial structure and so the Bankers' Guild was born; and then guilds for judges and notaries, followed by guilds for apothecaries (who also dealt in spices and precious stones from the orient and to which Dante belonged). The last of the most important guilds was that of the Furriers. Each had its own banner and anyone bankrupted had to make a public declaration of the fact in the Mercato Nuovo, today's Piazza Repubblica, by striking the 'carroccio', the symbolic chariot of the city that stood there, with his bare bottom.

There were 14 minor guilds, the most important of which were the butchers, who had their stalls in the Mercato Vecchio, today's Piazza Vittorio-Emmanuele. Then came the blacksmiths, shoe-makers, carpenters, tavern-keepers, hotel-keepers, tanners, dealers in oil, salt and cheese, bakers and so on. This was the situation towards the end of the fourteenth century, but naturally it altered according to circumstances. Perhaps what is most interesting about all this is that despite corruption in government or the jostling for power among the guilds, all this colour and variety was changing the outlook of people. Citizens had a broader world view, were becoming perhaps, by the end of the fourteenth century, less conscious of the world merely as a place where one's time was served before going to God and more aware of it as a source of infinite possibility, a place to celebrate one's very humanity. People were growing in confidence. Society remained very superstitious and conscious of religion but prosperity made people less fearful of the hereafter. Religious observance remained crucial of course but piety was often more for show than through any sense of devotion. It was possible, for example, to buy wax dolls in the Via dei Servi which bore a resemblance to the purchaser and which could then be hung in church while the purchaser went about his business.

Not that society was short of genuinely devout men. The eminent Florentine bookseller, Vespasiano Bisticci (and it is a measure of the times that a bookseller was a noted citizen), refers to one Bishop Antonio, a man whose piety made him afraid to accept the post of Archbishop but who would thunder at the wantons and the idlers in Santa Maria del Fiore, who would leave in fright.

The rise of the Medici

In the early part of the fifteenth century, therefore, Florence had become one of the most powerful cities or states, in Italy and, indeed, Europe. Politically it held together but stability of government was not a strong point. Economically it was strong, with far-reaching influence; and much of Tuscany was in its thrall. It had already produced several great artists but by 1420 changes were afoot, for Florence was on the edge of its greatest period – the Renaissance.

Power at the beginning of the fifteenth century was in the hands of an oligarchy dominated by families, the best known being the Albizzi, who were supported by the principal guilds – a comparatively small number of people. Not everybody was happy with this arrangement. One family, the Medici, had supported the

Ciompi uprising and had been popular with the people ever since, much to the irritation of the Albizzi, who did their best to dispossess them. The head of the Medici, Giovanni, living just off the Mercato Vecchio, managed nonetheless to become one of the richest men of Florence, whilst remaining conscious that power lay only with the will of the people. His descendants were to succeed in becoming princes without title, who ruled whilst remaining private individuals, through the careful manipulation of public support. They used severe measures whenever necessary to achieve this: by outward shows of piety (including the patronage of churches and the use of devices like holding regular remembrance services throughout Florence for members of the family) and the careful cultivation of the myth of the Medici as 'fathers of the country'. Finally they ensured a Medici network by marriages into the important families of other Italian states:

'... the rise of the Medici, who became de facto masters of the city in 1434, with Cosimo, did not so much open a new phase in Florentine history as consummate the forming and consolidation of an oligarchic regime, begun some decades before' (*History of the Italian People*, Giuliano Procacci).

Giovanni's son Cosimo enlarged the family fortune, based on banking, still farther. He was seen by the Albizzi as a threat, and a plot was hatched to get rid of him. Although an attempt to kill him failed, he was exiled to Padua in 1433. Just a year later the Albizzi were themselves banished and Cosimo asked to return. He came back discreetly but when the moment was right struck at his former enemies and established his authority. His revenge was thorough. All his enemies were hanged, their identities and fate commemorated with ghoulish portraits painted on the Podesta walls.

The Medici years – dynastic rule

The following years were peaceful in comparison with the faction rent years that preceded the coming of Cosimo. Nonetheless, control had been obtained with ruthless efficiency to ensure that Medici interests were not threatened; and that control now penetrated to every part of Florentine society – Florence was the Medici. The people were not neglected, however, at least as far as spectacle was concerned. A sense of Florence's pre-eminence was instilled into the people by ensuring that Florence was a focal point for historic occasions. In 1439, for example, Santa Maria del Fiore was the venue

The genius of Donatello – his St. George gazes out from the Orsanmichele.

for the Council of Florence, during which the union of the Greek and Roman churches was proclaimed. Cosimo founded the first public library, with the help of the bookseller and diarist Vespasiano Bisticci, and, something of a scholar himself, convened the first meetings of the Platonic Academy, thereby gaining the support of artists, writers and humanists. He was something of a builder, restoring the Badia at Fiesole and enlarging the monastery of San Marco. Meanwhile the Medici bank prospered, lending money to the crowned heads of Europe. Politically, there were not many changes, except that government was now dominated by one man. Cosimo was powerful but thoughtful and modest. He died on 1 August 1464. It is recorded that as death approached, he shut his eyes. When his daughter asked why, he replied: 'It is to accustom myself to not opening them any more'.

Piero the Gouty (Il Gottoso)

Cosimo was succeeded by his 48 year-old son Piero who had served as a Priore, had been an ambassador to Milan, Venice and Paris and now became the last Medici Gonfaloniere. Piero lacked his father's flair but was reasonably popular, maintaining an even temper in the face of the crippling gout that afflicted him for much of his life. He married the remarkable and beautiful Lucrezia Tornabuoni (the model for Ghirlandaio's St. Elizabeth in the choir of Santa Maria Novella) who was a poet and the mother of his five children. His rivals, however, considered he was an unworthy successor to Cosimo. Luca Pitti (whose palace still stands), Agnolo Acciaiuoli and Dietisalvi Neroni stood against him so that Florence was again driven by faction – the Party of the hill (the supporters of Pitti) and the Party of the plain (Medici followers). When Piero made a few tactical errors in business, many merchants sided with Pitti who was then joined by Niccolo Soderini, a fine orator of venerable lineage who forced Piero to make changes that enabled Soderini to become Gonfaloniere. He failed, however, to introduce the reforms that he had promised and as his term of office drew to a close he was convinced that only arms would shift the Medici.

A coup, with the help of Ferrara and Venice, was mounted as Piero lay ill in his villa at Careggi. Piero was able to confirm what was happening and returned suddenly to Florence. The coup was foiled and a new, pro-Medici government elected. Pitti was forgiven, the others banished to Venice from where they continued to plot, ineffectually.

His rule secure, Piero was able to turn his attention to his city. He wanted to be a patron of the arts and a confidante of artists. He bolstered the Medici collections of books and coins; saw to it that Donatello was properly commemorated on his death, patronised Uccello, Luca della Robbia, Pollaiuolo, Botticelli and Gozzoli. (Botticelli lived in the Medici Palace with Piero and Lucrezia for a while and his portrait of Piero, as *Fortitude* is in the Uffizi, and Gozzoli's *Adoration of the Magi,* in the Medici Palace, contains a number of portraits of Florentine personalities.) Piero died on 2 December 1469 and was buried next to his brother Giovanni in the old sacristy of San Lorenzo.

Lorenzo – il Magnifico

Lorenzo, at the age of 21, followed his father as leader of the Florentines – the third Medici in succession, in what was supposed to be a republic. He and his 16 year-old brother Giuliano seemed, however, to have the support of many of the people and the nobles. Lorenzo made sure of his position by creating a constitution that involved citizens of comparatively low rank, who supported the Medici, but who themselves were in fact elected by high-ranking people closely allied to Lorenzo himself. His father had seen him married into one of the great Roman families, the Orsini. The engagement festivities, held in Piazza Santa Croce, were celebrated by the poet Luigi Pulci in *La Giostra di Lorenzo de' Medici*. The marriage itself took place a few months later, when there were five spectacular banquets at the Medici Palace. The bride left the Palazzo Alessandri in the Borgo San Piero one Sunday morning and rode in procession to the Medici Palace, where, as she entered the portal an olive branch was placed over her head. The guests were separated according to age and sex (young married women, young men, older women, older men) and each of the many dishes was heralded by trumpets. Clarice and Lorenzo were to be moderately happy, although she never really adapted to Tuscan ways and they had little in common.

Lorenzo himself was a strange mixture, a mixture that perhaps summed up the paradoxes of Florentine life. He was rather coarse in appearance but said to have a joyful nature and to be kind and considerate. He was a lover of the outdoor life, from farming to jousting but was also a gifted poet. He was not a particularly ostentatious man, as the austerity of the Medici palace demonstrated (he was, after all, a private citizen) but in the early years of his influence, Florentines were regularly treated to spectacles arranged by Lorenzo. One of the most famous has been celebrated in poetry. This was the tournament of 1475 in honour of his brother Giuliano who was awarded as first prize in the joust, a helmet designed by the artist Verrocchio. Poliziano's (called Politian) *Le Stanze Per La Giostra* (verses in honour of the tournament) is an early Italian humanist masterpiece.

The joy of politics

Meanwhile, of course, political manoeuvering was very much alive, although on the death of his father Lorenzo had accepted the good wishes of a delegation that had included members of the Pitti family. The conspirators of 1466 were still plotting from abroad and indeed took Prato, retaken by Lorenzo in double quick time. Yet Lorenzo, who merited special treatment because of his lineage, was still too young to be a member of the Signoria and was only admitted by special decree. Nonetheless, his was the voice that people listened for when decisions had to be made.

Tuscan cities subject to Florence were theoretically free to run their own affairs (except foreign policy) but in fact the truth was a little different. A consortium had been given the contract to mine alum near Volterra. Lorenzo was asked to arbitrate in a subsequent dispute between the consortium and the town and found in favour of the consortium. Violence ensued and Lorenzo, against advice, decided to put the uprising down. Volterra surrendered but the peace terms were broken and the city plundered. Lorenzo apologised personally but it was he who had made the decisions that led to the city's violation.

It was not long before Lorenzo had to deal with something closer to home and which showed something of his determined and ruthless character.

The Pazzi conspiracy

Florence was not the only Italian state growing in power. The popes were by now secular rulers of some standing, some among them seeing war as a legitimate part of their rule. When Pope Sixtus IV threatened to become Lord of the city of Imola, which stood on the frontier of Florentine territory, Lorenzo was appalled. He therefore asked of his banking colleague Francesco Pazzi, upon whom the Pope depended for the loan necessary to his purchase, that he not comply.

Pazzi, ambitious himself, and whose family was rather older than the Medici, informed Sixtus, who promptly took all Papal business from the Medici and replaced the Medici Archbishop of Pisa. In 1478 war broke out. Meanwhile, a plot was hatched by the Pazzi family and others (with the approval of the Pope) to remove Lorenzo and Giuliano, for good. It was decided to carry out the deed during mass at Santa Maria del Fiore on 6 April 1478 when the Cardinal Raffaelle Riario would be officiating and when the Medici brothers were sure to be in attendance. At a certain point the Palazzo della Signoria would be seized and Lorenzo and Giuliano assassinated. The bells rang – Giuliano was stabbed to death as he walked around the choir whilst Lorenzo was wounded in the neck but managed to escape into the sacristy. An attempt to take the Palazzo della Signoria was foiled. If the Pazzi thought that the citizens of Florence would willingly rise up against the Medici, they were wrong and in fact the citizenry were thirsty to revenge the death of the popular Giuliano. In the days that followed, Lorenzo ensured that everyone involved in the conspiracy was captured and put to an ignoble death, willingly assisted by the bloodthirsty populace.

The mood of the city is demonstrated by the fate of Jacopo Pazzi, the head of the clan. He was caught escaping into the mountains and executed (though buried in Santa Croce). There was a rumour, however, that he had sold his soul to the Devil, whereupon his body was disinterred to be reburied outside the city walls. Then he was dug up again, his stinking corpse paraded around the city until finally thrown into the Arno to drift down to the sea.

The Pope was furious – he sequestered all Medici assets in Rome and excommunicated Lorenzo and his fellow citizens. Then he declared war on Florence upon which his ally the King of Naples' son, the Duke of Calabria, took Montepulciano. The Pope persuaded Siena and Lucca to join with him. Lorenzo had no one to turn to and as the months passed the Duke of Calabria came within 30 miles of Florence. Lorenzo decided to throw himself upon the mercy of the King of Naples. After much discussion, during which Lorenzo spoke eloquently on the men of peace of antiquity and of the idea of a united Italy, the King changed sides, although Lorenzo was forced to pay an indemnity to the Duke of Calabria and relinquish to him certain parts of southern Tuscany. Nonethless, Lorenzo was more popular than ever.

The darker side of Lorenzo

Despite his popularity, the conspiracy and the events that followed seemed to have brought out the worst in Lorenzo who treated the merest hint of a threat with extreme violence. Nor were his business affairs all they could be. He reordered the Signoria so that he had greater control over Florentine affairs (although he never had total control, which sometimes suited him, for he was then able to avoid accepting responsibility). He did not have the business acumen of his grandfather and left affairs to his devious assistant Francesco Sassetti. This led to the closure of the London branch and others and to Lorenzo dipping his hand in the Florentine treasury – he could do this because all the members of the government were in his hands. And the Pope had still not withdrawn his excommunication, the Duke of Calabria remained a threat and the Tuscan borders were unsafe elsewhere. Then, a stroke of luck occurred: a Turkish army landed at Otranto and threatened to march north. The Duke of Calabria, forced to meet the challenge to Naples, had to hand back his possessions. Furthermore, to secure help from Florence, the Pope forgave Lorenzo who was careful to cultivate the Pope's successors and indeed marry into the family of Innocent VIII. By the end of Lorenzo's life, Florence had a strong influence over Papal affairs and his son Giovanni became a cardinal.

The people were entertained with spectacle, and both trade and cultural life flourished. Lorenzo loved to spend time at his villas with artists and scholars – the poets Poliziano and Pulci, the philosopher Pico della Mirandola (who at this stage of the Renaissance was attempting to bring back a more contemplative dimension to Humanism), the bookseller Vespasiano da Bisticci, the humanist translator of Plato, Marsilio Ficino, the musician Squarcialupi and the artists Lippi, Michelangelo (who lived at the Medici Palace) and

Botticelli. Lorenzo did not have the funds to commission as much work as his forebears but ensured, where he could, that commissions were obtained from others. His advice was often sought on artistic matters and he even entered the competiton for the Cathedral façade.

Printing came to Florence in 1477 and Lorenzo gave substantial funds to Florence University, the only place in Europe, it was thought, where Greek was well taught. The Pisans, inimical to Florence since their subjugation, were placated with the revival of their university and the expansion of their port. Lorenzo, no obsessive Humanist, continued to champion the Italian language with his own poetry, a mixture of the devotional, libidinous and rhapsodical and celebrates passion and the beauty of Tuscany and its way of life. His most famous lines are:

Quant'e bella giovenezza	How beautiful is youth
Che si fugge tuttavia!	And yet how fleeting!
Chi vuol esser lieto, sia;	Who wishes to be happy, so be it,
Di doman non c'e certezza.	For tomorrow is uncertain.

He died in 1492, considered by many as not only a glorious leader of Florence, but also an ornament to Italy.

Florence in the fifteenth century

Interregnum

Lorenzo was succeeded by his son Piero who lacked the political foresight of his father – he was ruthless but lacked charm. A spoilt child, he simply had no interest in affairs of state. Furthermore he quarrelled frequently with his cousins, Lorenzo and Giovanni, the sons of Pierfrancesco de' Medici, who were unlikely to do him any favours should the need arise. A strange combination of events was to lead to Piero's downfall.

Savonarola in Florence September 1494 – May 1498

In short a firebrand of a monk was be Florence's mentor for the next few years. Girolamo Savonarola was born in Ferrara. A pious child, he became a Dominican monk and set about wandering the country to warn of impending doom. In the last years of Lorenzo's influence, he finally settled in Florence, becoming lector at the convent of S. Marco. In his sermons he castigated the wealth of the church, the princes who thought of nothing but new taxes, and the learned who were more interested in the antiquity of Greece than in the scriptures. His considerable following included some surprises – the humanist Pico della Mirandola, the artists Botticelli and Signorelli, and Poliziano. Even Michelangelo and Machiavelli were said to fall under his spell and Lorenzo il Magnifico called him to his deathbed. Just why he was able to exert such influence is open to debate. Was it something to do with the approach of the end of the century, disillusionment with the Medici, disillusionment with society's emphasis on Humanism or just another 'tide in the affairs of men'? His followers were enthralled by his oratory: 'Through his words and actions they began to realise their own isolation and the powerlessness of an aristocratic culture to satisfy the needs of a society in crisis.'

Savonarola prayed for a purge and his prayers seemed to be answered. Charles VIII of France was persuaded by certain interests in Italy to reclaim the Kingdom of Naples, his inheritance, through the line of the House of Anjou. He marched south through Italy as far as Tuscany, which, whilst willing to offer safe passage, was determined to remain neutral. Charles sacked Fivizzano at which Piero, with unexpected alacrity, stood up to him. His fellow citizens, under the spell of Savonarola, did not join him and his treacherous cousins connived with the French until their arrest. Piero, emulating the action of his father some years before, went directly to Charles who made absurd demands to which Piero cravenly submitted. Upon his return the Signoria denied him access and Piero was forced to flee, the cries of 'Banish the Medici!' ringing in his ears.

Meanwhile Charles marched into Pisa and declared it freed from Florentine rule and Savonarola became de facto ruler of Florence. He was one of a delegation to Charles whose purpose was to repair the damage done by Piero. But for Savonarola, Charles was a saviour to whom he begged that Florence be spared. She was, but the French army barracked there anyway, entering through the Porta San Frediano in November 1494.

God's will

Savonarola proclaimed the refounding of the republic and set out the model for the constitution in his *Trattato Circa il Reggimento e Governo della Citta di Firenze*. Christ's law was to affect every aspect of city life. The government was to involve 3,000 citizens, the most broadly-based in the city's history. 'If you want a good government you must submit it to God' he said.' Of course trade, the real ruler of the city, went on as before but if the people needed a mentor, in the past the Medici, it was now Savonarola. He promulgated laws by preaching in the churches – many thousands would cram into the Cathedral to listen to his sermons. The atmosphere of the city changed completely. The spirit of enquiry which had at least flourished in the time of the Medici was abandoned. People became afraid to vent their opinions for fear that spies would report them for blasphemy. For Carnevale of 1497 he built a 'bonfire of the vanities' on which all vain and indecent art, written, painted or sculpted, was to be burnt.

The French left, having kept their word not to sack the city, marched south and took Naples. Meanwhile the new Pope, Alexander VI (Roderigo Borgia), formed a Holy League against Charles, in the name of a united Italy (a device to increase his own power). Charles, leaving a garrison in Naples, retreated north, clashed with the Holy League in July 1495 and returned to France. Florence, under the orders of Savonarola, remained outside the Holy League. The Pope was infuriated by Savonarola's claims of quasi divinity, forbidding him to preach further. Savonarola defied the Pope, even when excommunicated. This was too much for the Florentines who, remarking that many of the monk's predictions and promises were failing to bear fruit, began to grumble and then openly criticise him.

He was challenged by the Franciscans to prove the divinity of his mission by undergoing ordeal by fire on Piazza della Signoria. Prevarication ensured that the ordeal did not materialise; the people felt cheated and foolish. He was pursued and captured, tortured in the Alberghettino tower of the Palazzo Signoria, tried, and burnt at the stake in Piazza della Signoria.

A period of decline

Florence was no longer the great power it had been under Lorenzo. Four years after the death of Savonarola the constitution was adapted once again to circumstances and a republic was proclaimed under one Piero Soderini, a wealthy merchant who was declared Gonfaloniere for life. It was a difficult time, for the treasury – the resources of which were devoted to endless attempts to win back Pisa – was almost empty. Beyond the borders of Tuscany there was a restlessness among the Italian states that was far from comforting. Machiavelli, in his capacity as government official (before he wrote

The Prince,) was placed in charge of creating a standing army in the hope that it would be more reliable than mercenaries. Before long it was to have a chance to prove its worth.

The Medici, although scattered among the courts of Italy and Europe, were far from vanquished and entertained hopes still of returning to Florence. Piero had been linked with Cesare Borgia, son of the Pope, who had carved himself a kingdom in the Romagna. Then he threw in his lot with the French who, under the leadership of the new King, Louis XII, were eager to hang on to the Neopolitan throne. Following a defeat at the hands of the Spanish, Piero was drowned near Gaeta in 1503. The Medici revival was in fact to come about through his brother, the flabby Cardinal Giovanni.

In 1504 the Pope was Julius II, the grandson of a fisherman, who was eager to ensure the power of the Papal States in Italy. He formed the League of Cambrai with the Kings of France and Spain and with Emperor Maximilian. They successfully defeated the Venetians, after which Julius thought it was time to break up the alliance for fear it became too strong at his expense. Thus he first determined to drive the French back home. To the Pope's disgust, Florence wished to have nothing to do with the enterprise, an opinion shared by most other Italian states. The Pope turned to the Spanish. In an indecisive battle with the French near Ravenna at Easter 1512, Cardinal Giovanni, a favourite of the Pope, was taken prisoner by the French, who continued on their way to France. He escaped to discover that the Pope was eager to enforce a change of government in Florence, with Giovanni at its head.

The Spanish army arrived at the gates of Prato. Soderini, warning of the danger of allowing the return of the Medici, even with their protestations of wishing to return only as private citizens, obtained the support of the Florentines and determined to resist. This was to no avail, the standing army notwithstanding, for the Spanish broke through Prato's walls and pillaged the city. Medici supporters demanded the resignation of Soderini who wisely took his leave. Florentines were asked to accept the return of the Medici, the army was abolished and Florence joined the Holy League.

A new dynasty

In Florence a new parliament was formed to accommodate the change in circumstances. Giovanni, aware of the need to curry favour with the populace, made sure that the people were well entertained.

Soon, it became clear that Pope Julius II was dying. Cardinal Giovanni, ill himself, had to return to Rome where he arrived in time for the elections of the new Pope. To the surprise of many, Giovanni himself was elected, even with the agreement of Soderini's brother Cardinal Piero – won over by the suggestion of marriage between Giovanni's nephew, Lorenzo, and a member of the Soderini household. He became Pope Leo X. Naturally his election was greeted with euphoria in Florence whose citizens made merry for some days.

The new Pope was anxious to make his mark, like his predecessors, by 'uniting' central Italy under Medici rule. Although he had been advised, by Machiavelli among others, to accomplish this with the help of the vigorous new French King, Francis I, the Pope threw in his lot with the King of Spain, the Emperor and the Swiss. Francis marched into Italy anyway, dealt with the Holy League and continued to Bologna to confer with the Pope.

Giovanni, en route to Bologna, visited Florence, where Medici power was by now secure in the hands of his nephew Lorenzo, who had been Captain General of the Florentine Republic. He entered through the Porta Romana on 30 November 1515, to a Florence that had been transformed for the occasion by artists like Sansovino, Bandinelli and Andrea del Sarto. His meeting with Francis in Bologna, by contrast, was a sombre affair and he was forced to give way on most of the French King's demands. He returned to Florence to attend the death of his brother Giuliano, who left no heir, but an illegitimate son called Ippolito. Lorenzo, meanwhile, became the Duke of Urbino (later to marry a cousin of the French King and father Catherine who would become Queen of France), which meant that Giovanni seemed to be on the verge of creating his Medici-dominated central Italian state. Giovanni returned to the Vatican where he squandered funds and offered preferment to friends and family, including his cousin Giulio who became Archbishop of Florence.

Lorenzo returned to Florence where he died unmourned by the grumbling populace. Now it was up to Cardinal Giulio to ensure that Medici rule continued; and in fact Florence did enjoy a short period of prosperity under his tutelage. The Medici inheritance was far from sure, however, for the family was running out of legitimate male heirs. Meanwhile the Pope created Catherine Duchess of Urbino and annexed the Duchy to the Papal States. New problems were apearing on the horizon, however, for the new Emperor was Charles V (ambitious and therefore regarded with suspicion by both the Pope and King Francis). Martin Luther, the decidedly anti-Vatican church reformer, was also in the ascendant. It was fear of the latter that compelled Pope Leo to abandon any alliance with the French and join instead Charles V, despite his reservations. The Emperor was to deal with Luther in exchange for territorial considerations in Italy. Thus they formed an army to relieve the French of their Italian possessions. Then Leo X (Giovanni) died in 1521. Cardinal Giulio de' Medici, having left Florence in the hands of the two bastard Medicis, Alessandro and Ippolito, aimed to become Pope. He failed at the first attempt; but when Leo's successor, Adrian VI, died, he succeeded and became Clement VII.

By 1524 Clement had reversed the policy of his predecessor and allied himself to France. This proved less than astute for the French were immediately defeated by Charles who took Francis prisoner. This did not prevent the Pope and Francis cementing their alliance once Francis was released. Charles reacted by asking his allies to attack Rome, 'to teach the Pope a lesson he would never forget'. Meanwhile a Lutheran force from Germany attacked Rome from the north. Clement was in some trouble and although he was assisted by the sculptor Benvenuto Cellini (who in his famously inaccurate and egotistical autobiography makes great claims for his marksmanship), he was forced to submit. He escaped to Orvieto where he received the request from Henry VIII of England for divorce from Catherine of Aragon, a request he was in no position to grant.

The return of the Medici

In Florence Ippolito and Alessandro, supposedly in the charge of Cardinal Silvio Passerini, the Pope's representative, had failed to win over the populace. Even the historian and influential government employee Guiccardini, generally pro-Medici, despaired of them; and there was rejoicing in Florence when the fate of the Pope became known. Passerini and his charges slunk away, the republican constitution was re-established and a new Gonfaloniere, Niccolo Capponi, a follower of Savonarola, elected. The Pope, determined to see the Medici back in Florence, connived with Charles, who agreed to help, provided he was recognised as Emperor. The Florentines determined to resist. The militia was reinstated and Michelangelo employed to extend the city defences.

The Florentines, under their commander Francesco Ferrucci, held out against the imperial (mostly Spanish) forces for ten months but finally capitulated, their cause not helped by the condottiere

Malatesta Baglioni (in overall charge of the operation), who, it was thought, was in league with the enemy. Certainly the population was starving and plague-ridden. The city surrendered and so died the last resistance to the Emperor and a dramatic period of Italian history that had begun with Charles VIII's invasion, continued with Savonarola, the hopes of an alliance of religion and Humanism and 'Machiavelli's vision of a total regeneration of Italian life on the model of the great foreign monarchies' (Giuliano Procacci, *History of the Italian People*) came to an end. The Medici were back.

More of the same

Yet another constitution was formed and brutal revenge exacted. The new ruler was to be Alessandro de' Medici, while Ippolito was made a cardinal by Clement, who died not long after in September 1534. The Florentines were afraid that Alessandro would now become impossible, and indeed he did, being proclaimed hereditary Duke in the process, though continuing nominal consultations with government councils. But his insensitive and incessant glorification of the Medici name, with no action to justify it, irritated citizens to the point where they appealed to Emperor Charles V. The charges they made were rebutted by Guiccardini and Charles did nothing. However, Alessandro was soon to die at the hands of another Medici, Lorenzaccio, a distant and dissolute cousin who arrived in Florence from Rome. Though forming a sort of friendship with Alessandro, it must have been based on jealousy, for Lorenzaccio contrived a strange plan for his assassination. He challenged Alessandro to seduce Caterina Soderini Ginori, a woman known for her propriety – Lorenzaccio would bring her to his room. But it was Lorezaccio who came and stabbed Alessandro as he lay waiting, though Alessandro succeeded in almost biting off his assailant's finger. His fate was kept secret for long enough to ensure that no anti-Medici revolution broke out.

The Medici supporters met to decide what to do. Some were in favour of restoring the republic but Guiccardini declared that he could not bear even the possibility of mob rule, as had occurred with the Ciompi uprising many years before. In the end it was settled that Cosimo, another cousin, would become Duke. Guiccardini rather fancied that he would be able to act as a sort of regent; but Cosimo was not to be so easily reigned in.

TEN

The Late Renaissance and the Modern Era

The Grand Duchy of Tuscany

Italy continued to be rent by war during the mid-sixteenth century, in which time the boundaries of present day Tuscany were practically established – only Lucca remained outside Medici rule. The style of rule changed too, so that Florence's dependent territories, previously thought of as subjects, came to be ruled homogeneously from the capital. And they accepted, even welcomed it. The old republican institutions existed but without any real power – instead, power passed into the hands of the 'pratica segreta,' a team of civil servants who worked under the Duke. He calmed the old patriciate by giving them important posts and allowing them guarded critisism. He married into the Spanish empire and happily. As this bureacracy grew so did the space needed for it – hence the construction of the Uffizi, close to the Palazzo Vecchio.

'The contrast between the character of these two buildings, the practical sobriety of the earlier one, the swaggering exuberance of the later, is the most effective illustration of the whole parabola of Florence's history, from its mercantile commune origins to its Grand-Ducal finale.' (Giuliano Procacci, *History of the Italian People*).

In 1569, Cosimo succeeded in acquiring the title of Grand Duchy from the Pope. Yet Florence lost much of its former impetus without becoming a modern state and entered a period of relative decline, becoming a city of rentiers and civil servants. The decline began at the beginning of the sixteenth century, but was in fact gradual, for the silk industry continued to flourish until the beginning of the seventeenth century and Florentine bankers were still important in

Lyons, where indeed many exiles settled. At home it was land that was now the biggest investment and thus large estates were formed. The rush for land was not accompanied by attempts to improve agriculture, as elsewhere. No city in Italy built less in the sixteenth century, if only because Florence remained jealous of its own traditions.

The Rule of Cosimo

Cosimo was unexpectedly resolute in his rule and determined to maintain Florentine traditions. Florence was first of all an economic organisation dedicated to trade, banking and manufacturing. Political uncertainty had rendered it a shadow of its former self; but Cosimo knew that one way of maintaining independence was through money. Economic stability was maintained by means of persevering with traditional trade, which, whilst reasonably successful, stifled innovation. On the other hand the new peace encouraged sustained business which had not entirely lost its old vitality. As for politics, Cosimo at first had little idea how to reanimate the body politic. In the end the best that he could do was build up a bureaucratic state, which, since it was to be based on efficiency, meant the reorganisation of the administrative offices and changing office holding requirements from wealth and influence to technical competence. The Church, too, was to change. Cosimo succeeded in easing corruption but the church remained inimical to new ideas, although Cosimo enjoyed the support of the population who, not surprisingly, were anti-clerical.

Cosimo's second principle was continuity. Thus, the constitution of the republic remained intact (in the same way that former Florentine constitutions had allowed other Tuscan cities to keep their constitutions) and although the final decision rested with the Duke at least there was deliberation. He listened but made up his own mind.

Another principle was the implementation of justice: the legal system was overhauled. Thus Cosimo's power was never quite as absolute as in other cities and though severe this was partly to force people to adhere to principles. The fourth principle was equality - everyone was entitled to the protection of the law. The new concept of liberty came to mean being allowed to get on with one's affairs in peace rather than involvement in public affairs.

Cosimo also tried to break down the old distinctions between dominant and subject cities and between city and country dweller. Subjection to Florence had drained many parts of Tuscany of talent and resources, so that to visit other parts of Florence's dominion was to go back in time. His remedy was to leave much of the traditional administration intact but to increase the authority of governors appointed from Florence and to tighten the chain of command between local and central authorities. Simultaneously, he eased ecomomic restrictions, sponsored the revival of the silk industry in Pisa, founded new settlements on Elba, constructed a modern port at Livorno and drained the Maremma. And he bothered to visit subject towns.

The difficulties of rule

But his consuming interest in so much had a bad effect too, for it tended to stifle initiative and esprit de corps. At first there were problems in the other Tuscan cities which took advantage of the situation (the Pisan occupation of Livorno, for example; feuding in Borgo San Sepolcro and in Pistoia). Cosimo had to show that he was strong in such cases for weakness, even if compassionate or merciful, might prove to be an excuse for the Emperor, already a sort of absent landlord, to take full control. Guiccardini supported him, for as he said:'The duty of good citizens when their country is in hands of a tyrant is to get into his confidence in order to persuade him to do good and desist from evil'. He garnered support from the lower classes, amongst others, which helped to obviate any threat from exiles – for example that of the Strozzi family, who were routed at Prato. And although Tuscany remained in some ways an imperial fief, Cosimo persuaded the Spanish to withdraw her troops and protectors from Tuscany. He learnt, furthermore, to play off the Pope against the Empire (for the Popes were always trying to expand), whilst remaining basically in the Spanish camp.

It was important, too, to keep the peace with the four minor states of Tuscany, particularly Siena which still controlled the southern third of Tuscany and which was always liable to boil over because of internal rivalries which might let in the Emperor. Piombino, on the coast, was needed for defence. Lucca kept mostly quiet, accepting Florence as an unofficial protector. The principality of Massa Carrara was a problem but Cosimo allowed the feuding families to squabble between themselves, as long as the marble mines remained safe.

However, it was no easy task that he had set himself, despite his dexterity. As time went on he found it necessary to be severe and even ruthless. He spent a lot of time (1554-57) in bringing Siena to heel, devastating it in the process. He had abandoned his policy of benevolent neutrality in 1553 when the appointment of his enemy Piero Strozzi as commander in chief of the French forces in Tuscany threatened to make Siena a bastion of the French or the Spanish or of exiles with grudges. Florence and Siena were both impoverished in the process.

Florence regains her pride

Cosimo proved to be an able military commander – increasing the size of the state by one third – and a sensitive diplomat, for he was able to win conquered peoples over quite quickly. In 1571 Florentine galleys played a significant role in the defeat of the Turks at the battle of Lepanto; it was Cosimo who had created the navy.

Florence also regained some of its reputation in the arts. Cosimo recognised the Florentine inheritance but many intellectuals had left following the problems between the death of Lorenzo il Magnifico and the arrival of Cosimo in 1537. He tried to stem the tide with the creation of new academies and the revival of Pisa University and he succeeded in luring back some distinguished citizens, like Vasari; although he failed with Michelangelo. Freedom of expression was tolerated up to a point, so that independence of thought and judgement gradually reasserted themselves, the community once again becoming involved in new projects; the importance of a common heritage bound them together. There was not a particularly anti-Renaissance sentiment, but a desire to condemn its worst aspects (pedantry, for example) enabled Florentines to be critically detached from their heritage. Certain of the old Humanist texts were discarded. Aristotle became more important than Plato. It was the epoch of the discovery of the importance of natural science as distinct from religion.

In 1560 Duke Cosimo moved from the Palazzo Vecchio, which he left for the use of his son Francesco, to the Pitti Palace, which had been bought from the Pitti family by his wife. Behind the Palace land was bought that was to become the Boboli Gardens. Private building was encouraged and soon other families followed him across the river, the Via Maggio becoming the most elegant street in town.

Towards the end of his life Cosimo handed over everything to Francesco except the running of foreign affairs. He died in 1574 but not to popular mourning. Although he was credited with having brought back more entertainment (eg chariot races around Santa Maria Novella where posts still mark the limits of the course), with releasing Florence from direct dependence on Spain, for the construction of a fleet and the enlarging of the state's frontiers, people resented a certain loss of freedom and an unscrupulous use of monopolies in trading. There were many other achievements of note, however. Cosimo had made improvements in farming methods (drainage and irrigation), in the construction of canals, in the cultivation of olives and in mining silver. He had ensured unity with the other towns of Tuscany, developed Pisa and Livorno and promoted Pisa University. He built the Ponte Santa Trinita and rebuilt the Ponte Carraia, built a tapestry factory, the Boboli Gardens, the Medici Mausoleum at San Lorenzo and the Pisa School of Botany. He also encouraged the cultivation of music and patronised Vasari, Bronzino, Pontormo and Cellini.

Grand Duke Francesco

With the demise of Cosimo it was down hill in some respects for Florence and Tuscany – the years of power and creative impetus had gone. Tuscany was no longer a power to be reckoned with, just a pawn in the politics of the superpowers, important only in small ways (the port of Livorno, for example). The rulers of Tuscany merely enjoyed themselves and did as little as possible. Francesco was not very ambitious and his wife, the Archduchess Joanna of Austria, loathed living in Florence, though Cosimo had tried to please her by having the Palazzo Vecchio courtyard painted with scenes of Austria. When she died at the age of 30, leaving no heir, Francesco married his mistress, Bianca Capello, and built the remarkable Villa Pratolino for her. The rest of his family were even less responsibile than Francesco, or just as feckless. His brother Pietro murdered his wife, and his sister Isabella, having taken a lover, was strangled by her husband.

Francesco did support the silk industry by cajoling farmers into planting mulberry, but farming, still prosperous though subject to disastrous failures, had become a subject for philosophy rather than practicalities.

Still, with careful diplomacy he ensured Tuscany remained free of invaders. His policy was based on the following: not brooking any interference with his absolute interference in internal affairs and avoiding any temptation to involve himself in the affairs of others. But people were chronically poor, despite the apparantly overflowing treasury, which gave rise to the problem of brigandage. Francesco had a weird private life and took little notice of his duties as ruler, rather he spent his time at Pratolino feeding his goldfish and planting rare shrubs and making scientific experiments. Altogether it was a time of dilettantism and at best a time of recognition of the achievements of the past. In the Uffizi Francesco created an art gallery and studios for young artists. He established the Accademia della Crusca dedicated to the purity (and superiority) of the Florentine language. He became an expert in making vases and invented a way of cutting rock crystal and a revolutionary method of making porcelain. He and Bianca both died on the same day in October 1587.

Ferdinand I

Francesco's other brother had been a cardinal since the age of 15 and was something of a contrast. His rule was benign and efficient, and he was determined to maintain Tuscany's independence at any cost, by force if necessary. The government became less corrupt and the finances more stable. Trade and farming flourished (although there were signs of stagnation there due to antiquated farming and business methods) whilst business began to go out of fashion among the intellectuals. The essence of Ferdinand's foreign policy was to preserve the peace and independence of all Italy and since he recognised the declining power of Spain, he acted accordingly to gain concessions. He protected himself against the French by seeing his niece Maria marry Henry IV. He built hospitals in Florence and colleges in Pisa. Livorno prospered still further with his promise of religious tolerance which drew Protestants and Jews to live and trade there (and Livorno still has the largest Jewish population of any Italian city). He endeared himself to his subjects by personally supervising disasters and by making efforts to help the poor. He was fairly extravagant with money which he poured into the embellishment of the Pitti Palace and Boboli Gardens, the enlargement of the Uffizi and the purchase of Egyptian antiquities; he was determined to maintain the fame of the Medici. Spectacle and entertainment continued to be important and on the occasion of his marriage to Christine of Lorraine no expense was spared. In the business world Pisa became the centre of international credit but Ferdinand presided nonetheless over the steady decline of Florentine initiatve and commerce. Bankers were banking on the wrong things, businesses were no longer following the precepts of sound commerce though the silk industry continued to prosper. This attitude was reflected in the construction of new palaces, the beauty of which depended on an ornate façade but lacking substance within. Ferdinand died in 1609.

Cosimo II

Ferdinand's son continued the family tradition of lavish entertainment. When he married to the Archduchess Maria Maddalena, sister of Emperor Ferdinand II, there was a spectacular display on the Arno:

'... the stage was the whole stretch of the river between the Ponte alla Carraia and the Ponte Santa Trinita, which was embellished with statues for the occasion. The audience, sitting in immense grandstands erected in the Lungarni, were treated to a performance of the Argonautica in which Jason, avoiding the hazards presented by gigantic dolphins, lobsters and fire-spitting hydra, sailed round an artificial island, captured the Golden Fleece and presented the Archduchess with six re apples symbolic of the Medici 'palle' or crest. (Christopher Hibbert, *The Rise and Fall of the House of Medici).*

Cosimo II extended the Pitti Palace and reconstructed the villa of Poggio Imperiale near Arcetri where Galileo was offered sanctuary.

Galileo Galilei

Galileo, astronomer and scientist, was born in Pisa in 1564, the son of a distinguished musician, and one of the founders of the Florentine Camerata, which is credited with the revival of Italian musical life. Perhaps Galileo's genius for mathematics in some measure derives from this, for music too is order and harmony.

He studied medicine and then maths and physics at the University of Pisa, where he exasperated his tutors by his questioning, presumptions and quick temper. He was offered a chair but his colleagues were not very welcomong so he went to Padua University for 18 years until he was invited to Florence by Cosimo II who had been his pupil. He spent the last years of his life under the protection of the Medici. Galileo was the man who took the world out of the shadows of potential, as recognised by Leonardo, to the world of precision and realisation. He began by rejecting Aristotelian science and accepting that of Copernicus. He saw that the infinite was measurable and this was heresy for it implied that God's ways were not necessarily that mysterious. Galileo recognised that his science was also philosophy, for he was on the edge of a new age and it was only mental laziness that prevented his discoveries manifesting themselves in other forms of culture. His view was that human understanding was as perfect as that of God within the limits of its knowledge. For the Church, the universe was immutable; for Galileo,

Santa Croce, Florence – the last resting place of many of the world's illustrious and great.

there was movement. His ideas spread across the country and though there were hiccups – Galileo's trial for heresy, the Counter Reformation – there was to be no looking back.

Cosimo died in 1620, at the age of 30. When Galileo died in 1642 the Church forbade any monument to his memory, although Ferdinand II, the son of Cosimo II had him buried in the Novices' Chapel of Santa Croce.

Ferdinand II

Since he was only ten at his accession, Tuscany was ruled by Ferdinand's mother and grandmother until he came of age. He did not seem very promising, although when older he at least showed compassion to his subjects during a bout of plague, remaining in Florence to help. He turned out to be unostentatious and good natured, with a preference for the companionship of men. He was a generous patron of science and letters and both he and his brother Leopoldo were students of Galileo and took a general interest in things scientific. Ferdinand was quite practical, helping to develop the Florentine craft of creating mosaics in 'pietra dura'. The Pitti palace was provided with more galleries to make way for new acquisitions and adorned with murals by accomplished artists.

Ferdinand's political policies were governed by a desire to avoid all trouble, although there was a brief war with the Pope's Barberini relatives. He avoided offending the Pope by not pursuing his claim to Urbino. He had one difficult brother Gian Carlo (who also provided the funds for the construction of a theatre in Via della Pergola) who, although a cardinal, created many problems over his pursuance of women. Ferdinand had one son, later Cosimo III who, according to the Lucca ambassador, was 'dominated by melancholy to an extraordinary degree'.

Family decline

Ferdinand's son, Cosimo was married off as soon as possible to Marguerite-Louise, daughter of the uncle of Louis XIV, Gaston d'Orleans. This was not a marriage made in heaven and she led him quite a dance. She hated Tuscany and though they hardly spent time together she managed to produce a son, Ferdinando. Nonetheless she said that Cosimo was a fornicator and that therefore she must enter a convent (in France) to which Louis replied that if she returned to France it would be to the Bastille. There was a reconciliation and she bore a daughter, Anna Maria Luisa. Then problems surfaced again at which point Ferdinand thought it sensible to send Cosimo on a tour to England and Holland. He was well received in English academic circles owing to his family's protection of Galileo. He returned and tried again with his wife as his father was dying, which he did, in May 1670.

Cosimo III

Despite Ferdinand's personal sense of economy and rigid and extensive system of taxation, there had been no improvement in the finances of Tuscany whose trade was rapidly declining and whose population was decreasing due to malaria, plague and food shortages, the result of backward agriculture. At first Cosimo tried to deal with it but then withdrew to a chapel life. His wife bore another son, Gian Gastone, but then the marriage began to fail completely. Finally she was allowed to return to France, from where her demands for more money came thick and fast.

Meanwhile Cosimo became ever madder and more zealous, imposing severe punishments on lawbreaking of any kind, no matter how absurd the crime: he tried, for example, to prevent Jews in Livorno frequenting Christian prostitutes. In deference to the Inquisition, no encouragement was given to scientists. Public executions reached 2,000 in one year. Many new taxes were imposed; further funds were obtained by selling off merchants' exclusive rights to the disposal of flour and salt. Some of the money was used to make purchases for art collections but mostly it was frittered away. In 1698 crowds of peasants gathered outside the Pitti Palace crying for 'bread and work'. Any idea of justice had evaporated; and yet, in common with most other states, autocratic rule was still regarded as a Divine right. And in some respects life in Florence, at least, was good – foreign visitors were astonished at the level of cleanliness.

Cosimo worried that his dissolute brother, Cardinal Francesco Maria, was having a deleterious effect on his heir Ferdinando, who was a gifted musician. He too showed a sexual preference for men; his father married him off to the boring Princess Violante Beatrice of Bavaria, whom he ignored.

Before his death in 1723, Cosimo turned to Gian Gastone, who became the next duke.

Gian Gastone

Married to a Bohemian duchess who was persuaded to leave her homeland only under duress, Gian Gastone's youthful promise was dissipated in debauch and vice. Nonetheless, at first he eased the tax burden and rescinded some of the more ridiculous laws. But eventually he lost interest – he let the country run itself and spent the final eight years of his life in bed. In any case, his attitude reflected events outside Italy, where the great powers were in the process of carving up Europe, a process in which Italy, not much more than a series of impotent fiefdoms, had no say.

When Gian Gastone died in July 1737, the Duke of Lorraine annexed Tuscany, which became another part of the Austrian Empire, the Medici crest being replaced with the Cross of Lorraine, eagle and fleur-de-lis. The last Medici was Anna Maria, the Electress Palatine and Gian Gastone's wife, who was allowed to see out her days in the Pitti Palace. She died in 1743. Independent Florence and Tuscany was no more.

Dependent Tuscany 1743-1859

Thus it was that in the eighteenth century Italy became a patchwork country whose little states and duchies were used by the bigger powers. Tuscany had become a Lorraine seigniory, ruled by an absent duke in Vienna, although Lucca continued to enjoy a measure of independence. Tuscans were never able to accept their new overlords, even if attempts were made to win them over and even if their own aristocracy was visibly decadent.

Nonetheless, in the second half of the eighteenth Italy enjoyed a long period of peace. The first coach route across the Alps, built in 1771, went through Brenner to Modena, across the Apennines by way of Abetone to Florence, passing through all the territories that belonged to the house of Austria, of which Lorraine was a part. Livorno and Pistoia were joined by canal. A return to the land was much in vogue: agricultural academies multiplied of which the best known was the Florentine 'Accademia dei Georgofili', formed in 1753, the 'supreme council' of Tuscan landowners. Land reclamation projects were initiated. New industries such as straw and porcelain were inaugurated and the Austrian Empire did at least provide new markets for Tuscan silk. A spirit of reform was engendered by the next Austrian Grand-Duke, Peter Leopold, who was steeped in the ideas of the Enlightenment.

In 1799 the French invaded, and by 1808, nominally independant, Tuscany was part of Napoleon's Empire. After the fall of Napoleon, the Austrians restored its Grand-Duchy status; but by then the forces for the unification of Italy were marching and in 1859 Tuscans voted for their annexation to Piedmont-Sardinia, after which her fate was tied to that of Italy, of which Florence was briefly capital from 1861-1875.

Tuscany from 1875 to the present

Whilst it is invidious to sum up more than a century in a mere paragraph, it is fair to say that Tuscany's proudest days were already passed. The newly-formed state of Italy needed several decades to settle into place – many would say that many more are required – and Tuscany fell into a quiet repose. The area suffered considerably during the Second World War but at least efforts were made by the Germans to avoid much destruction of the occupied city of Florence. Nonetheless, all the bridges except the Ponte Vecchio were blown up as the Germans retreated before the advancing allies who, with the help of the resistance fighters who had harried the invader from the Appenines, arrived in August 1944. After the war Tuscany was noted for its Communist sympathies. In 1966 the Arno burst its banks and many works of art were lost or damaged. Since then the development of industry and a generally more favourable economy throughout Italy has brought prosperity to the region, which is thriving once again.

ELEVEN

The Artists and a Glossary of Art and Architecture

An index of important artists

Alberti, Leon Battista (1404-72), architect and writer, a theoretician of Renaissance and Humanistic style.

Allori, Alessandro (1535-1607), Florentine Mannerist.

Ammannati, Bartolommeo (1511-92), Florentine architect and Mannerist sculptor.

Andrea del Castagno (1423-57), early Renaissance Florentine painter who worked in an energetic and heroic style.

Andrea del Sarto (1486-1530), predecessor of Mannerism, a gifted draughtsman and painter.

Fra Angelico (1387-1455), monk and painter whose Gothic style is transformed by an intense use of light.

Spinello Aretino (died 1410), falls between Giotto and the International Gothic.

Arnolfo di Cambio (1245-1302), architect and pupil of Nicola Pisano, noted for Florence Cathedral and the Palazzo Vecchio, whose architecture represents the spirit of Republican and pre-Renaissance Florence.

Baccio Bandinelli (1488-1559), court painter to Cosimo I.

Barna da Siena (active c.1350), follower of Martini.

Bartolo di Fredi (died 1410), pupil of A. Lorenzetti, noted for use of colour.

Domenico Beccafumi (1486-1551), Sienese Mannerist.

Benedetto da Maiano (1442-97), Florentine sculptor

Sandro Botticelli (1445-1510), Florentine Renaissance painter who in many ways is the epitome of his time.

Agnolo Bronzino (1503-72), Florentine Mannerist and portrait painter, with a personal, refined Classical style.

Filippo Brunelleschi (1377-1446), Florentine architect who rediscovered the building skills of antiquity and who was one of the progenitors of the Renaissance. The cupola of Florence Cathedral is one of his greatest achievements. His greatest innovation was the use of perspective.

Bernardo Buontalenti (1536-1608), Florentine mannerist.

Benvenuo Cellini (1500-71), Florentine sculptor and goldsmith of skill. An adventurer whose autobiography is an excellent read.

Cimabue (1240-1302), Giotto's predecessor accredited with the beginning of a drift away from standard Byzantine painting.

Matteo Civitali (1435-1501), Lucca painter of skill.

Coppo di Marcovaldo (mid/late thirteenth century), Florentine contemporary of Cimabue.

Bernardo Daddi (1290-1349), Florentine painter of altarpieces in Giotto style with great use of clour.

Desiderio da Settignano (1428-61), Florentine sculptor, follower of Donatello.

Domenico di Bartolo (1400-46), Sienese painter.

Donatello (1386-1466), highly individual Florentine Renaissance painter, perhaps the greatest of his time. He studied the ancient ruins of Rome with his friend Brunelleschi. Like him he mastered the use of perspective.

Duccio di Buoninsegna (died 1319), Siena's answer to Giotto.

Franciabiagio (1482-1525), Mannerist pupil of Andrea del Sarto.

Taddeo (father, 1300-66) and Agnolo (son, died 1396) Gaddi, Florentine followers of Giotto and Orcagna.

Gentile da Fabriano (1360-1427), international Gothic master.

Lorenzo Ghiberti (1378-1455), one of the legends of the Renaissance, a master with bronze, notably the doors of the Florence Baptistry.

Domenico Ghirlandaio (1448-94), great painter of fresco cycles.

Giambologna (1529-1608), from Flanders. Mannerist court sculptor to the Medici.

Giotto (1266-1337), the first painter to depart from the Byzantine style with new treatment of space and the human figure.

Giovanni di San Giovanni (1592-1633), Baroque painter.

Benozzo Gozzoli (died 1497), Florentine painter who used colour and narrative to good effect.

Leonardo da Vinci (1452-1519), a singular Florentine genius of the High Renaissance – painter, scientist and dabbler, strangely ignored by il Magnifico.

Fra Filippo Lippi (died 1469), Renaissance painter and monk of great skill who had an affair with one of his models.

Filippino Lippi (1457-1504), son of Filippo.

Ambrogio and Pietro Lorenzetti (died 1348), Sienese brothers and both innovators.

Lorenzo di Credi (1439-1537), follower of Leonardo.

Lorenzo Monaco (1370-1425), Sienese monk who painted in Florence.

Rutilio Manetti (1571-1639), Sienese Baroque painter.

Simone Martini (died 1344), Sienese artist of the International Gothic and one of the great innovators.

Masaccio (1401-1428), Florentine painter considered the touchstone for the Renaissance.

Maso di Banco (active mid-fourteenth century), Florentine follower of Giotto.

Masolino (died 1447), Florentine genius and contemporary of Masaccio but more of the International Gothic school.

Matteo di Giovanni (1435-95), Sienese Renaissance painter.

Michelangelo Buonarroti (1475-1564), Florentine student of Ghirlandaio; a temperamental genius who does not fit easily into any category but who sculpted and painted his vision of perfect, Classical man. He marks a break with the Humanist aspect of the Renaissance as practised by Brunelleschi and Alberti and was also a poet.

Michelozzo di Bartolomeo (1396-1472), Florentine sculptor and architect beloved of the Medici who, in common with other wealthy families, were keen to implement the tenets of Humanist architecture, as exemplified by Michelozzo's master, Brunelleschi.

Mino da Fiesole (1429-84), Florentine sculptor specialising in tomb work and an admirer of Donatello.

Nanni di Banco (1384-1421), Florentine sculptor.

Andrea Orcagna (died 1368), Florentine artist of the mid-fourteenth century, in the intricate International Gothic style. Also his brothers Nardo and Jacopo di Cione.

Piero della Francesca (died 1492), painter from Sansepolcro, a genius and innovator.

Piero di Cosimo (1462-1521), Florentine painter.

Pietro da Cortona (1596-1699), Baroque painter from Cortona

Pinturicchio (1454-1513), painter from Perugia noted for his use of colour.

Nicola Pisano (1258-78), one of the greatest of Tuscan sculptors, ahead of his time.

Giovanni Pisano (1265-1314), carried on the family tradition.

Andrea Pisano (died 1348), teacher to Orcagna and who brought his family's artistic inheritance to Florence with the Baptistry doors. Gothic influences still strong. Also his son, Nino.

Antonio Pollaiuolo (died 1498), a fine Florentine painter and sculptor who advanced the arts with his elegance and sense of balance. Also his brother, Piero.

Jacopo Pontormo (1494-1556), eccentric Florentine Mannerist of genius.

Jacopo della Quercia (1374-1438), Siena's greatest sculptor.

Luca della Robbia (1400-82), follower of Donatello and first of the family of sculptors whose distinctive coloured terracotta glazework is everywhere in Tuscany. The other Della Robbias are his nephew Andrea (1435-1525) and Andrea's son Giovanni (1469-1529).

Bernardo Rossellino (1409-64), Florentine architect and sculptor. His brother Antonio (1427-79) was also a noted sculptor.

Rosso Fiorentino (1494-1540), Florentine Mannerist of drama and skill.

Francesco Salviati (1510-63), talented Florentine painter.

Giuliano da Sangallo (1443-1516), Florentine Humanist architect much used by Il Magnifico.

Antonio da Sangallo (1455-1537), brother of Giuliano and architect.

Il Sassetta (1390-1450), Sienese Renaissance painter.

Luca Signorelli (died 1523), imaginative and influential painter from Cortona.

Il Sodoma (1477-1549), Sienese by adoption, mildly Mannerist.

Pietro Tacca (1580-1640), Baroque sculptor and pupil of Giambologna.

Taddeo di Bartolo (1363-1422), great Sienese artist.

Francesco Talenti (early fourteenth century), architect noted for completing Florence Cathedral and the last three storeys of the Campanile in classicised Gothic style.

Paolo Uccello (1397-1475), unique stylist with colour and perspective

Giorgio Vasari (1511-74), painter and architect of moderate skill and author of *Lives of the Artists*.

Il Vecchietta (1412-80), Sienese painter and sculptor.

Andrea del Verrocchio (1435-88), teacher to Leonardo and Botticelli, a master of intellectual robustness in his art.

Glossary of artistic, historic and religious terms

Abbazia – abbey
Affresco – fresco
Architrave – the horizontal frame above the door

Arte – old word for guild

Badia – abbey

Basilica – a church with aisles but without transepts

Borgo – suburb or arterial street

Bottega – workshop

Campanile – bell tower

Cantoria – choir gallery

Cappella – chapel, often not much more than an altarpiece along the aisle of a church

Carroccio – wagon used as a sort of mascot in battle

Cenacolo – a painting of the Last Supper

Chiaroscuro – light and shade

Chiesa – church

Chiostro – cloister

Ciborium – casket or tabernacle

Comune – Medieval city state and now a municipality

Condottiere v commander of an army of mercenaries

Crete – eroded chalk cliffs

Corbel – projecting stone block

Cupola – dome

Duomo – cathedral

Greek cross – cross with arms of equal length

Intarsia – wood or stone inlay

Latin cross – cross with long vertical arm

Lunette – semi-circular space, often painted

Maesta – Madonna and Child enthroned

Opera – a work or undertaking

Palazzo – loosely, palace, but any large, imposing building

Pieta – Virgin with dead Christ

Pietre Dure – semi-precious stone in mosaic or decorative use.

Pietra Forte – fine sandstone used in Florence

Pietra Serena – fine dark sandstone that is good for carving

Pieve – parish church

Polyptych – painting in several sections

Predella – sectioned painting below altarpiece

Putto – representation of naked cherubic child

Sinopia – sketch for a fresco made on the wall

Stoup – vessel for Holy Water

Tempera – a sort of paint (see History section)

Tondo – round picture

Travertine – hard, pale building stone

Triptych – painting in three sections.

TWELVE

Introduction – Florence, North of the Arno

Introduction – What to see and do in Florence

Tourist Information

The largest office is at Via Manzoni 16 (Tel: 247 81 41/234 62 80), which is not very conveniently situated. There are others, however, at the station (see chapter 3); at Via Tornbuoni 15 (Tel: 216544); just to the south of Piazza della Signoria on Via de' Baroncelli; and along Via Cavour south of Piazza San Marco. It is worthwhile visiting one of them – they are helpful and will give you information about everything, but you are advised to go on a weekday morning, opening hours being otherwise rather erratic.

Tours

Sightseeing tours of the city and environs are organised by CIT at Via Cavour 54.

Cafés and ice cream

There are cafés in almost every street. The most famous are on Piazza della Repubblica – Gilli and Giubbe Rosse. Elegant, too, is the Rivoire at Piazza della Signoria 5r.

The most famous ice cream parlour, practically an institution, is Vivoli, Via Isola delle Stinche 7r, closed Mondays. But there are many, many places and biggest is not necessarily best.

Nightlife

Italian cities are surprisingly quiet at night – there is no real equivalent to a pub culture and few shows or clubs. Eating is a major preoccupation and there are plenty of restaurants. The medieval atmosphere is a pleasure in itself and can be enjoyed at leisure seated outside the cafes of the city. However, Florence is not entirely bereft of entertainment and there are several publications which tell you what is going on:

Florence Today (from the Tourist Office)
Florence Concierge Information (as above plus hotels)
Firenze Spettacolo (newspaper kiosks)
Local newspapers (eg *La Nazione*).

Cinema
Cinema Astro, Piazza San Simone for films in English (except Mondays).

Bars and discotheques
For bars try Rifrullo, Via San Niccolo, Oltrarno; Café Voltaire, Via della Scala 9r, Piazza Santa' Maria Novella; Stonehenge, Via dell'Amorino 16r.

As for discotheques (discoteca), try Yab Yum, Via dei Sassetti 5 and Space Electronic Disco, Via Palazzuolo 37. Bars and discos come and go in popularity, however, so the listings magazines will be useful here. Or ask some likely-looking character in a bar, 'Qual'e il migliore bar/discoteca da questa parte?' (Which is the best bar/discotheque around here?).

Swimming pools
Costoli, Campo di Marte
Le Pavoniere, Viale degli Olmi (Cascine)
Bellariva, Lungarno Colombo 8.

North of the Arno

'Magnificently stern and sombre are the streets of beautiful Florence', Charles Dickens. The main things to see are itemised here as a rough guide to the acknowledged highlights but there is plenty more, all of which is mentioned in the text and simply walking around any given area is a pleasure in itself:

Piazza del Duomo and surroundings, Piazza della Signoria and Palazzo Vecchio. The Bargello, Orsanmichele and Uffizi Gallery. Ponte Vecchio, Palazzo Pitti and Boboli Gardens. The Accademia

Gallery. Piazza SS. Annunziata, San Marco, Santa Croce, Santo Spirito and Santa Maria del Carmine. San Miniato al Monte and Piazzale Michelangelo. Casa Buonarroti, Palazzo Medici-Riccardi, San Lorenzo. Santa Maria Novella.

The best way to see Florence, for the most part, is undoubtedly on foot. Most of what is of interest in Florence is within the old city walls, which have now all but gone. Thus, as far as is possible, everything is included within the compass of the following walks.

Piazza del Duomo and Piazza San Giovanni

These adjacent squares, in the heart of Florence, contain some of the most evocative of Florentine monuments which characterise the competitive spirit of the Renaissance. It is dominated by one of the city's most distinctive buildings, the Duomo (cathedral) of Santa Maria del Fiore, surmounted by Brunelleschi's miraculous dome. Here, it is said, the great humanist Leone Battista Alberti would support his left foot against the wall of the Cathedral and throw an apple right over the dome. The square has been the scene of many splendid events. When the Medici Pope, Leo X, visited Florence in 1515, he of course visited the Duomo where a special façade had been built by Iacopo Sansovino, adorned with chiaroscuro illustrations by Andrea del Sarto. In the square itself a gilt horse trampled a giant armed with a shield. In the evening the square was lit with candle lanterns, even in the windows of the campanile (as a result of which all the tradesmens' tents near the Baptistry were destroyed by fire). The fifteenth-century poet Poliziano had a flat nearby and Michelangelo's workshop was not far away. The winter of 1510 was particularly harsh – artists created snow lions at the foot of the campanile. It is still the site of two ancient pageants each year – the Scoppio del Carro at Easter and, on 24 June, the ceremony which honours the city's patron saint, John the Baptist.

The Duomo of Santa Maria del Fiore

The church of Santa Reparata stood on this site from the tenth century, until the rapidly increasing prosperity of the city prompted the construction of something far grander, under the patronage of the wool guild, (the Arte della Lana). Work started in 1296, but it was only completed in the mid-fifteenth century. The basic design

The entrance to Florence Duomo – hub of the city.

belongs to the first architect, Arnolfo di Cambio, whose death in 1302 brought work to a halt. He was considered by the Council Of One Hundred as 'the most celebrated and expert master in the art of church building of any known in the region' and was one of the main channels of Gothic influence in Italy. Some of his sculptures for the unfinished façade are in the Museo del Opera del Duomo (see below). Giotto was put to work in 1334 until he died in 1337, but it is thought that he became too engrossed in the campanile (bell-tower).

In 1357 work began again under Francesco Talenti, who revised and enlarged the original plan, which was then adapted over the years to the new precepts of the Renaissance. It became one of the largest buildings in the world at the time, though progress was slow - by 1380 the naves were finished and vaults covered; by 1421 the tribunes around the octagon were finished; the dome in 1434. The exterior is decorated in a geometric design of green, white and pink marble. The main (west) façade was never completed according to the original design and in fact the part completed was demolished in 1588 and the present façade, though inspired by fourteenth-century styles, was built only between 1881-88 by Emilio de Fabris. Though acceptable it is not highly considered. The bronze doors date from the end of the nineteenth century.

On the southern façade are the doors of the Porta dei Canonici in Gothic style, with sculptures of 1397 by Lorenzo di Giovanni d' Ambrogio and Piero di Giovanni Tedesco. The Porta della Mandorla (Almond), by Giovanni d'Ambrogio, on the north side is interesting, for there is clear indication that the Gothic style is beginning to give way to the Renaissance. Note the *Annunciation* in the lunette by Davide and Domenico Ghirlandaio (1490), the *Assumption* by Nanni di Banco (1421) in the gable. The two busts of prophets on the inside of the gable are probably by Donatello.

The dome, with its perfect form, in keeping with the surrounding hills, represents for many everything that the Renaissance was supposed to be. It was the architect Brunelleschi's aim to build the biggest and most beautiful dome in Italy, using a system of bricks that would support themselves as he did it. The basic foundation consisted of eight ribs, visible from inside, bound by chains.

In Brunelleschi's time measurements were vague (arms and palms of the hand, which were rather variable) – which renders his achievement all the more incredible. Architecture was not yet seen as a separate craft and Brunelleschi was trained as a goldsmith, although his father, a notary (notaries, curiously, produced a lot of innovative children then), is thought to have been against it. Brunelleschi was not brought up in the craft tradition and the fact that he, and other sons of professionals, wanted to become artists, demonstrates either the power of art at the time or, as in our own time, the power of rebellion.

Brunelleschi concerned himself with every detail, examining each brick to make sure it had been properly baked, fussing about the oven and supervising the mixing of sand and lime. He was also a sculptor and spent much of his time measuring antique ruins, which gave him the idea for the double cupola (which everyone else thought mad). He was convinced that ancient design could be turned into a mathematical formula for materials and dynamic pressure. Although he offered to build the dome in 1417, he had to compete with Lorenzo Ghiberti for the privilege. This did not please him, leading him to feign illness. 'Go and talk to Lorenzo' he would say. 'But he will do nothing without you' they replied. 'Well, I can do perfectly well without him' he retorted. Brunelleschi may be called the discoverer of perspective. He participated in the government as Prior in 1425.

The dome's diameter is 148 feet (45 metres) and the height 370 feet (112 metres). The sun dial on the cupola is by Toscanelli, who also helped to form the idea of Columbus's voyage west.

The interior

Open 1000–1730.

The Duomo is not only of enormous beauty but has been also the scene of much that has passed into Florentine folklore. It was here that the Franciscan Bernardino da Feltre persuaded the people to expel the Jews and where Bishop Antonino would glare so sternly during his sermons at the women and the young idlers whispering together they would slip away without waiting for more. Here it was that in 1439 that the Council met that was to proclaim the union of Greek and Catholic Churches and here, on 6 April 1478, Giuliano de' Medici was murdered in the Pazzi conspiracy, Lorenzo il Magnifico being forced to lock himself in the sacristy. In 1492 the cupola was struck by lightening. 'On which side?' asked the dying Lorenzo il Magnifico. He was told: 'On the side nearest my home. I'm done for.' In 1494 the French King, Charles VIII, upon entering the city, kissed the altar illuminated with thousands of candles and later reached an agreement to withdraw from the city in an orderly manner. Savonarola preached here many a time, to crowds of up to 14,000 citizens who had reserved seats for the occasion from dawn, children sitting on tiers of benches each with a red cross in hand. Following Savonarola's death, the citizens gave themselves up to an orgy of hooliganism, letting loose in the Cathedral an aged horse, tormenting it until it collapsed on the porch steps. In 1512 the Spanish army sold the booty here they had seized in the sack of Prato. Fires were lit on the summit of the campanile in celebration of the return of the Medici. In April 1473 a peasant hid under the altar of

Our Lady on Easter night in order to steal relics and jewels – he was caught and hung from the campanile. A sacred place, yes, but which reaches out into the lives of the citizens of Florence.

The nave

The mosaic in the tympanum of the central portal is fourteenth century and attributed to Gaddo Gaddi. The stained glass was designed by Lorenzo Ghiberti. Paolo Uccello painted the prophets on the clock which uses the 'hora italica' method of counting time, current in Italy until the eighteenth century. The last hour of the day ends at sunset or with the Ave Maria. To the right as you enter is the tomb of Bishop Antonio d'Orso (1321) with a statue attributed to the influential Tino di Camaino.

Nearby is the crypt of the former Santa Reparata, itself built on a fifth-century basilica. Brunelleschi's tomb was discovered here in 1972.

South aisle

The bust of *Brunelleschi*, in the corner by the entrance, is by his pupil and adopted son, Buggiano (1447). The statue of *Isaiah* next door is by Nanni di Branco and the bust of *Giotto* by Benedetto da Maiano (1490) with an inscription by Poliziano. Near the side door is a bust of *Marsilio Ficini* by Ferrucci (1521). The Gothic font (a copy - the original is in the Cathedral museum) near the pillar dates back to 1381. Behind it, on the pillar, a panel painting of *Sant' Antonio*, Bishop of Florence, by Il Poppi (1589).

On the second altar are painted sepulchral monuments by Bicci di Lorenzo (fifteenth century). The octagonal marble rail enclosing the choir is by Bandinelli and G.Bandini (1555). The high altar is also by Bandinelli with a wooden Crucifix of 1497 by Benedetto da Maiano.

The cupola was decorated in part by Vasari at the end of his life (1572-74) and is not highly considered. The stained glass windows in roundels were designed by Uccello, Donatello, Andrea del Castagno and Ghiberti.

At the back are the three apses. The Old Sacristy (south) on the right has a terracotta lunette (Ascension) over the doors by Luca della Robbia (1444) whose many children used to play in the choir-loft that used to rest above and is now in the Duomo museum. The doors of the New (north) sacristy, through which Lorenzo il Magnifico escaped in 1478, as his brother lay dying following the Pazzi conspiracy, are by Michelozzo and Luca della Robbia, and bear portraits of Lorenzo and his brother Giuliano. The lunette

(*Resurrection*) is also by Luca della Robbia. Within are beautiful intarsia cupboards from 1436-45 by Giuliano da Maiano and others.

In the chapel of the central apse is a bronze reliquary urn of the first Bishop of Florence, San Zanobi, (died 417) by Ghiberti. Michelangelo's *Pieta* is now in the Museo dell'Opera del Duomo.

In the pavement of the left apse notice on the floor a gnomon, or meridian sun dial, of 1475, struck every year by a beam of sunlight at the summer solstice.

North aisle

This is on the left as you enter. The painting of *Dante* (for biography see History section), at the east end of the north aisle, with the *Divine Comedy* in his hand and Florence behind him, is by Domenico di Michelino from 1465 – on one side are Purgatory and Hell, on the other, Paradise. The equestrian frescoes are of condottieri, or mercenary soldiers. One, on the right, is *Sir John Hawkwood*, the illustrious English soldier honoured for his services to Florence; it was painted by Paulo Uccello in 1436. The other, by Andrea del Castagno in 1456, is of *Niccolo Marucci da Tolentino*. The nearby statue of *Joshua* is probably the work of B. Ciuffagni and Nanni di Bartolo but has also been attributed to Donatello. The painting at the west end of the aisle, *San Zenobi* with *Cruelty* and *Pride* underfoot, was painted by G. del Biondo in 1375.

The entrance to the cupola is near the Dante fresco. You may climb the 463 steps and see how Brunelleschi built it. There is an inner and outer dome which provide enough strength to avoid buttressing – the inner is 13 feet (four metres) thick, the outer seven feet (two metres) and it weighs 25,000 tons.

(You may need to buy tickets outside from the booth just to the south of the Cathedral). Open 1000-1730, closed Sunday.

Giotto's Campanile

Open every day 09.00-19.30 (17.30 in winter).

The originality of the design of this campanile, a fusion of Gothic and Classical that is one of the finest in Italy, is indicated in its name. Giotto in fact had comparatively little to do with it – he only started on it in 1334, three years before he died, although it is supposed to be his design. Andrea Pisano continued the work, the two levels with double arched windows, which was completed by Talenti between

1350-59. Note the typical Florentine feature of alternating colours of marble. The bas reliefs representing the Planets, Virtues, Liberal Arts and the Sacraments, by Giotto, Arnoldi, Luca della Robbia, and A. Pisano and the allegorical scenes of the Creation of Man and Arts and Industries by Pisano and Luca della Robbia are fakes – the originals are in the Duomo museum. Nonetheless, they testify to a growing awareness of man's place in the Universe. The upper bas reliefs are probably by pupils of Pisano and Andrea Orcagna. There are 414 steps to the top, which is 279 feet (85 metres) up.

Baptistry

The Baptistry is dedicated to the city's patron saint John the Baptist ('mio bel San Giovanni' as Dante famously called it) and has always been an object of special affection for Florentines. On the feast day of San Giovanni all the guild workshops would be decorated with silks and gold cloth, and paintings. At noon a procession of the clergy would form, escorted by parishioners dressed as saints and angels, with music and song. In the evening the citizens would walk in pairs according to their quarter to offer candles in the Baptistry. Still widely used, it is built on the site of a Roman building and incorporates the remains of a church started in the sixth century. It is an example of Tuscan Romanesque architecture of the eleventh and twelfth centuries by an unknown architect. Much of the work done on it was the responsibility of the cloth guild, the Calimala, who commissioned Ghiberti to make his famous doors – although only just, for his supposed illegitimacy almost told against him. The deep green marble is from Prato and the rectangular apse was constructed in the thirteenth century, roughly at the time that the dome was covered with the current pyramid roof. There are three sets of bronze doors on the north, south and east façades.

East doors (The Gates of Paradise)

These, the doors facing the entrance to the Cathedral, are the most famous, and Lorenzo Ghiberti's masterpiece. He was given the commission in 1425 and finished them only in 1450. The Calimala guild gave him a free hand in the execution of them (based on his work on the North doors), although the humanist Leonardo Bruni was consulted by the guild beforehand as to suitable subjects which demonstrates that humanism was something that brought artists and intellectuals together. As art became subject to dissection as to its intrinsic qualities, essential ingredients were decided upon – one was 'richness', which Ghiberti admitted to aiming for in his doors. Bruni suggested they should be 'illustri', meaning 'feeding the eye well with variety of design.' The ten panels depict scenes from the Old Testament. They are, from left to right (starting top left): story of Adam and Eve, Cain and Abel, Noah, Abraham and Isaac, Isaac, Rebecca and Esau, Joseph sold by his brothers, Moses receiving the tablets on Mount Sinai, Joshua and the fall of Jericho, David and Goliath, and Solomon and the Queen of Sheba. It has been suggested that some of the stories carry political significance, e.g. the Abraham and Isaac panel hoping for divine intervention from the Milanese threat.

The panels are surrounded by small figures of prophets, sibyls and busts of contemporary artists, including Ghiberti himself (on the right hand side of the left door, between the third and fourth panels going from top to bottom) a sign of the growing sense of artists' self esteem. Originally these doors were gilded. Ghiberti, like his contemporary Brunelleschi, was a goldsmith by trade. This is an astounding work of art – detailed, yet with vast scenes in a small space. The door frame is also by Ghiberti. The bronze group in the architrave, *The Baptism of Christ* is by Andrea Sansovino (1502) and an *Angel* by Spinazzi of 1792.

North doors

These were made between 1403 and 1424 following a competition in 1401 between the principal artists of the city, based on trial panels on the subject of the sacrifice of Isaac, a fairly common thing in the achievement orientated republic. The main stipulation was that they should be similar in form to the south doors, already in place, with 28 panels. Many eminent artists became involved, including Jacopo della Quercia, Brunelleschi and Lorenzo Ghiberti – Ghiberti won (much to the disgust of Brunelleschi) as he won another later one for the tomb of St. Zanobi in the church. The panels show episodes from the 'Life and Passion of Christ', 'the Evangelists', and 'Doctors of the Church'. The bronze figures of the architrave are later work, by Giovanni Rustici, 1511, with the probable help of Leonardo.

Nearby is the column of San Zanobi, first bishop of Florence, erected in memory of his last miracle. As his body was being carried to its final resting place in the Duomo, having been buried before outside the walls, (an early set of which used to run just about here), a dying elm burst into leaf.

South doors

The earliest Baptistry doors and the first monument to be made in Florence of bronze, executed by Andrea Pisano (1290-1349) by 1330 from wax models. They are divided into 28 panels showing the life of St. John the Baptist, and allegories of virtue. It is Gothic in style, but of considerable natural grace.

The interior

Baptisms took place only once a year, on 21 March (New Year's Day according to the old calender) which accounts for the large size of the Baptistry. The granite columns decorating the lower half of the walls are from a Roman building. The mosaic floor, with the signs of the Zodiac, dates back to 1209, and used to support a font in the middle – the font to the right of the entrance is of 1371. The Renaissance tomb to the right of the thirteenth-century altar is that of the anti-pope John XXIII (died 1419) who was deposed in 1415 by the Council of Constance, obtaining his place here thanks to the Medici whom he had made Curia bankers. The tomb is by Donatello (who also made the bronze of the Pope) and Michelozzo. The two sarcophagi are Roman.

The mosaics in the cupola were started in the early thirteenth century and finished in the fourteenth, showing considerable variation in style from the comparitive immobility of the Byzantine style to the dynamism of the Renaissance. Among the many artists who worked on them, perhaps, was the great Cimabue. The mosaics are most important because they demonstrate the first beginnings of a change in Florentine art that would culminate in Giotto's work. The most impressive is the *Last Judgement* – it has been pointed out that Dante may well have been inspired by these scenes in writing the inferno section of the *Divine Comedy*. The others, from the centre outwards are: *The Hierarchy of Heaven, Genesis, Life of Joseph, Life of Christ*, and *Life of St. John the Baptist*.

Around the square

Just south of the Baptistry is Via dei Calzaiuoli (Hosiers Street), leading to Piazza Signoria. On the corner is the fourteenth-century **Loggia del Bigallo**, originally built for a charitible institution, the Misericordia, who looked after victims of the plague. The Loggia was where orphans were shown to the public and announcements made to the populace. Later the Misericordia was absorbed into another organisation named Bigallo. On wedding days, trumpets would sound above the Loggia, as the marriage party proceeded past, each trumpet boasting a square pennon with a red lily on a white background. At nearby Piazza San Giovanni, 1 is the interesting

Museo del Bigallo, exhibiting works of art collected by the Bigallo which include a fresco showing the earliest view of Florence (1342), a Gerini of 1386 showing orphans being settled with foster-mothers and a Ridolfo del Ghirlandaio showing a burial in front of the Loggia.

The Misericordia moved to a new building opposite, across Via de' Calzaiuoli, in 1576. This lay confraternity, the brothers distinctive in black capes and hoods, continues to help the needy. The charming **Oratory** to the left of the entrance to the Misericordia contains work by Andrea della Robbia and Benedetto da Maiano.

Further along the square, between Via dello Studio and Via del Proconsolo, is the **Sasso di Dante** (Dante's Stone), a stone plaque marking the spot where the poet is supposed to have sat and passed the hours in contemplation of his city. The medieval streets behind are traditionally associated with Dante and are very attractive – Via Sant' Elizabetta, Via delle Oche (Geese Street), Via dello Studio and Via della Canonica.

Museum of Florence's Past

Open 09.00-14.00, 08.00-13.00 Sunday. Closed Thursday.

In the south-east corner of Piazza Duomo at Via dell' Oriuolo, is the seventeenth-century Palazzo Guadagni-Riccardi. Via dell' Oriuolo takes you to number 4 and the former Convento delle Oblate, now the Museo di Firenze com' era (Museum of Florence's Past), with maps, paintings and documents relating to the topography and social history of the city since the fifteenth century.

Museo dell' Opera del Duomo (Museum of Florence Cathedral)

This museum, at Piazza del Duomo, 9, which opened in 1892 in the building that housed the committee responsible for the maintenance of the Duomo, is mostly dedicated to the works of art connected with the Cathedral, Baptistry and Campanile, and to their planning and construction. In the courtyard there are marble panels from the Duomo choir by Bandinelli and Bandini; in Room I is a drawing of the old façade designed by Arnolfo di Cambio, as well as several sculptures from the old façade by the same man. The four seated evangelists, also from the façade, are by Nanni di Bianco, Donatello, Ciuffagni and Lamberti. There are two rooms concerning Brunelleschi, with his death mask, models of the cupola and apparatus used in its construction. In Room II are models entered for the competition of the new façade in 1588 by Buontalenti, Giambologna, Giovanni Dosio and Giovanni de' Medici.

Michelangelo's *Pieta*, formerly in the Duomo, is on the stair landing. It was intended for the artist's own tomb; the head of Nicodemus is thought to be a self-portrait. The arm and left leg of the Christ are not original – Michelangelo removed them in dissatisfaction and the replacements were added by a pupil, Calcagni, who also completed Mary Magdalen.

On the first floor: Room I has the 1430 cantorie or organ lofts by Donatello (with a frieze of running putti, and the extraordinary wooden Mary Magdalen beneath) and Luca della Robbia (children playing instruments, singing and dancing) as well as 16 statues that used to decorate the Campanile.

In neighbouring room are bas-reliefs, formerly on the campanile, by Andrea Pisano and perhaps Giotto, illustrating the Creation of Man and celebrating his genius.

Room II on the first floor has Baptistry door panels by Ghiberti; needlework panels with life of John the Baptist by craftsmen of the Calimala; the fourteenth-century Baptistry altar in silver gilt, with life of John the Baptist. *St. John* is by Michelozzo and the side reliefs by Verrocchio and Antonio del Pollaiuolo.

The rest of the Cathedral Square

On the square the sixteenth-century **Palazzo Strozzi-Niccolini** at Piazza del Duomo, 28, is on the site of Donatello's workshop, whilst several of the buildings here date back to the fourteenth century. Along Via dei Servi is the church of **San Michele Visdomini**, first built in the eleventh century nearer to Piazza del Duomo, demolished in 1368 to make way for the new Cathedral and rebuilt here soon after. Visdomini is the name given to that part of the episcopal administration concerned with church land. In the secnd chapel on the right is a *Holy Family and Saints* by Pontormo (1518), a Mannerist masterpiece.

Once back in the area of the Baptistry, you will notice the fourteenth century so-called Pillar of San Zanobi (see 'Baptistry – north doors' above).

The west end of the square is dominated by the **Palazzo Arcivescovile** (Archbishop's Palace – a sixteenth-century remodelling of a medieval building, the loggia of which was walled up in the fourteenth century to make way for shops) which incorporates the church of San Salvatore al Vescovo, the Romanesque façade of which is visible from Piazza dell' Olio behind.

Santa Maria Nuova and Sant' Egidio

By following Via dei Servi from Piazza Duomo and turning right into Via Bufalini you will come to the hospital of **Santa Maria Nuova**. It was founded in 1286 by Folco Portinari, the father of Dante's great love Beatrice, the subject of much of his poetry, and is still doing service. Its portico of 1574 is by Buontalenti.

The Church of **Sant Egidio** beneath it dates back to 1420. The striking high altar ciborium in pietra dura is of 1666. The Portinari tomb is to the right of the entrance. On the left is a 1450 marble tabernacle by B. Rossellino and a replica of a Ghiberti bronze door (the original is in the Presidenza on the floor above, open to scholars by arrangement). Admission to the ancient cloister, with a *Pieta* by G. della Robbia, is through the hospital grounds. In a courtyard, left of the church, is the tomb of Portinari's servant Monna Tessa, who persuaded her master to found the hospital; and a tabernacle with a fresco of *Charity* by Giovanni di San Giovanni. The more modern pavillion is a memorial to one of the hospital's benefactors, Count Galli Tassi.

Via Bufalini, 1, is the site of Ghiberti's workshop.

Museo Fiorentino di Preistoria (Florence Museum of Prehistory)

Open 0.930–12.30, closed Sunday.

The entrance is at Via Sant Egidio 21, the continuation of Via Bufalini. It has some interesting exhibits from Italy (including a human skull from the Paleolithic era) and around the world.

The Medici Palace, San Lorenzo and the Medici Tombs

The Palazzo Medici Riccardi is open 09.00-13.00 and 15.00-17.00, closed Wednesdays and Sunday pm at 12.00.

The road leading north from between the Baptistry and the Duomo is Via de' Martelli, soon becoming Via Cavour (formerly Via Larga or

Broad Street). On the left corner of Via Cavour is the old **Palazzo Medici-Riccardi**, the former home of the Medici and, though it must be remembered that the first generations of Medici were in fact private citizens, this was a sort of unofficial court until Cosimo I moved to the Palazzo Vecchio in 1540. It was built in 1444, making it the oldest Renaissance palace still standing, by Cosimo il Vecchio, father of Lorenzo il Magnifico, to a design by Michelozzo that was much influenced by Brunelleschi (and Alberti). The later ground floor windows are by Michelangelo. Later it was purchased by the Riccardi family, who owned it until until 1809. Michelozzo (1396-1472), much used in Florence, was noted by Vasari in his 'Lives of the Artists' as the most 'well-ordered' architect of his day. Cosimo evidently saw greatness on the horizon for his family who, until then, had lived in greater modesty near the Mercato Vecchio. In Lorenzo's time many of the greatest minds of his day were often visitors here, as were many of the masterpieces they produced. In fact it was Lorenzo's aim to ensure that the family palace did not become too much like a ducal court and informality was the order of the day. The door was always open to family and friends. Now it is the city prefecture.

The courtyard is delightful and the gardens quintessentialy Renaissance, with the hedges, at one time, shaped into animals. Family marriages were celebrated here, and discussions took place among the artists and intellectuals. The most memorable of the marriages was that of Clarice Orsini to Lorenzo il Magnifico, with 50 dancing ladies attending the table of the bride. From the upper windows ducats were distributed to the populace on the election of the Medici Pope Leo X and the Via Larga was the scene of races and entertainment.

Two rooms are open to visitors. The Medici Museum on the ground floor is of interest mostly to scholars – better to head for the Medici family chapel on the first floor (from a staircase on the right of the courtyard) to see the frescoes of Benozzo Gozzoli (1420-98), pupil of Fra Angelico. Commissioned by Piero di Cosimo, they depict the *Procession of the Magi*, travelling through the Tuscan countryside on their way to Bethlehem. In the entourage are many faces of contemporaries: the Emperor of Constantinople rides with Lorenzo (in a white robe as one of the Magi, on a grey horse) and other members of his family, recognisable by the family emblem of three ostrich feathers. Notable humanist scholars are in the procession too, as well as Gozzoli himself, at the middle towards the top, wearing a red hat with his name on it. The painting may well have been inspired by the meetings between the eastern and western churches in Florence in 1439 and is one of the most colourful and vivid displays of Florentine pride and self-confidence during a new age. The *Nativity* on the altar is a copy of one by Filippo Lippi by Pier Francesco Fiorentino.

By mounting another staircase off the downstairs courtyard (there is a lift, too), you may visit the gallery, to see the 1670 ceiling by the Neapolitan Luca Giordano in Baroque style - called 'the Apotheosis of the Medici', it features Cosimo III and his son Gian Gastone, not, it will be remembered the most noble of their line.

Opposite the Palazzo Medici Riccardi, on Via de' Gori, is the sixteenth-century Renaissance church of **San Giovannino**, by Ammannati.

Continue along Via de' Gori until you reach Piazza San Lorenzo and the Church of San Lorenzo.

Piazza San Lorenzo and area

This is one of the liveliest areas of the city, not least because of its market specialising in leather goods, prints, knitwear and colourful souvenirs. In fact the market (open every day except Sunday and Monday) extends along Via Dell' Ariento to the Mercato Centrale, the main food market, built in the late nineteenth century and open Monday-Saturday. On the other side of the market is Via Panicale, noted for its clothes stalls, off which runs Via Chiara, Cellin's birthplace. Via dell' Ariento finishes at Via Nazionale where there is a tabernacle above a fountain, attributed to G. della Robbia.

On the other side of the Piazza San Lorenzo is Borgo San Lorenzo. The French writer Montaigne stayed at number 14 in 1580-81.

The square in front of San Lorenzo, covered in market stalls, is distinctive also for the sixteenth-century equestrian statue of *Giovanni delle Bande Nere*, father of Cosimo I, by Bandinelli.

San Lorenzo (Church of St. Lawrence)

Open 07.00-12.00 and 15.30-18.30.

The church, built on an earlier fourth-century chapel (probably the oldest in Florence), is very much a Medici edifice and one of the most beautiful of the early Renaissance. It was in fact the Medici parish church, hence their interest and their love of the name Lorenzo

– indeed Lorenzo the Magnifico was married here to Clarice Orsini. This church was commissioned by the father of Cosimo il Vecchio, Giovanni di Bicci de Medici, the man whose wealth and influence provided his descendents with the wherewithal to control the city. He commissioned Brunelleschi, who worked on the church from 1425 until his death in 1446. Antonio Manetti and Pagno di Lapo Potigiani carried on after him but the façade was never completed, even though Michelangelo offered to take it on (his model for it is in Casa Buonarroti). The campanile is of 1740.

Although Brunelleschi experimented with the interior by using different coloured materials, in grey and white, the atmosphere is of classical simplicity. The decoration on the whole is rather plain. The second chapel along the right aisle has a Marriage of the Virgin of 1523 by Rosso Fiorentino, a leading 'mannerist'. Here too is a tomb of one of the few musicians of the Renaissance of whom we know anything, Francesco Landini, the blind organist of Florence Cathedral and composer of ballads (secular music was popular at the time) who died in 1397. He is remembered as a humanist and performer on the hand-organ capable of attracting the nightingale.

At the end of this aisle is a tabernacle by Desiderio da Settignano (1430-64), who came from the village of Settignano near Florence, famous for its stone quarries. Donatello's last works, the two bronze pulpits in the nave, date from 1465. The panels of the pulpit to the north illustrate *The Agony in the Garden, St. John the Baptist*, and *The Death of Christ*. The pulpit to the south continues the story of *The Death of Christ, Pentecost, The Martyrdom of Saints Lawrence and Luke*, and *The Mocking of Christ*.

In the right transept is a *Nativity* attributed to D. Ghirlandaio or C. Rosselli. In the chapel on the corner of the right aile and right transept is a Crucifix by A. del Pollaiolo.

In the choir are some grills in the floor that indicate the crypt where Cosimo il Vecchio is buried, with the words 'Pater Patriae' (Father of the Nation). In the left transept, in the chapel to the left of the high altar, is a charming wooden Madonna attributed to Alberto Arnoldi.

Beyond the neighbouring chapel, with its painting of saints by the School of Ghirlandaio, is the entrance to the Old Sacristy (1420-29), considered one of the finest and purest works of the Renaissance, by Brunelleschi, with decoration by Donatello, who is responsable for the terracotta and plaster lunettes in the cupola, and the frieze below it, as well as the bronze panels of the doors of the two chapels. Brunelleschi and Donatello were friends and rivals – a story is told of how Brunelleschi reproached Donatello for the peasant qualities of his Crucifixion. Donatello told him to do better. Some time later Donatello came to Brunelleschi's house with a basket of eggs, saw a carving Brunelleschi had executed and dropped the eggs, so amazed was he. 'Alright' he said – 'you do the Christs and I'll do the peasants.' The bust of San Lorenzo is attributed to Donatello or D. da Settignano. In the dome of the altar are some fine frescoes showing the sky as it was in 1442.

To the left of the entrance to the sacristy is the sarcophagus of Piero and Giovanni dei Medici, in porphyry and bronze, by Verrocchio (1472). In the centre is the tomb of Giovanni di Bicci de Medici, for whom the chapel was built, and his wife. The body of Allessandro De Medici was lain here for a while after he had been killed by Lorenzino.

On the corner of the left transept and aisle is the Martelli chapel with a monument to Donatello, the artist being buried below. The *Annunciation* on the altarpiece is by Filippo Lippi from 1440.

In the left aisle, close to the Martelli Chapel, the fresco (1559) of the martyrdom of San Lorenzo is by Bronzino. Bianca Capello, the mistress and, later, wife of Francesco de' Medici is reputed to be buried secretly here, since she was not allowed to take her place in the family vault. The cloister, a peaceful haven by Manetti, dates back to 1457 – from it you can reach the Laurentian Library.

Biblioteca Medicea Laurenziana

Open 10.00-13.00, closed Sundays.

Designed and started by Michelangelo (1524) and realised by others to house the collection of manuscripts founded by Cosimo il Vecchio (though named after Lorenzo who enlarged it), the Biblioteca is in marked contrast to the classically simple lines of Brunelleschi and heralds the Baroque. The ornate Vestibule was completed by Vasari and Ammannati (1559-71), to Michelangelo's design (the remarkable staircase is also by Michelangelo). Ammanati designed the reading room, which is in marked contrast to the Vestibule, but the feel is Michelangelo's, who also designed the furnishings. The collection of manuscripts is one of the most important in the world and one of the glories of Humanism. Here are early examples of the works of Virgil, the eighth-century *Codex Amiatinus* written in Jarrow, England; Petrarch's copy of *Horace*, Dante manuscripts, the records of the Council of Florence, illuminated manuscripts and Cellini's original autobiography.

The Medici Chapels and Tombs (Cappelle Medicee)

Open 09.00-14.00 or 13.00 on Sunday. Closed Monday.

The entrance is on Piazza Madonna degli Aldobrandini, behind the church of San Lorenzo. At number 4 is the Palazzo Mannelli-Riccardi with sixteenth-century façade and bust of Ferdinand I.

A staircase leads to the first floor and the Chapel of the Princes (Capella dei Principi, 1604), from the Chapel crypt which contains the tomb slabs of many family members. The Chapel itself was designed by Giovanni dei Medici, the illegitimate son of Cosimo I, and contains the tombs of the Grand Dukes and is decorated with the mosaic arms of the 16 towns of Tuscany. It is neo-Classical in style. The walls are of marble, the altar of pietra dura, the floor of marble mosaic, the tombs of Egyptian granite, of granite and of Corsican green jasper. Behind the altar you can see the mitre of Leo X. The dome frescoes are dated 1828.

A passage leads to the New Sacristy, a counterbalance to the Old Sacristy in the church (although unconnected). This is by Michelangelo, a theatrical piece of Baroque begun in 1520. He left Florence for political reasons without finishing it. It is built in pietra serena and marble, producing a suitably funereal atmosphere. Two of the tombs are by Michelangelo – left of the entrance is that of Lorenzo, Duke of Urbino, grandson of Lorenzo il Magnifico. He sits, absorbed (some think it was the inspiration for Rodin's *Thinker*); beneath are figures of Dawn and Dusk. Opposite, is the tomb of Giuliano, Duke of Nemours, son of il Magnifico, in his armour, with the two allegories at his feet of Day and Night. The first is incomplete, the second, finished, represented by a languid, sensual woman. Time and death are the underlying motifs of both of them, after the fall of Florence to Imperial forces in 1530. Michelangelo, who was also a poet, wrote:

> 'I long to sleep, but more, to be of stone,
> Amidst such infamy and shame'.

The pessimistic themes are perhaps on account of the youth of the two princes in question.

The tomb monuments of Lorenzo il Magnifico and his brother Giuliano were never finished, although Michelangelo did complete a beautiful *Madonna and Child* for Lorenzo il Magnifico (on his tomb, with two statues of saints either side).

In 1975 a passage was discovered behind the altar, decorated with drawings attributed to Michelangelo, probably for an unknown project; or he may have hid here following the return of the Medici in 1530. Conducted visits are arranged from the ticket office.

Via Faenza and Cenacalo di Foligno

This leads away from Piazza Madonna degli Aldobrandini, crossing bustling Via Sant' Antonio. At 42 is Perugino's 1493-96 fresco, *Cenacolo di Foligno* (Last Supper) with its beautiful landscape, in the former convent of the Tertiary Franciscans of Foligno. Admission can only be gained on Mondays at 11.00 by previous arrangement with the Sezione Didattica degli Uffizi (tel: 284272).

Via Faenza meets Via Guelfa at Piazza del Crocefisso. It is thought that the Della Robbia family, whose terracottas are to be seen decorating churches, loggias and palaces all over Tuscany, had their workshops here.

The church of San Barnaba on Via Guelfa has a fourteenth-century entrance (with Della Robbia lunette) and, inside, a Baroque organ.

Piazza Santa Maria Novella

This was an impoverished part of Medieval Florence, attractive to the mendicant order of St. Dominic who were preaching a renewal of faith based on vows of brotherhood and poverty. They were eventually granted an old church which grew into Santa Maria Novella. This square was also the scene of the Palio dei Cocchi, a chariot race every 24 June introduced by Cosimo I and marked by the two marble obelisks on bronze tortoises by Giambologna. Facing the church across the square is the Loggia di San Paolo of 1496, with lovely arches above which the terracotta lunettes by Andrea and Giovanni della Robbia – the first on the left is a self-portrait of Andrea; the last on the right is of Luca della Robbia, their uncle. The lunette beneath the arcade shows the *Meeting of St. Francis and St. Dominic*. The **Loggia** is currently used as a bus shelter.

Note the plaque to the American poet Longfellow on the building next to the church. Henry James lived in the house on the corner of Via della Scala. At Via della Scala, 16, is the **Farmacia di Santa Maria Novella**, still producing perfumes and medicines to ancient recipes. The shop is in a fourteenth-century chapel with nineteenth-century neo-Gothic decoration. On request, you may see the other rooms, including the original pharmacy overlooking the Great Cloister of Santa Maria Novella.

Via delle Belle Donne leads from the square to a crossroads and the granite Croce del Trebbio, thought to commemorate a massacre of heretics.

Santa Maria Novella

Open 07.00-11.30 (except Sunday) and 15.30-18.00. Cloister open 09.00-14.00, 13.00 Sunday. Closed Friday.

This is one of the finest examples of Gothic in Tuscany. It stands on the site of the 1094 church of Santa Maria delle Vigne. The land passed to the hands of the Dominican order who decided to build a new church in 1246. Two Dominican monks, Sisto and Ristoro, designed the main body of the church, whilst the remainder was added by Fra' Jacopo Talenti in the fourteenth-century. He was also responsible for the lower part of the Tuscan-Romanesque marble façade, completed by Leon Battista Alberti in 1456-70, according to a commission from Giovanni di Paolo Rucellai. The friezes bear the Rucellai family emblem, a ship's sail, and that of the Medici, a ring with ostrich feathers. The result is a pleasing mixture of the spare lines of the Gothic and the decorative skill of the Renaissance. To the right of the façade is the old cemetery and the arcaded family vaults of high-ranking Florentines. The Campanile was incorporated into an earlier watch tower.

The interior
The interior is spacious, notable for the vaulting and arches highlighted by the use of grey pietra serena. The simplicity of the original Florentine Gothic design, with its French Cistercian style predominates, despite the additions of Vasari's sixteenth-century Rood Screen and the nineteenth-century chapels along the nave. The rose window at the west end is fourteenth-century; and the restored *Nativity* fresco over the door is an early work of Botticelli; possibly it is still being restored.

The south aisle, right, has several sixteenth-century altarpieces, among which you find a *Martyrdom of San Lorenzo* by Macchietti and a 1451 monument to Villana delle Botti by B. Rossellino (first altar); works by Naldini (second, third, fourth with to the right of the latter a 1528 *Deposition* in extravagant Mannerist style by S. Cosini), and painting of *San Vicenzo Ferrer* by Del Meglio (fifth). Notice too

(Opposite) *A typical town in the Casentino.*

the modern statue of *Madonna with Rosary with St. Dominic*.

Behind the fifth altar is the Cappella della Purita, with fourteenth-century frescoes; and the sixth altar has a *Miracle of San Raimondo* by Ligozzi.

In the south transept are three Gothic tombs, of Bishop Aliotti (1336), Fra' Aldovrando Cavalcanti (1279) and of Joseph, Patriarch of Costantinople who attended the 1439 Council of Florence (the attempt to unite the western and eastern churches) and who died in Florence in 1440; the accompanying fresco has his portrait. The nearby Cappella Rucellai contains a *Madonna and Child* by Nini Pisano and a bronze tomb of the Dominican, Francesco Dati, by Ghiberti.

In the corner is the Cappella dei Bardi with lunettes by Cimabue (1285). Next to it is the Cappella Filippo Strozzi, for use by the great Florentine banker of the same name. The walls are adorned with some remarkable frescoes by Filippino Lippi from 1502, in a style which contrasts markedly with other frescoes of the period and which tell the story of the lives and deaths of St. Philip (crucifixion and killing of dragon) and St. John the Evangelist. He also designed the stained glass window. The tomb of Filippo Strozzi behind the altar is by Benedetto da Maiano. It is interesting to note that in Boccaccio's *Decameron*, (a hundred stories told by a group of young people as a form of escapism in the plague-ridden Florence of 1348) the story-tellers met at this spot.

In the Sanctuary behind the main altar (with Crucifix by Giambologna) are the marvellous frescoes by Domenico Ghirlandaio, helped it is thought by the young Michelangelo. They portray the *Lives of Dominican Saints*, *St. John the Baptist* and the *Virgin*. But it is a also an evocation of the Florence of the time, the late fifteenth century, in which he uses portraits of his contemporaries. There is also a self portrait on the left wall (in the group on the right, which also includes other artists), wearing a red hat, in the *Expulsion of St. Joachim from the Temple*. The stained glass windows are also by Ghirlandaio.

On the other, left, side of the altar is the Cappella Gondi. In here is the famous Brunelleschi wooden Crucifix reputed to have so astonished Donatello that he dropped a basket of eggs.

Next door is the Cappella Gaddi and then the Cappella Strozzi very

(Opposite) Top: *The roof tops of Siena from the Torre di Mangia.*
(Opposite) Bottom: *One of the most elegant squares in the world – The Campo Siena, with the Fonte Gaia.*

much in its original fourteenth-century style. The frescoes are by Nardo di Cione. On the vault you see *Thomas Aquinas and the Virtues*; on the right wall is *Hell* (a rendition of Dante's *Inferno*); on the left, *Heaven*. The fine altarpiece of the *Redeemer giving the Keys to St. Peter and the Book of Wisdom to St. Thomas Aquinas* is by Nardo's brother, Andrea Orcagna.

In the Sacristy the stained glass windows are of 1386. The terracotta basin is by Giovanni della Robbia. Above the door is a Crucifix by Giotto.

Among the altarpieces of the left, north aisle are *Saints* by Allessandro Allori (in the chapel by the Sacristy); two chapels down is Vasari's *Resurrection and Saints*; and next to it, above a skeleton on a sarcophagus (with a warning that we shall all come to this) one of the most remarkable paintings of the Renaissance, Massaccio's 1428 *Trinity* and Virgin and St. John the Evangelist. It is particularly noteworthy for its manner of composition and use of perspective.

The pulpit was designed by Brunelleschi – from it Galileo was denounced for his astronomical theories. The altar nearest the west door is the *Resurrection of Lazarus* by Santi di Tito.

The entrance to the left of the church façade leads into the cloisters which once formed part of one of Florence's richest convents. During the Council of Florence it played host to the Papal Court. The first cloister is the Romanesque Chiostro Verde (green cloister) with Dominican saints in the roundels. The cloister takes its name from the hues used in its decoration, the frescoes by Paolo Uccello tell the story of *Genesis*. Uccello uses here to great effect the two features for which he is most associated – animals and perspective.

The Great Cloister to the left of the Green Cloister, with frescoes by Bronzino and others, is now a police barracks – it can be seen through a glass door. Between the two cloisters is the Cappella degli Ubriachi (literally, Chapel of the Intoxicated – in fact the Ubriachi were an eminent Florentine family whose tomb slab is here) built by Francesco Talenti in 1365 and now a museum of Sacred Art. Among the exhibits are busts of the prophets by Orcagna, originally in the church; and sinopie of some of Uccello's frescoes from the Chiostro Verde.

Next to it is the Refectory with impressive vaulting also by Talenti. The inner fresco on the entrance wall, of the *Virgin between St. Thomas Aquinas, St. Dominic, St. John the Baptist and St. Peter the Martyr*, is attributed to the school of Agnolo Gaddi painted at the time of the building's construction. The other sixteenth-century frescoes are by Alessandro Allori.

The Great Spanish Cloister

At the far end of the cloister is the Cappellone degli Spagnuoli, or Great Spanish Chapel. Originally the Chapter House, it acquired its name in the sixteenth-century when the Duchess Eleanora of Toledo gave it to her Spanish retinue for their use. The famous frescoes in Sienese style are by an otherwise almost unknown fourteenth-century artist by the name of Andrea di Buonaiuto. His theme is the Cosmology of the Dominican Order, their view of Vice, Virtue and Philosophy. In the vault you see the Resurrection, Ascension, Navicella and Descent of the Holy Spirit. On the right wall you see the Works of the Dominican Order – notice the artist's impression of a finished Duomo in front of which is a representation of the Church Militant with Pope and Emperor; and in the right foreground the purported portraits of Dante, Petrarch, Boccaccio, Cimabue and Giotto. Notice too St. Dominic unleasing the Hounds of God, the representaion of Vice by four seated figures surrounded by dancers; and a Dominican monk showing the path to salvation.

The left wall portrays St. Thomas Aquinas enthroned as the personification of the Triumph of Catholic Doctrine. Beneath, in the choirstalls, the female figures are symbols of Art and Science.

The entrance wall shows the life of St. Peter the Martyr; the altar wall the Via Dolorosa, the Crucifixion and the Descent into Limbo.

The oldest part of the convent is to be found through an entrance to the right of the Spanish Chapel. This is the 1270 Chiostrino dei Morti (The Little Cloister of the Dead) with fourteenth-century frescoes and a tabernacle by G. della Robbia. The large statue of S. Giovanni di Salerno is by Girolamo Ticciati.

The Station and the Fortezza del Basso

Behind the Church of Santa Maria Novella is Piazza Stazione and the station itself, built in 1932-34 by Giovanni Michelucci in so-called 'Rational' style. Beyond it, right, on Viale Filippo Strozzi, is the **Fortezza da Basso** (only accessible when there are exhibitions), designed by Sangallo the Younger in 1534 on the orders of Alessandro de'Medici. It came to be regarded as an symbol of Medici tyranny – indeed Alessandro was assassinated here by his cousin in 1537. An important example of military architecture, it has been used over the centuries as a prison, among other things. Now it has become a garden and is the scene of annual exhibitions and fashion shows.

From Piazza Santa Maria Novella take **Via de' Fossi** named after the twelfth-century moat that ran along here, until you reach **Piazza Goldoni** (with a statue of the eighteenth-century Venetian playwright, and, on the east side, with coats of arms, the fifteenth-century Palazzo Ricasoli). The bridge before you is the **Ponte alla Carraia**, originally built in wood in 1218. Constructed after the Ponte Vecchio, it was known as the Ponte Nuovo (New Bridge) and was then rebuilt in 1333, perhaps to a design by Giotto. It was blown up during the war and reconstructed. Turn right along Borgo Ognissanti (you will pass the Church of **San Giovanni di Dio** – the building next to it incorporates the house where Amerigo Vespucci was born) which leads slightly inland again and brings you to the church of Ognissanti.

Ognissanti (All Saints)

Open 07.30-12.00, 15.00-18.30. Convent open 09.00-12.00 Monday, Tuesday and Saturday; ring the bell for admission.

This church was founded in 1256 by the Benedictine order of Umiliati in the city's main wool manufacturing area. Since 1561 the church has been owned by the Franciscans and was rebuilt in Baroque style in the seventeenth century. The 1637 façade is by Nigetti.

Interior

In the pavement below the second altar, right, is the tomb of the Vespucci family who were silk merchants. Amerigo Vespucci (1451-1512), after whom America is named, was a Medici agent who made two recorded voyages to the New World. The painting above the tomb is an early work by Davide and Domenico Ghirlandaio legend has it that the young boy between the Madonna and the becloaked man is Amerigo himself. Between the third and fourth altars is Botticelli's St. Augustine of 1481. On the floor of the Baroque chapel in the south transept is Botticelli's round tombstone; his real name was Sandro Filipepi.

In the Sacristy there is a *Crucifixion* and its sinopia by Taddeo Gaddi; and a *Resurrection* by Agnolo Gaddi. On the north side between the third and fourth altars is *St. Jerome* by Domenico Ghirlandaio.

To the left of the church is the entrance to the Convent. In the Refectory is a delightful 1480 *Last Supper* by Domenico Ghirlandaio, with a charming background of trees and exotic birds.

At Piazza Ognissanti, 2, on the corner of Borgo Ognissanti, is the fifteenth-century **Palazzo Lenzi**, now the French Consulate. In front of Piazza Ognissanti is the river and Lungarno Vespucci. Going back towards the centre, it becomes **Lungarno Corsini**. At number 10 is the distinctive seventeenth-century **Baroque Palazzo Corsini**, crowned with statues. The Corsini were an illustrious family from the fourteenth to the eighteenth century – Pope Clement XII was a Corsini. The palace contains a remarkable staircase as well as the most eminent private collection of art in the city in its Galleria Corsini. Dating from 1765, it contains work by Signorelli, Raphael, Bellini and others, as well as furniture. Entry is by appointment only; call 218994.

Beyond at number 4, is the **Palazzo Gianfigliazzi** of 1459, home in 1827 to the great writer Alessandro Manzoni, best known for 'I promessi sposi' (the *Betrothed*). Next to it is the Palazzo Masetti which is now the British Consulate. It was where the widow of Prince Charles Stuart the Pretender, the Countess of Albany, lived, and where her lover and second husband, the poet and dramatist Alfieri, died.

Via Tornabuoni and San Trinita

Via Tornabuoni, linking the Ponte San Trinita (see Ponte Vecchio) with Via del Trebbio and so to Santa Maria Novella, is the main thoroughfare of a fashionable area but also feeds a variety of interesting smaller streets. In the days of Florence's mercantile prosperity, wealthy merchants built their lavish palaces here, on the edge of the wool making district.

If you start from Ponte San Trinita, you see **Palazzo Spini-Ferroni**, right, built for Geri degli Spini in 1289 by, perhaps, Lapo Tedesco, the master of Arnolfo di Cambio. Fortress like, it was supposed to guard the newly-built Ponte San Trinita. A little way on, left, is the Church of **San Trinita** which has unusually, the accent on the first syllable. It is open 07.00-12.00 and 16.00-19.00.

The present Gothic form, by Neri di Fioravante, dates back to the fourteenth century but there has been a church of the Vallombrosan Order of Cistercians on the site since 1077. The façade is a late sixteenth-century addition by Buontalenti (though the interior façade is the original Romanesque). The bell tower is from the 1390s.

Inside, it is worth looking at the Bartolini-Salimbeni Chapel (fourth right) with its magical *Marriage of the Virgin* (1422) by the Sienese Lorenzo Monaco, who also painted the *Annunciation*.

The Sassetti Chapel in the choir contains a 1495 masterpiece by Domenico Ghirlandaio, a *Life of San Francesco* painted for the merchant Francesco Sassetti. It is a very Florentine picture – above the altar Francis receives the Rule of the Order from Pope Honorius in Piazza della Signoria as Sassetti (right foreground) and Lorenzo Medici il Magnifico look on with Antonio Pucci. On the steps is the Humanist poet Poliziano with Lorenzo's sons. Beneath is a Miracle taking place in Piazza San Trinita showing the old bridge and original Romanesque façade. *The Adoration of the Shepherds* altarpiece is one of the artist's best known works, pure Renaissance Humanism with many Classical images and allusions. The kneeling figures are Francesco Sassetti and his wife Nera Corsi.

The chapel to the right of the high altar contains a painted Crucifix, originally in San Miniato, that is supposed to have nodded in approval at the temperance of San Giovanni Gualberto in forgiving the murderer of his brother; whereupon he went on to found the Vallombrosan order in the Casentino area. The Sanctuary vault has fine frescoes of Biblical figures by Alesso Baldovinetti.

In the second chapel to the left of the High Altar is a 1454 Luca della Robbia masterpiece, the tomb of Bishop Benozzo Federighi, Bishop of Fiesole. In the fourth and fifth chapels on the left of the nave are frescoes illustrating events in the life of San Giovanni Gualberto by Neri di Bicci and Bicci di Lorenzo.

The Crypt, which may need to be opened by the sexton, is eleventh-century.

Back on the square in front of the church stands the granite Column of Justice, a gift to Cosimo I from Pope Pius IV, originally in the Baths of Caracalla in Rome. Several interesting streets lead east and west from Piazza San Trinita – they are dealt with a little later (see below).

On the near corner of Via delle Terme (Baths Street), right, is the **Palazzo Buondelmonti** by Baccio d'Agnolo. The **Palazzo Bartolini-Salimbeni** on the other corner of Via delle Terme is also by Baccio d'Agnolo (1520), one of his finest works, with an interesting courtyard. It was a much discussed creation – note the plaque over the door. In 1839 it became the Hotel du Nord and host to several eminent writers including Emerson and Melville.

The street is lined with other palaces – an early one is the fourteenth and fifteenth-century **Palazzo Minerbetti**, left, at number 3. Above the door of number 7 is a bust of Francesco I by Giambologna. Soon, right, you will come to the massive **Palazzo**

Strozzi, built in 1489 for Filippo Strozzi the wealthy banker and the last of the great Renaissance palaces. Still retaining the distinctively fortress-like characteristics of the period, it was begun by Benedetto da Maiano. Filippo died in 1491, when only the part facing Piazza Strozzi (on the other side) was almost finished. It was completed by Cronaca. The Strozzi family were at first closely allied to the Medici but Filippo's son later led a failed conspiracy against them. The Palace is the home of several organisations and institutions and is also used for exhibitions and fairs. There is also a small museum devoted to the history of the Palace (It is open 16.00-19.00, Monday, Wednesday and Friday.)

Via Tornabuoni is joined by Via della Vigna Nuova (New Vineyard Street) and Via della Spada (Sword Street), left, and Via Strozzi, right. This point marks the western extremity of the Roman city. Between the two streets on the left is the Palazzo used by Sir Robert Dudley in 1614 whilst he was helping in the construction of the Livorno Arsenal.

Along Via della Vigna Nuova you will come to, left, the beautiful **Palazzo Rucellai**. Giovanni Rucellai was a Renaissance intellectual and wealthy merchant. It seems that the Palace was designed by Leon Batista Alberti (the Humanist and all-round Renaissance man) and its construction overseen by Bernardo Rossellino in the mid-fifteenth century. Its unusually delicate design (for the period) was highly influential. The Rucellai and Medici arms are clearly seen. Across the street is the **Rucellai Loggia**, also by Alberti.

The Palazzo Rucellai contains the **Museo di Storia della Fotografia 'Fratelli Alinari'** concerned with the history of photography. The pioneering Alinari Brothers' photographic studio was founded in 1852. It is open 10.00-19.30 except Mondays.

From here carry on until Via Palchetti, right; proceed along it to Via de' Federighi and turn right until you reach **Piazza Pancrazio** and one of the oldest churches in the city – founded before 1000 AD. The porch of the current building is by Alberti. Now deconsecrated, it has been converted into a museum of the sculptural works of **Marino Marini**. (Open all year: 10.00-13.00 and 16.00-19.00 or 10.00-18.00 June-August).

Turn right into Via della Spada. At 18 is the **Cappella di San Sepolcro** built for Giovanni Rucellai by Alberti. It is often closed but contains a beautiful marble model of the Holy Sepulchre in Jerusalem. Continue back to Via Tornabuoni, passing, left, **Via delle Belle Donne** (Beautiful Women Street), once known for its brothels, and turn left.

On the left, at number 19, you will see the post-Renaissance **Palazzo Larderel** of 1580, attributed to Giovanni Dosio. Opposite is the Baroque Church of **San Gaetano**; inside is a *Martyrdom of San Lorenzo* by P. da Cortona and lunettes by Lorenzo Lippi in the Cappella Ardinghelli. On Piazza Antinori, left, is **Palazzo Antinori**, built in 1461 for the Antinori family probably by Giuliano da Maiano.

Turn right along Via degli Agli and then third left to the church of **Santa Maria Maggiore**, another early church founded in the eighth-century and rebuilt in the thirteenth century. The internal façade is by Buontalenti. There is a chapel of interest next to the choir with a column from the tomb of Brunello Latini, Dante's teacher, and a lovely thirteenth-century enthroned *Madonna*.

Turning left out of the church and heading along Via de' Vecchietti eventually will bring you face to face with the fourteenth-century **Palazzo Davanzati**, at Piazza Davanzati, 9. This is an excellent example of a Florentine nobleman's house and is now the **Museo della Casa Fiorentina Antica** (Museum of the Ancient Florentine House), which recreates Florentine life from the fourteenth to the seventeenth-century. Perhaps most impressive is the fourteenth-century Parrot Room (Sala dei Pappagalli). The entrance is on Via Porta Rossa and it is open 09.00-14.00 or 13.00 Sundays; closed Mondays.

Turn right out of this Palace and walk along Via Porta Rossa (Street of the Red Gate). Turn right down Via Pellicceria to the fourteenth-century **Palazzo di Parte Guelfa** (Palace of the Guelf Party – see History section), completed by Brunelleschi. Nearby is the famous pig and market as described elsewhere. This backs onto Via delle Terme from where you may get to the parallel **Borgo SS Apostoli**, a fascinating medieval street and former Roman road which will bring you back to Piazza San Trinita. Passing along it you will meet, at number 19, the thirteenth-century **Palazzo Usimbardi** which, as the Grand Hotel Royal, played host to many eminent literatti like Dickens, Henry James and Longfellow. Right, on the corner of Via delle Bombarde, is the fourteenth-century towered **Palazzo Altoviti**. Just before it, left, is **Piazza del Limbo**, with some handsome palaces and the Romanesque church of SS Apostoli which, legend has it, was founded by Charlemagne in 786. In fact it dates back to the tenth century, and is thus one of the oldest churches in the city. The interior is notable for its green marble columns and, at the end of the north aisle is the 1507 Tomb of Prior Oddo Altoviti by Benedetto da Rovezzano and a lovely *Tabernacle* by Andrea della Robbia.

Piazza and Church of Santissima Annunziata and the Spedale degli Innocenti

The Via dei Servi, lined with a number of sixteenth-century palaces (number 15 is particularly attractive) runs north-east from the Cathedral Square (Piazza del Duomo) and brings you to **Piazza della Santissima Annunziata**, perhaps the most harmonious square in Florence and a true attempt to put the tenets of the Renaissance into practise. It was designed by Brunelleschi to provide a perfect view of the Duomo (down Via dei Servi). If you are walking from the Cathedral Square, you will pass the vast **Palazzo Pucci** – the Pucci being one of the oldest of eminent Florentine families. Left, on the corner of Via de' Pucci and on the same square is the church of **San Michele Visdomini** with work by Pontormo, Poppi and others. You may care to make a diversion by taking the Via del Castellaccio, right, which leads to the so-called **Rotonda di Brunelleschi** or Rotonda di Santa Maria degli Angeli, one of Brunelleschi's last works (1434). It is an octagonal chapel, based on Roman centralised structures, built in memory of the soldier Filippo degli Scolari but unfinished due to lack of money. The accompanying convent became absorbed into the Ospedale di Santa Maria Nuova. From here turn left into Via degli Alfani and then right into Via D. Fibbia which will bring you to Piazza della Santissima Annunziata.

The equestrian statue in the centre is of *Ferdinand I*, the last work of Giambologna (1608). It is made of bronze cannonry captured from the Turks at the Battle of Lepanto. Beyond it is the church of **Santissima Annunziata** and the Servite convent. On the left is the 1516-25 colonnade by by A. da Sangallo and Baccio d'Agnolo. On the corner of the square and Via dei Servi is the **Palazzo della Regione** (administrative offices for Tuscany), otherwise known as the Palazzo Ricardi-Mannelli, begun in 1557 by Ammannati and finished by Buontalenti and Giambologna. On the right is the **Spedale degli Innocenti** built by Brunelleschi in 1419, the first hospital for foundlings in Italy and still functioning. It was commissioned by the Arte della Seta, the Silk Guild. (Open 09.00-14.00 or 13.00 on Sundays; closed Wednesdays.)

The Spedale portico is to a Brunelleschi design, classical proportions adapted to the traditional Romanesque architecture of Tuscany – the pillars are Greek in style, the width of the arches Roman. The last bays right and left were added in the nineteenth century. It is decorated with the beautiful 1487 terracotta tondoes of infants by Andrea della Robbia, added to encourage people to provide for dying infants, who, left on the steps of the church, were passed through a special window at the left of the portico. Within are two cloisters: the main Chiostro degli Uomini (Men's Cloister) with clock tower and emblems of the Arte della Seta; and the Chiostro delle Donne (Women's Cloister) with lovely Ionic colonnades. The stairway to the Hospital Gallery of Painting is off the main cloister. Here are works by Luca and Andrea della Robbia, Andrea del Sarto, Pontormo, Botticelli, Filippo Lippi and Ghirlandaio – his *Adoration of the Magi* has a self-portrait (he is the second figure to the right of the Virgin). Others are members of the wool guild who founded the spedale. One room is dedicated to eighteenth-century painting.

Santissima Annunziata (Church of the Most Blessed Annunciation)

Open 07.00-12.30 and 16.00-18.45.

Perhaps the best loved church in Florence, it was first built as an oratory in 1250 by Founders of the Order of Servites, rich merchants dedicated to the cult of the Virgin Mary. The Virgin was always adored by the Florentines because the day of the Annunciation fell close to the old Florentine New Year. It remains the traditional place for Florentine brides to take their bouquets after their marriage. Somehow it was always a favourite place of devotion of a more pagan kind. In the fifteenth century the worried citizen would buy little wax dolls, in his own likeness, to hang in the church to obtain the protection of the Virgin.

This church was built by Michelozzo between 1441 and 1455, with some help from Alberti. The Chiostrino dei Voti in front has the delightful *Nativity* by Baldovinetti, the *Visitation* by Pontormo, the *Birth of Mary* and *Adoration of the Magi* by Andrea del Sarto and others. The interior is covered in donations from citizens, giving a rather Baroque effect, masking the construction by Michelozzo, a little. The ceiling has been frequently altered over the centuries.

On the left as you enter is a fifteenth-century 'Tempietto' (little temple) housing a thirteenth-century Annunciation, painter unknown. It is said that the painter, having completed the angel and body of the Virgin, fell asleep; upon waking he found that the face had been completed by an angel. The chapel next to it has lovely panels inlaid by the Opificio delle Pietre Dure (see Workshop of Pietre Dure, below).

Along the left nave beyond are two chapels with frescoes by Andrea del Castagno of the 1450s, painted over and only rediscovered in 1864. Of Castagno it is said that 'he was taken from keeping animals by a Florentine citizen who found him drawing a sheep on a rock'. Although the detail of the story is open to question (several painters, including Giotto, are said to have begun in similar ways) something of the kind must have happened to allow anyone of humble origins to reach this sort of position, not least because peasants were tied to the land. Castagno gained the nickname Andrea degli Impiccati (Andrea of the hanged men) because he was also well known as the painter of criminals, placed on the walls of the Palazzo della Podesta, both to shame them and as a deterrent.

In the fourth chapel on the left is a *Crucifixion* by Perugino. The chapel in the left transept contains a terracotta Baptist by Michelozzo. At the east end of the church are nine semi-circular chapels with work by Perugino (third chapel from left), a *Resurrection* by Bronzino (fourth chapel), work by Giambologna in what he hoped would be his burial place (fifth chapel). The circular and unusual Tribune at the east end is by Michelozzo and Leon Battista Alberti. To the left of the arch, beneath a statue of St. Peter, is the grave of the painter Andrea del Sarto.

On the south side there are more chapels. In the second on the right is a wooden Crucifix by A. da Sangallo. In the fifth is the 1456 monument to Orlando de' Medici by B. Rossellino. In the right transept chapel is a painted Crucifix by Baldovinetti. In the chapel beyond it to the east is a *Christ Supported by Nicodemus*, whose head is a self-portrait of the sculptor Bandinelli. Behind is another portrait of the sculptor with his wife.

Over the door into the Chiostro dei Morti (Cloister of the Dead) in the left transept there is one of Andrea del Sarto's finest and most sensitive works, the *Madonna del Sacco* (the Madonna of the Cushion). The entrance to the cloister is actually outside the church, to the left of the façade. The frescoed lunettes in the cloister illustrate the origins of the Servite order. In the Cappella di San Luca, which has belonged to the artist's guild since 1565, are the graves of several eminent artists, Cellini and Pontormo among them. The chapel altarpiece has a self portrait by Vasari.

The area around Piazza Santissima Annunziata

Via G. Capponi leads north to the right of Santissima Annunziata. At number 4 is the delightful cloister of the **Compagnia di San Pierino** (ring the bell on the door of the Societa D. Alighieri) with sixteenth-century frescoes by B. Poccetti and others. At 26 is the seventeenth-century **Palazzo Capponi**, the house of the statesman after whom the street is named. On the corner of Via Micheli, number 15, is the **Palazzo di San Clemente**. This once belonged to Charles Stuart the Young Pretender; from here his wife, the Countess of Albany, who was having an affair with the poet Alfieri, fled to a convent in 1780.

Archeological Museum

Open 09.00-14.00 or 13.00 on Sunday; closed Monday.

Via della Colonna, leading east from Piazza Santissima Annunziata, leads to the Archeological Museum (Museo Archeologico) at number 36. It is housed in the Palazzo della Crocetta, built for the Grand Duchess Maria Maddalena of Austria in the seventeenth century.

On three floors it features many of the antiquities from the Medici collection. There is a unique collection of Etruscan pieces (see History section) of which the most famous is the Chimera bronze; antiquities from Ancient Rome (notably the bronze Arringatore or Orator), Greece (including the magnificent Francois Vase) and Egypt. The Etruscan section is arranged according to discovery sites.

Further along Via della Colonna, on the right at the junction with Borgo Pinti, is the church of **Santa Maria Maddalena dei Pazzi**, named after a canonised nun of the Pazzi family. It was built in 1492 by Giuliano da Sangallo in classical Renaissance style for the Cistercians. The chapter room has a fine *Crucifixion* by Perugino – you may need to ask permission to see it. There is an unusually good example of Florentine Baroque in the sacristy. (See section 'Sant' Ambrogio and Santa Maria Maddalena dei Pazzi').

Continuing north along Borgo Pinti brings you to another work by Giuliano da Sangallo at 97 – the late fifteenth-century **Palazzo di Bartolomeo della Scala**. Scala was secretary of state under Lorenzo il Magnifico.

To the Accademia

To the left of Santissima Annunziata, as you face it, is Via C. Battisti, leading to Piazza San Marco. As you emerge into the square the Accademia delle Belle Arti (Academy of Fine Arts) is on the left, founded by Grand-Duke Leopold in 1784, as a paeon to Florentine art from the thirteenth century to the Renaissance. In front of it is the Loggia dell'Ospedale di S. Matteo, built in 1384 and one of the oldest in the city. Over the doors of the Accademia are lovely Della Robbian lunettes.

Galleria dell'Accademia delle Belle Arti

Open 09.00-14.00 or 13.00 on Sundays; closed Mondays.

The entrance to the Galleria dell'Accademia is at Via Ricasoli, 60, the street taking its name from a nineteenth-century mayor of Florence. The gallery features many works by Michelangelo, including the original *David*.

You will first enter the Pinacoteca, with paintings by many of the great Florentine artists from the fifteenth and sixteenth centuries. Of particular note are the *Descent from the Cross* by Filippino Lippi and the *Madonna with Saints and Angels* by Fra' Bartolomeo. In the Galleria itself are many of the works of Michelangelo, particularly his *Four Prisoners* (1521), intended for the tomb of Julius II and his unfinished, by accident or by design, *St. Matthew* (San Matteo) (1504-1608), commissioned by the Opera del Duomo.

Off to the right are three more rooms mostly dedicated to fifteenth-century painting. Among the highlights are Room II: *Cassone Adimari* panel by Lo Scheggia (1440-45), showing wedding guests in front of the Baptistry; and the Maestro di Castello *Nativity*. Room III: early Botticelli, *Madonna and Child*; Baldovinetti, *Trinity and Saints*. Room IV: Lorenzo di Credi, *Adoration of the Infant.*

In the Tribune Michelangelo's *David* (1501-04) is exhibited, sculpted when he was 29 and removed from Piazza della Signoria in 1882. Commissioned by the city fathers to stand outside the Palazzo Vecchio as a symbol of Republican liberty, it is Michelangelo's most famous creation and shows David at the moment of his victory over Goliath. Its size is remarkable but it is an unsettling piece - on the one hand there is a sort of perfection in it, on the other it is somehow at variance with the ideals of the Renaissance. The statue's arm was broken in the anti-Medici riot of 1527.

The Tribune walls are covered in paintings by R. Ghirlandaio (two portraits), Bronzino (*Deposition*) and Pontormo (*Venus and Cupid*), among others.

Left of this are three more rooms of the pinacoteca, devoted to thirteenth and fourteenth-century Tuscan painting. Room V: note the

Crucifix from the Sienese school. Room VI: *Madonna and Child* by A. Orcagna. Room VII: a *Pieta* by Giovanni da Milano and works by T. Gaddi from the Sacristy of Santa Croce. In this area is a room devoted to the work of nineteenth-century members of the Academy.

On the first floor are four more rooms devoted to the art of the fourteenth and fifteenth centuries. Room I: work by Lorenzo Monaco. Room II has triptychs by Orcagna (Pentecost, formerly on the high altar of the Church of Santi Apostoli), Giovanni del Biondo and others. Room III: sixteenth to eighteenth century Russian art, including icons. Room IV: works by Mariotto di Nardo, Agnolo Gaddi and Lorenzo Monaco.

The Museum of Musical Instruments and the Workshop of Pietre Dure

Open 09.00-14.00, closed Sundays.

By turning left out of the Accademia and left again into Via degli Alfani you will come to two small museums - the Museum of Musical Instruments (Museo degli Strumenti Musicali) and the Workshop of Pietre Dure (Opificio delle Pietre Dure). The first, at number 80, consists of a collection started by the Medici and includes violins by Stradivarius and a harpsichord by Cristofori. It has recently been housed in the Palazzo Vecchio so you may need to check on the latest situation. The second, at number 78, is dedicated to the Florentine speciality of pietre dure (literally 'hard stones') which is the inlay of semi-precious stones used in many of the churches and tombs of the city. It was popularised by the Medici Grand Dukes notably Ferdinando I who founded this workshop in 1588. There is some beautiful work to be seen here as well as the instruments used by the craftsmen.

The University and its museums

Across Via C. Battisti from the Accademia, on Piazza San Marco, is the Universita degli Studi, founded by the commune in 1321, and its several museums. This building originally served as the Ducal stables. Nearby, at Via Micheli, 3, is the Giardino dei Semplici, the Botanical Gardens (open 09.00-12.00, Monday, Wednesday and Friday), founded by Cosimo I in 1545. At Via La Pira, 4, is the entrance to various university museums: the Botanical Museum (open 09.00-12.00 Monday to Friday), contains one of the oldest herbariums in the world; the Geology and Palaentology Museum, the most important in Italy (open 14.00-18.00 Monday, 09.00-13.00 Tuesday, Wednesday, Thursday, and Saturday); and the Minerology and Lithology Museum which includes several Medici artefacts worked in stone (open 09.00-13.00; also 15.00-18.00 Wednesdays).

Education in the Renaissance was fairly well organised and Florence had a high percentage of literate citizens. There were three types of school. The basic school taught reading and writing; for arithmetic there was the abacus school; for Latin a child went to the 'master of grammar'. Otherwise there were private tutors, or you could be attached to a court as a page. Painters and other artisans were mostly apprenticed; lawyers, doctors, scientists and humanists were the ones who ended up at university. Students might be only 16 on going to university. First they would study liberal arts – grammar, logic, rhetoric, arithmetic, geometry, music and astronomy, and then perhaps theology, law or medicine. Teaching was in Latin and it was expensive. Florence, surprisingly, never had one of the great Italian universities. This was due partly to expense – war, famine, and new building tended to eat into funds – but also for political reasons. It was decided that Pisa University should be allowed to develop in order to placate its citizens, angry at their loss of liberty.

Piazza San Marco

Piazza San Marco has a number of cafes popular with students. It is classical in style with, on the corner of the Accademia, the fourteenth-century **Loggia dell' Ospedale di San Matteo**. On the left, as you face the church, is the **Court of Appeal** (Corte d'Appello) by Buontalenti in 1574, with nineteenth-century adornments. The Medici gardens were here, where Lorenzo il Magnifico founded a school of sculpture, placed under the direction of a pupil of Donatello and where, so it is said, Michelangelo was a pupil. It was quite informal, il Magnifico himself often taking his place among the artists. The square was also the scene of more unsettling events, when Savonarola decreed that all licentious books and works of art be burnt – the bonfires of the vanities - celebrations followed here. A cross was set up with three circles around it: in the innermost were the Dominican monks with boys dressed as angels; next a group of young laymen and clerics; and finally a circle of old men priests and burghers dancing with flowers. But after Savanarola's death the crown of the Virgin in the church was set triumphantly upon the head of a courtesan.

The square takes its name from the thirteenth-century church, which with the convent and museum of the same name, dominates the north side of the square. The church of **San Marco** was founded in the thirteenth-century but was redesigned by Giambologna in 1588. The Baroque façade is of 1780. Inside, note the Crucifix by the school of Giotto above the portal, and the 1508 Virgin by Fra Bartolomeo on the second altar on the right. The third altar, right, boasts a wonderful Byzantine mosaic of 705. Sant' Antonio, former bishop of Florence - from whom, it is recorded, a single glance would still the chattering children during services at the Duomo - is buried here, as are the eminent humanist Pico della Mirandola and the poet Angelo Poliziano (Politician).

The Convent and Museum of San Marco

Piazza San Marco, 1. Open 09.00-14.00 or 13.00 on Sunday; Closed Mondays. The entrance is to the right of the church.

The Dominican convent is thirteenth-century, though rebuilt by Michelozzo in 1452. Though a haven of 'holy quietness', it is associated with artists of some renown, and one of Renaissance Florence's more controversial figures, Girolamo Savonarola, who was Prior here. Two artists of note, Fra Bartolomeo and Fra Angelico were monks here, Fra Angelico remembered with particular affection. He came from a poor background in the Mugello countryside. Whilst undoubtedly a highly skilled artist, his work is characterised by love of pure spirituality; for him pictorial art was a meditative aid. The walls are covered in his works, becoming part of the daily lives of all the monks. He blends realism, Tuscan landscapes and buildings with spiritual values – he is the 'blessed' Angelico. He is also at odds with the Dominican tradition which was concerned with the fear of God while he emphasises love and compassion. It is said that he would never add to his paintings once completed because they had been created through the will of God.

(Opposite) Top: *A Renaissance portrait – nuns in the cloister of a church in Certaldo.*
(Opposite) Botom: *The Camposento, Pisa. Badly damaged in the war, it remains a stunning adjunct to the cathedral and famous leaning tower.*

First, visit the Cloister of Sant' Antonio (who was also Prior here) with sixteenth and seventeenth-century frescoes depicting Antonio's life, by Poccetti. Some frescoes here are by Fra Angelico including *St. Dominic* at the foot of the cross (on the wall opposite the entrance) and above the door of the Pilgrims' Hospice, *Christ as a Pilgrim Received by the Dominicans*.

The Pilgrims' Hospice is filled with Fra Angelico's works, many of which were formerly in various Florence churches. The most famous is the *Tabernacolo dei Linaioli*; commissioned by the Linen Guild to whom the Blessed Angelico promised to use 'the best and finest colours that can be found'. Patrons were careful with their money; the guild insisted on seeing the design before the painter went ahead. The predella showing scenes from the life of saints Cosmos and Damien, intended for San Marco Church, shows a burial scene taking place in Piazza San Marco. The pictures of the *Life of Christ* and the *Virgin* come from a polyptych that was in Santissima Annunziata, some by Fra Angelico, some by his pupils. The Paradise part of the *Last Judgement* is also by Fra Angelico, as is a *Descent from the Cross* with a portrait of Michelozzo as *Joseph of Arimathea*.

The Lavatorium and the rooms off it are devoted to the works of Fra Bartolomeo, a later resident of the convent; there is a *Last Judgement* by him in the Great Refectory. In the Chapter House is one of Fra Angelico's masterpieces, the *Crucifixion*. In the small refectory is a *Last Supper* by Ghirlandaio.

In the Foresteria, the old guest quarters, is a small museum devoted to material saved from the demolition of the Mercato Vecchio and the Ghetto (where Piazza della Repubblica is now).

On the first floor are the cells of the Dormitory, each decorated by a fresco, mostly by Fra Angelico. The *Annunciation* at the top of the stairs is one of his finest works.

Cosimo il Vecchio used cells 38 and 39 for his retreat; they have works of Fra Angelico and Gozzoli. Savonarola used rooms 12 to 14; there is a portrait of him here by Fra Bartolomeo. It was from here that he was dragged to his death in 1498. Cell 31 was used by Sant' Antonio, 32 by Fra Angelico himself.

(Opposite) Top: *The unique beauty of the Tuscan countryside.*
(Opposite) Bottom: *Buying furniture in comfort – an outdoor shop in Lucca.*

The library, between cells 42 and 43, was built by Michelozzo in 1441-44 and is the oldest in Europe. One of the finest works of the Renaissance, it was started by Cosimo Medici il Vecchio and is the precurser to the Lorenzian Library.

Chiostro dello Scalzo

Open 09.00-14.00 or 13.00 on Sundays; closed on Mondays. Ring the bell on the door.

Via Cavour runs north-south to the left of the Church of San Marco as you look at it. Turn on to it and go north. A little way up on the left, at number 69, is the Chiostro dello Scalzo.

This is all that is left of the Confraternity of San Giovanni Battista with its monochrome frescoes of the *Life of John the Baptist* by Andrèa del Sarto (1514-24). Andrea del Sarto was the son of a tailor (hence his name) and was at first a goldsmith. Eventually he married his pretty, vain mistress, Lucrezia, when her husband died, inheriting all her dependents. His colleagues thought him mad but he was said to be bewitched. His skill took him to the Paris court but his homesickness drove him back to Florence, with a promise to return to Paris. Lucrezia would not allow it; soon he was once again poor but isolated from his friends. His shrewish wife and his art were to be his only consolations for the remainder of his life.

Continuing up Via Cavour and turning left into Via Salvestrina will bring you to the **Palazzo Pandolfini**, a commission given to Raphael in 1520 by the Archbishop of Troia, Giannozzo Pandolfini. It is still owned by the same family.

Via Cavour going south in the direction of the Duomo, passes the seventeenth-century **Marucelliana Library**, right, before reaching the **Palazzo Medici-Riccardi**.

Cenacolo di Sant' Apollonia (Benedictine Convent)

Open 09.00-14.00 or 13.00 on Sundays; closed Mondays.

Across Via Cavour from Piazza San Marco is Via degli Arazzieri (where the tapestry makers worked) which crosses Via San Gallo and becomes Via Ventisette Aprile. Here at number 1 is Andrea del Castagno's 1440 masterpiece, in the former Benedictine convent. The *Last Supper* was painted for the Refectory – there are also a *Crucifixion*, *Entombment*, and *Resurrection*.

Last Suppers and Crucifixions (flesh and blood, bread and wine) had been popular as refectory subjects since the fourteenth century. The addition of the Resurrection here shows spiritual optimism.

Castagno is noteworthy as the first artist to use contrast of light and colour to express drama – the lively colours of landscape in the upper part of the mural, the heavier colours of the sense of imminent tragedy at the supper.

This little museum is of particular interest because Castagno's fresco working methods are clearly visible. His work has a splendid robustness; his realism gave him the nickname 'Andrea degli Impiccati'. There are also works by Paolo Schiavo and Raffaele da Montelupo.

Via Ventisette Aprile leads into **Piazza della Indipendenza**, Florence's first nineteenth-century square. There are statues of two city mayors and on the top right corner the Villino Trollope where Anthony Trollope wrote *Doctor Thorne* in 1857. Thomas Hardy also stayed here.

Via San Gallo

Just before reaching Via Ventisette Aprile you cross Via San Gallo which leads, right, to Piazza della Liberta and in so doing passes the 1500 **Loggia dei Tessitori**. This is all that is left of the old Weavers' Guildhouse. Also here is the church of **San Giovannino dei Cavalieri**, with a large *Crucifixion* by Lorenzo Monaco in the Tribune and in the right aisle, an *Annunciation* by the Maestro della Nativita di Castello.

Via San Gallo leads south towards the Duomo and Baptistry. On the way it passes some notable palaces including, at number 10, the 1630 **Palazzo Marucelli**. Also, as it becomes Via dei Ginori, at number 15, stands the fifteenth-century **Palazzo Taddei**, famous for its Michelangelo tondo (now in the Royal Academy, London) and where Raphael stayed in 1505. At number 14 is the **Biblioteca Riccardiana**, a private library forming an extension to the Medici Palace and open to the public since 1718. It retains its original shelves and many valuable manuscripts.

THIRTEEN

To the heart of Florence

Piazza della Signoria, Piazza della Repubblica and Orsanmichele

From Piazza del Duomo, Via de' Calzaiuoli leads south to Piazza Signoria, passing Orsanmichele. Formerly the principal street of Florence, it is now a pedestrian precinct widened in the mid-nineteenth century at the cost of something of its medieval character. Via Speziali, right, leads to **Piazza della Repubblica** which is also the result of the same nineteenth-century desire to 'modernise' the city. It was the site of the Roman forum and became the medieval Mercato Vecchio (old market), the chief food market of the city. (Even then, veal was the favourite meat but minestra was the more important part of the meal.) Later it became the Jewish Ghetto, created in 1571. All this was cleared away in the name of progress and is undistinguished architecturally. But it has the advantage of space and is not an unpleasant place for an (expensive) drink in the Giubbe Rosse, among others, haunt of intellectuals at the turn of the-century. The **Triumphal Arch** celebrates the construction of the square as a new beginning. The main post office, where international calls are possible, is on this square, as is the Edison cinema dating back to 1901. The column near Gilli's bar used to support a representation of *Abundance* by Donatello, the first occasion that a market was protected or celebrated by art that was not directly religious.

Continue south from Piazza della Repubblica along Via Calimala in the south-east corner, named after the guild of cloth importers who had their warehouses here. Before visiting Orsanmichele, along Via dei Lamberti, left, you are recommended to first continue a short way along Via Calimala to the **Mercato Nuovo** (new market, also known as the straw market). This has been a market since the eleventh-century, and was in the middle of the old area of banks, of which there were 72 by 1421. The beautiful **Logge del Mercato Nuovo** were built in 1547 as a merchants' exchange specialising in silk (sericulture was introduced in 1420) and gold, and later, straw to comply with the fashion for hats. Within is a plaque, said to mark the spot where the 'carroccio', or battle-wagon, was placed following a military triumph. It remains a daily market (closed Sunday and Monday in winter) dealing in leather goods and so on. Florentines call the market the *Porcellino* after the bronze boar, a copy of 1612 by Tacca of a classical antique in the Uffizi. To rub his snout is supposed to bring good luck.

Return to Via dei Lamberti, and meet the tall, imposing Orsanmichele, with its niches and statues, on the left.

Orsanmichele

Open: 08.00-12.00 and 15.00-17.30.

This unlikely-looking church is in the form of a tall rectangle built on the site of the ninth-century San Michele ad Hortum, destroyed in 1239 to make way for a grain market, which continued to attract pilgrims because of a miraculous icon of the Virgin. This led to the founding of a brotherhood, with Guelf sympathies, who did charitable works for Guelf followers and became rich in the process, probably paying for the tabernacle inside. The first grain market burnt down in 1304 and was replaced by the current edifice in 1337, built by Francesco Talenti and others. The upper floors were used as a granary while the exterior design was undertaken by the Arti (Guilds) whose influence in Florence's affairs from the end of the thirteenth-century until the rise of the Medici was immense. Something of the area's original religious character lingered on so that provision was made for the guilds to adorn the building with their patron saints.

After 1380 the building became a church again but the connection with the guilds continued for, as the importance of art in daily life grew, so they competed with one another to commission more innovative and more beautiful art. Hence the extraordinary collection of statues in the niches around the building by some of Florence's greatest artists. Refreshingly, here is great, original work not in a museum but amid the bustle of everyday life, though the originals of some of these are in museums. The change of direction of sculpted statuary is particularly evident in the Humanist-influenced work of Donatello, Ghiberti and Nanni.

Anti-clockwise from the corner on Via de' Calzaiuoli (with Via de' Lamberti) you see:

St. John the Baptist by Ghiberti (1414, Calimala Cloth Guild)
St. Thomas by Verrocchio (1466, Merchants' Court)
St. Luke by Giambologna (1601, Judges and Notaries)
St. Peter by Donatello (1408, Butchers)
St. Philip by Nanni di Banco (1415, Tanners)
Four Crowned Saints by Nanni di Banco (1415, Stonemasons and Carpenters)
St. George by Donatello (1417, Armourers)
St. Matthew by Ghiberti (1419, Bankers)
St. Stephen by Ghiberti (1428, Wool manufacturers)
St. Eligius by Nanni di Banco (1417, Farriers)
St. Mark by Donatello (1411, Linen Merchants)
St. James by Lamberti (1430, Furriers)
Madonna of the Roses attributed to Giovanni Tedesco (1400, Doctors and Apothecaries)
St. John by Baccio da Montelupo (1515, Goldsmiths and Silkweavers).

The Orsanmichele is linked by an arch to another building at the back. This, the Palazzo dell' Arte della Lana (1308), was the seat of the Wool Merchants' Guild, one of the most important in a city where perhaps a third of the population were at one time involved in the industry. Across Via Orsanmichele, to the right of Orsanmichele church as you look at the entrance, is Palazzo dell'Arte dei Beccai (Butchers' Guild) distinguishable by the symbol of a goat high on its wall.

The interior of the church is dark. Many of the pilasters and vaults are decorated with patron saints and there is some fine Gothic stained glass, but the principal attraction is the mid-fourteenth-century Gothic *Tabernacle* by Andrea Orcagna, in marble and coloured glass, his only work of sculpture. The base is surrounded by reliefs of the Life of the Virgin. Behind the altar are more reliefs of the Transition and Assumption of the Virgin. The painting of the *Madonna* is by Bernardo Daddi. The upper floors are used for exhibitions.

Piazza della Signoria

Via de' Calzaioli leads into the city's main square. The principal building with the tower across the square, left, is the **Palazzo**

Vecchio. The arcaded building next to it or behind it (just off the square) is the **Uffizi Gallery**. Just about opposite Via Calzaioli, filled with statuary, is the **Loggia della Signoria** (or dei Lanzi or dell' Orcagna). The bronze equestrian statue is of *Cosimo I* by Giambologna (1595). On it there are depictions of his conquest of Siena and of his inauguration as Grand Duke. The uninspiring **Neptune Fountain** (known as 'Il Biancone' or the 'big white thing'), built to help expunge the memory of Savanarola, is by Ammannati, with the help of Giambologna, and others. Next to it is the Marzocco, or heraldic lion of Florence, by Donatello.

At number 7, opposite the left side of the Palazzo Vecchio, is the striking sixteenth-century **Palazzo Uguccione**, in Roman Renaissance style. To the right of it at number 10, covered in coats of arms, is the fourteenth-century **Tribunale di Mercanzia**, or Merchants' Court, which was also a public post-office. At 5 is the **Gallery of Modern Art**, called 'Alberto della Ragione' (open mornings only; closed Monday) which contains recent work by De Chirico, Morandi, De Pisis, Severini, Carlo Levi, Guttuso, Scipione and others.

The square has been the scene of many important events in the history of Florence – it was and is the natural gathering place for citizens and visitors alike. Recent excavations have shown that the Roman baths were here but with the construction of the Palazzo Vecchio at the end of the thirteenth-century it became the site of the Piazza del Popolo (People's Square). The square grew in size with the expansion of Florentine power. By the end of the fourteenth-century it had reached its current dimensions. When the city was threatened, or when a Parliament was convened, the populace gathered here. The Pazzi conspirators were hanged from the Palazzo Vecchio in 1478. When the Medici returned here in 1530, the citizens gathered to cheer. Here Savanarola ignited his Bonfire of the Vanities and was himself later burnt at the stake. This is commemorated by a plaque in the eighteenth-century paving, near the Ammanati fountain.

Palazzo Vecchio

Open 09.00-19.00.Closed Saturdays and Sunday pm. Admission is expensive but free as far as the first courtyards, where you will also find public lavatories and the ticket office.

If anything symbolises the growth of Florence, it is this building, part fortress, part palace, built 1299-1302 on the site of a formerly

Ghibelline area of the city that was razed by the Guelphs. They commissioned Arnolfo di Cambio, responsible for the basic design of the Duomo, to build it. The design he came up with was to serve as a model for many other buildings in Florence and later all over Tuscany. Before the rise of the Medici it was known as the Palazzo del Popolo. The tower was for long the tallest in the city at 310 feet (94 metres). It was used as a prison (called the 'alberghetto' or 'little hotel') for some celebrated inmates, Savanarola and Cosimo il Vecchio to name but two. The Medici, private citizens in theory, finally moved here in 1540, after which it was known as the Palazzo Ducale. By 1549, however, the dukes had moved to the Pitti Palace after which it took on the current name. It is built of pietra forte on a trapezoidal plan and although plenty of additions have been made over the centuries, what you see on the Piazza is essentially the fourteenth-century original. At the main entrance, in its original position, is a copy of Michelangelo's 1501 *David*, commissioned as a symbol of Republicanism over tyranny. The original was moved to the Accademia in 1873. The other statue, of *Hercules and Cacus*, is by Bandinelli (1534) and is considered a poor imitation of the *David* – it was commissioned by Cosimo I who was present, with its sculptor, when Cellini gave his unflattering opinion of the effort. Today the Palace is both the town hall and a museum.

The interior

Although it started life as the seat of a popular government, its interior decoration is largely the result of the brief occupation by the Medici who commissioned Vasari to embellish it. They are only of average artistic merit but interesting as an illustration of contemporary events.

The first courtyard, reconstructed in 1453 by Michelozzo, is decorated with sixteenth-century frescoes of Austrian cities by Vasari painted when Cosimo I's son Francesco married Joanna of Austria. The fourteenth-century Armoury (Sala d' Arme) is the only other room open on this floor.

On the first floor is the grandiose Salone dei Cinquecento (grand hall of the five hundred), built in 1495 by Cronaca, which held the the assemblies of the General Council of the People, a result of Savanarola's reforms during the short-lived Republic. The walls of this room were to have been frescoed with the Battles of Cascina and Anghiari by Michelangelo and Leonardo, but were never completed. The wall decoration you see is by Vasari and others in celebration of victories over Pisa and Siena; indeed all the decor is calculated to glorify the Medici – the ceiling shows the Apotheosis of Cosimo I. The Udienza is the raised part, decorated with statues of various Medici by Bandinelli, De'Rossi and Caccini. The sculptures showing the Deeds of Hercules are by De' Rossi. Here too is *Victory* by Michelangelo, intended for the tomb of Julius II.

Next to it is a beautiful example of Mannerist art, the windowless Studiolo of Francesco I by Vasari in 1570, filled with works by Bronzino and others dedicated to the Duke's passion for natural history. The Sala dei Dugento (room of the two hundred), where the town council meets, is named after the council of citizens who met here, to the left of the Udienza in the Sala dei Cinquecento. It has a magnificent ceiling which was rebuilt by the Da Maianos in 1472-77; the tapestries were made in Florence by Bronzino and others. Another door leads from the other side of the Sala dei Cinquecento to the Quartiere di Leone X, all the rooms of which are dedicated to members of the Medici family and frescoed accordingly by Vasari.

The following route can be reversed, starting in the Sala dei Gigli:

On the second floor is the Quartiere degli Elementi (apartment of the elements), five rooms frescoed by Vasari with allegories of the elements. From here you can reach the Siviero Museum of works of art recovered after World War II or from illegal export, including works by Masaccio, Masolino, Veronese and others.

Also on the second floor, on the other side of the Salone dei Cinquecento, is the Apartment of Eleonora of Toledo, wife of Cosimo I. Eleanora's Chapel is decorated with magnificent frescoes by Bronzino. Next to this is the Camera Verde, the roof of which is decorated by Ridolfo del Ghirlandaio (1540). The next four rooms were painted by Vasari with allegories of female Virtues; one has a 1557 painting of the lost Leonardo fresco of the *Battle of Anghiari*.

After these rooms a passage with fourteenth-century ceiling leads to the Cappella della Signoria (Signoria Chapel, 1511) decorated by Ridolfo di Ghirlandaio; note the *Annunciation* with a view of of the Church of Santissima Annunziata. The Sala d' Udienza (audience hall) boasts a marvellous ceiling by Giuliano da Maiano and doors with figures of Dante and Petrarch. The murals by the Mannerist Salviati (1545), are scenes from the life of the Roman Marcus Camillus. Donatello's *Judith and Holofernes*, which used to be in Piazza della Signoria, has been moved here.

The Sala dei Gigli (hall of lilies) is named after the symbol of the city with a fine ceiling and a fresco of St. Zenobius, between St. Stephen and St. Lawrence. Next is the Cancelleria (Chancellery,

1511) used by Machiavelli, with a *Putto with Dolphin* by Verrocchio. The Guardaroba or Sala delle Carte Geographiche has a collection of remarkable maps painted in 1563.

Also here, in the Quartiere del Mezzanino, is the Loeser Collection left to the city by the American art critic Charles Loeser, comprising Tuscan art from the fourteenth to the sixteenth-century. The collection of musical instruments from the Conservatorio Cherubini is currently here too. The Alberghettino is closed to visitors.

Loggia della Signoria

Located on Piazza della Signoria close to the entrance to the Palazzo Vecchio, this is sometimes called the Loggia dei Lanzi after the German lancers who acted as Cosimo I's guards, or the Loggia Orcagna after the artist responsible, it is believed, for the design. It was built by Benci di Cione and Simone Talenti in 1376 and had a largely ceremonial role. The building now houses some important works of art of which the most important are *Perseus Proffering Medusa's Head*, by Cellini (1545); and the distinctive Mannerist spiralling *Rape of the Sabine Women* by Giambologna (1582).

The Badia and Bargello and the medieval streets in the area of Piazza della Signoria

Via Calimaruzza (on the right of the square looking towards the Palazzo Vecchio) was formerly the headquarters of the most important of Florentine guilds, the Arte di Calimala (the cloth guild). At number 2 you can still see their symbol, an eagle clutching a cotton bale.

Attractive Via dei Cerchi leads you north from the square towards the Duomo. You will soon come to Via della Condotta; turn left and soon, right, you will come to Vicolo dei Cerchi with, on the corner, the thirteenth-century **Palazzo Cerchi**.

Return to Via dei Cerchi; on the other corner with Via della Condotta is the medieval **Palazzo Giugni**. Continue along Via dei Cerchi and turn right into Via dei Cimatori, then left into Via dei Magazzini (further along Via dei Cerchi is Via dei Tavolini and its twelfth-century **Torre Greci**).

Via dei Magazzini passes the part of the Badia that is now the Law Courts and leads into **Piazza San Martino** with the fine thirteenth-century **Torre della Castagna**, the former residence of the city governors before the construction of the Palazzo Vecchio.

The church here is **San Martino del Vescovo**, dating back to 986 and patronised by the Alighieri (Dante) family. The current building is of 1479, when it was the seat of a charitable institution, and has some very interesting frescoes, illustrating the life of San Martino, by Francesco d' Antonio del Chierico. There is a bust of St. Antonius (founder of the Compagnia dei Buonomini charity) by Verocchio on the altar; and two *Madonnas*, one thought to be by Perugino.

Via Dante Alighieri is to the north of the square. Across this street is Dante's House, **La Casa di Dante**. (It is open 09.30-12.30 and 15.30-18.30, but closed Wednesdays and Sunday pm.)

This is allegedly the birthplace of the poet and it displays items relating to his life. Behind the house is the twelfth-century church of Santa Margherita de' Cerchi where Dante married Gemma Donati. Behind the church is Via del Corso and, left, the 1508 church of Santa Margherita in Santa Maria de' Ricci with eighteenth-century interior.

Further along Via del Corso are several medieval towers. Going east along Via del Corso you pass **Via dello Studio** (an attractive street and which leads to the Duomo, passing pretty Via della Canonica).

Just after the entrance to Via dello Studio is, left, **Palazzo Salviati**, now a bank, built in 1470 by the banking Portinari family and later bought by the Salviati who were related to the Medici. Inside is a *Madonna and Child* fresco and there is also a lovely courtyard.

Via del Corso crosses Via del Proconsolo and becomes imposing **Borgo d' Albizzi**, named after one of the most famous and wealthy fourteenth-century Florentine families. The two palaces at its beginning are described as you continue down Via Proconsolo - but a diversion along Borgo d' Albizzi is worthwhile. At number 28 is the sixteenth-century **Palazzo Vitali** by Ammannati, at 26, also by Ammannati, the **Palazzo Matteuci Ramirez di Montalvo**. At 18 is the early fifteenth-century **Palazzo Altoviti** with portraits of eminent sixteenth-century Florentines. Number 12, is the **Palazzo degli Albizi**, partly fourteenth-century. Opposite, at 15 is the fine fourteenth-century **Palazzo degli Alessandri** where the sculptor Canova later had his studio. In Piazza San Pier Maggiore is the thirteenth-century **Torre Donati**.

Turn right down Via del Proconsolo passing on the corners of Borgo d' Albizzi the **Palazzo Nonfinito** (the unfinished palace) at number 12, started in 1593 by Buontalenti. It now houses the **Museo**

Nazionale di Antropologia ed Etnologia (National Museum of Ethnology and Anthropology) and is open 09.00-13.00 Thursdays, Fridays and Saturdays. (Also the third Sunday of the month except in July, August and September.) One of the most important collections in Italy, it has rare exhibits from Indonesia, South and Central America, Asia and Africa and even includes material collected by Captain Cook from the Pacific in 1779. Nearby is the Palazzo Pazzi Quaratesi thought to have been built by Giuliano da Maiano between 1458 and 1469. The Pazzi were an old Florentine family and rivals of the Medici. In the Pazzi Conspiracy of 1478 Francesco de' Pazzi murdered Lorenzo de'Medici's brother Giuliano and was lynched by the mob from the Palazzo Vecchio.

Badia Fiorentina

Open daily 09.00-12.00 and 16.00-1800.

Further down Via del Proconsolo, right, is the entrance to this Benedictine abbey, founded in 978 by Willa in memory of her husband Uberto, the Margrave of Tuscany (the Margraves were Imperial plenipotentiaries of the Holy Roman Empire). It became one of the most important institutions of the city used in its time as a hospital, from 1031, and the meeting place of the Consiglio del Popolo. It was rebuilt by Arnolfo di Cambio, the architect of the Duomo, in 1284-1310; the interior is mostly from 1627.

The lovely Campanile is Romanesque (1310) at the bottom and Gothic above (1330). The tympanum of the main door contains a terracotta *Virgin* by Buglioni, a pupil of Della Robbia.

Within you may see fragments of the original interior on the west wall. It has a very fine ceiling. Also worthy of note is a 1485 *Madonna and San Martino* (north wall) by Filippino Lippi and a 1464-69 altarpiece (south wall) by Mino da Fiesole who also sculpted the statue of *Justice* on the tomb of the Florentine statesman Bernardo Giugni (1396-1466) in the right transept. Here, in the Baroque chapel, is a lovely 1558 organ. In the left transept is the 1469-81 monument to Ugo, son of Willa and Uberto, by Mino da Fiesole, with, above, an *Assumption* by Vasari. In the chapel frescoes removed from the nave are displayed.

To the right of the Choir (from which frescoes, some attributed to Giotto, have been removed) stairs lead to the Chiostro degli Aranci (cloister of the orange trees) where orange trees were once grown. The fine frescoes by an unknown artist illustrate the life of St. Benedict.

The Museo Nazionale del Bargello

Open 09.00-14.00 and 13.00 on Sundays; closed Mondays.

Opposite the Badia is the fortress-like Bargello, not unlike the Palazzo Vecchio, once Florence's prison and now home to one of the finest collection's of fourteenth to seventeenth-century sculpture and objets d' art in the country. Built from 1254, the Bargello was to have been the Palazzo del Popolo but became instead the residence of the chief magistrate or Podesta until 1502. Until 1574 it was the seat of the Council of Justice and then the office of the Captain of Police (known as the Bargello) and prison, and functioned thus until the mid-nineteenth-century, although the habit of painting the portraits of condemned criminals (from which the painter Andrea del Castagno obtained his nickname Andrea degli Impiccati, or Andrea of the hanged) was abandoned long before. Executions took place in the delightful courtyard. Presumably it is here to which Dickens, who was here in 1845, refers as being the prison hard by the Palazzo Vecchio:

> '...a foul and dismal place... where some men are shut up close, in small cells like ovens; and where others look through bars and beg; where some are playing draughts, and some are talking to their friends, who smoke, the while, to purify the air; ... before the hour is out, an old man, 80 years of age, quarrelling over a bargain with a young girl of 17, stabs her dead, in the market-place full of bright flowers; and is brought in prisoner, to swell the number.'

The tower, which is 175 feet (75 metres) high, is known as the Volognana. The Bargello still preserves its fourteenth-century aspect; but within it is possible to see and understand the progress of the Renaissance – much of the work on display here has been brought from elsewhere.

The main ground floor vaulted gallery is given over to works by Michelangelo (including a *Brutus*, the only bust he ever executed), Cellini and Giambologna (including his most famous *Mercury*). There is also a bust of Michelangelo by Daniele da Volterra and a marble *Leda* by Ammannati which is a surviving copy of a painting by Michelangelo which was destroyed. Cellini's *Narcissus*, *Apollo* and his *Hyacinth* were only identified earlier this-century, when they were discoverd in the Boboli Gardens. In other rooms, on the other side of the courtyard, are the works of Paolo di Giovanni, Tino di Camaino and international Gothic.

The Gothic courtyard is magnificent. It is surrounded by several interesting sculptures and the fine 1638 cannon of San Paolo (with portrait of San Paolo) made for Livorno Castle. Upstairs from the courtyard to the Loggia are arrayed Giambologna's bronze birds (made for the Medici Villa di Castello).

On the walls of the Salone del Consiglio Generale (the old court room) on the first floor are the trial reliefs for the second set of Baptistry doors by Brunelleschi and Ghiberti, both depicting the *Sacrifice of Isaac*. The room is filled with masterpieces from the Renaissance, notably Donatello's *David*, his *San Giorgio* from the Orsanmichele, his *Marzocco* (stone lion and city mascot) that once stood on the Ponte Vecchio, his *Cupid*, all fine examples of his remarkable originality. There are also works by Verrocchio, Luca della Robbia and others.

Elsewhere on the first floor there are rooms devoted to Islamic art, Renaissance jewellery, clocks, ivory (including an eighth-century chest from Northumbria), maiolica and others. There is also the Cappella del Podesta with its frescoes from the school of Giotto. The *Paradise* above the altar is attributed to Giotto with, bottom right, a portrait of Dante in red behind the kneeling figure. The lectern is from the Church of San Miniato.

On the second floor are fine works of the della Robbia workshop, works by Antonio Pollaiuolo, and by Verrocchio, including the lovely bust of a lady holding flowers. As well as medals and armour, there is also the most important collection in Italy of small bronzes, which became fashionable in Florence in imitation of the Ancient Romans and are often copies of antique art or miniatures of art of the time.

Emerging from the Bargello and turning left will take you to Piazza San Firenze, dominated by the eighteenth-century Baroque church of **San Firenze**, now mostly used as law courts. By then turning right into Via Gondi you will pass the lovely 1489 **Palazzo Gondi by Giuliano da Sangallo** (right, number 2) completed only last-century. Continue on to Piazza della Signoria.

You may prefer to continue on to Santa Croce, either by following the next route, or by taking Via della Vigna Vecchia, to the right of the Bargello. This passes the fourteenth-century **Palazzo Covoni** (at number 9) and a little after, the Church of **San Simone** with seventeenth-century wooden ceiling, a 1363 tabernacle with Della Robbia enamel work and the excellent 1307 *San Pietro* (first altar on the right) which is by the Master of Santa Cecilia. Bear right here, cross Via Anguillara, follow the curve of Via Bentaccordi (the contour of the old Roman amphitheatre) to Piazza Peruzzi and then Via dei Rustici to the back of San Remigio where you may rejoin the route below.

Santa Croce and its vicinity

If you go east from Piazza della Signoria, take Via dei Ninna to the right of the Palazzo Vecchio (as you look at the main entrance) which then becomes Via dei Neri, on the corner of which is the **Loggia del Grano** (corn market), dating from the time of Cosimo II and beyond it the fourteenth-century **Palazzo Fagni**. It passes Via de' Magalotti which leads to the eleventh-century church of **San Remigio** (open for services) which has a fine Gothic interior with fresco fragments from the school of Giotto and, in the left aisle, a lovely *Madonna and Child* by the Master of San Remigio, a follower of Cimabue. Also worth a look is the 1591 *Immaculate Conception* by Empoli, in the chapel to the left of the high altar.

Via dei Neri crosses Via de'Benci into Corso dei Tintori. Before proceeding along it go left along Via de' Benci until, on the far side of Borgo Santa Croce, right, is the thirteenth-century **Torre degli Alberti** with fifteenth-century loggia. **Borgo Santa Croce** is a highly attractive street with some fine palaces including number 8, the **Casa Morra**, which belonged to Vasari and number 6 with its fine courtyard.

Museo Horne

On Via de' Benci in the other direction is (at number 6) the Palazzo Corsi, by Cronaca, now the Museo della Fondazione Horne, which has a good collection of fourteenth and sixteenth-century paintings, sculpture, furniture and objets d' art. These were formerly in the possession of the English art historian Percy Horne, who died in 1916, bequeathing his collection and house to the Italian nation. There are works by Dosso Dossi, Giambologna, Pietro Lorenzetti, Gozzoli, Signorelli, Giotto, Filippino and Filippo Lippi, and it includes a contemporary copy of Leonardo's lost *Battle of Anghiari*. (Open 09.00-13.00; closed Sundays.)

At Via de' Benci, 5, is the 1430 **Palazzo Bardi alle Grazie**, thought to be by Brunelleschi and once famous for its opera productions. Number 1 was built on the site of the residence of the Alberti family, from whom sprung the great Renaissance man Leon Battista Alberti, who died here.

On Via dei Tintori (dyers street) is the late fourteenth-century **Palazzo Alberti**, opposite the Museo Horne. This street then leads to Via Magliabecchi, which leads, left, to Piazza Santa Croce.

Via Magliabecchi passes, left, the attractive **Palazzo Rasponi-Spinelli** at number 10, and, right, the **Biblioteca Nazionale** (National Library), built from 1911 and based on the collections of the seventeenth and eighteenth centuries bibliophile A. Magliabecchi, the Biblioteca Palatina-Medicea and Ferdinando III. Next to it is the entrance to the Museo dell'Opera di Santa Croce and the Cappella dei Pazzi.

Museo dell' Opera di Santa Croce and Cappella dei Pazzi

Open 10.00-12.30 and 14.30-18.30 or 15.00-17.00 in winter.

The entrance leads to the fourteenth-century First Cloister of Santa Croce with, under the arcade to the left, nineteenth-century works from the demolished Chiostro dei Morti. This First Cloister was itself originally divided into two by a building that ran from the church to the refectory. On the lawn is Henry Moore's *Warrior* (a gift to the city). At the back is the Pazzi Chapel, beneath the nineteenth-century neo-Gothic campanile; the Museum is to your right.

The Franciscan monastery grew with the church. The fourteenth-century saw the construction of a refectory, dormitory, infirmary and library. Fire destroyed some of these buildings in 1423 - they were rebuilt with help from the government and wealthy families like the Medici and Pazzi. The monastery was to produce three Popes and 32 two bishops. Dante also began his education here. Although much reduced, the monastery continues to function.

In the old refectory is Cimabue's *Crucifixion*, one of his masterpieces, and a 1340 *Last Supper* by Taddeo Gaddi, the earliest of many in Florence. On the other walls are the remains of the Orcagna frescoes, the *Triumph of Death* and *Hell*, that formerly decorated the church, as well as other fragments. Also here is Donatello's bronze *St. Louis of Toulouse*, cast for the Orsanmichele. In the small refectory next to it is a fifteenth-century *Madonna and Child* attributed by some to Uccello; and a *Madonna Sewing* by the Master of the Bambino Vispo. The third room (the former Cerchi Chapel) contains a terracotta altarpiece by A. della Robbia and frescoes by Niccolo di Pietro Gerini. In the corridor is a fine fresco from the tomb of a cardinal. In the fourth room are sketches from the Pazzi Chapel including the head of *St. John the Baptist*, attributed by some to Donatello and another haloed head attributed to Desiderio da Settignano. There are also detached frescoes from the fourteenth and fifteenth centuries Tuscan school. In the fifth room is the reconstructed tomb of Gastone della Torre by Tino da Camaino. In the last, sixth room are seventeenth-century works, including ceiling paintings of angels by Matteo Rosselli.

Just before the exit from the cloister is a monument to Florence Nightingale, who was born in the city. On the other side of the museum is the tranquil Second Cloister, by Brunelleschi.

At the back of the First Cloister is the Cappella (chapel) dei Pazzi, one of Brunelleschi's most perfect works, commissioned as a Chapter House by the Pazzi family in 1429. Brunelleschi died in 1446 and the work was completed only in the 1470s. The portico may have been designed by Giuliano da Maiano. The cherubs' heads on the frieze are by the Della Robbia workshop. The cupola of the colonnaded entrance has terracotta decoration by Luca della Robbia and the Pazzi arms surrounded by a garland of fruit.

The interior is one of the masterpieces of the Renaissance - it is of classical clarity, restful and uncluttered. The white background is relieved by the use of carved pietra serena. Note the 12 roundels of the seated *Apostles* by Luca della Robbia; the roundels of the *Evangelists* in the cupola by Donatello or Brunelleschi; and the stained glass, attributed to Baldovinetti, in the sanctuary.

Santa Croce (Church of the Holy Cross)

Open daily 07.30-12.30 and 15.00-18.30.

Next door is the church itself where, according to Dickens, 'every stone in the cloisters is eloquent on great men's deaths'. It looks out over a busy and interesting square, for many centuries a gathering place for citizens, who might have come to listen to the sermons of San Francesco, or to enjoy tournaments and festivals (like the famous jousts of 1469 and 1475 which inspired Poliziano's 'Stanze per la Giostra'), as well as the traditional 'calcio' (football) game which still takes place in June in traditional costume. The game, a rather anarchic one, takes place between the four 'quartiere' of Santa Croce, San Giovanni, Santa Maria Novella and Santo Spirito. Originally the Arno forked around this area, creating an island. Later the square and its surrounding area was the centre of the Florentine wool industry and was surrounded by poor houses. A noticeable medieval feature of the square are the houses, whose upper storeys rest on supporting brackets or 'sporti'. There are two buildings worthy of special note: at number 1, the late-fifteenth-century Palazzo Cocchi-Serristori at the far end opposite the church, (now attributed to G. da Sangallo) and built above a medieval house; and at number 21, the highly decorated Palazzo dell' Antella. The ungainly statue of Dante by the church, which once stood in the centre of the square, is nineteenth-century.

Built over an earlier Franciscan oratory, Santa Croce, was designed for the Franciscans, probably by Arnolfo di Cambio, in 1294. The Franciscans, sent by San Francesco, chose a spot outside the city walls and a poor one at that, in keeping with their vows of poverty. Construction of the new church began at the apse which would have adjoined the old church (which continued to function as building progressed). By 1320 the new church was being used though it was consecrated only in 1442. There were frequent accusations of vainglory by upholders of the faith and indeed funding ceased after 1504, leaving the façade, like many in this city of ancient but uncompleted churches, unfinished until the nineteenth-century. In the period of the Counter Reformation the painter Vasari was asked to redesign the interior. As in many churches, the simplicity of the earlier lines, theoretically a reflection of the spiritual values of the Franciscans, were broken by gaudy, fussy altars and chapels. Between 1254 and 1782 the church was the headquarters of the Holy Inquisition.

The façade was started at the end of the fifteenth-century to a design of Il Cronaca (Simone del Pollaiolo) but ceased following disagreements between financiers and church administrators. It was finally completed in 1863, designed by Nicola Matas, (who is buried beneath the steps) and financed by the Englishman, Sir Francis Sloane (as in Sloane Square, London). Much marble was used in this imitation of Gothic style but the fussiness of the nineteenth-century still detracts from the basic simplicity of the interior. Note the *Triumph of the Cross* above the main door and the fourteenth-century arcade to the left of the church.

The interior

The fifteenth-century rose window above the entrance is attributed to Lorenzo Ghiberti, but immediately noticeable are the windows of the apse at the far end, of kaleidoscopic beauty. The three round windows, immediately above the sets of double windows, are probably the oldest in Florence and may well have been designed by Giotto. The nave is 345 feet (115 metres) long, 120 feet wide and 120 feet high; it is divided into three by pilasters of pietra forte. Although the feeling of simplicity has been retained, there is a lot of decoration along the aisles added in the sixteenth-century. At the same time some of the original decoration (Orcagna's fresco cycle, the choirstalls before the altar and some neighbouring chapels) was destroyed.

To the left as you enter is the monument to Gino Capponi, the historian; to the right the monument to the historian and poet, Giovanni Battista Niccolini – this statue is supposed to have inspired the more famous Statue of Liberty in New York.

Right aisle

A series of altars with sixteenth-century paintings line the wall, the theme is the Passion of Christ. The first is the Antella Chapel with a *Crucifixion* by Santi di Tito. Against the nearby pilaster is the lovely 1478 *Madonna del Latte* (Madonna of milk) by Antonio Rossellino, the younger brother of Rossellino da Settignano. Next is the monument to Michelangelo Buonarroti by Vasari – the artist's death mask was used in the creation of the bust. The next altar is the Buonarroti Chapel, with an *Ascent to Calvary* by Vasari. You then come to the brooding nineteenth-century Monument to Dante (he was buried in Ravenna where he died in exile). He sits grimly above two figures – Italy, left, and Poetry, right. Beneath Dante's feet are the words from the *Divine Comedy* 'Onorate l'altissimo poeta' (bestow honour on the greatest of poets). The third altar is the Zati Chapel, followed by the 1810 monument to the great Italian poet Alfieri, by Canova. The marvellous nearby fifteenth-century pulpit, one of the best from the Renaissance, is by Benedetto da Maiano - the work is of exceptional quality, a perfect example of balance and perspective.

The fourth altar is the Corsi Chapel, then there is a bronze plaque to the poet Carducci, and then the tomb of the great political theorist and playwright, Niccolo Machiavelli, who was Secretary of the Republic of Florence between 1498 and 1512. The 1787 monument, representing *Diplomacy* is by Innocenzo Spinazzi. Next is the tomb of P. Micheli, the botanist.

The fifth altar is the Pazzi Chapel (not to be confused with the other one in the cloister), the family tomb. Next is the tomb of P. Lanzi, art historian and prefect of Florentine Museums. Next to that is the tabernacle containing Donatello's *Annunciation*, made for a now destroyed chapel after a visit to Rome.

Beyond the door is a fine mid-fifteenth-century work by Rossellino da Settignano, the tomb of Leonardo Bruni, the great humanist, philosopher and politician. This piece of Renaissance art, in which the influence of Brunelleschi's architecture is clear, is an attempt to fuse the arts of painting, architecture and sculpture into a whole suggestive of peace and immortality. The nineteenth-century tomb of the composer Rossini is next door – it attempts to emulate Bruni's tomb but is clumsy in comparison.

The sixth altar is the Serristori Chapel. Beyond is the tomb of the nineteenth-century poet Ugo Foscolo, who was re-interred here after being buried first in St. Nicholas churchyard, Chiswick, London. Note the floor tombs near the right transept, among them that of Giovanni Acuto, or Sir John Hawkwood, the English mercenary who often fought for the Florentine Republic. In the transept is also the tomb of Francesco da Barberino Valdelsa (1294-1348) with an epigraph said to have been written by Boccaccio himself. Note too the monument to Prince Neri Corsini with two unpublished poems by Carducci (1835-1907), who was considered the first modern Italian poet.

The first chapel in the transept is the Castellani Chapel, built with money left for the purpose in 1383 by Michele di Vanni di Ser Lotti de' Castellani and dedicated to Sant' Antonio Abate. The frescoes are by Agnolo Gaddi (son of Taddeo) and school. On the walls, from left to right, are episodes from the lives of St. John the Evangelist, Sant' Antonio Abate (note especially his temptation by devils), St. John the Baptist, and St. Nicola of Bari. The altar front is a fourteenth-century sarcophagus of the Pisan school showing the three Marys. The fifteenth-century marble tabernacle is by Mino da Fiesole. The fourteenth-century *Crucifixion* above is by Nicolo di Piero Gerini.

Note the tomb of the Countess of Albany, the wife of Charles III the Pretender to the English throne (who settled in Tuscany, eventually, after the Battle of Culloden) and the lover of the poet Alfieri; and the Polish nobles Oginski and Skotnicki.

The next chapel is the Baroncelli Chapel. Before entering, note the Gothic tomb by the Pisan Giovanni di Balduccio with the Baroncelli coat of arms above its arch and a *Madonna and Child* by Taddeo Gaddi within. The chapel is dedicated to the Virgin of the Annunciation and the *Stories of the Virgin* were also painted by Taddeo Gaddi, one of the greatest painters of the fourteenth-century, a pupil of Giotto. The window, showing the Stigmata of St.Francis, is also by Gaddi. On the altar is a *Coronation of the Virgin* by Giotto.

Nearby a corridor leads to the Sacristy. The beautiful marquetry doorway is probably by Brunelleschi; the sacristy itself is filled with fine fifteenth-century woodwork and, in a corner, a fourteenth-century cabinet. Note the bust of *Christ* by G. della Robbia. The frescoes on the right wall are a *Crucifixion* by T. Gaddi, an *Ascent to Calvary* by Spinello Aretino, and a *Resurrection* and *Ascension* by N. di Pietro Gerini. Behind the 1371 gate is the Rinuccini Chapel dedicated to San Francesco and St. Mary Magdalen, with frescoes (1363-66) by Giovanni da Milano. The lower parts were completed by another artist, probably due to contractual problems. The left wall illustrates events from the life of the Virgin (note the Gioacchino expelled from the Temple, with the ladies holding lambs); on the right, the life of Mary Magdalen. Next to the Sacristy is a shop and the Little Cloister of the Novitiates, now used for the leather workshop (scuola del cuoio).

The Medici Chapel is at the far end of the corridor outside the Sacristy. Cosimo il Vecchio ordered its construction which was undertaken by Michelozzo in 1445. The sixteenth-century *Adoration of the Shepherds* is Florentine School and the fifteenth-century *Madonna Enthroned* is by Paolo Schiavo. On the altar is a blue and white *Madonna and Child* by A. della Robbia. In the glass window, by Baldovinetti, are the saints Cosmas and Damian, to whom the Chapel is dedicated. The *St. John the Baptist* is by Spinello Aretino.

Returning to the main body of the church, head for the chapels either side of the main altar. The one nearest the right transept is the Velluti Chapel, dedicated to St. Michael Archangel. The fourteenth-century frescoes, telling the life of St. Michael were attributed to Cimabue but are now thought to be by Jacopo del Casentino. Next is the Bellacci or Calderini Chapel, dedicated to St. Andrew the Apostle, which was designed by Gherardo Silvani in 1620, with ceiling frescoes by Giovanni da San Giovanni.

The Giugni Chapel is dedicated to all the Apostle saints and once was patronised by the Bonaparte family. Charlotte Bonaparte, niece of Napoleon and daughter of the King of Naples, was buried here in 1839.

The Peruzzi Chapel, dedicated to St. John the Evangelist and St. John the Baptist, is covered in frescoes by Giotto, only rediscovered in 1841, since they had been whitewashed in the eighteenth century. Early attempts to repair the damage have sometimes been clumsy, added to which Giotto's dry plaster method of fresco has a tendency to crumble. They are from a late period of Giotto, 1320-25, and display confidence and maturity. The paintings show (left wall, from top lunette to bottom): *St. Zaccaria* and *Annunciation; Birth of St. John the Baptist*; *Salome and the Head of St. John*; and, right wall:

Vision of St. John the Evangelist; the *Saint Resuscitates Drusiana; St. John Taken to Heaven*. The tomb on the right wall is of V. Peruzzi (1789-1847), a Chancellor of Florence, by Fantacchiotti.

The Bardi Chapel next door, dedicated to St. Francis, was also frescoed by Giotto, the illustrations of the life of the saint considered by many to be his finest work. From the left wall, (from lunette downwards): *St. Francis Divests; St. Francis Appears to Monks at Arles*; the *Death of the Saint* (the two figures on the far left may represent Giotto and Arnolfo di Cambio). Right wall: the *Approval of the Franciscan Rule*; *Trial by Fire Before a Sultan*; the *Vision of Bishop Guido di Assisi*. Above the chapel arch, outside, is *St. Francis* receiving the stigmata. On the altar is a painting on wood of *The Life of St. Francis* from the thirteenth-century Lucca school.

Beyond the high altar is the Major Chapel, dedicated to the Holy Cross and formerly the chapel of the Alberti family. The fourteenth-century frescoes, illustrating the *Legend of the Cross*, are by Agnolo Gaddi. On the right wall (from top): Planting of a Branch of the Tree of Good and Evil over Adam's Tomb; the Tree is Cut Down to Construct the Temple in Jerusalem but is Used to Construct a Bridge; Prediction by the Queen of Sheba that One will Rest on the Wood and Decree the End of the Kingdom of Judas; the Wood Remains Buried Underground; St. Helena Recognises the True Cross.

The left wall comprises: St. Helena Carries the Cross to Jerusalem; the Cross is Stolen by the King of the Persians; the Dream of the Emperor; and the Cross is Returned to Jerusalem.

The Crucifix suspended over the altar is by a follower of Giotto.

To the left of the main altar is the Tolosini Chapel, dedicated to the Assumption of the Madonna. The frescoes are nineteenth-century. Next door is the Benci Chapel, proclaimed the Chapel of the Motherland in honour of World War I soldiers' mothers. The *Pieta* is by Libero Andreotti.

The Ricasoli Chapel, dedicated to St. Anthony of Padua, is decorated with nineteenth-century paintings of his life by Luigi Sabatelli. Next door is the Pulci-Beraldi Chapel dedicated to the Holy Martyrs and covered with the only known frescoes by Bernardo Daddi (1290-1348), a pupil of Giotto. It is thought that Daddi was also responsible for the round part of the window (with Crucifixion) but the contrast with the rest of the window is such that it must have been finished by others. The terracotta on the altar is by G. della Robbia.

The Bardi Chapel is dedicated to Pope San Silvestro and covered with fourteenth-century frescoes by another pupil of Giotto, Maso di

Banco. They illustrate events from the lives of Pope Silvestro and Emperor Constantine. The window is by the same artist.

The chapel in the corner behind a fine seventeenth-century gate is the Niccolini, first dedicated to the Virgin of the Laudi and then, following the fine seventeenth-century reconstruction by G. Dosio, to the Assumption of Mary. The frescoes in the vault are by Baldassare Franceschini, known as il Volterrano.

The Bardi di Vernio Chapel, dedicated to Ludovic of Tolosa, St. Bartholomew and to the Crucifixion, contains, at the altar, a magnificent wooden *Crucifixion* by Donatello. Legend has it that the figure was criticised by Brunelleschi for being too 'peasant' like. In the little chapel next door is a fine fourteenth-century Pisan school sarcophagus with a sculpture of a member of the Bardi family.

The last of the major chapels is the Machiavelli or San Lorenzo Chapel, dedicated first to saints Jacob and Francis by Guido Machiavelli and later to San Lorenzo by the Salviati family. On the altar is a beautiful *Martyrdom of San Lorenzo* by Jacopo Ligozzi (1547-1626). Also notable is the nineteenth-century tomb of the Polish noblewoman Sofia Zamoyska by Lorenzo Bartolini.

Outside the chapel is the monument to the Florentine musician Cherubini (1760-1842), after whom the musical conservatory is named.

The north aisle, like the south aisle, is lined with altars. The first is the Biffoli, with a painting of the Pentecost by Vasari. Nearby is a plaque to Toscanelli dal Pozzo, the fifteenth-century geographer and astronomer and to Amerigo Vespucci, the explorer after whom America is named. Here too is another plaque in memory of Vespasiano da Bisticci (1421-1498), the bookseller who has bequeathed so much information about his time and contemporaries.

The organ, made in 1926, is one of the largest in Italy and incorporates the older one of 1579, within it. Beyond is the tomb of the humanist and politician Carlo Marsuppini by Desiderio di Settignano (1428-64). It is interesting to compare this tomb with the one of Bruno Latini on the other side of the church.

The second altar is the Asini Chapel with, adjacent, a lovely tabernacle and *Pieta*, by Bronzino. Note too the fine floor tomb, with eagle emblem, of Lorenzo Ghiberti, creator of the Baptistry doors.

The third altar is the Guidacci Chapel with altar piece by Vasari. At the base of a nearby pilaster is the tomb of Giorgio Vasari himself. Nearby is a memorial to the painter Raphael Sanzio who is buried in Rome. The fourth altar is the Berti Chapel with a *Supper of Emmaus* by Santi di Tito. Nearby is a memorial to Leonardo da Vinci, who is buried in France. The fifth altar is the Medici Chapel with a *Resurrection* by Santi di Tito. Then, the tomb of Galileo Galilei (1564-1642), the mathematician and astromomer (see History section). It was financed by Galileo's pupil Viviani who wanted to be buried with his master. Most of the tomb was built after 1734 to an earlier baroque design by G. B. Foggini. The statues represent Astronomy and Geometry. The sixth altar is the Verrazzano Chapel.

In the middle area of the nave is the floor tomb of Giovanni (John) Catrik who died in 1419 and was the English ambassador to the Florentine Republic.

From Santa Croce to the Casa Buonarroti

To the left of Santa Croce runs Via di San Giuseppe, leading past Via delle Pinzochere (which leads to Michelangelo's house) to the churches of Santa Maria della Croce al Tempio (closed) and San Giuseppe (open 17.00-19.00) built in 1519 by Baccio d'Agnolo. Within are some winsome eighteenth-century frescoes, an eighteenth-century organ and a triptych by T. Gaddi. Anthony Trollope, the English writer, lived in the house next to Santa Croce.

The **Casa Buonarroti**, Michelangelo's house, is at Via Ghibellina, 70. In fact it consists of three houses bought by Michelangelo in 1508 which were left to his nephew, Leonardo who made a single house of them. In 1612 Leonardo's son turned part of it into a gallery, in memory of the great artist. The museum took on its present form in 1858.

The house was decorated by Florentine artists at the beginning of the sixteenth-century. The museum contains an interesting collection of Michelangelo sculptures including the *Madonna of the Steps*, his earliest known work when he was about 16; a clay and wood torso intended for the Medici Chapel; and a wooden Crucifix found only in 1963. There are also drawings as well as works by his descendants and works by other artists. Interesting, too, is a bronze bust of Michelangelo by Daniele da Volterra. (Open 09.30-13.30; closed Tuesdays.)

Sant' Ambrogio and Santa Maria Maddalena dei Pazzi

From the Casa Buonarroti you can continue along Via Ghibellina and turn left along Via de' Macci until you reach the thirteenth-century church of **Sant' Ambrogio** with its nineteenth-century façade. On the way you may care to have a look at the market (mercato) of Sant'

Ambrogio, just east of Via Macci and south of the church on Piazza Ghiberti. This farmers' market is housed in a cast-iron building of 1873.

In the church, to the right of the choir, is the Chapel of the Miracle with a beautiful 1481 tabernacle, containing a miraculous chalice, by Mino da Fiesole who is buried here, and a fifteenth-century fresco of a procession of the miraculous chalice by Cosimo Rosselli. On the north side, near the fourth altar, with its *Saints* and *Annunciation* attributed to Raffaellino del Garbo, is the tomb of the artist Verrocchio (Leonardo's teacher), who died in 1488. On the north wall is an *Angels and Saints* by A. Baldovinetti and on the west a *Martyrdom of San Sebastiano* by A. Gaddi. On the south side, by the first altar, is the tomb of the painter Simone del Pollaiuolo, known as Il Cronaca; by the second altar, a fine fresco of *Madonna and Saints* by the Orcagna school.

From the church, Via Pietrapiana leads to **Piazza dei Ciompi** (named after the 1378 revolt of the clothmakers), graced by the 1568 Loggia del Pesce, designed by Vasari as a fish market following the demolition of the Mercato Vecchio. A flea market (mercatino) takes place in this square, once the home of Lorenzo Ghiberti, creator of the Doors of Paradise on the Baptistry.

Via Pietrapiana continues to Via de' Pepi, right. Take this to Via dei Pilastri; turn left and then right into Borgo Pinti. (If you turn right at Via Pilastri and then left into Via Farini you will come to the nineteenth-century **Synagogue**, built after the Jewish community was freed from the ghetto in the area of Piazza della Repubblica where they had been confined since 1571. There is a small museum upstairs. For opening hours, telephone 245252 between 09.30 and 13.00.)

At 58 Borgo dei Pinti is the Church of **Santa Maria dei Pazzi** named after a canonised Carmelite nun, a member of the eminent Pazzi family. The church was founded in 1257; a Cistercian convent arose from 1321, later becoming a Carmelite convent. The church was largely rebuilt by G. da Sangallo in 1492. Baroque additions were made in the seventeenth century.

To the right of the entrance to the Convent is the **Lily Chapel** (Cappella del Giglio) with some good 1600 frescoes by Poccetti. You may need to ask at the Convent for admission.

The ceiling painting dates from 1677 and is by J. Chiavistelli and M. Molinari. The main east chapel is a particularly fine example of Florentine Baroque. The third chapel on the left (north) side has an altarpiece, *Agony in the Garden*, by Santi di Tito and stained glass by

Ponte Santa Trinita from the Ponte Vecchio.

Domenico del Ghirlandaio. Above all the church is known for a fine fresco in the Chapter House (entered from the crypt). This is a Perugino masterpiece, a *Crucifixion and Saints*, in an excellent state of preservation. The church also has a beautiful cloister.

Borgo Pinti continues north past the late-fifteenth-century **Palazzo Ximenes** (68, right, on the corner of Via della Colonna), once the home of the Sangallo brothers, the noted fifteenth-century architects. It then passes Via G. Giusti which, left, leads to the **German Institute** and the former house of the painter, Andrea del Sarto. Borgo Pinti continues past the **Palazzo della Gherardesca** at 99 (built by G. da Sangallo), which has a lovely garden. It finishes at **Piazza Donatello** with its nineteenth-century Protestant cemetery, often known as 'the **English Cemetery**', since several eminent English people are buried here, notably the poet Elizabeth Barrett Browning (to the left of the main path). Walter Savage Landor is also buried here, as well as many Protestants from around the world.

Borgo Pinti southwards takes you to Piazza San Pier Maggio, and along Via Palmieri to Via de' Pandolfini (right) where number 14 was the **Palazzo of the Valori** who led the siege of Florence in 1530. Via Palmieri then crosses Via Ghibellina with the fourteenth-century **Palazzo Salvati Quaratesi** on the corner. Along Via Ghibellina to the right is **Palazzo Borghese** at 110, built by the husband of Napoleon's sister Pauline to celebrate the marriage of Ferdinando III. The entrance to the **Teatro Verdi** is at Via Ghibellina, 99. Via Ghibellina brings you out near the Badia and the Bargello.

The Uffizi Gallery

Open 09.00-19.00; closes at 13.00 on Sunday. Closed on Mondays.

Containing one of the most important collections of art in the world, the Galleria degli Uffizi extends from Piazza della Signoria, between the Palazzo Vecchio and the Loggia dei Lanzi, to the river. It was built by Vasari, a commission from Cosimo I, to be government offices ('uffici' hence 'uffizi'). His innovation was to use iron reinforcement on the sandy ground. It incorporates the old mint which produced gold 'florins' and the church of S. Pier Scheraggio. Provision was also made to house the Medici art collection which became public property in 1737. The State Archives, dating back to the eighth-century, were housed here until 1988. Outside, the pilasters of the long arcade have nineteenth-century statues of illustrious Tuscans in their niches.

The entrance is under the colonnade on the left as you leave the Palazzo Vecchio. The collection, arranged chronologically by school, is vast and well labelled, so only the highlights are mentioned here. There are plans afoot to reorganise the collection, and although there is a tradition of delay in Italy, the following information will need to be reconfirmed when you visit.

The remains of San Pier Scheraggio, once one of the largest churches in the city, are beyond the entrance hall. Here are Andrea del Castagno's 1450 frescoes from the Villa Pandolfini with portraits of Dante, Boccaccio and Petrarch. Beyond are works by Maestro di San Martino alla Palma and Giovanni del Ponte from the original church. In the corridor nearby is Botticelli's *Annunciation* from San Martino della Scala.

The galleries are on the third floor. The staircase passes the theatre by Buontalenti for Francesco I and the Prints and Drawings room, open to scholars by arrangement. There is a lift for disabled visitors. The stairs bring you to the Vestibule in the east corridor, with Room I to your right and Rooms II-XXIV to your left.

Highlights

Room I is devoted to ancient Greek and Roman sculpture. **Room II:** Thirteenth-century Tuscan school, notably a *Madonna* painted by Cimabue for San Trinita, the *Rucellai Madonna* by Duccio di Boninsegna (commissioned for Santa Maria Novella) with original frame, and a *Madonna* by Giotto for the Church of Ognissanti. The Polyptych of the *Badia* is also by Giotto. **Room III:** Fourteenth-century Sienese school. Note the A. Lorenzetti *Presentation of the Temple* and the *Annunciation* by Simone Martini. **Room IV**: Fourteenth-century Florentine school with Orcagna's *St. Matthew*, Giottino's *Deposition* from the Church of San Remigio. **Rooms V and VI**: Late Gothic with Lorenzo Monaco's *Adoration of the Magi* and Gherardo Starnina or Fra Angelico's *Thebaid Hermits*. **Room VII**: Fifteenth-century Florentine school. Veneziano's *Madonna and Saints*, Piero della Francesca's portrait of *Federico di Montefeltro and his wife, Battista Sforza*, and Paolo Uccello's *Battle of San Romano*, formerly in Il Magnifico's bedroom in the Medici Palace are featured.

Room VIII: Early fifteenth-century Florentine school. The works of Filippo Lippi are included with A. Baldovinetti's *Annunciation*. **Room IX**: Features the works of the Pollaiolo Brothers and early Botticelli.

Rooms X-XIV: These are now one room with part of the old Medici Theatre exposed. The works of Botticelli include his *Annunciation*, his *Adoration of the Magi* (with self-portrait on far right and portraits of Medici courtiers around Il Magnifico), his *Primavera/Spring* and *Birth of Venus*; also Lorenzo di Credi's *Venus*. **Room XV**: contains early Leonardo da Vinci and Verrocchio.

Room XVI: This is La Sala delle Carte Geografiche, or the map room, with maps of Tuscany by Stefano Bonsignori (1589). **Room XVII**: The Sala dell' Ermafrodito (The Hermaphrodite Room) includes a copy of a Greek work of 200 BC.

Room XVIII: The 1584 octagonal Tribuna with mother-of-pearl dome by Buontalenti was designed to display the most highly valued objects of the Medici collection, now confined to sculpture, including *The Medici Venus* and other antique works. The cabinet in ebony and pietre dure (1650) belonged to Ferdinando II. On the walls there are portraits of the Medici family and court members by Bronzino plus works by Pontormo and others.

Room XIX: This contains the works of Perugino and Signorelli. **Room XX**: Dürer and the German School. **Room XXI**: Venetian school, particularly Giorgione and Bellini; also Carpaccio. **Room XXII**: German and Flemish work with portraits of *Sir Thomas More* and *Sir Richard Southwell*. **Room XXIII**: Includes Mantegna's portrait of *Cardinal Carlo de'Medici* and *Adoration of the Magi*, *Circumcision* and *Ascension* triptych.

Room XXIV: Contains a collection of fifteenth to eighteenth-century miniatures. The short south corridor (with good views of Florence), is lined with mostly antique sculpture.

The west corridor

Room XXV: The works of Michelangelo include his only completed oil painting. **Room XXVI**: The works of Raphael include portraits of Medici Pope *Leo X* and Cardinal *Giulio de' Medici* plus Andrea del Sarto's *Madonna of the Harpies*.

Room XXVII: The works of Pontormo. Room **XXVIII**: The works of Titian (Tiziano), particularly the *Venus of Urbino*.

Rooms XXIX/XXX: Sixteenth-century Emilian School with Parmigianino's Mannerist *Madonna dal collo lungo* (Madonna with long neck).

Rooms XXXI/XXXII: Veneto (Venice region) School. Works of Dosso Dossi and Sebastiano del Piombo's *Death of Adonis*.

Room XXXIII: An equestrian portrait of *Francis I* by Francois Clouet and Alessandro Allori's portrait of the writer *Torquato Tasso* are included. **Room XXXIV**: The works of Veronese, Moroni and the Venetian school are displayed.

Near here is the entrance to the Vasariano Corridor, lined with a series of self-portraits, and running across the Ponte Vecchio (see 'Ponte Vecchio' below). Permission to see this is generally granted by previous appointment from the administrative offices on the third floor near the entrance to the gallery.

Room XXXV: The works of Tintoretto and Bassano. **Room XXXXI**: Works of Rubens and Van Dyck, and a portrait of *Galileo* by Sustermans. **Room XXXXII**: The Niobe Room, frescoed in the 1770s by Tommaso Gherardini. The name of the room is taken from a Roman copy of a Greek original of Niobe and her children found in Rome in 1583.

Room XXXXIII: Works of Caravaggio. **Room XXXXIV**: Works of Rembrandt. **Room XXXXV**: Eighteenth-century work including Goya's portraits of *Maria Theresa*, and of *Alfieri and the Countess of Albany* by Francoise Xavier Fabre.

At the end of the corridor is a door to the roof of the Loggia on Piazza della Signoria.

San Stefano al Ponte (St. Stephen by the Bridge)

This church sits a little way from the river bank between the Uffizi and the Ponte Vecchio. The first church was built on the site in 969. The Romanesque façade is from 1233; inside there are works by Santi di Tito and others including some fine Mannerist altar steps by Buontalenti.

FOURTEEN

Florence – Oltrarno

The area on the other side of the river from the political centre is known as Oltrarno (beyond the Arno), a quieter, less fashionable area of the city but in a sense its residential heart. In general there are fewer people here so you are able to explore to your heart's content. It is known as an antique centre and was and still is an artisanal area, filled with workshops devoted to carpentry and woodcarving, the work spilling out on to the streets, most notably on Via Santa Monica, Borgo San Iacopo, Borgo San Frediano, Via Maggio and Via Sant' Agostino.

The Ponte Vecchio and the Ponte San Trinita bring you into the area.

The Ponte Vecchio and the Pitti Palace

The Uffizi is linked to the Pitti via the Vasari Gallery and the Ponte Vecchio. **The Corridoio Vasariano** was built in 1565 on the occasion of the marriage of Francesco de' Medici and Joanna of Austria, its purpose to connect the new residence, the Pitti, with the old one and the Uffizi and runs along the top of the Ponte Vecchio and, to quote Charles Dickens 'it takes its jealous course among the streets and houses, with true despotism'. It is lined with a notable collection of self-portraits and other paintings (see Uffizi Gallery above).

The **Ponte Vecchio** itself is distinguished by the medieval shops that line it. Until 1218 the only bridge in the city was at this, the narrowest point, close to the site of the old Roman bridge. This construction dates back to 1345 and is probably the work of Taddeo Gaddi. The very pretty jewellery shops extend over the edge of the bridge, supported by brackets and devoted to the art of the goldsmith,

The Ponte Vecchio from Oltrarno.

associated with Florence since the fifteenth-century – they replace the butcher shops that were once there. The most famous of Florentine goldsmiths (and many artists were trained as goldsmiths) is Cellini whose bust is in the middle of the bridge. During World War II special orders were given to the retreating Germans not to blow it up.

Florence's other famous bridge, the **Ponte San Trinita** which you see to the right as you cross from the Uffizi side, was not so lucky. However, with great difficulty it has been reconstructed according to the design by Ammannati in 1567. Reproduction of the three elegant arches was remarkably difficult, demonstrating once again the astonishing skills of early architects and engineers. Its *Four Seasons* statues were recovered from the river.

After the Ponte Vecchio you cross Borgo San Jacopo and enter Via Guiccardini which leads to Palazzo Pitti. You will pass Piazza Santa Felicita, left, with a granite column of 1381 marking the site of an early Christian cemetery. The church of **Santa Felicita** (a Roman martyr) is one of the oldest in the city, though this construction is from only 1736. The original was built by Syrian Greek merchants who settled in and introduced Christianity to the area in the second-century. The interior is noteworthy for some fine sixteenth-century Florentine art: by Pontormo and Bronzino in the Capponi chapel (first on right): and a *Madonna and Child* by Taddeo Gaddi in the Sacristy.

Just before the point where the street opens up to reveal the Pitti Palace you pass, left, the **Palazzo Guicciardini** built on the site of the residence of Luigi di Piero Guicciardini, a Gonfalonier of Justice, razed during the Ciompi uprising of 1378. The historian and political philosopher Francesco Guicciardini was born here in 1483. Machiavelli lived in a house on the site of number 18.

Among the attractive houses facing the Pitti Palace, number 21 was the home of the Russian writer Dostoyevsky while he wrote *The Idiot*.

Palazzo Pitti and its museums

The Galleria di Palazzo Pitti (Galleria Palatina) is open 09.00-14.00 or 13.00 on Sunday. Closed Mondays.

The Museo degli Argenti (Treasure Museum) has the same hours as the Galleria.

Appartamenti Monumentali (Ducal apartments) are open 09.00-14.00 or 13.00 Sundays).

Museo delle Porcellane (Porcelain Museum). Visits by prior arangement; call 212557.

Galleria del Costume (Costume Museum) and Galleria d'Arte Moderna (Gallery of Modern Art), have hours as the Galleria.

Collezione Contini Bonacossi has visits on Tuesdays, Thursdays, and Saturdays at 10.00 by previous appointment with the Uffizi offices; call 218341.

Check what your ticket buys you for it is quite likely to be valid for two or more of the museums. Tickets are purchased just off the courtyard inside the entrance.

This massive palace was started in 1457, the design attributed to Brunelleschi, although Luca Fancelli and another unknown architect are known to have been involved in its construction.

The Pitti family were powerful banking rivals to the Medici. The palace was bought by Cosimo I's wife, Eleanora di Toledo in 1549. Soon after it became the official residence and seat of the Medici Grand-Dukes and was used by the rulers of Florence until 1919, after which it was presented to the state.

Originally it consisted only of the central section, until 1616 when it was enlarged by Giulio and Alfonso Parigi. The two wings at right angles to the main building were added in the eighteenth and nineteenth centuries. You enter into an Atrium by Pasquale Poccianti of 1850. This leads to a courtyard, the Cortile dell'Ammannati, a marvellous example of Florentine Mannerist architecture which was used for entertainments. The 'Fontana del Carciofo' (the artichoke fountain) on the terrace is by Susini (1641) and originally was crowned by a bronze artichoke. Beyond are the Boboli Gardens (see below).

To the right is the entrance to Florence's other major art collection, the Galeria Palatina, and to the ducal apartments. The collection was started by the seventeenth-century Medici dukes and was substantially supplemented until 1713. The paintings were arranged in 1771, as they are today, in rooms decorated by Pietro da Cortona and Ciro Ferri. The collection was opened to the public in 1833 and although some of the paintings have been moved to the Uffizi, the presentation is just as it was in 1833 and feels very much like a private collection. They are not in chronological sequence but are well labelled.

Galleria Palatina

The entrance is up the Grand Staircase (no lift) by Ammannati. The Anticamera (Sala degli Staffieri, the footmen's room) contains sculpture by Bandinelli and Francavilla. The neighbouring **Galleria delle Statue** is filled with Florentine tapestries as well as other statues and seascapes by Van der Velde the Elder. Left of this room is the **Sala delle Nicchie** (room of nooks and crannies) in neo-classical style by G. Terreni and G. Castagnoli.

Straight on from the Galleria delle Statue is the **Sala del Castagnoli** decorated by the artist of the same name. The table in pietre dure was made in 1837-50 in Florence. The *St. Sebastian* is by Sodoma. Left of this room is the **Sala di Venere** (Venus room) with ceiling by Pietro da Cortona, who also did the four rooms to the right of it. In the Sala di Venere are works by Titian (Tiziano), Rubens, and others, sculpture by Canova and seascapes by S. Rosa.

Sala di Apollo (Apollo room): Andrea del Sarto's *Holy Family*; Rosso Fiorentino's *Madonna and Saints* painted for Santo Spirito; Titian's *Portrait of a Gentleman* and *Mary Magdalen*. **Sala di Marte** (Mars Room): Titian, Tintoretto, Van Dyck, Rubens's *Consequences of War* and *Four Philosophers* including a self-portrait, Veronese and Murillo. **Sala di Giove** (Jove's Room): The Medici Throne Room. Raphael's *Portrait of a Lady*; Verrocchio's *Head of St. Jerome*; Fra' Bartolomeo's *Deposition*; Andrea del Sarto's *St. John the Baptist*. **Sala di Saturno** (Saturn Room): Raphael's tondo the *Madonna della Seggiola* (Madonna of the Chair) and portraits of *Maddalena Doni* and *Agnolo Doni*; Perugino's *Deposition*.

Sala dell'Iliade (Iliad Room): Ceiling decorated with scenes from the Iliad by Sabatelli (1819). Portrait of *Elizabeth I* of England; Raphael's portrait of *Pregnant Woman* (La Gravida); works by Titian; Andrea del Sarto's two *Assumptions*.

To the right is the first of a series of rooms in neo-classical style. These rooms, worth visiting for their sumptuous appointments, contain smaller works of artists including Botticelli, Pontormo, Lippi, Raphael, Rubens and many others.

Appartamenti Monumentali (Ducal Apartments)

These are usually entered from the Sala delle Nicchie (see above). They were mostly decorated in the nineteenth-century by the dukes of Lorraine and are filled with portraits of the Medici by Sustermans, the Flemish painter who was attached to the Medici court from 1619-81, and eighteenth-century Gobelins tapestries.

Left of the Sala delle Nicchie is the **Sala Verde** (green room) with *Allegory of Peace between Florence and Fiesole* by Luca Giordano and 1680 cabinet made for Vittoria della Rovere. Next is the **Sala del Trono** (throne room) and then the **Sala Celeste** (celestial room), the **Cappella** (chapel), the **Sala dei Pappagalli** (parrot room), the **Sala Gialla** (yellow room), **Camera da Letto della Regina Margherita** (Queen Margaret's bedroom) with hunting tapestries featuring Louis XV, the **Toilette della Regina** (Queen's dressing room) in Chinese style, and Sala di **Musica della Regina** (Queen's music room).

The entrance to the Appartamenti di Umberto I is from the Sala dei Pappagalli, with more Sustermans portraits.

The Galleria d'Arte Moderna

This is on the floor above, in rooms decorated by the last Grand-Dukes, and features Tuscan art from the eighteenth century to World War II, including the work of the nineteenth-century Tuscan Impressionists, the 'Macchiaioli'.

The Museo degli Argenti

This is entered from the left side of the main courtyard. It is arranged in the summer apartments of the Grand-Dukes and contains the more eclectic items of the Medici treasury, including a collection of Roman vases in pietre dure that belonged to Lorenzo il Magnifico. In the

Grotticina there is a limewood relef by Grinling Gibbons presented by Charles II to Cosimo III in 1682. There is work by local craftsmen in the Chapel as well as the jewellery collection, church silver, gold and silversmiths' work, and Chinese and Japanese porcelain.

Both the **Collezione Contini-Bonacossi** (a collection of Italian and Spanish art and furniture from the fifteenth to the seventeenth-century, including El Greco, Goya, Veneziano, A. Gaddi, Tintoretto, A. Del Castagno and Bellini) and the **Galleria del Costume** (displaying the history of costume from the eighteenth to the twentieth-century) are in the Palazzina della Meridiana, which is an extension of the Pitti reached by going up the steps from the main courtyard to the Boboli Gardens and turning right.

The Boboli Gardens

The main entrance to this marvellous example of the ornate Italian garden is through the Bacchus Gate to the left of the Pitti Palace. There are also entrances at the Ammannati Courtyard of the Pitti Palace, the Porta Romana, the Forte di Belvedere and the Annalena Gate on Via Romana. In general the Pitti, Bacchus Gate and the Porta Romana entrances are open during the day.

The gardens, used as a setting for the 'Maggio Musicale Fiorentino' every May, were designed to follow the natural contours of the land by Niccolo Pericoli and completed by Ammannati and Buontalenti. They date from 1560, with some alterations made by Parigi in the seventeenth-century. Many celebrations took place here, notably several marriages of the Medici family. They were opened to the public in 1766. The various highlights are well signposted.

The fountain just inside the Bacchus Gate has a statue of Bacchus modelled on a dwarf from the court of Cosimo I. A path leads from here to the artificial grotto by Buontalenti (1583) decorated with statuary, among which a fine *Venus* finishing her bath, by Giambologna, and, in the corners, casts of Michelangelo's 'slaves'. The path winds up behind the Pitti Palace and Artichoke Fountain (see above), offering fine views of the Duomo.

Behind the Palace, a little further up, is the **Amphitheatre** designed by Ammannati as a garden in 1599 with a basin from the Caracalla Baths in Rome and obelisk from Thebes. The theatre was added in 1630. There are Roman statues on the first terrace behind the Amphitheatre. (A path, left, leads to the 1776 Rococo Kaffeehaus by Zanobi del Rosso which opens in Summer.) On the next terrace the pond has a Baroque bronze *Neptune* fountain by Stoldo Lorenzi. The third terrace has a statue of *Plenty* by Giambologna and Tacca.

Still higher up, offering marvellous views, is a garden built on a bastion designed by Michelangelo (Giardino del Cavaliere) with the Fontane delle Scimmie (Fountains of the Apes) by Tacca. From here you see, left, the Belvedere Fortress and San Miniato, and, right, the Bobolino area from which the garden takes its name. The eighteenth-century building here houses the **Museo della Porcellana** (porcelain museum) with Sevres, Berlin, Meissen, Worcester, Capodimonte and other porcelains.

Descending again, turn left onto the Prato dell'Uccellare and take the wide and elegant tree-lined alley (the Viottolone) which leads to the Porta Romana exit. In doing so you will pass the **Piazzale dell' Isolotto**, a Parigi-designed water garden with a small island and Ocean Fountain by Giambologna inspired by Hadrian's gardens at Tivoli outside Rome. Just outside the Porta Romana, left, is the entrance to the former Royal Stables, now the Art Institute.

If you exit via the Annalena Gate you will notice the 1785 **Orangery** by Zanobi del Rosso.

Via Romana

Just past the Pitti Palace Via Romana leads to **Piazza San Felice**. The church here has been attributed to Michelozzo (1457). Inside there is a *Pieta* attributed to Gerini (first altar, right), *a Virgin and Saints* by Ghirlandaio (sixth altar, right), a Neri di Bicci triptych (sixth altar, left) and a School of Giotto Crucifix on the wall of the choir.

Opposite at 8, Piazza Felice, is the **Casa Guidi**, home of the English poets, Robert and Elizabeth Browning after they eloped from London.

At Via Romana, 17, in the Palazzo Torrigiani, is the **Zoological Museum 'La Specola'** which has two sections. One is devoted to an array of stuffed fauna from all over the world, including the hippo which lived in the Boboli Gardens in the eighteenth-century. (Open Mondays, Thursdays, and Fridays 09.00-12.00, and the second Sunday of the month 09.30-12.30.)

The other is the **Museum of Waxes** which displays a series of anatomical models of humans in diseased state commissioned by the morbid Cosimo III. It was opened in 1775. Dickens visited it in 1844 and noted:

'Few admonitions of our frail mortality can be more solemn, and more sad, or strike so home upon the heart, as the counterfeits of Youth and Beauty that are lying there, upon their beds, in their last sleep.'

Also here is the Tribune of Galileo, an 1841 room created in honour of the scientist with inlaid marble and frescoes celebrating the scientific discoveries of the Renaissance. (Open Tuesdays and Saturdays 09.00-12.00, and the second Sunday of the month, 09.30-12.30.)

The **Porta Romana** at the end of the street from the last Comune walls (1284-1333) was designed by Orcagna and built in 1327.

The streets beyond the Arno to Santo Spirito

From the Ponte Vecchio turn right along the Borgo San Iacopo to Piazza Frescobaldi with Palazzo Frescobaldi on the right. Turn left along Via Maggio, passing the fifteenth-century Palazzo Rosselli del Turco at number 40, left, and the **Casa di Bianca Cappello** at 26, right. The latter was designed by the architect Buontalenti in 1566 and is covered in colourful frescoes. Bianca Cappello was the mistress of Francesco dei Medici, the family heir. When his wife died, she persuaded him to marry her so that she became the Grand Duchess. Cardinal Ferdinando dei Medici thus saw his chance of becoming Duke disappear, but when the couple died after a meal at Poggio in 1587 he was deemed the culprit. It is a romantic story and she was a beautiful woman as is clear from the numerous portraits of her in Florence's galleries.

Turn right across Borgo Tegolaio which was the street of brick makers in the Middle Ages to the attractive **Piazza Santo Spirito**. It is a popular place for painters and sellers and was landscaped in the nineteenth-century. The church of Santo Spirito is at one end; the Palazzo Guadagni with its pioneering top portico, (attributed to Il Cronaca, Simone del Pollaiuolo in 1503) at the other. At number 29, to the left of the church, you will find the **Cenacolo di Santo Spirito** in the remains of a fourteenth-century Augustinian monastery, with a 1360 fresco by Orcagna, one of his major works. The refectory contains works by Donatello, Jacopo della Quercia and others, a collection donated by the antiquarian Salvatore Romano in 1946, the Fondazione San Romano. (Open 09.00-14.00, 13.00 on Sundays; closed Mondays.)

Santo Spirito (Church of the Holy Ghost)

Open daily 08.30-12.00 and 15.30-18.30.

A church has stood here since 1292 but this one was started in 1444 to a design by Brunelleschi who died two years after. The project was completed only near the end of the-century to an altered design by Manetti. The façade is eighteenth-century but the interior is a Brunelleschi Renaissance masterpiece, beautifully proportioned in the form of a continuously arcaded Latin cross. It contains a number of fine works of art.

Starting from the right, in the following chapels these include:

Second chapel – a 1549 copy of Michelangelo's *Pieta* in Rome.
In the right transept (15th chapel) there is a 1490 *Virgin with Saints and Donators* by Filippino Lippi.
In the 17th chapel – a 1458 sarcophagus of Neri Capponi attributed to Rossellini.
In the apse (18th chapel) *Virgin and Saints*, school of Lorenzo di Credi.
In the 23rd chapel – fifteenth-century *Annunciation* of Florentine school.
In the 24th chapel – *Nativity*, school of Ghirlandaio.
In the 25th chapel – *Virgin*, Raffaellino del Garbo.
In the left transept (26th chapel) *Santa Monica*, by F. Botticini or Verrocchio.
In the 27th chapel – 1481 *Virgin and Saints*, Roselli.
The 28th chapel – 1492, is designed by Andrea Sansovino.
In the 32nd chapel – *Calvary*, M. Ghirlandaio.
In the left nave (33rd chapel) *Maesta*, Fra Bartolomeo.
In the 37th chapel – *Virgin, St. Anne and Saints*, M. and R. Ghirlandaio.
In the 40th chapel – *Resurrection of Christ* by T. Landini based on work by Michelangelo in Rome.

Below the organ is the fifteenth-century vestibule by Cronaca and the octagonal sacristy by Sangallo. The vestibule leads to the seventeenth-century cloister, likely to be closed.

Santa Maria del Carmine

The other major monument in the area of Oltrarno is the church of Santa Maria del Carmine. From Piazza Santo Spirito turn right at the Palazzo Guadagni end of the square, with your back to the church, into Via Sant' Agostino. Cross Via Maffia and Via de' Serragli (with several handsome palaces) to Via Santa Monaca, crossing Via dell'Ardiglione, where the painter Filippo Lippi was born, to Piazza del Carmine. On the corner of Via Santa Monaca note the 1427 tabernacle with *Madonna and Saints* by Lorenzo di Bicci.

Santa Maria del Carmine and Brancacci chapel

Open 10.00-17.00, or 13.00-17.00 Sunday; closed Tuesdays.

The original Romanesque-Gothic church was destroyed by fire in 1771, though the exterior, sacristy, seventeenth-century Corsini chapel and the Brancacci chapel were saved. The interior was reconstructed in late Baroque style by Giulio Mannaioni.

The church is interesting for the marvellous frescoes in the Brancacci chapel (right transept but entered through the cloister) commissioned by F. Brancacci, a wealthy merchant, later exiled by the Medici. They were started in 1424 by Masolino da Panicale, continued by his pupil Masaccio in 1426, (until he went to Rome where he died when only 27), and finished by Filippino Lippi in 1485. Mostly they deal with the life of St. Peter. The work of Masolino and Lippi are quite similar but the style of Masaccio is unique and his work here is his greatest with a tremendous sense of spatial arrangement – this fresco had enormous influence on fifteenth-century Florentine art. The frescoes are as follows:

Upper, left to right: *Adam and Eve expelled from Paradise* and *Payment of the Tribute* (Masaccio).
St. Peter Preaching (Masolino).
St. Peter Baptising and Healing a Cripple (Masaccio).
St. Peter Raising Tobias from the Dead (Masolino and Masaccio).
The Temptation of Adam (Masolino).

Lower, left to right: *St. Peter visited by St. Paul in Prison* (Lippi).
St. Peter raising the Emperor's Nephew from the Dead (Masaccio and Lippi).
St. Peter in the Pulpit, St. Peter Healing the Sick, and *St. Peter Giving Alms with St. John* (Masaccio).
Crucifixion of St. Peter, St. Peter Before the Consul and *The Angel Delivering St. Peter from Prison* (Lippi).

The **Gothic Sacristy** has frescoes from the life of Santa Cecilia by school of Bicci di Lorenzo. In the rooms off the lovely seventeenth-century **Cloister** are works by Filippo Lippi and others. The **Choir** contains the funerary monument to Piero Soderini, Gonfaloniere of Florence, who died in 1522.

San Frediano in Cestello and Porta San Frediano

Near Santa Maria del Carmine (leave Piazza del Carmine at the end opposite the church and then turn left into Borgo San Frediano) is the late seventeenth-century church of San Frediano in Cestello with a fine dome. Further on, in good condition, is the 1324 Porta San Frediano (with its old locks) and remains of the Comune walls of 1284-1333 that protected the road from Pisa.

In the direction of Ponte Vecchio, Borgo San Frediano becomes Via Santo Spirito and passes, right, the seventeenth-century **Palazzo Rinuccini** and fifteenth-century **Palazzo Manetti**, home from 1740-86 of Sir Horace Mann, British envoy to the Tuscan court, and famous for his correspondence with Horace Walpole. Further along, left, is the **Palazzo Guicciardini** which is now the British Institute.

Borgo San Jacopo

Via di Santo Spirito ends at Piazza dei Frescobaldi, and becomes Borgo San Jacopo. The first building, left, is the seventeenth-century **Palazzo Frescobaldi**. Next door is the **Church of San Jacopo sopr'Arno**, open only for concerts, with Baroque interior and Romanesque pillars. The second altarpiece, left, is by the Englishman, Ignazio Hugford (see Impruneta). On the corner of Via Toscanella is the **Torre Marsili** di Borgo, a medieval tower with a Della Robbia *Annunciation* over the entrance.

Via de' Bardi

This street, named after a wealthy medieval banking family who owned several palaces here, runs east along the Arno for a short way from the Ponte Vecchio and then forks, right, up and away from the river. It is lined with fine buildings, notably at 36, the **Palazzo Capponi delle Rovinate**, with its fine courtyard, the church of **Santa Lucia dei Magnoli** at 24, and on Piazza dei Mozzi, the thirteenth-century **Palazzo dei Mozzi** where Pope Gregory X stayed in 1273.

On the same square is the **Museo Bardini**, an art collection left to Florence in 1922 by the collector and dealer Bardini which includes works by Tino da Camaino, A. Pollaiuolo and others as well as old musical instruments, Persian carpets, armour and funerary objects including an altarpiece by A. della Robbia. (Open 09.00-14.00, 08.00-13.00 on Sunday; closed Wednesday.)

A Symbol of the Republic – Michelangelo's David.

Via di San Niccolo

Via de' Bardi becomes Via di San Niccolo and takes you to the fourteenth-century **San Niccolo sopr'Arno** with a fine Baldovinetti fresco in the sacristy, the *Madonna della Cintola* (Madonna of the girdle). The street passes the **Porta San Miniato**, right, and finishes at **Porta San Niccolo**, built in 1340.

FIFTEEN

Additional sights in the city and suburbs

Above Florence – Bellosguardo to the Belvedere Fortress to San Miniato

The best view of Florence is said to be had from Bellosguardo ('beautiful glance'). **Piazza di Bellosguardo** lies to the west of the Porta Romana, close to the Boboli Gardens.

The scenic area above Florence to the east of the Boboli Gardens is served by the so called **Viale dei Colli** (Avenue of the Hills), linking Piazzale di Porta Romana with Piazza F. Ferrucci by way of Piazzale Michelangelo. In doing so it changes name several times. This road dates back to 1865 when it was constructed as a route for passengers in horse drawn carriages to enjoy the breathtaking view of the city below.

The **Belvedere Fortress** (open 09.00-20.00) can best be reached on foot following pretty Costa di San Giorgio from Piazza Santa Felicita as it climbs past gardens and villas, among them number 19 which belonged to Galileo between 1610 and 1630. The church of San Giorgio sulla Costa has a fine Baroque interior and an early Giotto. Porta San Giorgio is the oldest gate in the city and marks the entrance to the fort designed by Buontalenti in 1590 and opened to the public in 1958. It has fine views and is used for exhibitions. The fort can also be reached from the Boboli Gardens or by car from the Viale dei Colli. To reach San Miniato from here take Via di Belvedere along some well-preserved thirteenth-century walls to Porta San Miniato.

If, however, you wish to explore the rural suburbs of Florence follow Costa di San Giorgio as it becomes Via di Leonardo, an equally delightful street of villas and trees and which passes the charming Romanesque church of **San Leonardo in Arcetri** (open for services or ring the bell at number 25). Via di Leonardo then crosses the wide Viale Galileo (part of the Viale dei Colli) and then forks left to become Via Via Viviani. It forks left again to become Via del Pian dei Giullari (now called Via Guglielmo Righini), passing the road to the Observatory, right, and then forks right, with the fourteenth-century Gallo Tower ahead, left, to the village of **Pian de' Giullari** just over one mile (two kilometres) from Belvedere. In the village, at number 42 is the **Villa di Gioiello** (the Jewel Villa), the home of Galileo from 1631 to his death in 1642 and where he was visited by Thomas Hobbes and reputedly by the poet Milton.

San Miniato al Monte

This church which overlooks the city can be reached on foot from Porta San Miniato beneath Piazzale Michelangelo following the Stations of the Cross up Via di San Salvatore al Monte. If you do not like the idea of the climb, or are short of time, you may go by car or by taking the number 13 bus (from the station or from Piazza dei Giudici by the Uffizi).

To the right of the church is the 1295 Bishop's Palace. Behind the church is the **Holy Doors** cemetery of 1839, the resting place of many local artists.

San Miniato church is one of the masterpieces of Florentine Romanesque architecture and one of the most beautiful churches in Italy, at its most peaceful early in the morning. It was one of the three most important churches in the city. Miniatus was a third-century martyr who was buried here; Benedictine monks started to repair here for the sake of tranquility. In 1018 they decided to build this church to replace a former chapel. The marble and mosaic façade is twelfth-century, with a representation of Christ between the Virgin and San Miniato. The eagle was the symbol of the Calimala cloth guild who paid for part of the decoration. The bell tower was built in 1518.

The unique eleventh-century interior is sombrely faced in green and white marble and the floor is decorated with signs of the zodiac; the pillars were removed from Roman temples. The frescoes on the aisle walls are fifteenth-century. The 1448 ciborium at the end of the nave was made by Michelozzo and decorated in terracotta by L. della Robbia and in paint by A. Gaddi.

The Chapel of the Cardinal of Portugal (1459-66) by Brunelleschi's pupil Manetti, is off the left aisle. It was built for the tomb of Cardinal Jacopo di Lusitania, nephew of King Alfonso of Portugal who died in Florence in 1459. The vault medallions, among his masterpieces, are by L. della Robbia and the painting of saints above the altar and the frescoes of angels on either side are by A. and P. del Pollaiuolo. The cardinal's tomb is by Rossellino.

The eleventh-century crypt with fourteenth-century frescoes by T. Gaddi and the bones of the martyr is at the back of the nave. The raised choir with twelfth-century altar and inlaid wooden stalls of 1470 is charming. Note too the pink alabaster windows. The 1387 sacristy, to the right of the choir, is decorated with the *Life of St. Benedict* by S. Aretino. This in turn leads to the cloister with the remains of frescoes by Paolo Uccello. Permission to enter may be obtained from the monks.

Below San Miniato, towards Piazzale Michelangelo, is the church of San Salvatore al Monte by Cronaca. Michelangelo called it his 'bella villanella', his lovely country maid. In the second chapel, left, is a restored terracotta *Deposition* attributed to G. della Robbia.

Just below the church is Piazzale Michelangelo, offering a splendid view of the Arno, the Ponte Vecchio and the area of the city around the Duomo.

Museo Stibbert

Open 09.00-12.45 or 09.00-12.30 on Sundays. Closed Thursdays. On Sundays only rooms 2-7 and 9 are open. The park is open from 09.00 till dusk every day. Take bus 4 from the station or Duomo. Group tours are conducted every half hour.

This museum, located in the north of the city at Via Stibbert, 26, near Via Vittorio Emanuele, is a wonderful curiosity, the perfect offspring of the Anglo-Italian love affair. Frederick Stibbert (1838-1906) was born in Florence to an English father and an Italian mother. His wealth came from a legacy – he travelled, became an artist and collector and fought with Garibaldi. He built this villa in 1878-1905 to be part residence, part museum. The rooms were each designed to complement different parts of his collection. The park, also Stibbert's, is well worth investigating. Stibbert bequeathed his collection to the British Government, who in turn presented it to Florence.

The collection itself is eclectic in the extreme. Each of the rooms has a name – the Malachite Room, the Dutch Room, the English Room, and so on - that refers to its style, its use or its contents. They contain armour (including the finest collection of Japanese armour in Europe), spurs, porcelain, tapestries, paintings (school of Botticelli, Crivelli, Giordano), furniture, ceramics and costume.

Further north along Via Vittorio Emanuele is Via dei Cappuccini, right, and the **Church of the Convent of the Cappuccini di Montughi**. Within are good paintings from the seventeenth-century Florentine School.

Further south along Via Vittorio Emanuele at 48 is the **Villa Fabbricotti** where Queen Victoria stayed in 1894. Now the Foreigners University, the park is open to the public.

The Viali

The Viali are the broad roads circling the city running pretty well where the old walls were and linking the city gates that remain. Some points of interest have already been mentioned in the course of other visits. Others worth visiting include:

Cascine
Take bus 17C from the station or Duomo.

This is a vast public park, near the Arno west of Ponte della Vittoria, made on land acquired by Alessandro de'Medici and used as hunting land and for celebration and spectacle. It was opened to the public in 1811. At the far end is a monument to the Maharajah of Kolhapur who died in Florence in 1870.

Russian Church
This is located at Via Leone X, west of the Fortezza da Basso. It was consecrated in 1904 and built with the money from the nineteenth-century aristocratic families who used to winter in Florence. The architects were Russian. There are services on the third Sunday of the month.

Giardino dell' Orticoltura
A horticultural garden of 1859 with a particularly fine greenhouse, at Via Bolognese, north of Piazza della Liberta; open daily.

Via Scipione Ammirato
The best examples in Florence of Art Nouveau are to be found at numbers 99 and 101.

Former Convent of San Salvi
Via San Salvi, 16. Open 09.00-14.00, 13.00 Sundays; closed Mondays.

Montepulciano – building on the past.

This is due east of Piazza Beccaria and can be reached by taking bus number 6 from the Duomo. The Vallombrosan abbey church has fourteenth-century origins. In the convent gallery are works by Poppi, Vasari, Michele di Ridiolfo del Ghirlandaio and carved reliefs by Benedetto da Rovezzano. In other rooms are works by Pontormo and Franciabiagio. The best known work, in the Refectory, is Andrea del Sarto's notable *Last Supper* (1511-27), a fresco masterpiece.

SIXTEEN

Chianti and the Near South

The Way to Chianti

If there is one Italian wine that foreign drinkers are familiar with, it is Chianti. Wine has been produced here since the time of the Etruscans and as early as the sixteenth-century it was being exported to England.

So where is Chianti? The word is derived, it is said, from the Latin 'clango' meaning the 'blowing of horns'. Others think that it derives from 'Clante', the name of an eminent Etruscan family. The first recorded use, however, of the word Chianti dates back to the thirteenth-century to describe the area now known as the Chianti hills. Later the three communities of Castellina, Radda and Gaiole formed the Lega di Chianti (League of Chianti), using the symbol of a black rooster, a sort of consortium to protect local interests including wine. Nonetheless, as is always the case in defining the limits of an area that has no official boundaries, just where is Chianti?

It might be said that there are three Chiantis: first, geographical Chianti, which is generally the area lying between the Arno Valley between Florence and Arezzo, the main Arezzo-Siena road and the A1 Autostrada del Sole. Secondly there is wine growing Chianti which refers to a much larger area. This includes Chianti Classico with the addition of the general wine growing areas of Montalbano, the Colli Fiorentini (including Rufina), the Colli Senesi, the Colli Aretini, the Colline Pisane and the Colline Pistoiese. Thirdly there is the Chianti Classico area to the south of Florence, within the provinces of Florence and Siena, starting roughly in the area of Impruneta in the north, and reaching almost to Siena in the south; and lying between the A1 Autostrada del Sole in the west and a variable line between San Polo in Robbiana (north east) and Castelnuovo Berardenga (south east) in the east. The name of Chianti Classico

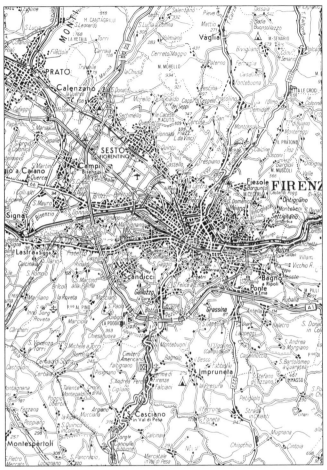

Florence and surrounding area (from the provincial map of Florence, courtesy of Litografia Artistica Cartografica (L.A.C.), Florence).

was adopted in 1924 by producers interested in protecting the wine's reputation and who took the emblem of the Black Rooster, the symbol of the old Chianti League. This area of 172,900 acres or 70,000 hectares, with some 800 farms and estates, includes Castellina in Chianti, Radda in Chianti, Gaiole in Chianti, Greve in Chianti, and parts of San Casciano Val di Pesa, Barberino Val d' Elsa, Tavernelle Val di Pesa, Castelnuovo Berardenga and Poggibonsi. This area corresponds closely to a definition in an edict of 1716 by the Grand Duchy of Tuscany which defined a wine production area for the first time.

It might be said that all three definitions meet in the area known as Chianti Classico, which is supposed to produce the best Chianti wine, has the most obvious Chianti identity and is also the most picturesque. This section, therefore, covers only that area, and those places on its border that have not been covered elsewhere.

Chianti – a rural history

Chianti is essentialy a rural area, where the largest towns, none in fact very large, are market towns. In the Middle Ages it was an area of villages and cultivated land, usually on sunny, well watered hills, linked by paths. Villages usually took their name or part of it from the patron saint. Even today many of the villages consist of nothing more than a turretted noble residence and a few peasant houses clustered around a church and they have barely changed for several hundred years. Feudalism has long disappeared of course and yet in many ways the way of life in these areas is remarkably similar too; ancient terraces are still worked and patches of vine are mixed with other crops. Larger, better organised estates have to a large extent, however, become the norm but the landscape, happily, largely retains a feeling of historical continuity.

Changes began to come about already several centuries ago with the rise of urban capitalism, the influence of which began to make itself felt in the countryside. Villages expanded as houses were built for additional workers and villas were built by the new class of landowner, often of urban background. These villas gradually lost their fortified aspect and took on the loggias and gardens that marked an easier way of life.

Certain families, with their own coats of arms, naturally predominated, and whilst many have dwindled to nothing, some 40, the earliest dating back to 1071, are still producing wine.

Chianti – where to go

The main road to Chianti from Florence is also the Siena road and takes you through the suburbs of Impruneta and Galluzzo. There are two roads in this direction: the older N2 and the superstrada. From the Porta Romana you will pass near the **Villa di Poggio Imperiale** at the top of the Viale del Poggio Imperiale. This sixteenth-century villa with early nineteenth-century neo-classical façade was confiscated by Cosimo I from the Salviati family in 1565. It remained the property of the royal family, taking its name from the Grand Duchess Maria Maddalena. In 1865 it became a boarding school for girls and is now also a state school and international lycee. Inside are some lavishly decorated rooms, the earliest by Matteo Rosselli in 1623 and, the room known as the Sala di Cosimo II, by O. Vannini in the same year. The Sala Verde (green room), overlooking the garden, has some pretty landscapes by G. Angiolini. The Sala di Diana is decorated with some charming hunting scenes by Giuseppe del Moro. In the upstairs loggia, the Peristilo, is a fine sixteenth-century Roman table.

Certosa del Galluzzo

On the way south you will eventually pass the Certosa del Galluzzo (or di Val d'Ema or di Firenze – 'certosa' means Charterhouse or Carthusian monastery), overlooking the road and giving a name to a motorway exit). It was founded in 1341 by Niccolo Acciaiuoli, a wealthy Florentine merchant and banker; it has been run by Cistercians since 1958 when they returned to Florence for the first time since their expulsion in 1782. The buildings are grouped around a fine 1545 courtyard and two cloisters, including the Great Cloister (Chiostro Grande) with majolica tondi by A. and G. della Robbia, overlooked by the monks' cells. To the side is the church adorned with works from the sixteenth-century and the Baroque period; and which incorporates the church of Santa Maria originally built in 1404, with stained glass by Niccolo di Pietro Gerini and some particularly fine tombs of the Acciaioli family, the one of Cardinal Agnolo II thought to be by Francesco da Sangallo. The hostel (Foresteria), formerly a lodging place for popes and kings, is in front of the church.

The **Palazzo degli Studi**, built for Florentines to study the liberal arts, has a fine Gothic hall. There is also a gallery with work by Pontormo formerly in the Great Cloister (painted here between 1522 and 1525 during a residency enforced by an outbreak of plague), Ridolfo del Ghirlandaio, the School of Orcagna and others. Near the entrance is the Pharmacy which sells liqueurs made on the premises.

The Chapel of Santa Caterina dell' Antella

East of Galluzzo is Ponte a Ema and, about half a mile outside it (follow signposts for Bagno a Ripoli), is the charming little chapel of Santa Caterina dell' Antella, built by the Alberti family in 1387. The fresco cycle of Santa Caterina's life is a major work by Spinello Aretino (1373-1410).

Impruneta

South of Certosa, off the N2 a side road leads to the town of Impruneta, noted for its pottery and terracotta tiles (which decorate the roof of Florence Duomo). The traditional horse and cattle fair of St. Luke, visited by the Venetian painter Tiepolo when he wished to draw donkeys, is still held in October in the main, arcaded square overlooked by the principal attraction, the ancient **Collegiata of Santa Maria dell' Impruneta**. This is an ancient building, rebuilt after World War II during which, in its most recent, fifteenth-century Renaissance incarnation, it was badly damaged. Originally it was built in the eleventh-century to house a miraculous painting of the *Madonna and Child*, turned up by a plough in the tenth-century and, according to tradition, the work of St. Luke himself. It was often transported to Florence in times of turbulence to exercise a benign influence. The tower is thirteenth-century; the 1634 portico is by Silvani.

Inside, there are two chapels by Michelozzo of particular note, to the left and right of the choir. To the right is the chapel of the Cross, built to house a fragment of the True Cross, with a marvellous majolica ceiling by Luca della Robbia, who also made the fine tabernacle containing a Crucifixion. The chapel of the Madonna to the left, houses the icon supposedly by St. Luke in a tabernacle flanked by statues of St. Paul and St. Luke by Luca della Robbia, who also made the beautiful ceiling. The story of the restoration of the Madonna in the eighteenth-century by the English artist Ignazio Hugford is entertaining. It had not been visible for centuries, and when in the mid-eighteenth-century the governor of Tuscany expressed a desire to see it, it was discovered that the painting had all but faded completely away. With admirable concern for the spiritual wellbeing, not to say gullibility, of the flock, it was decided to ask Hugford, a painter living in Florence, expert in copying, to paint a

Madonna in Byzantine style, which is what you see today. Ignazio, and his brother Enrico, were the sons of Ignatius Hugford, an English Catholic who had fled from England at the end of the seventeenth-century and who had become watchmaker to the Grand Duke of Tuscany, Cosimo III. The two sons became well known. Enrico became an Abbot who in his early years at the monastery of Santa Reparata di Marradi and discovered a way of working scagliola (plaster made from selenite and which can be made into imitation marble) delicately enough to be used in pictures. He later became Abbot of Vallombrosa where he continued to work on his secret recipe for the preparation of scagliola. Unfortunately his recipe was ever imparted only to one person, his pupil Gori; there are a few of his works at Vallombrosa and also at the Opificio in Florence, which also has work by Gori; and it is thought there must be examples of his fine work in English country houses, since he performed many commissions. Ignazio was an artist of middling quality but a great connoisseur. He did some work at Vallombrosa, as well as other churches, but came to devote more time to collecting and dealing. His collection was pretty good – the Uffizi bought more than 3,000 items from it on his death, including a self-portrait. It seems he was a genial fellow, much loved and respected by the likes of Reynolds and Adam; but not above faking, as we have seen.

The fourteenth-century cloister is to the right of the church. On the first floor (entrance to left of church) the treasury displays, among other things, a fine fifteenth-century silver cross attributed to Lorenzo Ghiberti and a marble relief, probably by a follower of Donatello, illustrating the discovery of St. Luke's icon.

Sant' Andrea in Percussina

On the other side of the N2 is the town of Sant' Andrea in Percussina, where Machiavelli spent his exile, passing the time with wood-cutters in his employ, reading Dante and Petrarch, amusing himself in a local tavern and writing *The Prince*. He describes the vicissitudes of his day to Francesco Vettori in a letter dated 10 December 1513. In the tavern there were rows over gambling

'... and for the most part the row is over a farthing and yet they can hear our shouts from San Casciano. Thus, wallowing in all this lousiness, I keep the mould from my brains, and vent my rage against the malice of my fate, glad to be downtrodden this way, in the hopes of her becoming ashamed of it.'

He is philosophical about his fate but in the same letter he mentions his new pamphlet (*The Prince*). He laments that his expertise is ignored by the Medici but dedicates the book to Giuliano de' Medici

> '... and anybody should be glad to make use of one who is full of experience gained at the expense of others. Nor should there be any doubt as to my fidelity, as having always kept faith, I have no call to learn now how to break it: and he who has been faithful and good for forty-three years, which is my age cannot presumably change his nature; and of my fidelity and goodness my poverty stands as witness'.

The tavern he mentions is still in business, trading somewhat on his name but also serving good Tuscan food. It is called the Tavernetta Machiavelli (Tel: 055 828471; closed Mondays). His house, the Albergaccio, is now a museum devoted to his life.

The nearby **Spedaletto** is also of some interest, a hamlet which is really a group of buildings once used to lodge travellers and pilgrims. A little way south, just off the N2, is the **Poggio Torselli**, a villa originally built by the Corsini family and now one of the largest and most elegant villas in the area. A lane of cypress trees leads up to it; it sells its own wine.

Near Chiesanuova is the **Palazzo al Bosco**, which sells wine and olive oil, and which as one of the most handsome villas in the area, is said to have been designed by Michelangelo. Between Chiesanuova and Cerbaia is the early fifteenth-century **Villa Tattoli**, in pure Tuscan style; it too sells wine and olive oil.

Continuing along the N2

San Casciano in Val di Pesa is a largish town with an historic centre of some charm. It belonged to the Bishops of Florence until 1272 when it became part of the Republic of Florence. Since it was an outpost, it was vulnerable to attack: its walls, of which there are considerable remains, were built by the Duke of Athens in 1342. The Collegiata contains an *Annunciation* by Ghirlandaio; whilst the 1335 church of Santa Maria del Prato ('of the meadow'), near a complete city gate, has retained its fourteenth-century interior and an impressive pulpit by a pupil of Andrea Pisano, Giovanni Balducci da Pisa. There is also a Crucifix attributed to Simone Martini, a painting on the pilasters by T. Gaddi and a tryptych by Ugolino di Neri. The

Virgin Enthroned in the sacristy is attributed to Bartolomeo della Porta.

In the vicinity of the area of San Casciano is the the **Villa Borromeo** (on the right of the Certaldo Road) and, just over a mile along the Mercatale Val di Pesa road is the **Villa le Corti**, owned by the eminent Corsini family for over 600 years and which sells its own wine. The handsome **Villa Caserotta** is also off this road; its current aspect is due to the influence of the eminent Strozzi family who once owned it. From Le Quattro Strade a road leads to the **Villa Palagio**, dating back to 1320, and the village of Campoli, with its Pieve di San Stefano a **Campoli** containing a tabernacle from the Della Robbia school, a *Madonna and Child* by Bugiardini and a wooden sixteenth-century pulpit.

North west of San Casciano is Mucciana and the **Chiesa di San Jacopo** which goes back to the early eleventh century and which is in severe need of repair. Further south is **Bibbione**, on the road to Montefiridolfi, an interesting fortified village with the remains of the fourteenth-century castle, originally erected by the Cadoningi Counts in the tenth century. It eventually came to belong to a branch of the Machiavelli family and is still in the hands of the Marquis Rangoni-Machiavelli. It is now a farm and winery. The same family also owns the nearby Villa Tidi (Il Mocale), which once belonged to the Medici.

Tavarnelle Val di Pesa is an agricultural centre with the Gothic church of Santa Lucia al Borghetto with beamed ceiling and, nearby, the Romanesque Pieve di San Pietro in **Bossolo** with a thirteenth-century painting by Coppo di Marcovaldo.

The **Badia a Passignano** (the Tavarnelle exit from SS2) is an abbey resembling a fortified village once one of the most famous in Tuscany. Most of what you see dates back to the fourteenth century when it was renovated by the Buondelmontis; more work was done in the seventeenth century. In the Abbey Church of San Michele are the paintings of the local painter Domenico Cresti (Passignano) and works by Allori and Ghirlandaio.

North-east of here, just off the road south of Quattro Strade, is **La Torre a Luciana**, a well preserved medieval hamlet once the property of the Pitti family. To the south of Badia is **Rignana**, another small medieval hamlet. **Barberino Val d' Elsa** is a medieval town that has kept much of its fourteenth-century character. The nearby Pieve di San Appiano retains many tenth-century elements.

San Donato in Poggio was the site of the signing of two peace treaties between Florence and Siena in 1176 and 1255 and preserves its medieval layout. In the main square is the fourteenth-century

Gothic church of Santa Maria della Neve ('of the snow'). The Romanesque Pieve di San Donato has an interesting campanile and sixteenth-century terracotta font. To the east of San Donato is the sixteenth-century church of Madonna di Pietra Cupa, with works by Passignano and Paolo Schiavo.

Cortine, on the road from San Donato to Poggibonsi, is a hamlet consisting of the mansion-castle, church and farm buildings. **La Paneretta**, to the east of the superstrada and to the north of Monsanto, is a fifteenth-century fortified mansion that belonged to the Vettoris, a member of whom was Machiavelli's famous correspondent. **Monsanto** has one of the oldest religious buildings buildings in the Chianti region, the Romanesque San Ruffiniano a Monsanto.

The Chiantigiana

The route known as the Chiantigiana, the most scenic and 'typical' through Chianti, is the N222, which passes through or close to the heart of vinicultural Tuscany. It can be reached from Galluzzo by joining the A1, exiting at Firenze Sud and then heading for Grassina. Or, if you have been visiting Impruneta, it can be joined from there. On the way to Greve, the centre for Chianti, there are a few things of interest: the Romanesque church of **San Stefano di Tizzano** and the eleventh-century **Castello di Tizzano**; beyond it is **San Polo in Robbiana**, famous for its irises to which is dedicated a festival in May. The nearby Romanesque church of **San Miniato di Robbiana** dates back to before the tenth century.

The **Castello di Mugnana** on the Dudda road, a castle of strategic importance for one thousand years, sits atop an outcrop overlooking a gorge. It was here, in 1198, that the Tuscan League agreement was signed by Florence and a number of other communes. It is in good repair.

At Chiocchio the road to Passo dei Pecorai and then to Mercatale Val di Pesa leads to the **Castello di Gabbiano**, a restored castle formerly belonging to the Bardi family in the tenth century and then the Soderini in the fifteenth century. It is one of the most interesting buildings in the area and sells wine and olive oil.

Vicchiomaggio, in the loop between Le Bolle and Passo dei Pecorai, once played host to Leonardo da Vinci. There is a castle and hamlet and the small twelfth-century church of Santa Maria a Vicchiomaggio, its fourteenth-century bell the oldest in Chianti.

A narrow street, found in almost every Tuscan town. This one is in Lucca.

Uzzano with its castle formed one of the strongest fortified strongholds in the Greve Valley between the thirteenth and fifteenth centuries. It gradually changed its character, becoming a villa-farm, so that only the bases of the powerful walls have survived from the original building. The Uzzano were an important family in Florence; Niccolo Uzzano and Gino Capponi ran the Florentine Republic at the end of the fourteenth-century.

Verrazzano, on the other side of the SS 222, has its castle too: in it was born the navigator and explorer Giovanni da Verrazzano in 1485. He was the discoverer of New York harbour where the entrance and bridge across it still carry his name. He died mysteriously on another expedition to Brazil in 1528.

Greve

Colognole castle appears on the right of the 222 and soon you are in **Greve**, considered the capital of the area.

Although there was certainly a castle in the area as far back as the eleventh-century, and a church, Greve seems only to have become a town comparatively recently. In 1551 there were only 92 inhabitants; by 1845 there were over 10,000. Until the fifteenth-century there was a monastery of Franciscans on a nearby hill: the chapel is still there with rose window of the school of Della Robbia. The parish church of Santa Croce was rebuilt in 1833. Within are a *Madonna* by a disciple of Fra' Angelico and a triptych by Lorenzo di Bicci. Most impressive of all is the oddly-shaped Piazza del Mercatale fringed by loggias, with a statue of the navigator Giovanni da Verrazzano in the centre. A market is held here each Saturday. There is a wine fair each September.

West of Greve is **Montefioralle**, still surrounded by much of its wall. Much of the town has been restored. By the Middle Ages this castle or fortified town was already the residence of many noble families, including the Ricasolis, the Vespuccis and the Bencis. After 1250 it became the seat of the Lega di Greve until the fall of Siena after which Greve subsequently began to increase, slowly, in importance whilst the nobles moved to Florence. The church of San Stefano has some interesting works of art whilst the twelfth-century Romanesque Pieve di San Cresci a Montefioralle, outside the walls, is dedicated to an early Florentine evangelist and, unusually in Tuscan Romanesque, has a portico in front. Further west is the Badia a Passignano (see below).

East of Greve is **Canonica**, with almost unaltered Romanesque church. To the south is Vignmaggio, the site of an old villa of the Gherardini family a member of which called Lisa married Francesco del Giocondo and later posed for Leonardo da Vinci's *Mona Lisa*. A little beyond it is **Lamole**, a fortified village.

Further south of Greve is **Panzano**, formerly a member of the Lega di Greve, with the ruins of its once important castle and which remains noted for its embroidery. The nearby **Pieve di San Leolino**, two miles south, has a triptych by Mariotto di Nardo. Further south is the church of **San' Eufrosino** (containing the relics of the Chianti evangelist), well located for views.

Grignano Castle has been well restored; **Pietrafitta** is a pretty and well preserved village easy to miss because of woodland.

Castellina

Castellina in Chianti is the next major centre you encounter. It was formerly an important link in the chain of fortifications built by Florence from the Val d' Elsa to the Val d' Arno and was built as a fortified village on the border of Florentine territory. After the defeat at Montaperti, the Florentines tightened up their defenses, which gave rise to the idea of Leagues (the League of Chianti for example). In 1452 the town successfully withstood a siege of 40 days by the Duke of Calabria. In 1478 the town was besieged again and eventually fell to the Sienese who remained there for five years. When Siena itself finally fell in 1555 Castellina became less important, the walls being used as house foundations. The town has been well preserved, however, and remains an interesting place to visit. The walls are in good condition as is the Rocca or fortress at the town centre. The church of San Salvatore contains a *Madonna and Child* by Lorenzo di Bicci. Of interest too is the Via delle Volte, a covered street that was part of the town's defensive system. About half a mile away is a recently restored sixth-century BC Etruscan tomb (the Ipogeo Etrusco di Montecalvario).

The Castellina area

The village of **Cispiano**, to the west of Castellina, off the road to Poggibonsi, is graced with the pretty Romanesque church of San Martino while **Sant' Agnese** also has a church of some interest, containing a *Madonna and Child with Saints* by Bicci di Lorenzo. **San Quirico** has a church in simple Romanesque style with a fine portal.

South-east of Castellina is **Badiola** (in the area of Casalecchi), an ancient church also known as Santa Maria al Colle, and one of the oldest in Chianti. South west is **Fattoria della Leccia**, another fortified hamlet and beyond it **Lilliano**, with the attractive Pieve di Santa Cristina. Further south-west still is **Cerna** and its Villa which boasts a double circuit of bastions.

South of Castellina on the 222 is well-preserved **Fonterutoli**, a town often used by Siena and Florence for hammering out territorial disputes. The **Pieve di San Leonino** in Conio, a little further south, is of ancient foundation. West of it is the **Castello di Campalli**, which served as the headquarters of Alfonso of Aragon during the siege of Castellina. **Quercegrossa** was the birthplace of the great fifteenth-century sculptor Jacopa della Quercia ('quercia' means 'oak').

The Hills of East Chianti

Radda in Chianti and environs

Radda lies at an altitude of 1,700 feet (533 metres) and is an agricultural centre. In the Middle Ages it was fairly insignificant, although it began to develop when the populations of smaller hamlets in the area settled here, perhaps after the construction of the fifteenth-century Franciscan Monastero. It is not a place with a tumultous history, although it was attacked by the Sienese in 1230, by Charles d'Anjou in 1268, and destroyed in 1478. In common with many other towns, it changed after the fall of Siena in 1555; rather than a fortfied frontier town it became a popular site for nobles' villas. It now lives off the sale and production of wine.

The streetplan remains essentially medieval, with some interesting houses, among them the fifteenth-century Palazzo del Podesta. Portions of wall are still in place and just outside them is the Monastero.

To the north of Radda is **Montevertine** with its Piccolo Museo del Chianti (little museum of Chianti) devoted to rural life in the area. A little to the west of here is the **Pieve di Santa Maria Novella**, a large church once responsible for a large area. Although substantially rebuilt, it contains some interesting pillars and capitals in the nave, with marked Lombard characteristics, and an altarpiece of the Della Robbia school. Further north is the well-preserved village of **Montemaggio**, while **Volpaia** is a fortified village in excellent condition. It used to be of some importance but with the fall of Siena, lost its strategic use. The fifteenth-century Commenda di Sant' Eufrosino, within the walls, is of some interest: deconsecrated in 1932 it used to possess an altarpiece by Cosimo Rosselli. It is now used for an important annual exhibition of contemporary art.

To the south of Radda is the attractive eleventh-century church of **San Giusto in Salcio**, in a beautiful location and the well-preserved medieval villages of **Galenda** and **Ama**. Further south still is **San Polo in Rosso**, with its Pieve of the same name. This church is rather unusual since it seems to have been incorporated into a set of fortifications when it found itself on the Siena-Florence frontier.

Vistarenni, to the east of Radda, boasts the sixteenth-century Villa di Vistarenni built by the Strozzi family. Further east, near the junction with the N429 and N408, is the **Badia a Coltibuono**, an abbey probably founded in 770 and which later became a monastery of the Vallombrosan order. It was consecrated by Pope Nicholas II in 1058 and reconstructed in 1160; the cloister dates from 1427 and various alterations were made in the sixteenth and seventeenth centuries. The church of **San Lorenzo a Coltibuono** is one of the finest examples of Romanesque in the Chianti area and dates back to 1049. The Abbey became quite important, controlling the monasteries of Spineta, Ardenga and San Jacopo in Siena. Later it was in the protection of Cardinal Giovanni de' Medici, who became Pope Leo X. In 1810 the monastery closed following an edict by Napoleon; now it flourishes as a farm and winery.

Gaiole in Chianti and environs

South of it is **Gaiole in Chianti**. It has always been a market town of some importance in the area, yet was never protected by walls or towers. It is a fairly modern town, with some well-preserved buildings in the old centre. Just to the south of the town is the **Pieve di Spaltenna**, a medieval church in excellent condition. The mighty castle of **Meleto** is a little further south, not far from the well-preserved village of **Rietine**. East of Meleto is **Castangnoli** or Castello di Castangnoli (not to be confused with the other near Castellina), with a fine castle and well-preserved medieval village. Further east is the panoramic area of **Monteluco** at 2,756 feet (840 metres) and nearby **San Vincenti**, a fine example of Romanesque and which, to judge from its size, must once have been of some considerable importance. **Tornano**, to the south of Lecchi, has a fine castle. Not far from it is **San Sano**, which holds an unusual celebration to the 'rana beona' or 'drunken frog'. East of here is **Brolio** with its imposing castle, just off the SS484, once of considerable importance because of its location on the Siena-Florence border. In common with many it was destroyed and rebuilt several times, including in 1533 just before the final Florence-Siena war, after which it lost its strategic significance and rested in the hands of the Ricasoli family. It was decided to restructure the castle again in 1860 although some of the older buildings (the keep, some turrets, the glacis and the chapel with polyptych by Ugolino di Nero) can still be seen. It was here that the 'Iron Baron', Bettino Ricasoli, conceived his formula for Chianti wine. Further to the south, on a side road off the SS484, is the **La Pagliaia** with a charming eighteenth-century villa. East of here is the fortified village of **San Gusme**, formerly a Sienese possession and in direct confrontation with the formely Florentine Brolio.

To the west of Gaiole is **Vertine** and its fine castle with walls and donjon. **Gittori**, to the north, was the home of the Bandinelli family, whose most famous member was the sculptor Baccio Bandinelli, Michelangelo's great enemy. To the east of Gaiole is **Barbischio** with some interesting remains from its past as a fortified village. Nearby **Montegrossi** used to have two castles and was a place of considerable strategic importance. The hill above the castle ruins offers one of the finest views in the area.

Chianti, far south

The fortified church of **Pieve Asciata**, between Vagliagli and Pianella, is one of the oldest diocesan churches in the Siena area. **Pontignano** has an interesting certosa, founded in 1343 and sacked in 1554. At the beginning of the seventeenth century the church was rebuilt and frescoed by Poccetti among others. The great cloister was added later in late Renaissance style; it thus became one of the largest Carthusian monasteries in the Grand Duchy. Then it was suppressed again by order of Napoleon in 1810. In the 1950s the Certosa was purchased by Siena University to be used as a students' residence and conference centre.

East of here is **Vitignano**, not far from the hill of Montaperti where the Florentines were epically defeated by the Sienese in 1260, with its villa formerly the property of the canons of Siena Cathedral.

SEVENTEEN

Northern Tuscany

The areas to the north

Fiesole

A town of considerable intrinsic interest, Fiesole (pronounced 'fee-yez-ohlay'), a hill-top neighbour to the north-east of Florence, also offers a fine view of the city. There are frequent bus services (number 7) from the Duomo, the Station and Piazza San Marco.

Walking to Fiesole from Florence

To walk would take between two and two and-a-half hours and could be undertaken by taking Via Sacchetti from Piazza delle Cure and then Via G. Boccaccio which passes (at 126 on the right) Villa Palmieri, the setting for one of the scenes of the *Decameron*. This road skirts the Villa Schifanoia and then, with the Via San Domenico along which the bus runs, arrives in Piazza San Domenico. The church dates from the early fifteenth century with seventeenth-century portico and campanile. Within it are some lovely Renaissance pietra serena arches; note the sixteenth-century benches near the altar and in the first chapel on the left, north side, a fine 1430 *Madonna and Saints* by Fra Angelico with added background by Lorenzo di Credi in 1501. The Convent was where Fra Angelico and St. Antoninus first took religious orders (later they moved to San Marco). The Chapter House (you may need to ring at number 4) has a fine *Crucifixion* by Fra Angelico.

Across the road is Via della Badia dei Roccettini which leads to the Badia Fiesolana. This was Fiesole Cathedral until 1028 and it was built by Bishop Donato (thought to have been an Irish pilgrim) in the ninth-century. There are fine views to be had from here. The charming black and white Romanesque façade is still in place though the church was rebuilt around it in the fifteenth-century by

Brunelleschi, under the orders of Cosimo il Vecchio. The monastery buildings have become part of the European University. The church, with elegant interior, opens only for the Sunday 11 am service.

From here return to the main road, turn left and then left along the Via Vecchia Fiesolana, a steep and winding but very pretty road that will bring you to Fiesole proper at Piazza Mino da Fiesole, which is where the bus also stops. The road also passes, left, the Convent of San Girolamo and, right, the Villa Medici (not open to public), built by Michelozzo for Cosimo il Vecchio in 1458 and much favoured by Lorenzo il Magnifico. There is a Tourist Information Office at Piazza Mino da Fiesole, 37 (Tel: 055 598720).

History

Fiesole is older than Florence. There has been a settlement on the twin hills of San Francesco and Borgunto for four thousand years; it became one of the most important of Etruscan towns. It was captured by the Romans, and remained important as Faesulae. But in the ups and downs that characterised the Roman era, Fiesole was sacked several times and, as Florence prospered, so it declined. From the ninth-century the two cities were administered together but Fiesole retained a measure of independence until 1125 when it was defeated by Florence definitively – although it is now once again a separate commune. It has for long been seen as a retreat from the hurlyburly of Florence below, best characterised in Boccaccio's *Decameron*. But it has been celebrated in words by many an artist, among them Milton, who refers to it in *Paradise Lost*, and by Anatole France, and Mark Twain.

What to see

The main square, Piazza Mino da Fiesole, named after the fifteenth-century sculptor who lived here, is dominated by the **Duomo**, founded in 1028 and altered or enlarged in the thirteenth and fourteenth centuries (the campanile in 1213) and heavily restored in the nineteenth century. Some of the interior pilasters are Roman. Note the statue of *St. Romulus*, Bishop of Fiesole, by G. della Robbia above the door. Over the main altar is a fine 1440 altarpiece by Bicci di Lorenzo and on the right, south, is the Cappella Salutati which contains two fine works by Mino da Fiesole: the Altar front and the 1465 Tomb of Bishop Leonardo Salutati.

At the top of the sloping piazza is the fifteenth-century town hall, the former **Palazzo Pretorio**, covered in coats of arms. Below it are the 1906 equestrian statues of Garibaldi and Victor Emmanuel II meeting at Teano. Next door to the town hall is the Church of Santa Maria Pimerana, dating back to the tenth-century and rebuilt in the sixteenth-century with the addition of the portico. In the Gothic presbytery are frescoes from the school of Taddeo Gaddi. There is also a Crucifix by the Della Robbia workshop and a marble bas-relief by F. da Sangallo which includes a self portrait.

Behind the Duomo is the Roman Theatre (**Teatro Romano**) and Archeological Museum, in a pretty setting amid groves of trees overlooking the Mugnone Valley. The area has been plundered over the years for Roman building materials which have contributed to the construction of the Duomo here and San Miniato in Florence. The theatre dates back to 100 BC and would have held some 2,500 spectators – it is still used for summer performances. The baths (calidarium, tepidarium, and frigidarium), to the right as you look at the valley, were built 200 years later. Beyond the theatre you may have a good view of the fourth-century BC Etruscan walls, best viewed from Via delle Mura Etrusche. Steps opposite lead to two superimposed temples, one Etruscan, the other Roman.

The Museum contains artefacts from all periods found at Fiesole among which are a bronze lioness, urns, Roman and Etruscan tablets (notably the fifth-century BC 'Stele Fiesolana' showing a wake), and a Roman frieze. The nearby Antiquarium Costantini, with its collection of Greek vases and recent local finds, can be visited with the same ticket.

Also behind the Duomo, to the left of the entrance to the Roman Theatre, is the **Museo Bandini**, devoted to Florentine art. It includes work by T. and A. Gaddi, Lorenzo di Bicci and Neri di Bicci.

At the other end of the square is the seventeenth-century Seminary and Bishop's Palace, and, next to the Duomo, the priest's house. Via San Francesco leads between them up to fine viewpoints, war memorials and the Church of **San Alessandro**, perhaps founded in the sixth century on the site of an Etruscan-Roman temple to Bacchus. The interior is notable for its Roman marble columns.

At the top of the hill, once the Etruscan and Roman citadel, is the early fourteenth-century church and monastery of **San Francesco**, restored at the beginning of the twentieth century. It was built as a retreat for Florentine women, but it passed to the Franciscans in 1399. Within, is an *Annunciation* by Raffaellino del Garbo (second altar, left) and an *Immaculate Conception* by Piero di Cosimo (second altar, right). The monastery has several pretty cloisters and a Franciscan Missionary Museum, displaying objets d' art from around the world, notably China and Egypt.

Behind the Palazzo Pretorio, Via A. Gramsci leads to the ancient suburb of Borgunto, once the entrance to the Roman Via Cassia. It meets Via G. Matteotti; on nearby Via A. Mari is part of the Etruscan wall and on Via del Bargellino the remains of Etruscan tombs. Via F. Ferrucci takes you out of the town and eventually bears right onto **Monte Ceceri** – where Leonardo da Vinci conducted his flying experiments – into some lovely woods and fine views. Alternatively, take Via Santa Maria, to the right of the Palazzo Pretorio and then Via Belvedere, right, until it meets Via A. Mari (with its Etruscan wall) and bear right to Via Montececeri. This also leads to the woods of Monte Ceceri, and the site of the quarries for pietra serena used in the construction of much of Florence.

Settignano

Bus number 10 from Florence station takes you to Settignano. The road passes Ponte a Mensola, where, in the Villa di Poggio Gherardo, the first episodes of Boccaccio's *Decameron* are set. In the nearby **San Martino a Mensola** there is a Benedictine church founded by the Scotsman St. Andrew in the ninth century. The fifteenth-century interior contains some fine art – a *Triptych* by T. Gaddi, and another on the high altar by a follower of Orcagna (1391). In the north aisle is a *Madonna and Saints* by Neri di Bicci. The casket in the museum formerly contained the body of St. Andrew.

Settignano produced several eminent sculptors including Desiderio da Settignano and the Rossellino brothers. In the Church of Santa Maria is an enamelled *Madonna* by A. della Robbia.

The Mugello and Valdisieve

This is a region of hills and valleys around the river Sieve north and west of Florence, noted for its wine and home to the painters Fra Angelico and Giotto, and where the Medici family originated. It has for long been considered one of the most beautiful areas of the region, its slopes covered in woods, vineyards and olive groves. To get an idea of the whole area (in one day) you could follow the following basic route which describes a sort of circle, first north and then east and so back to Florence.

The main road from Florence in this direction is the road to Bologna, the N65. Just north of Careggi is the charming Romanesque church of Cercina.

Some 7¹/₂ miles (12 kilometres) to the north is the town of **Pratolino**, well known for one of the last Medici villas, the Villa Demidoff, built in the sixteenth century for Francesco I dei Medici. In the grounds, by Buontalenti, there is the impressive statue of the *Appenino* by Giambologna. A little way north-east of here is the monastery of Monte Senario, at 2,700 feet (817 metres) where the mendicant Servite Order was founded by some wealthy Florentines in 1233. Some of the original cells are still visible as is the newer sixteenth-century monastery. As the height suggests, tremendous views are to be had from here.

Further north, west of the road before it forks at Novoli, is a turning for the **Castello del Trebbio** with attractive garden built by Michelozzo in 1461 for the Medici. The gardens are open at the usual hours but the house is open only on the first Tuesday of each month. The gardens of the grand Villa Cafaggiolo, to the north after the fork, can be visited but not the villa itself which, transformed from a fortress by Michelozzo, was the favourite of Cosimo il Vecchio and of Lorenzo il Magnifico. In the nearby Bosco ai Frati (Friars Wood) is a little church by Michelozzo with a Crucifix by Donatello.

Further north is the little town of **Barberino di Mugello**, which belonged in the fourteenth-century to the Visconti of Milan, and has a fifteenth-century Pretorial Palace and the Medici Loggia designed by Michelozzo. The road continues to the Passo della Futa at 2,980 feet (903 metres) an important point in the German defences during World War II and which offers tremendous views. From here you can take the road east to Firenzuola (or continue north into Emilia-Romagna) and back to Scarperia and San Piero a Sieve.

Had you forked right at Novoli on the N503 you would have arrived at **San Piero a Sieve**. In the parish church is an unusual terracotta font by Luca della Robbia. The town is dominated by the Medicean fortress of San Martino designed by Buontalenti in 1571. A little further on is **Scarperia**, a handsome town that overlooks the valley, well known for the manufacture of cutlery and finely worked thrust weaponry. Here you will find the 1306 Pretorian Palace, with frescoes from the school of Giotto. The Madonna di Piazza Oratory has a *Madonna and Child* by T. Gaddi in a tabernacle attributed to A. della Robbia. The propository church contains work by B. da Maiano and a tabernacle by Mino da Fiesole. In the Madonna dei Terremoti Oratory (Madonna of earthquakes) is a *Madonna* attributed to Filippo Lippi. Nearby is the Mugello International Car Racing Track.

West of the road a little way to the north of Scarperia is the lovely Romanesque church of **Santa Agata**. Within are beautiful columns, paintings by Giovanni del Biondo and A. Gaddi and a tabernacle by Giovanni della Robbia. The pulpit dates from 1175.

North of Scarperia is **Firenzuola**. It was badly damaged during World War II but has been rebuilt with care. The 1371 Palazzo del Popolo is on Piazza Agnolo Firenzuola, named after the sixteenth-century author. Nearby, to the west at Cornacchia, is a church dating back to Carolingian times.

The N551 from near San Piero a Sieve leads east to **Borgo San Lorenzo**, which fell to the Florentines in 1291. The town is noted for two interesting churches. The church of San Lorenzo dates back to the twelfth century and possesses an unusual 1263 hexagonal campanile, a mixture of Gothic and Romanesque. The church of San Giovanni Maggiore, 1³/₄ miles (3 kilometres) to the north, boasts an octagonal campanile and a lovely marble pulpit. In the Oratory of SS. Crocefisso dei Miracoli is a ninth-century painting illustrating the plague.

From Borgo San Lorenzo you may continue east to Vicchio. If you wish to explore the area to the north of Borgo you should take the N302 which soon forks, the left fork becoming the N477. On it is **Palazzuolo sul Senio** which has the fourteenth-century Palazzo dei Capitani (where Pope Julius II and Machiavelli once stayed) with its Ethnographic Museum, and the nearby Susinana Abbey of 1373, later turned into a villa. The Misileo church has a crypt of some interest. The right fork continues as the N302 to **Marradi** with its Palazzo Fabroni and eighteenth-century theatre.

East of Borgo San Lorenzo the N551 leads to the town of **Vicchio**, birthplace of the painter and monk Fra Angelico 'the Blessed Angelico', whose work graces the Monastery of San Marco in Florence. In the Palazzo Pretorio is a museum named after him with local archeological discoveries, detached frescoes from the schol of Giotto, and a rare thirteenth-century holy water stoup. The neighbouring hamlet of **Vespignano** was the birthplace of one of the greatest of Italian painters, Giotto di Bondone. Here you may visit the Casa di Giotto, where he is supposed to have been born and see the bridge where Cimabue is supposed to have discovered the young shepherd painting sheep on a rock.

The road continues to **Dicomano**, an industrial town with a fourteenth-century church containing works by Vasari and Santi di Tito. The Chapel of SS. Annunziata houses a painting from the school of Piero della Francesca. The Sant' Onofrio Oratory has a fresco by Filippo Lippi.

The road east from Dicomano, the N67, passes close (right) to the nearby Abbey of **Santa Maria ad Agnano** with eleventh-century campanile and continues to the Muraglione Pass at 2,993 feet (907 metres). These hills are known as the Alps of San Benedetto. The village of **San Godenzo** where Dante was present at a meeting between the White Guelfs and Florentine exiles in 1302 is here with its eleventh-century Benedictine Abbey in the church of which is a raised marble presbytery and a polyptych by the Giotto school. A road from here leads to the foot of Monte Falterona, 5,458 feet (1,654 metres), and the village of **Castagno d' Andrea**, the birthplace of the artist Andrea del Castagno (1423-57) who was also known as Andrea degli Impiccati for his paintings of condemned criminals on the Bargello and whose masterpiece is the *Cenacolo di Sant' Apollonia* in Florence.

Over the border in Emilia-Romagna is the ninth-century Abbey of **San Benedetto in Alpe**, mentioned rather mysteriously by Dante in *Inferno* XVI, along with the pretty Acquacheta waterfall.

South of Dicomano the N67 follows the river Sieve. The N556 soon leads east to **Londa**, lying prettily next to an artificial lake and near to the villages of **San Leolino** and **Santa Elena a Rincine**, both of which have interesting churches.

The N67 passes through the town of **Rufina** with the sixteenth-century Villa di Poggio Reale. This is a wine-producing area and in **Poggio Reale** there is a small Wine Museum. On the other side of the river, at **Acone**, is an interesting church, Santa Maria, and a castle.

Pontassieve, on the confluence of the Sieve and Arno, is an industrial town but which still has its Medicean bridge and ancient clocktower. South of the town is **Rosano**, with the St. Mary Convent with intersting campanile and altar by Orcagna. To the east the N70 takes you on a pretty route up to the Passo della Consuma, at 3,376 feet (1,023 metres), and on to the Romena Castle and the Casentino (see relevant section).

Medici villas

Not far from Florence are several beautiful country houses formerly in the hands of the Medici.

Villa della Petraia
Bus 28 from Florence station. Open: 09.00-16.00 or 13.00 in winter.

This was rebuilt by Buontalenti in 1557. It is worth a look for its Baroque interior, Cantonese paintings and beautiful park.

Villa di Castello
Bus 28 from Florence station. Open: 09.00-16.00 or 13.00 in winter.

This villa, the best known, was bought in 1477 by Lorenzo di Pierfrancesco and Giovanni de'Medici. The garden was much admired in the sixteenth and seventeenth centuries and is open to the public. The villa is now the seat of the Accademia della Crusca devoted to the study of the Italian language.

Villa Careggi
Viale Pieraccini, 17. Bus 14C from Florence station or Duomo.

This was rebuilt by Michelozzo for Cosimo il Vecchio in 1434. It soon became one of the launching pads for Humanism, where Poliziano, Pico della Mirandola, Ficino and others regularly met to discuss philosophy with Lorenzo il Magnifico, as members of their Platonic Academy. Lorenzo died here, as did Cosimo il Vecchio before him. It was restored in the nineteenth-century by Sir Francis Sloane. The gardens are open to the public but the villa, now part of a hospital, can be visited only by prior arangement.

From Florence to Pisa – Route One

A railway line – built by the Englishman, Ralph Bonfield, in 1848 – and an autostrada (A11) run north of Monte Albano, touching or almost touching Prato, Pistoia, Montecatini and Lucca on the way to Pisa. These towns are each of considerable interest.

Sesto Fiorentino
This small town is noted for the Villa Corsi Salviati and its eighteenth-century garden and the Museo delle Porcellane di Doccia (Doccia Porcelain Museum), at Via Pratese, 31, which exhibits much of the ware produced in the local Doccia factory. Founded by Carlo Ginori in 1737, since 1896 it has been known as Richard-Ginori. Open 09.30-13.00 and 15.30-18.30; closed Sunday and Monday.

Prato

From Florence take the A11 at Peretola in the direction of Pisa and Viareggio). There is no parking in the centre, but there are two railway stations – Centrale and Porta Serraglio (nearer to centre). Tourist Information is located at Via L. Muzzi, 51. (Tel: 0574 35141.)

With a population of 150,000 Prato is the third town of Tuscany and its industrial heart. As in the past it is mainly important for textiles, particularly the recycling of rags. It has plenty to offer in the way of sights, nonetheless, for its medieval wealth enabled it to be embellished with art. Prato means 'meadow', a reflection of the fact that the garrison and commercial activity was based in a field outside the city walls.

Founded in the ninth century, it became a commune in 1140 and the most important wool town in Europe. However, in the fourteenth-century Florence was on the up and ultimately, after a tussle, purchased the city. Prato retained some autonomy though, until the Spaniards sacked it mercilessly in 1512 after which its fate was entwined with that of Florence.

What to see

Everything is within walking distance. Although an industrial town, the old town is still of some charm, its narrow streets retaining the names of the crafts and arts practised there, for example Via dei Tintori (Dyers Street).

Castello dell'Imperatore, Viale Piave

This was built in 1237 by the Holy Roman Emperor, Frederick II, the only one like it in the north of Italy. He resided in Palermo, as heir to the Norman kingdom of South Italy, and rarely visited his far dominions. This may have been built by Apulian architects. There is nothing special inside but it offers good views.

Nearby is **Santa Maria delle Carceri**, the late fifteenth-century Brunelleschian church by Giuliano da Sangallo. It is supposed to embody all the philosophical qualities of Humanistic architecture and was built to celebrate a miracle of a talking image of the Virgin on a prison wall. The exterior is of polychrome marble; the interior is considered a masterpiece of Renaissance architecture with some decoration by Andrea della Robbia. Behind, on Via Cairoli, is the famed Metastasio Theatre.

Nearby is the thirteenth-century church of **San Francesco**, which contains the tomb of the Merchant of Prato, Francesco di Marco Datini, one of the richest people of his time (the late fourteenth-century), through dealing in everything from wool to slaves. Thousands of documents, mainly concerning business transactions have been preserved so it has been possible to build a comprehensive picture of his life and so of his times. He was obsessed with business to the point where a friend wrote to him:

'Your business is just accounts, here today and gone tomorrow...
Cut yourself off from the church, you cut yourself off from God.
And I know, and you know, how your work has cut you off.'

He dabbled extensively in art patronage and it is interesting to see
that even then art was already being seen as a commodity. Skill was
recognised, though in the case of Datini it was a question of best
value rather than highest quality. In a letter he says to an agent:

'These two panels should have beautiful figures. I want them for
people who are asking for fine work . . if you find something cheap
and likely to be profitable, take it.'

On the nearby Via Rinaldesca is his old palace, the Palazzo Datini,
from the 1390s.

Piazza Comune has a nineteenth-century statue of Datini, the
Palazzo Comunale has some fifteenth-century frescoes and portraits
of the Grand Dukes, the medieval Palazzo Pretorio dates back to
Prato's independence and contains the Galleria Comunale with works
by Filippino Lippi, who was born here, Bernardo Daddi, Signorelli
and Filippo Lippi.

The **Duomo** (Santo Stefano) was begun in the thirteenth century in
Pisan style. It has an interesting campanile and on the façade, the
delightful Pulpit of the Sacred Girdle designed by Michelozzo and
decorated by Donatello. The girdle, Prato's most holy relic, is the
Virgin Mary's belt, displayed from the pulpit on Easter Day, May 1,
August 15, September 8, and Christmas Day. The interior is
Romanesque in style. The chapel of the Sacred Girdle has a statue of
the *Madonna and Child* by Giovanni Pisano and in the choir, Filippo
Lippi's frescoes; the model for Salome was the girl with whom the
painter monk eloped. In the next chapel some frescoes by Uccello
and Andrea di Giusto. Next door is the Cathedral Museum with
works relating to the Duomo.

The **Museo del Tessuto** (weaving museum) on Viale della
Repubblica, 9, has a collection of fabrics, costumes and looms. The
Museum of Mural Painting is in the convent of San Domenico,
formerly the residence of the painter Fra Bartolomeo and Savonarola.
The Gothic church next door is late thirteenth-century.

The Church of **Sant' Agostino** on Piazza Sant'Agostino has works by
Vasari and San Fabiano on Via del Seminario 30, has a fine pre-
Romanesque mosaic. The **Spedalinghi Palace** (now the Prato Academy
of Medicine and Science) has some rare thirteenth-century frescoes.

The **Mercatale Square** was the traditional market place, the original 'prato' perhaps. Craftsmens' shops, specialising in copperware, were situated under the archways. There is still a market here on Mondays. The sculpture on Piazza San Marco is *Square Form With Split*, 1964/70 by Henry Moore.

Byway: Val di Bisenzio area

This valley, via the N325 road, runs north of Prato, once the fiefdom of the Albertis of Prato. Each of the following small towns has something of interest or is beautifully situated. **Vaiano**: a Benedictine abbey church and campanile, and Alberti's twelfth-century Cerbaia 'Rocca' or fortress. **San Quirico di Vernio**: Alberti castle, town hall, oratory, and, one mile outside the town, the Abbey of St Mary's. **Cantagallo**, higher up off the N325, with good easy walks from here up to the Pian della Rosa at 3,133 feet (1,001 metres) and **Monte della Scoperta** at 4,217 feet (1,278 metres). This last location might be easier from **Montepiano** where there is also an old abbey with its original gate, and some frescoes.

On the minor road from Prato to Pistoia that goes via Maliseti and Montale, you will pass through **Montemurlo**, a pretty old Etruscan town with medieval castle and Rocca mentioned by Dante and important in the Guelf/Ghibelline struggles and anti- Medici struggles in sixteenth-century. The Church of San Giovanni Decollato has works of Giovanni da Prato, and a fine campanile.

Pistoia

This is situated just off the A11. The station is about half a mile (0.75 kilometres) from the city centre. Cars are banned in the city centre but parking is easy. Tourist offices at Piazza Duomo (tel: 0573 21622) or Corso Gramsci 110 (tel: 0573 34326).

The word 'pistol' is said to derive from the town's name and coincides with its history which is particularly brutal. A Roman town on the old Via Cassia, it prospered through agriculture and craftsmanship under the Lombards and subsequently became a commune. Its reputation developed during the Guelph-Ghibelline struggles, the factional fighting between Black and White Guelph which spread to Florence supposedly starting here. Dante curses her several times in *The Divine Comedy* (notably in the 25th canto of The *Inferno* where he says:

'Ahi Pistoia, Pistoia, che non stanzi d' incenerarti si che piu non duri, poi che in mal far lo seme tuo avanzi?'
(Oh Pistoia, Pistoia, how is it that they haven't razed you to the ground, since your evil is greater even than that of your forbears?).

From 1306 its fate was mostly tied in with that of Florence. Noted for iron working in the past - daggers and then pistols being a speciality - it now produces ornamental trees and light trains; the population is 94,000.

The old town is quite intact, some of the buildings dating as far back as the eleventh century.

Piazza del Duomo

A fine medieval L-shaped square, this is the artistic and historic centre of the town and the site of the Giostra dell'Orso (bear joust). This medieval joust used to be a contest between 12 knights and a bear; nowadays the bear has been replaced by wooden dummies.

The Cathedral dates back to the twelfth-century. The façade is Romanesque, though the loggias are more typical of the Pisan style. The lunette above the main door is a *Madonna and Child* by Andrea della Robbia. The quaint campanile was originally a watchtower. The much altered interior abounds with interest, the most precious item is in the Chapel of St. James in the south aisle, an altar-frontal of 1287-1456 made from a ton of silver, with the *Nine Stories from the Life of St. James* by Leonardo di Giovanni (a fee is payable) – one of the finest examples of silverwork in Italy. Also worth noting: the tomb of the thirteenth-century poet and lawyer Cino da Pistoia, a friend of Dante (south aisle); the fifteenth-century bronze candelabra, left of the altar; the monument to Niccolo Forteguerri near the entrance; the bust of Bishop Donato de'Medici by either Verrocchio or Antonio Rossellino in the Chapel of the Sacrament (north of choir); a fifteenth-century font by Benedetto da Maiano and Andrea Ferrucci; and a *Madonna and Child between St. John the Baptist and St. Zeno* by Verrocchio and Lorenzo di Credi, on the south wall.

Next to the Duomo is the **Bishop's Palace** (Palazzo dei Vescovi) with its Cathedral Museum containing the famous treasury also mentioned by Dante in *Inferno* XXIV. In the basement is the Archeological Museum.

The octagonal Baptistry, completed in 1359 to a design of Andrea Pisano, is considered one of the finest Gothic buildings in Tuscany; note the bas reliefs on the architrave telling the Story of John the Baptist.

The fourteenth-century **Palazzo del Podesta** (or Palazzo Pretorio), now a law court (west side of square) has a courtyard with a stone table and bench for the judge and a bench for the accused. Its military aspect is a reflection of the bloody goings-on of the twelfth and thirteenth centuries.

The thirteenth-century Guelf **Palazzo del Comune** on the east side of the square, contains the Galleria Comunale with work by Beccafumi, Lorenzo di Credo, Gerino Gerini, a Pistoiese, Andrea del Brescianino, Foggini, Buglioni and others. The Palazzo also has a Hall of the Pages and a Ghibelline Hall, both worth seeing.

San Giovanni Fuoricivitas

This is on Via Cavour, reached by taking Via Roma from the Duomo Square. The name tells you that it was originally, in the eighth-century, outside the city wall. It was rebuilt between the twelfth and fourteenth centuries in Pisan style. The architrave over the doorway is decorated with an early bas-relief of *Jesus with the Apostles* of 1162 by Gruamonte. The beautiful pulpit is by Guglielmo Agnelli da Pisa from about the end of the thirteenth-century and a fine glazed terracotta *Visitation* by one of the della Robbias and a holy water stoup representing the three theological virtues by Giovanni Pisano and a polyptych by Gaddi.

Directly south is Piazza Garibaldi. **San Domenico** was built here at the end of the thirteenth century and contains a *Madonna and Child* by Fra Bartolomeo (1475-1517) and busts by Gian Lorenzo Bernini (1598-1680). The magnificent organ is of 1617; the two Renaissance tombs are by the brothers Rossellino. The painter Gozzoli is buried in the cloister; his most famous work is in the Medici Palace in Florence. Nearby is the **Cappella del Tau**, named after the 'T' the priests wore on their vestments, with interesting frescoes attributed to Masolino. (Open 08.00-13.45; closed Sunday.)

By taking Via 27 Aprile from Piazza del Duomo and turning right into Via delle Pappe you will come to Piazza Ospedale and the thirteenth-century *Ospedale del Ceppo* (hospital of the log, after the wooden device for collecting alms). The magnificent terracotta frieze is by the Della Robbia brothers, depicting the seven acts of charity. Not far to the west, on Via Sant' Andrea is the twelfth-century Sant' Andrea containing the fine 1298-1301 pulpit by Giovanni Pisano, one of his masterpieces.

Further west still is the church of **San Francesco** with fourteenth-century frescoes from the school of Giotto. Note too, the memorial outside to the politician Aldo Moro, kidnapped in 1978 by the Red Brigade and executed and dumped in the middle of Rome.

The sixteenth-century **Basilica della Madonna dell' Umilta**, on Via della Madonna, was built by a pupil of Bramante, Ventura Vitoni, with a dome by Vasari. **San Bartolomeo** in Pantano, on Via San Bartolomeo, has a pulpit of 1250 by Guido da Como and it is interesting to compare it, from the point of view of changing styles, with the later one by Pisano in Sant' Andrea. The eight reliefs depict scenes from the Passion of Christ.

From Pistoia to Lucca

The road from Pistoia to Lucca passes through a valley protected by the fourteenth-century castle of Serravalle Pistoiese with a Lombard tower.

Just south of the A11, is the resort of **Monsummano** with vapour baths in natural caves. The old town offers a ruined castle and Romanesque church.

Montecatini Terme

This is a fashionable spa town 10 miles (16 kilometres) to the west of Pistoia. By road it is off the A11. It may also be reached by train. Tourist information: Via Verdi 66. Tel: 0572 772244.

This is an expensive way to cure liver problems or relax in a mineral bath. Although used from at least the fourteenth-century the atmosphere is more northern here, the resort being developed by the Lorraine Grand Dukes from the eighteenth century, with Art Nouveau and Art Deco additions made in the twentieth century. The oldest and grandest establishment here is 'Tettuccio' – others offer mud baths, at Terme Leopoldine, or concerts, at Torretta. The baths are open from May to October; the Excelsior is open all year. A pleasant place to stroll or to take a funicular ride to Montecatini Alto for fine views.

Pescia

Continuing on the N435 will take you past Buggiano, a pretty hill town (not to be confused with Borgo a Buggiano), and bring you to Pescia, famous for its flowers. The fourteenth-century church of San Francesco has works by Bonaventura Berlinghieri including what is thought to be a good likeness of the saint and a *Crucifixion* by Puccio. The seventeenth-century Duomo has an attractive

Romanesque campanile and a triptych by Luca della Robbia. The Palazzo Comunale and Church of Sant' Antonio with frescoes by Neri di Bicci are also worth seeing. Uzzano, with its fourteenth-century church with fifteenth-century loggettas and frescoes by Gemignani, is within walking distance. North of Pescia is the twelfth-century church of Pieve di Castelvecchio.

Collodi

West of Pescia is Collodi, much visited by the Florentine author of the children's book *Pinocchio*, Carlo Lorenzo (1826-90) whose uncle worked in the castle. The Parco di Pinocchio offers a variety of attractions based on the story.

The seventeenth-century Castello/Villa Garzoni is considered to have one of the finest Italian gardens in the country, designed by Ottaviano Diodati da Lucca. (Open 08.00-20.00.)

North of Collodi is Villa Basilica with a thirteenth-century Pieve. Near Villa Basilica is the village of San Gennaro with a lovely twelfth-century ambo.

Lucca – a fairy commonwealth

Lucca is located just off the A11. There are several car parks, for example on Piazza Napoleone. The station is a little way to the south of the city walls. Bicycles may be hired on the Piazza opposite Porta Santa Maria. Tourist information at Piazza Guidiccioni 2 (Tel: (0583) 41205), or Via Vittorio Veneto 40 (Tel: (0583) 46915).

With a population of 90,000, Lucca is situated on the left bank of the Serchio, at the begining of the Garfagnana, in a vast and fertile plain. Originally a Ligurian settlement, it became a Roman colony (Luca) in 180 BC. It then became first the Goth and then Lombard capital of Tuscany; only under the Franks was the capital transferred to Florence.

Lucca started to develop its own civic culture from about 1000 and in 1119 it became one of the first independent communes, specialising in the manufacture of silk which generated the wealth that inspired its art and architecture. The architecture was much inspired by Pisan Romanesque, though developing its own style, rich in ornamentation and influenced by the northern Como school (because of the silk connection). Though temporarily under the tutelage of several neighbouring city states (particularly that of Pisa in 1314) one of the more remarkable episodes of its history involved one Castruccio Castracani, an exiled Lucchese noble who returned to restore Lucca's independence, extending the frontiers of this little empire briefly throughout most of west Tuscany.

In 1369 Lucca was granted republican status by Charles IV and so it remained (outside the Grand Duchy of Tuscany) until 1805 when Napoleon gave it to his sister Elisa Baciocchi. In 1847 it became part of Tuscany.

It retains a very special atmosphere – one eighteenth-century visitor called it 'a fairy commonwealth'. It was known as a model state, 'a peaceful, law-abiding, industrious, prosperous and independent little state which had successfully governed itself as a republic for several hundred years'. Firearms were removed from visitors as they entered the city gates.

What to see

The Walls
Undoubtedly Lucca's special character is partly attributable to its sixteenth and seventeenth-century walls which are two and a half miles (four kilometres) long and can be walked or driven in part, visiting some of the bastions en route. (Bastion San Paolino in the southwest of the city is open to the public). These ramparts are given the name 'Passegiata delle mura' (wall promenade) and are the best preserved in Italy, one reason being that though they were never really used they came to represent the city's independence (notice the inscription 'Libertas' over the most ornate gate of St. Peter near Piazza Risorgimento). The walls were originally built at a time when war seemed imminent but in the end, preserved and unused, one of Lucca's last rulers, Marie Louise (Napoleon's widow), embellished them with trees to make a pleasant walkway where even now the citizenry likes to stroll in the cool of summer evenings.

Piazza Napoleone and the Ducal Palace
The Palazzo Ducale was started in 1579 by Ammannati and was the seat of the republican government. Behind it, to the west, is the Romanesque church of San Romano with a fine work by Matteo Civitali (1435-1501), Lucca's greatest artist, and the tomb of San Romano.

To the Duomo

Adjacent to Piazza Napoleone, to the east, take Piazza Giglio with its neo-classical municipal theatre, then take Via Duomo. **San Giovanni**, the twelfth-century church on the left, has a beautiful twelfth-century carving over the portal and, being built on the ruins of a Roman building, incorporates Roman pillars inside. Next to it are the Gothic Baptistry, and the Palazzo Micheletti by Ammannati. Beyond is Piazza San Martino, the site of an antiques market on the third weekend of the month, and the **Cathedral of San Martino** itself, considered a fine example of the Pisan style and constructed between the eleventh and fifteenth centuries. The façade is a marvellous extravagance – the marble statue of *San Martino*, on horseback, and the *Beggarman*, the *Adoration of the Magi* by Nicola Pisano are particularly fine. The campanile was built between 1060 and 1261.

The interior, in multi-coloured marble, is late Gothic. Worthy of note are the tomb of Pietro da Noceto by Civitali in the right transept, the chapel of Liberty built in 1369 by Charles IV in the left transept and the Sanctuary Chapel with works by Fra Bartolomeo. The tomb of Ilaria del Carretto (wife of a member of the Guinigi family, despotic rulers of Lucca) by Iacopo della Quercia (1367-1438) in the middle of the left transept is considered one of his finest works. This has recently been the subject of controversy following its cleaning and restoration, thought by some to have ruined its original character. In the centre of the left aisle is the famous *Tempietto* or Tabernacle of the Holy Countenance by Civitali, which contains Lucca's most venerated relic, an image of Christ said to be sculped by Nicodemus, present at the Crucifixion, and mentioned in Dante's *Inferno* in Canto XXI. In fact the Crucifix probably dates from the eleventh or twelfth century but is paraded through the streets nonetheless in a candle-lit procession each September 13. In the sacristy, off the right aisle, there is a *Madonna* by Ghirlandaio. Many of the most valuable artefacts from the Cathedral are kept in the Museo dell'Opera del Duomo on Piazza degli Antelminelli nearby.

Further east is Via dell'Arcivescovato. Turn left (north), sparing a glance at the church of **Santa Maria Forisportam** (St. Mary Without the Gate) on your right, so-called because at the time of its construction, in the twelfth-century, it lay outside the old Roman walls. It is in the Pisan style. Behind it is one of the old gates and the remains of the moat.

Via Guinigi brings you to the Romanesque **Palazzo Guinigi** and next to it, with a tree blooming out of the summit, the **Torre Guinigi.**

Both belonged to the despotic family that ruled Lucca in the fourteenth-century. The tower provides a fine view of the city and surrounding countryside. (Open 09.00-19.00 April to September or 10.00-16.00 October to March). This quarter of the city takes you back to medieval and Renaissance Lucca, for much of it has barely changed in hundreds of years – anything much newer was built outside the Renaissance walls.

Walking along Via Sant' Andrea, turning right into Piazza del Carmine, and crossing Via A. Mordoni will bring you to **Piazza Anfiteatro**, a beautiful square shaped in the ellipse that was the original Roman amphitheatre. Traces of the original are visible here and there, but more impressive is its perfect transformation into a medieval market place.

North of here is Via Fillungo ('length of filament', something to do with the silk industry presumably) and beyond it Piazza **San Frediano** and the early twelfth-century church of the same name. The mosaic on the façade depicts the Ascension; inside there is a marvellous twelfth-century font by Roberto and works by Civitali and Andrea della Robbia.

Via C. Battisti leads from the square and passes the eighteenth-century **Palazzo Pfanner** with a fine garden, a collection of Lucchese silks, and costumes from the seventeenth to the nineteenth centuries (Open 10.00-17.00 April to September. Closed Mondays. For other times call 491449.)

The other church of particular interest is **San Michele in Foro** which lies to the south and may be reached directly by taking Via Calderia or indirectly by returning to Via Fillungo, and its shops, cafes and medieval palaces and tower (Torre delle Ore). Taking the latter, turn right into Via Roma which will bring you to **San Michele** and its Pisan-Lucchese façade, built over the old Roman forum ('foro'). It is probably the work of Guidetto da Como. Inside there is an enamelled terracotta *Madonna and Child* by Luca della Robbia and a panel by Filippino Lippi.

The Lucchese composer Giacomo **Puccini**, whose works include Madame Butterfly, La Boheme and Turandot, was born at nearby Via di Poggio 30 opposite the church, which is now a museum dedicated to him. The composer also played the organ in San Paolino on nearby Via San Paolino and was a choirboy in San Michele. (Open 10.00-18.00 April to September, 10.00-16.00 October-March; closed Mondays.)

By continuing along Via di Poggio and then Via del Toro you will come to the **Pinacoteca Nazionale** (art gallery) in the seventeenth-century Palazzo Mansi on Via Galli Tassi. It has works by Tintoretto, Pontormo, Botticelli and Bronzino as well as a display of furniture, including an extravagant Bridal Chamber. (Open 09.00-19.00, 09.00-14.00 Sunday; closed Mondays.)

Other items worth seeing in Lucca include: the Church of **San Francesco** (with the tombs of Castracani and the composer Boccherini); and the **Museo Nazionale Guinigi**, or Museo Civico, in the Villa Guinigi. This has medieval paintings and sculptures and archeological finds. (Open 09.00-14.00; closed Mondays). Also San Giulia, San Cristoforo, San Pietro Somaldi, San Giusto, Oratorio di Santa Maria delle Rose, and the Casa di Monna Vanna. The **Botanical Garden** is open 08.00-13.00 October-April; closed Sunday and Monday or 09.00-12.00, and 15.30-18.30 May-September; closed Monday. The sixteenth-century **Villa Bottini** with Salimbeni frescoes and a fine park is open 09.00-13.30.

Around Lucca – Villas and Puccini

There are several villas worth a look as follows: The lovely **Villa Mansi** with garden laid out by Juvarra in Segromigno to the north-east. (Open 10.00-12.30 and 15.30-17.00, closed Mondays). **Villa Torrigiani** in Camigliano, also to the north-east, with gardens and interesting interior decoration. (Open every day March-November 09.30-11.30 and 14.30-17.00, otherwise only on Sunday). The **Villa Pecci-Blunt** in Marlia, also to the north-east. (Guided visits 10.00-11.00, 16.00-18.00, Tuesday, Wednesday, Thursday, Sunday, July-September. In October, November, March, April, May, June, open every day except Monday 10.00-11.00 and 15.00-18.00. In December, January, February by appointment only. Tel: 0583 30108.) The house is not open but it is the site of the Lucca music festival in the summer.

To the east of Lucca, **Capannori** is of interest for its Romanesque churches. To the west is **Marina di Torre del Lago** where, on the banks of Lake Massaciuccoli, **Puccini** had a villa. The villa, which contains many of his possessions, including his piano, is open: 09.00-

(Opposite) Top: *The old public buildings of the Repubblica Massetana – Massa Marittima.*

(Opposite) Bottom: *Pistoia – one of the finest works of the Della Robbia workshop, the decoration on the Ospedale del Ceppo.*

12.00 and 15.00-19.00 April-September, or 09.00-12.00 and 14.30-17.00 October-March. He and his family are buried in the small chapel. There is a festival of his music here in August – for information contact Festival Pucciniano, Piazzale Belvedere Puccini, Torre del Lago. (Tel: 0584 343322.)

The Garfagnana and Lunigiana

North of Lucca are the Apuan Alps, source of the marble used to such great effect in Tuscan art. The valley of the Serchio is the Garfagnana; north-west of this is the Lunigiana, the area between the mountains and the coast that derives its name from the Roman town of Luni.

Garfagnana

This is essentially the route that follows the N12 and N445. Places of interest in the area are varied. They include: the church of **San Giorgio di Brancoli** near Vinchiana, **Diecimo**'s Church and campanile and **Borgo a Mozzano's** charming bridge. These, and **Bagni di Lucca** are spa villages, much loved by Browning and Shelley. The Valley of the Lima has picturesque villages and scenery like **Vico** (on roads off the N12), **Alpe Tre Potenze** and **Tereglio**. **Coreglia Antelmielli** has the Museo della Figurina, the museum of Garfagnana (plaster figures) and **Barga**, a marvellous cathedral (the museum is open 10.00-12.00 and 15.00-18.00). This is a charming town, with an opera festival in July/August.

 Castelnuovo di Garfagnana has a fortress and is a starting point for the scenic drive east to San Pellegrino in Alpe or the road west to the coast over the Apuan Alps. The **Parco dell' Orecchiella** is a nature reserve and the **Lago di Vagli** a scenic lake.

Lunigiana

This is an area of castles and rocky landscapes along the N445, N63 and N62, perhaps the least visited part of Tuscany, where local mountain produce like figs, mushrooms and sheep's cheese, is sold by women at the roadside. It is also well known for its chestnuts, as a

(Opposite) Top: *A corner of the Piazza Grande in Arezzo.*
(Opposite) Bottom: *The obsession with fashion – photo-shoots of models are a common sight in the streets of Tuscany.*

seventeenth-century English visitor, Francis Mortoft noted as he made the journey from Genoa to Massa:

> 'for some 60 Mile together the mountains were all covered with Chestnut Trees, whereof the People . . makes Chestnut Bread, which suffices them instead of others'.

Worth visiting are **Fivizzano**, a pretty town that belonged to the Malaspina family who ruled the Lunigiana in the early fourteenth-century, right up to 1829, and **Fosdinovo**, with Malaspina castle where Dante stayed; he mentions the family in *Inferno* XXIV. **Aulla** has a Genoese fortress and **Caprigliola** is a fortified village. **Villafranca in Lunigiana** has an Ethnographic museum devoted to life in Lunigiana. **Pontremoli** is the main town of Lunigiana with fortififications by Castracani, the Torre dell' Orologio, Duomo, the Church of San Francesco (with work by Duccio), and the Castello del Piagnaro with an archaeology museum devoted to the anonymous culture flourishing in Lunigiana from 3000 BC.

   Luni (Luni Antica on signs), the old Roman town from which the area takes its name and which flourished because of the importance of marble, is over the border in Liguria, not far from Marinella. The forum and amphitheatre remain, and you may visit the Museo Nazionale di Luni with a good display of Roman artefacts and modern architectural techniques. (Open 09.00-12.00 and 14.00-17.00; closed Mondays).

Carrara, Massa and the coast down to Viareggio

This is the area of the Riviera della Versilia. There are good bus services between these towns. The railway service is less convenient.

   The sea along this part of the Tuscan coast is no longer as inviting as it once was, because of the effects of pollution. The beaches themselves, however, are fairly clean, mostly because you pay to enjoy them and their facilities. Nonetheless beach life is on the whole a crowded, commercial affair, with one resort running into another. It all started at Forte dei Marmi when Leopold I, Grand Duke of Tuscany, built a fortress there. This was never used but the rich began to build villas in the area when bathing became fashionable in the nineteenth-century. From there it spread. **Marinella** is supposed to be the resort with the cleanest water; **Marina di Carrara** is not recommended for bathing on account of the marble port; **Marina di Massa** is quite lively; between Cinquale and Forte dei Marmi is an area of free beach; **Marina di Pietrasanta** has the Parco della Versiliana filled with Mediterranean forest and **Lido di Camaiore** is good for children.

Carrara

Tourist information: Piazza 2 Giugno, 14. Tel: (0585) 70894; or Marina di Carrara, Piazza Meconi. Tel: (0585) 632218.

Carrara is famous for its marble quarries and thus forever associated with Michelangelo, for whom the search for the perfect piece of marble was a quest in itself. The Romans were the first to quarry here, removing marble to build their city far away to the south.

The **Duomo** is the main building of the city, a Romanesque church started in the eleventh century and distinctive for its fourteenth-century rose window. John Ruskin said of this church 'a perfect gem of Italian Gothic, covered with twelfth-century sculpture of the most glorious richness and interest'.

The **Accademia delle Belle Arti** is in a palazzo at Via Roma 1, formally a castle belonging to the Malaspina family, also much enjoyed by Ruskin. Here there are artefacts found in Roman Luni and a Roman altar, the Edicola dei Fantiscritti, found in the quarry of the Fantiscritti (named after this altar) with bas reliefs of Roman gods and graffiti left by visiting artists to the quarry.

The marble museum (**Museo del Marmo**), on Viale XX Settembre, describes the quarrying process and shows examples of different marbles from around the world.

Carrara is synonymous with marble and the **quarries** are worth visiting. (The word for quarry is 'cave', pronounced 'ka', as in car, 'vay'.) As a nineteenth-century observer put it, the inhabitants of Carrara are 'peculiar people gather'd together from all parts of the world to search for good marble'. The quarries are a few kilometres outside the town, huge gashes in the hills that you cannot miss. A large amount is exported but it seems there is plenty left – the three principal quarries are Ravaccione, Colonnata and Fantiscritti, where Michelangelo is said to have obtained his pieces. The marble from Nelson's tomb comes from Carrara; and more recently the sculptor Henry Moore made his selections here.

There are strong British connections with Carrara. In the early nineteenth-century a good deal of marble was imported into Britain –

one William Walton went as far as emigrating to the area and purchasing a marble firm. He was one of the first to introduce sophisticated marble-working machinery here and ended by dominating the trade, helping to establish good trading links with America and Britain. He also became honorary British Consul. The citizens of Carrara were grateful enough for his enterprise to erect a memorial plaque to him.

Charles Dickens stayed with Walton when he passed through Carrara in 1844. Having witnessed the toil of removing the marble and later idling in a sculptor's studio he wrote,

> '...it seemed at first, so strange to me that those exquisite shapes, replete with grace, and thought, and delicate repose, should grow out of all this toil, and sweat and torture!'

Massa

Tourist information (Marina di Massa), Lungomare Vespucci 24. Tel: (0585) 240046.

This was the capital for the Malaspina family when they ruled the area. Both their seventeenth-century Palazzo Cybo-Malaspina (on Piazza degli Aranci) and eleventh-century castle/Renaissance palace higher up on Via della Rocca are here and are open to the public (09.00-12.00 and 16.00-19.00; closed Mondays). The fifteenth-century Duomo was built by the same family and contains many of their tombs.

Pietrasanta and the Apuan Alps

Pietrasanta

This is a medieval town notable for its fourteenth-century Romanesque-Gothic Duomo di San Martino. Inside there is a fresco of the Giotto school, seventeenth-century works by Rosselli and Dandini and a fine marble choir.

Pietrasanta is good as a base for drives or walks in the mountains behind. By car you might go via the following routes:

Pietrasanta-Capriglia-Capezzano-Pietrasanta; Pietrasanta-Pieve di SS Giovanni e Felicita-Valdicastello Carducci; Pietra-

santa-Seravezza-Ruosina-Levigliani-Terrinca-Cipollaio Tunnel-
Arni;   Pietrasanta-Querceta-Ripa-Strettoia-Castello   Aghinolfi-
Montignoso-Cerreto-Foce del Pasquilio-Pariana-S. Carlo Terme-
Massa-Pietrasanta; and Pietrasanta-Camaiore-Pieve SS Giovanni e
Stefano-Montemagno-Gombitelli-Lucese.

There is good walking to be had from Arni, Lucese and other places
in the area; obtain the latest information from the nearest information
office.

Camaiore
Camaiore is of interest for its Romanesque churches, namely Pieve di
SS. Giovanni and Stefano ($1^{1}/_{2}$ miles south west of the town) and the
Collegiata. Also worth seeing is the Badia dei Santi Benedettini, the
Benedictine abbey.

Viareggio

Tourist information: Viale G.Carducci 10. Tel: (0584) 48881. The
railway station is reasonably centrally located.

This is the main sea resort of Tuscany, growing in importance only
from the early nineteenth-century when Duchess Maria Luisa
developed what had been a village, important as Lucca's access to
the sea. It is a busy, colourful resort, worth a visit for its unusual
architecture and for a rather old-fashioned holiday atmosphere.
Interesting here is Italian Art Nouveau architecture by Galileo Chini
and Alfredo Belluomini from the 1920s, particularly the Gran Caffe
Margherita, the Bagna Balena, the Supercinema, all of which are to
found on the Passegiata Viale Regina Margherita, and Puccini's villa
on Piazza Puccini. In 1917 a fire burnt most of the wooden Art
Nouveau buildings for which Viareggio had been previously known
– one survives, the Negozio Martini, of 1900.
    Viareggio is also famous for its extravagant papier-mache floats
which appear during Carnevale on Shrove Tuesday.

EIGHTEEN

To the west of Florence

From Florence to Pisa – Route Two

The second route from Florence to Pisa follows the River Arno (the Middle Valdarno) and touches Empoli, Vinci, San Miniato, Castelfiorentino and Certaldo. Take the N67 towards Livorno (Leghorn) through the Florence suburb of Signa. There is a train service along this route from Florence, too.

On the way to Empoli

The Etruscan town of **Artimino** has a medieval castle, the Romanesque church of San Leonardo with traces of Lombard and Etruscan remains, and Fernandina Villa by Buontalenti with an Etruscan museum. **Comeana** has Etruscan tombs while **Carmignano** has the church of San Michele and its celebrated *Visitation* by Pontormo

> '...based on the dynamic twisting of the figures, deformed in the central swelling of the clothes, crooked like the reflection in a curved mirror, this painting follows a curly winding line in a shiny combination of cold, light and bright colours'.

Of Pontormo, Vasari noted:

> 'What most annoyed other men about him was that he would not work save when and for whom he pleased and after his own fancy.'

Poggio a Caino is well known for its Medici Villa, open 09.00-13.30, closed Mondays. The park is closed one hour before dusk. Originally the property of the Strozzi, it was bought by Lorenzo il Magnifico and redesigned by G. da Sangallo. Francesco I and Bianca Cappello died here on the same day in 1587. Occupied throughout the following centuries, it was ofen used to receive honoured guests before they entered the city. On the ground floor is a seventeenth-century theatre with the beautiful frieze attributed to A. del Sansovino. There are also works by Pontormo, Andrea del Sarto and Franciabiagio.

South of Scandicci is San Paolo a Mosciano and the **Villa Mirenda**, where D. H. Lawrence stayed in 1927 and where he completed *Lady Chatterley's Lover*. A short distance north west of Fornaci is the beautiful tenth-century Abbey of **S. Salvatore a Settimo**, fortified in 1371. (You may need to ring the bell for entry.) On the left of the high altar is a fine Tabernacle by G. da Sangallo and in the nearby chapel are frescoes by Giovanni da San Giovanni.

Lastra a Signa retains its city walls, as well as the Loggia di Sant' Antonio Hospital said to be built by Brunelleschi for the Silk Guild, the church of San Martino in Gangalandi by Alberti and Caruso's Villa di Bellosguardo. The church of Santa Maria has thirteenth-century frescoes.

In **Signa**, in the Church of San Lorenzo, are fourteenth-century frescoes and a fine marble pulpit. Montelupo Fiorentino is famous for ceramics and has a ceramics museum at Via Baccio Sinaldi, 45. The castle dates from 1203, the church of San Giovanni Evangelista has a *Madonna* by the school of Botticelli and the Villa Ambrosiana by Buontalenti (1587) is nearby; it may be viewed from the outside.

Empoli

It was here that the Sienese, having defeated the Florentines in the Battle of Montaperti in 1260, failed to take advantage by deciding not to sack the city. Thus Florence was allowed to go on to become the greatest city of Tuscany, perhaps Italy or even Europe. It is mostly a modern town, with one building of particular interest – the Romanesque **Collegiata Sant' Andrea** with a façade of which the lower part dates back to 1093. The church gives on to the art gallery with a particularly fine collection, including works by Masolino (*Pieta* fresco), the Rossellino brothers and Pontormo. (Open 10.00-12.00; closed Mondays.)

The fourteenth-century church of **San Stefano** (normally only open for mass on Saturday evenings) also has works by Masolino and a *Nativity* by Passignano.

Castelfiorentino and Certaldo

Eight miles south of Empoli on the N429 is **Castelfiorentino**, a hill town with thirteenth-century church of San Francesco with frescoes, and a *Pieta* panel attributed to a pupil of Filippino Lippi, and the eighteenth-century church of San Verdiana with a Baroque façade and paintings by Gherardini and Giovanni di Isidoro Baratta. In the adjacent rectory there is a good gallery with interesting fourteenth-century paintings including a Duccio and a Gaddi. Frescoes by Gozzoli are in the Cappella della Visitazione at Via Gozzoli, 55.

Certaldo (the old part known as Castello) is a delightful town some 13 miles south of Empoli which sits prettily on a hill within the old walls. It has a fourteenth-century Pretorial Palace with, in its chapel, Gozzoli's *Tabernacle of the Punished*, the church of San Jacopo and San Michele (with tabernacles from the della Robbia workshop, and Boccaccio's tomb), Boccaccio's house (open 09.00-12.00 and 15.00 - 18.00) is at Via Boccaccio, 18, where he spent the last years of his life. There is a very good little information office on the main street of the old town.

West of Certaldo is Montaione. West again is the Monastery of San Vivaldo in the woods surrounded by 20 chapels.

Empoli to Pisa

North of Empoli is the town of **Vinci**, home of Leonardo da Vinci who was the son of a lawyer and his maid. His father's house where Leonardo was born, is in fact a couple of miles to the south-east in Anchiano. (Open 09.30-12.00 and 14.30-18.00; closed Wednesdays.)

In Vinci itself you may visit the Conti Guidi Castle, now the **Museo Leonardiano**, where models of the inventions Leonardo never succeeded in building are displayed, along with reproductions of his drawings. Thus you can see his idea of a bicycle, an aeroplane and so on. (Open 09.30-12.00 and 14.30-18.00.)

Cerreto Guidi, nearby, is well known for its **Villa Medicea** by Buontalenti where Paolo Giordano Orsini murdered his wife Isabella, daughter of Cosimo I, in 1576 and which is approached by crossing the 'Medici bridges'. Inside there is a collection of Medici portraits and all the families into which they married. (Open 09.00-14.00 or 09.00-13.00 on Sundays; closed Mondays.) Cerreto also has its own palio every year.

San Miniato

San Miniato is sometimes called San Miniato al Tedesco – 'of the Germans' – from the days when northern Italian towns were forced to pay tribute to the Holy Roman Emperor (Barbarossa was one of the Emperors to have stayed here). It is a hill town on the old pilgrim route from Pavia to Rome with fine views of the surrounding countryside. Originally a Roman village, it was fortified either by Desiderius, the last King of the Lombards, or by the Emperor Otto I. Matilda of Tuscany came from here and it has been claimed that the Bonaparte family are from here originally. The poet Pier della Vigna, secretary to Frederick II, accused of treason by his master, is said to have committed suicide in gaol here, but it is more likely that it was in Pisa. His moving story is told by Dante in *Inferno* XIII, where he placed the suicides.

It was also an important fortress in the twelfth-century. There are two medieval towers, the Duomo campanile and the nearby taller Torrione. The twelfth-century Duomo boasts a Crucifix by Baccio da Montelupo and nineteenth-century frescoes by Gatti. Next to it is the Diocesan Museum which contains a bust by Verrocchio and a *Madonna* by Neri di Bicci. (Open 10.00-12.30 and 15.30-19.00.) Nearby also is the twelfth-century Imperial Vicar's Palace.

San Domenico, on Piazza del Popolo, has works by Masolino, Pisanello, Gaddi, Poppi and B. Rossellino. Also of interest are the Church of the Trinity and the Santuario del Crocefisso.

On the first Sunday after Easter San Miniato is host to the National Kite Flying Contest.

From San Miniato towards Pisa

Fucecchio, on the lower slopes of Monte Albano, has the eleventh-century collegiate church of San Giovanni Battista with a fifteenth-century Tuscan school *Madonna*. San Salvatore contains paintings by Vasari. Other places of some interest include **Montopoli** in Val d' Arno, a small eleventh-century town, Villa di Camugliano, Casciano Terme and Palaia to the south. Also worth a visit are **Vicopisano** with its castle, to the north and **Cascina**, with its walls and churches of San Benedetto a Settimo (with a fourteenth-century Irish altarpiece in alabaster), San Casciano and San Giovanni Evangelista. **Certosa di Pisa** is a Baroque abbey housing the University natural history collection started by the Medici. (Open 09.30-12.00 and 14.00-17.00.) **Calci** has an interesting church and a disused monastery, one of the finest in Italy.

Pisa

Pisa is the location for Tuscany's international and main domestic airport. It is served by trains from all major cities - the nearest station to the Leaning Tower is S. Rossore, though the main station is on the southern edge of the town. Tourist information can be found at Lungarno Mediceo, 42 (Tel: 050 20351), Stazione Centrale (Tel: 050 42291) or Piazza Duomo (Tel: 050 501761).

Pisa is one of those places so famous for a single item, the Leaning Tower, that you might be forgiven for thinking there is nothing else there at all. Of course there are plenty of other things to enjoy – after all the Republic of Pisa was, in its heyday, one of the most powerful states in Europe and initially the most powerful of the Tuscan republics.

It was a Roman settlement originally and became the first commune by virtue of the election of consuls in 1085; it retained its importance as a river and seaport (Pisa was then on the coast) and along with Genoa, Venice and Amalfi ruled the Mediterranean during the eleventh, twelfth and thirteenth centuries. Pisa was dominant, however, until defeat at the hands of the Genoese in 1284. It established an empire, ruling Corsica and Sardinia for a while and establishing trading colonies in Byzantium. Towards the end of theeleventh-century the republic's prosperity enabled it to embark on a building programme during which the Pisan Romanesque style was developed and which had a considerable effect on the architecture of the whole province. This spectacular growth can be measured by the expansion of the city walls: in the early days they enclosed only 74 acres, growing to 114 acres in 1162 and 185 acres by the end of the thirteenth-century. Pisa, powerful like other republics of the region, nonetheless had the advantage of being a port and acted as a conduit for all the new ideas from the countries it dealt with, architectural and otherwise.

Pisa's most famous son is Galileo Galilei (see History section), though there were others, and its scholarly tradition is shown by the importance of the university, much older and venerable than Florence. However, Pisa's fate was sealed when the prospering Florence needed a sure outlet to the sea – it became part of the Florentine empire in 1406.

The Campo dei Miracoli – Field of Miracles

Unusually the Cathedral is not in the centre of town but on the northern edge of the city. Ruskin, when he visited Pisa, wrote of 'the first sight of Pisa, where the solemnity and purity of its architecture impressed me deeply.' The break with Byzantine art happened in Pisa, not in Florence. And the first manifestation of this was in the building of the Cathedral in Romanesque and Gothic style. The architect was Greek; and this was the first time marble had been used since Classical times. Then came the Baptistry, the Leaning Tower campanile and the Camposanto. It is an astonishing ensemble, like a perfect picture of antiquity and an example of dedicated town planning.

The **Duomo** is one of the finest works of Pisan Romanesque, started by the Greek in 1063 and finished by Rainaldo in the twelfth-century. Buscheto is buried in the left arch of the façade. You are immediately struck by the sheer number of arches, the principal ornamentation on an otherwise straightforward exterior. The Gothic arches around the cupola were added after the dedication of the Cathedral. Notable are the bronze doors on the right apse, the Porte San Ranieri, by Bonanno Pisano, architect of the Leaning Tower.

The interior, partly destroyed by fire in the sixteenth-century, is notable for the pulpit, made sometime between 1302 and 1311 by Giovanni Pisano, one of the masterpieces of Italian art. It is a revolutionary mixture of the classical and the Christian – St. Michael supports the pulpit with Hercules and the Fates. The panels describe scenes from the life of Christ. The thirteenth-century mosaic *Lord in Glory* in the apse is by Cimabue. There is a portrait of St. Agnes by Andrea del Sarto at the entrance to the Choir and other portraits of saints by the same artist on the walls beneath the Cantoria.

Many of the pillars inside date from Roman times. Opposite the altar hangs a bronze lamp – its oscillations after being lit by the sacristan are supposed to have inspired Galileo's theory of the pendulum – even if this lamp happens to have been made some years after the publication of the theory. The tomb for Emperor Henry VII in the left outer aisle is by Tino di Camaiano. A fragment of mosaic by the altar dates back to the eleventh century.

The Baptistry

The first architect was called Diotisalvi ('May God save you') and he started work in the mid-twelfth-century; he completed the lower half in Pisan style. The upper Gothic portion was taken on by Giovanni and Nicola Pisano and only completed by Cellino di Nese towards the end of the fourteenth-century. The roof was originally open to the skies. The door facing the Duomo is decorated with a *Madonna* by Giovanni Pisano.

The interior is dominated by the thirteenth-century font by Guido Bigianelli from Como. The pulpit is by Nicola Pisano in 1260, the first to blend Gothic with Classical. The reliefs represent the *Nativity, Epiphany, Presentation in the Temple, Crucifixion* and *Last Judgement*. The famous echo ('eco' in Italian) may be demonstrated by the custodian, for a consideration.

The Leaning Tower (Campanile or Torre Pendente)

This was begun in 1173 by Bonanno Pisano, continued from the third floor by Giovanni di Simone in about 1275 and finished in the late fourteenth century by Tommaso di Andrea da Pontedera. It is 163 feet (50 metres) high and leans an astonishing 14 feet (4.3 metres). Still its famous idiosyncracy conceals the fact that it is one of the most unusual and elegant Romanesque designs in Italy or indeed Europe. The question is whether the lean is deliberate or not? It seems unlikely but there are those who find it impossible that the sandy soil could have subsided only after the first couple of floors had been built. Anyway, attempts are periodically made to shore the tower up but to no avail. Galileo carried out some of his experiments from the top of it. Currently closed, there has been some talk of reopening it to the public.

The Camposanto

Open 09.00-19.00 April-September or 09.00-17.00 October-March.

This is the sacred field or cemetery which owes its beginning, it is said, to Archbishop Lanfranchi, who having led the Pisans on the Crusade, brought back tons of holy soil to bury the dead. Started by Giovanni di Simone in 1278, it is a rather beautiful marble rectangular cloister with a Gothic tabernacle over one door. Over the centuries, its halls were decorated with frescoes by some of the greatest artists of their time. Unfortunately, it was badly damaged in World War II. Most of the frescoes have survived though some have been removed to the Museo delle Sinopie.

There are some 600 tombstones in the floor of the Gothic galleries, which are also lined with Graeco-Roman sarcophagi and sculptures. The frescoes are:

South Gallery (entrance): Gozzoli, *Fall of Jericho; Youth of Moses; Queen of Shebah and Solomon; Story of Joseph; Story of Abraham.*
Veneziano, *Return of St. Ranieri.*
A. Bonaaiuti, *St. Ranieri in the Holy Land* and *Conversion*;
Spinello Aretino, *Life of St. Ephysius*;
T. Gaddi, *Story of Job.*

North Gallery: Piero di Puccio, *Theological Cosmograph* (the circle in the centre represents a map of Asia, Europe and Africa, the lines representing the Mediterranean, the Black Sea and the Nile), *Cain and Abel; Adam; The Ark and the Flood.*
Benozzo Gozzoli, *Tower of Babel.*

Behind is the **Cappella Ammannati** with fourteenth-century frescoes variously attributed to Orcagna, Buffalmacco and others. Their theme, *Triumph of Death, The Last Judgement*, gave inspiration to Liszt (whose bust is here) for his 'Totentanz'.
The *Crucifixion* is by Maestro della Crocefisione di Camposanto.
The Patience of Job is by T. Gaddi.
At the east end is Gozzoli's *Wine harvest* and *Drunkeness of Noah.*

West Gallery: Left to right – the *Story of Esther* and the *Story of Judith*. The chains from the old port of Pisa are in the centre.

Museums

There are two museums on the Field of Miracles. The Museo delle Sinopie is dedicated to sketches for frescoes, especially those lost in the Camposanto fire. It is on the south of the square in the former Ospedale Nuovo di Misericordia. (Open 09.30-12.30, and 15.00-16.30.) The Museo dell'Opera del Duomo on nearby Piazza Arcivescovado in the Chapter House contains fragments and ornaments from the Duomo exterior, sculptures by the Pisano's and Tino di Camaino and models of the Duomo. Note especially Giovanni Pisano's ivory *Madonna and Child*. (Open 08.00-20.00 in summer, 09.00-17.00 in winter.)

Pisa city

The city is divided in two – north and south – by the River Arno.

North Pisa

The ancient centre of the old Republic is in the area of Piazza dei Cavalieri, reached by taking Via Santa Maria from near the leaning tower and turning left into Via dei Mille. Pisa, like other of the

Tuscan communes, was once a city of towers; in the 1160s the traveller Benjamin of Tudela described Pisa as 'a very great city, with about 10,000 turreted houses for battle at times of strife'. The height of the towers was restricted from 1100, to ensure that no single individual saw himself as above the Communal government, and fines were levied on any citizen daring to attack another tower. By the end of the twelfth-century they were destroyed. A new law stated, as the buildings grew shorter, that washing was not to be hung so low that it might impede a man on horseback.

If you care to visit the **Roman Baths** first, near the Porta Lucca, take Via Cardinale Maffi from near the tower instead. To the south-east of the Baths, on Piazza Santa Caterina, is the thirteenth-century church of **Santa Caterina** with fine Pisan façade and which contains works by Traini and Nino Pisano. To reach Piazza dei Cavalieri from here take Via Carducci from the Baths and turn right at Via San Lorenzo. The Cavalieri in question were the Knights of the Order of Santo Stefano, started by Cosimo I in 1562 to vanquish the Saracen. Their Palazzo dei Cavalieri (or della Carovana), designed by Vasari in the sixteenth century to replace the old republican Palazzo del Popolo (with a nineteenth-century external staircase), dominates the square and is now a school. Nearby is the church of **Santo Stefano dei Cavalieri**, also by Vasari, with a façade by Giovanni de' Medici. Inside is a bust by Donatello.

The beautiful **Palazzo Gherardesca** (or Palazzo dell' Orologio) is also by Vasari – it is thought to stand on the remains of the 'hunger tower' as mentioned by Dante in *Inferno* XXXIII, the circle of traitors. Count Ugolino della Gherardesca was of Ghibelline family but sold out to the Guelfs and eventually became Podesta of the city. Threatened by war, he ceded land to the Lucchese after which the Ghibellines, led by Archbishop Ruggieri, rose up and had him immured here, along with his sons and nephews, until they starved to death. Ugolino was forced to eat his own sons – 'ond'io mi diedi, gia cieco, a brancolar sovra ciascuno'. He is buried in the plain Gothic church of San Francesco, of the early thirteenth-century, on Via San Francesco. It has works by Tommaso Pisano, Taddeo Gaddi, Di Pietro Gerini and Di Bartolo.

The **Museo di San Matteo** on Lungarno Mediceo specialises in Pisan art from 1100 to 1400 but also has some works by other Italian artists. There are works by Martini, Traini, di Bartolo, Agnolo Gaddi, Turino Vanni, Antonio Veneziano, various Pisanos, di Bicci, da Fabriano, Masaccio, Donatello, Fra Angelico and Gozzoli. (Open 08.30-19.30 or 08.30-13.30 on Sundays; closed Mondays.)

Nearby is the sixteenth-century **Palazzo Toscanelli**, home to Byron in 1821, and the Prefecture which is housed in a thirteenth-century Medici palace. **San Michele in Borgo** dating from 990, off the Borgo Stretto (itself an attractive street with colonnaded doorways from 1000-1600) has an impressive fourteenth-century façade.

Also of interest is the twelfth-century **San Nicola**, just north of Lungarno Pacinotti, close to the Palazzo Reale. It has works by Jacopo della Quercia, Traini and Nino Pisano; in its campanile there is a fine staircase. **Galileo's House Museum** is on Via Santa Maria and Via delle Belle Torri contains some fine medieval houses.

South Pisa

If you cross by the Ponte di Mezzo (scene of the June 'Gioco di Ponte'), you will arrive in **Piazza XX Settembre** with its early seventeenth-century market hall called the Logge di Banchi. Beyond, going south, is the main shopping street of Pisa, the Corso Italia. Here you are close to **San Sepolcro** on the Lungarno Galileo Galilei, by Diotisalvi, architect of the Baptistry. Also on the Lungarno is the **Palazzo Scotto**, home to Shelley in 1822.

Near the Solferino bridge is the **Santa Maria della Spina**, 'of the thorn', a Gothic masterpiece. Its name comes supposedly from Christ's crown of thorns brought back from the Crusades. The church took on its present form in 1323, with exterior sculptures from the school of Giovanni Pisano and sculptures inside by Nino Pisano.

Further west along the Lungarno Sonnino is the fine church of **San Paolo a Ripa d'Arno** and Via Mazzini, 29, houses the Mazzini museum. The oldest bar in Pisa is the Antico Caffe dell' Ussero, Lungarno Pacinotti, 27.

Marina di Pisa

Marina di Pisa is a bathing resort with some Art Nouveau houses. On the way to it you may pass San Piero a Grado, an unusual eleventh-century Romanesque basilica built where St. Peter is said to have landed on his way to Rome.

Near Pisa

The coastal areas near to Pisa are mostly pine and scrub forest, quite similar to how the whole coast looked originally. The names of the areas here are Macchia di Migliarino, San Rossore and Tombolo. A section of San Rossore is open on Sundays, the entrance is on Viale delle Cascine.

NINETEEN

Southern Tuscany and the Coast

The coast from Livorno southwards

Livorno (Leghorn)

The train station is on the eastern edge of the city. Livorno is an important ferry port: there are daily departures to Corsica, a French Departement for which some nationals may need a visa. There are also services to Sardinia and to the Tuscan islands of Elba and Capraia. The Tourist Office is on Piazza Cavour, 6 (Tel: (0586) 33111) or at the railway station and at the port in the summer.

Traditionally this is the most important port on the Tuscan coast, now the largest container seaport in the Mediterranean. It is a purpose-built city of the sixteenth century by Buontalenti commissioned by the Medici to replace Pisa's silted harbour. It still bustles in the way it always has, a town where commerce has not stimulated the art that it has in the other cities of Tuscany. It has longstanding ties with Great Britain. Why the English have always called it Leghorn is a matter of debate; some say that it is a mispronunciation of the old name of Legiorno. There is good seafood to be eaten here; a famous Livornese dish is Cacciucco fish stew.

There was a small settlement here in the Middle Ages but the town grew in importance only after 1571. The Englishman Sir Robert Dudley constructed the original port area. The town continued to thrive particularly after Ferdinand I's declaration of religious liberty encouraged persecuted worshippers of many nationalities to reside

(Opposite) Top: *Home of noble wines – the main square of Montepulciano.*
(Opposite) Bottom: *Style – a jewellery shop in Lucca.*

here and after 1618 when it became a free port. It has continued to thrive despite being heavily bombed during World War II.

Shelley, Byron and Smollet lived here during their sojourns in Tuscany; the composer Mascagni ('Cavalleria Rusticana') and the artist Modigliani were born here.

What to see

Livorno is not rich in monuments although it is not without interest. The streets are still filled with people of a surprisingly wide variety of nationalities and the port remains busy. The entrance to it is on Piazza Micheli, which is also the site of the noteworthy bronze sculpture *Quattro Mori* ('Four Moors') made by Pietro Tacca in 1623 as a symbol of Tuscan supremacy on the sea. It is near a statue of Ferdinand I by Bandini from 1595. Near the harbour, to your right as you look out to sea, is the sixteenth-century **Fortezza Vecchia**, containing the eleventh-century 'Matilda Tower'.

Between the port and the Fortezza Nuova is an unusual area known as **New Venice** (Nuova Venezia), a small, tranquil quarter of houses and canals laid out in 1629-44. The nearby church of Santa Caterina has a *Coronation of the Virgin* by Vasari. The nearby Bottini d' Olio are early eighteenth-century warehouses for oil with a fine vaulted hall, now used for exhibitions.

Via Grande takes you from the port to Piazza Grande and the Duomo, in the city centre. The **Duomo** was designed by Inigo Jones in 1605 and had to be rebuilt after the war. Via Grande continues to the undistinguished Piazza della Repubblica and the Fortezza Nuova of 1590. From here Via Larderel, and then Viale Carducci takes you past the **Palazzo Larderel** (1832) and the **Cisternone**, a neoclassical water cistern (1829). Nearby, south, is **Piazza XX Settembre** and the Mercatino, a Saturday market specialising in imported goods.

Via Cairoli runs south-east from the Duomo and crosses the Fosso Reale (the former moat). On Via Verdi, right, at 59 is the **English Cemetery**, burial place of the writer Smollett in 1773 and various British and American former residents. (If closed, apply to the Misericordia.)

(Opposite) Top: *The sparkling mosaics of San Frediano in Lucca, showing Christ and the Apostles.*
(Opposite) Bottom: *The glorious Art Nouveau interior of a restaurant in Viareggio.*

Further south, less than one mile, is the **Museo Civico** in the Villa Fabbricotti, which contains works by the 'Macchiaioli' painters, Italy's nineteenth-century Impressionists, and Modigliani. (Open 10.00-13.00 and 16.00-19.00 on Thursdays. Closed Mondays.)

The coast road south of the port is Viale Italia and leads past the Terrazza Mascagni, a pleasant look-out point, and the aquarium. It goes on to pass the Naval Academy, some Art Nouveau houses and the pleasant town of **Ardenza** with its 1840 neo-classical crescent.

On a hill five miles (nine kilometres) to the south is the town of **Montenero**, which can also be reached by funicular railway (funicolare, pronounced fooneekohlaray). Smollett lived and wrote here, and Byron and Shelley were frequent visitors. The Pilgrim's Church has an ornate Baroque interior and is brimful of paintings and offerings made by worshippers thankful to have been saved from shipwreck by the Madonna of Montenero, the patron saint of Tuscany.

The coast south of Livorno is well endowed with well-used beaches. Among the best are in the vicinity of the otherwise undistinguished resort of San Vicenzo. In the hills behind is the pretty little town of **Suvereto**.

Populonia

About nine miles (15 kilometres) north of Piombino is this old Etruscan town, possibly one of the 12 cities of the Etruscan federation. There is a small Museo Etrusco, which is closed on Sundays. The Etruscsan Necropolis date back to 900-300 BC. (Open 09.00-12.00, 16.00-20.00 and 14.00-18.00 in winter.) The port, which runs into neighbouring Porto Baratti, was where the iron ore from Elba was unloaded and smelted in the Etruscan period.

The Tuscan Islands

Elba

The steel town of Piombino is the principal mainland port for Elba. There are two companies operating regular sailings of car ferries: Toremar, whose main office at Scali del Corso, 5, Livorno (Tel: 0586 22772); and Navarma at Piazzale Premuda, 13, Piombino (Tel: 0565 33032). There are at least three sailings a day all year round and the crossing takes one or two hours depending upon the route. Toremar runs hydrofoil services in the summer which are faster and more expensive. There is also a daily five-hour service from Livorno. There is an air service from Pisa.

Cars can be hired at Portoferraio (Tel: 915368) and Porto Azzurro (Avis Tel: 95000) and there is a good bus service. Passengers without cars should disembark at Portoferraio. The tourist information is at Calata Italia, 26, Portoferraio (Tel: 0565 916350), near where the ferries dock.

Although tourism has replaced steel as the most important industry on Elba, the island has retained much of its charm. Tourism here is reasonably discreet, with lots of small resorts. The island is 18 miles (29 kilometres) long and 11 miles (18 kilometres) wide.

Elba (which is derived from the Greek word for iron) has always been important for its minerals; copper and iron were sought here by the Etruscans, Greeks and Romans, who colonised it and for whom it became a home for their villas. It changed hands many times in the centuries following the fall of Rome until it became part of the Pisan empire in the eleventh-century. It remained Pisan until the sixteenth-century when Cosimo I took it for Florence. Then it was partitioned between Spain and the Grand Duchy of Tuscany until the eighteenth-century when it was briefly held by the British and 1802 when it was taken by Napoleon. Following his defeat at the hands of the British, Napoleon was offered the governership of Elba in 1814. He raised standards of education, built roads and took the iron industry in hand. All of this was accomplished quickly for within nine months of his arrival he had escaped to raise another army. Elba became part of Tuscany again.

Portoferraio ('Iron Harbour') population 11,000, is the island's capital. The walls, built by Cosimo I, mostly remain complete and include the Porta a Mare and Torre del Martello. The old quarter lies beyond the 1637 fortified gateway. Beyond the Porta is Piazza Cavour from which Via Garibaldi leads to the Palazzino dei Mulini, the former residence of Napoleon, which contains many items of contemporary interest. (Open 09.00-13.30 and 09.00-12.30 on Sundays. Closed Mondays.) Two churches on Via Garibaldi contain Napoleon's death masks. Near to the Palazzino are the two Medici fortresses, one of which, Falcone, can be visited from the Porta a Terra on the sea front. The heart of the town is Piazza della Repubblica. Here is the Museo Archeologico della Linguella.

Out of the town, at **Bagnaia**, there is a charming twelfth-century church, Santo Stefano. Napoleon's summer residence, the **Villa Napoleonica di San Martino**, with charming frescoes, is west of

Portoferraio. In the **Le Grotte** district, three miles (five kilometres) south-east, are the ruins of an Imperial Roman villa, close to the Terme di San Giovanni, where sufferers from rheumatism and throat and skin ailments can take the waters.

For mineralogists the picturesque mining town of **Capoliveri** will be of interest, where you may search for the likes of gold pyrites. **Rio nell' Elba**, at the east of the island, is another old mining centre with plenty of old mines from different periods in the vicinity. At **Rio Marina** there is a mineralogical museum. **Porto Azzurro**, built by the Spaniards and called Porto Longone until 1947, is well known for its fortress, built in 1603, which became a prison. North of the town is the Santuario di Monserrato with its well known Black Madonna dating from 1606.

The town of **Marciano** is charming with remains of the old fortress and wall, and an archeology museum. The town offers fine views from the summit of Monte Capanne, which may be reached by cable car.

The best beaches are at **Procchio** and **Marciana Marina** though there are plenty of good small ones for those with a boat, which can be hired. There are also sporting facilities for golf, tennis, sailing, riding and scuba diving. Tropical plants flourish here as well as the native Mediterranean vegetation. Some very good DOC wines, both white and red, are produced here. Fish, of course, features a great deal in the local cooking.

Gorgona

To visit this island, administered by Livorno, you will need special permission from the Ministry of Justice (Ministero di Giustizia). This is because there has been a prison here since the time of Pope Gregory the Great. Its most interesting feature is its barrenness. There is also a museum of archeology.

Capraia

The third largest of the islands, Capraia may be reached from Livorno and Elba by ferry. It is of interest for flora and the Fortezza San Giorgio, a fifteenth-century castle built by the Genoese. There are good views from Monte Arpagna and beautiful water lilies on the lake at Lo Stagnone. In the town of Capraia Isola is the church of S. Antonio, an eleventh-century chapel dedicated to the Vergine Assunta, a pair of towers, a ruined Roman villa and the fifteenth-century Genoese Fortezza San Giorgio. The Grotta di Parino cave near Monte Pontica is a sacred place of meditation.

Pianosa

A very flat island nine miles (14 kilometres) from Elba. It is also a prison island that sometimes may be visited by gaining permission from the judicial authorities in Piombino. On the east of the island there is a ruined Roman villa, to which Postumio Agrippa was banished by his uncle Augustus.

Montecristo

Probably ancient Artemisia, Montecristo (where Dumas set his *The Count of Montecristo*), is 25 miles (40 kilometres) from Elba. Dumas's inspiration was a legend of buried treasure left by Benedictine monks who occupied the ruined monastery. Cone shaped, it was the hunting reserve of Italian kings and is now a nature reserve for rare flora and fauna, among which is a wild goat said by the locals to have gold teeth. It is possible to visit a very small part of the island (Cala Maestra) privately or on excursions from Elba. The mountain, hunting lodge and all else are out of bounds.

Isola del Giglio (Lily Island)

The second largest island can be reached from Porto Santo Stefano by car ferry. The island's name is a corruption of the Roman Aegilium. There is a bus service from Giglio Porto, with its beaches, to the delightful fortified village of Giglio Castello. Here there is a castle, medieval walls and church with early frescoes and an ivory Christ by Giambologna. It also keeps the arm of San Mamiliano, a sixth-century hermit from Montecristo whose death prompted so much excitement in the area that it was decided to divide his corpse among the claimants. Giglio won an arm. On the island there are holiday villages, a camping site and a sandy beach at Campese.

Giannutri

This is the southern-most of the Tuscan islands. Though privately owned it can be reached by scheduled ship from Porto Santo Stefano. It is very green, covered in vineyards and olive groves. In the north there is a ruined Roman harbour and villa.

The Maremma – a sweet wilderness

The Maremma is Italy's answer to the Camargue - a coastal area to the south of Piombino of pine groves and marshland forest following the curve of the Golfo di Follonica and on to Grosseto. For the Etruscans it was an important agricultural and commercial area as the remains of several Etruscan towns testify. It was neglected by the Romans, however, who allowed it to degenerate into swamp, thus encouraging the mosquito and a reputation in the Middle Ages for malaria and disease.

In the eighteenth-century efforts were made to rehabilitate the region and though there have been a few hiccups, malaria has long gone and the Maremma is once again prosperous whilst retaining something of its wild flavour, with cowboys and long stretches of pine-backed beach and unspoiled spaces.

Follonica is essentially a new, busy resort town with beaches and the Museum of Iron and Cast Iron in an 1830s foundry. It is also the nearest railway station for the beautiful town of Massa Marittima – see below. **Punta Ala** is an exclusive marina resort with good beach, golf and polo facilities. **Castiglione della Pescaia** is an older resort and ancient fishing village with sixteenth-century Aragonese castle. It is the burial place of the writer Italo Calvino (1923-85).

Inland from Castiglione by 14 miles (23 kilometres) is the town of **Vetulonia**, where Etruscan burial grounds, (with, in particular, the Tomba della Pietrera and Il Diavolino) lie at the foot of the pretty medieval town which also boasts Roman mosaics and other Etruscan remains.

Another Etruscan ruined town is **Roselle**, off the N223 about seven miles (ten kilometres) north-east of Grosseto; there is a large section of Etruscan wall surrounding the town dating from 600 BC to 200 BC. There are the remains, too, of an amphitheatre, forum and baths (the Romans occupied the town later) and Etruscan dwelling houses and shops. These, along with the medieval remains and the view, combine to give an impressively desolate view of the decline of successive civilisations.

Massa Marittima

This is a beautiful hill town set among olive and oak some 12^1/$_2$ miles (20 kilometres) from the coast, 19 miles (30 kilometres) from Grosseto, 41 miles (65 kilometres) from Siena. The nearest train station is at Follonica. Tourist information is in the museum opposite the Duomo (Tel: 902289).

This was an Etruscan city, then a medieval bishopric and city state, La Repubblica Massetana, which became Siena's second city in 1337, before finally being taken by Florence. The old town is mostly Romanesque, the new town Gothic. It was the birthplace of Santa Bernadina di Siena and became prosperous through silver and copper mining.

The artistic centre is Piazza Garibaldi, a beautiful example of medieval town planning, dominated by one of Tuscany's greatest monuments, the **Duomo**, started in Romanesque style, completed in Gothic. The magnificent travertine façade, lower half Romanesque, upper half Pisan Gothic, with the story of San Cerbone over the doorway, conceals an airy interior. The campanile dates from the early fifteenth century. Inside there is a beautiful travertine font dating from 1267 by Giroldo da Como, with fifteenth-century tabernacle; behind the high altar is the 1324 tomb of San Cerbone by the Sienese Goro di Gregorio, the reliquary chapel and the Gothic monument to Giuseppe Traversi. There are also some fourteenth-century frescoes, a *Madonna* by Duccio di Boninsegna in the left transept and some Lombard reliefs from the eleventh-century church on which the Duomo was built.

To the left of the Duomo is the Bishop's Palace; then the Palazzo dell'Abbondanza, its name 'abundance' stemming from the time it served as a granary for the Sienese. To the right of the Duomo is the thirteenth-century Romanesque **Palazzo Pretorio del Podesta**, with the coat of arms of the city and the she-wolf of Siena. It was the seat of government of the city throughout its years of prosperity and now contains the city's museums – the Pinacoteca, the Archeological Museum and the Garibaldi Museum. Here, in the Pinacoteca is the town's greatest treasure, which originally decorated the Palazzo Comunale – the *Maesta*, depicting Faith, Hope and Charity, by Ambrogio Lorenzetti dating from 1330. (Open 10.00-12.30 and 15.30-19.00 April-October or 09.00-15.00 and 17.00 November-March; closed Mondays.) The current municipal offices are across the square in the thirteenth-century Palazzo Communale.

From the square Via Moncini leads up to the so-called Citta Nuova or New Town of the fourteenth-century, passing a Sienese fortress built when they captured Massa in 1337. At the top is the tower of the older thirteenth-century fortress, the **Torre del Candeliere** which may be climbed every day except Mondays. Here is **Piazza Matteotti** with fine views of the walls and nearby is **Piazza delle Armi** with its museum of the history of mining and mining art. The main street of this area is Corso Diaz which leads to the fourteenth-century **Sant' Agostino** with a lovely cloister and paintings by Manetti.

Near the Duomo is Via Corridoni and the excellent mining museum built into an old mine. (Guided tours only. Open 10.00-12.30 and 15.30-19.00 April-September, or 11.00-13.00, and 16.00-17.00 October-March.)

Grosseto

Tourist office: Via Monterosa, 20 (Tel: 0564 22534).

This is the capital of the province and of the Maremma. It is not considered one of Tuscany's ornaments but is not without interest. It was subject first to Siena and then to Florence. The town's most striking feature, the hexagonal **city wall** built by the Medici in 1574-93, and which surrounds the old town, dates from the Florentine era. Parts of the wall were turned into raised gardens in the nineteenth century by the Lorraine Dukes, although they still bear something of their military aspect in places. The **Duomo**, built between 1190 and 1250, was restored in the sixteenth century and again, badly, in the nineteenth. Inside there is a valuable ciborium.

The **Archeological and Art Museum** of the Maremma on Piazza Baccarini contains many artefacts from Vetulonia and Roselle – terracottas, urns and so on. In the same building is the art gallery with works by Sienese artists from the thirteenth-century onwards, and works formerly in the Cathedral. (Open 09.30-13.00 and 16.30-19.00 or 09.30-13.00 Sundays; closed on Wednesdays.)

Near the museum is the church of San Francesco with a Crucifix by Duccio di Buoninsegna. The new town has several grandiose edifices dating from the Mussolini period.

On the N223 (to Siena) some 12 miles north-east of Grosseto is the pretty walled village of **Paganico** with church of San Michele and its fourteenth-century frescoes by Bartolo di Fredi. Further still is the walled spa-town of Bagni di Petriolo.

Monti dell' Uccellina

South-east of Grosseto on the coast is the **Maremma Nature Park** and the Monti dell'Uccellina (mountains of the little henbird), reached from the Via Aurelia. These coastal hills are favoured by migrating birds. It is now a park filled with several defence towers including the Bella Marsilia Tower; a reminder of the night in 1543 when the pirates of Khair-ed-Din Barbarossa killed all of the Marsili family except a young daughter who became favourite of Sultan Solimani. There are also caves and the ruined eleventh-century monastery of San Rabano. The landscape varies from macchia (Mediterranean scrub) to swamp and is alive with wild boar, deer, horses which are herded by the local cowboys, the 'butteri', and a wide variety of birds from birds of prey to water fowl. Guided tours are available, call 0564 407098. The visitors centre is at Alberese.

At the southern-most tip of the Park is **Talamone**, a little walled village on an outcrop of rock which used to be Siena's conduit to the sea when the harbour was clear, as illustrated in Siena City Hall. A sixteenth-century Spanish castle looms over the village.

Monte Argentario

This quasi-island connected to the mainland by only the slenderest of links is of considerable interest with attractive towns, mountain scenery and pretty coastline. Once, it was an island but over the centuries the currents deposited sand to the point where sandbars ('tomboli') now connect it to the Tuscan coast. The middle one is partly artificial, completed by the Romans for the town of Orbetello.

These northern and southern tomboli create the **Laguna di Orbetello**, cleft in two by the central tombolo. This lagoon is rich in birdlife, the northern half being a reserve, open to visitors on Thursdays and Sundays (at 10.00 and 14.00). The entrance is on the main coast road between Albinia and Orbetello Scalo. The name of the island could be translated as 'silvery mountain' though it is unclear why it was given that name. The beaches here are quite good and usually rather quieter than elsewhere in Tuscany.

The town of **Orbetello** was originally an important Etruscan port and remained so through the Middle Ages, then being ruled by Spain from 1559 to 1707. It was from here that Italo Balbo made his trans-Atlantic flight to Chicago in 1933. The town retains a certain Spanish feel, with its walls and palm- fringed waterfront. Near the main gate is the Spanish-built Polveria Guzman, the old gunpowder factory and arsenal. The Museo Civico on Piazza della Repubblica contains Etruscan sculptures and the beautiful second-century pediment ('frontone') from an Etruscan temple at Talamone. The Duomo, on the same Piazza, has a delightful fourteenth-century façade and Romanesque altarpiece. The interior was rebuilt in the early seventeenth-century.

There is a road all the way around the island. **Porto Ercole** is worth seeing for its Spanish fortresses and delightful old town with Piazza Santa Barbara and Spanish Governor's Palace, and the church of Sant' Erasmo where the artist Caravaggio, who drowned in the Laguna, is buried. **Porto Santo Stefano**, on the north side of M. Argentario, is larger and busier, acting more as a port for luxury yachts and the ferry that serves Isola del Giglio.

Between the two towns is **Il Punto Telegrafo**, the highest peak on the island, offering fine views. The road up to it passes the Abbey of the Passionist Order, founded by St. Paul of the Cross in 1720.

On the coast a few miles to the south are the ruins of the Etruscan and Roman town of **Cosa**, later called Ansedonia. It sits on a hill, with fine views and an excellent museum open in the mornings. The Roman remains – walls, forum, temple and Capitolium - are quite extensive. The old port was at one time connected to the nearby Lago di Burano before silting took its toll, and to the sea first by a natural cleft and then by another cut by the Etruscans to prevent silting and now known as the 'Tagliata Etrusca'. The nearby **Torre Puccini** was where the composer wrote part of Tosca. (**Lago di Burano** is now a bird sanctuary, closed June and July, otherwise tours operate on Thursdays and Sundays at 10.00 and 14.00.)

The border with Lazio

Inland from Ansedonia is the pretty medieval settlement of **Capalbio**, a walled hill town with castle and twelfth-century frescoed church surrounded by forest.

A little further west on the border with Lazio is the town of **Pescia Fiorentina** and its old iron foundry. Returning to Orbetello and going north to Albinia you may care to take the N74 road that leads west through lovely south Tuscan countryside in the direction of Pitigliano. Shortly, left, the N323 heads for Scansano, passing through **Magliano in Toscana**, another medieval town with fine walls and gates, a couple of interesting churches, and the 1,000 year-old Ulio della Strega (witches olive tree). Close by, south-east, is the ruined eleventh-century Romanesque/Lombard church of San Bruzio.

If you prefer, the N74 the route takes you through the old Sienese fortress town of **Manciano** with its Museo di Preistoria e Protostoria della Valle del fiume Fiora (closed on Mondays) which houses local finds from the eras before recorded history. From Manciano another road leads on to **Montemerano**, another walled town with church and fifteenth-century frescoes; and from there another road leads on to **Saturnia** with ancient walls and medieval ramparts. This is a spa town with baths used since Roman times. It lays claim to being the first city founded in Italy, by Saturn himself.

The N74 continues from Manciano to **Pitigliano**, famous for its white wine, in a magnificent location on a volcanic outcrop amid the gullies of the Meleta, Lente and Prochio ravines. It is the former seat of the Orsini family where their crenellated fourteenth-century fortress, sacked in 1547 during a local revolt, survives still, as does the Orsini Villa with statues carved from the rock. The Baroque Duomo is on the main piazza.

Near Pitigliano is the village of **Sovana**, the birthplace of Pope Gregory VII and host to an Etruscan burial ground with interesting tombs and remains of an Etruscan road (the 'Cavone'). Here too are the remains of the Aldobrandeschi family (of which Gregory was a scion), the Romanesque church of Santa Maria with ninth-century ciborium, several palaces and the splendid eleventh-century Duomo.

Near Sovana is another medieval village worthy of note: **Sorano**, also splendidly located, was declared too dangerous for habitation in 1929 due to landslides but has since been mostly restored. It has a fifteenth-century castle and Orsini palace.

South Tuscany

Siena

The toll-free SS22 takes you to Siena from the north, whilst the N222 and the N2 are rather more scenic and curvy. There are several parking areas around the city walls, some free, some where you must pay. The railway station is one mile (1.5 kilometres) from the centre on Viale G. Mazzini from where there are regular bus services to the old town. Tourist information is located at Via di Citta, 43 (Tel: 0577 42209).

Siena, ancient enemy of Florence, remains the city in Tuscany most likely to rival Florence for its range of attractions. Some prefer it for its location and its Gothic beauty. It is situated between the valleys of the Orbia and Elsa and extends over three hills. The 1604 Porta Camollia has this inscription above it: 'Cor magis tibi Sena pandit' ('Siena opens her heart even wider to you'), a welcome originally reserved for a visit by Grand Duke Ferdinand I. Siena is said to be the home of the best or most authentic spoken Italian.

History

Siena was a Roman town founded by Augustus as Soena Julia, on earlier Etruscan remains. The Siennese symbol remains the she-wolf to this day, since the legendary founder of the city was thought to be the son of Remus. In the time of Charlemagne it was ruled by counts, becoming a republic at the beginning of the twelfth century, basing its prosperity on wool, a silver mine acquired from Volterra and, later, banking. As in all the Tuscan cities the nobles were forced within the walls where they built their towers, losing much of their

A glorious but unrealised ambition – Siena Cathedral.

power but remaining troublesome to the commune for years. Siena was essentially a Ghibelline town, siding with the Holy Roman Emperor in the Ghibelline-Guelph struggles of the thirteenth-century, defeating Florence at the Battle of Montaperti in 1260, after which Florence only just escaped being razed through the pleading of Florentine exiles in the Sienese army. Eventually, following the defeat of the Ghibellines, the city came to be ruled by a Guelph middle class Council of Nine, not dissimilar to the arrangements in Florence, although infighting continued to be a feature of Sienese government for a long time. Nonetheless, this was a time of prosperity and growth, Siena ruling most of southern Tuscany.

It suffered during the plagues of the fourteenth-century, which provoked the beginning of economic decline and political instability, fought Charles IV and then fell to the Viscontis of Milan in their attempts to contain the power of Florence. This was followed by a period of freedom, a period of autocracy under the Petruccis, a further period of liberty which included another defeat of Florence and then occupation by the Spanish in 1530. Cosimo il Vecchio of Florence had the city besieged in 1555 and it fell after 18 months.

A large number of Sienese families were determined to preserve their ancient freedom and maintained a Sienese republic in exile at Montalcino, which lasted some four years before succumbing to Medici power. Henceforth the history of Siena was that of Florence and Tuscany, the city declining into almost total obscurity, until its rediscovery by lovers of art and history in the nineteenth-century. The event most associated with medieval Siena is the Palio which is discussed below.

Sienese art and architecure made their own distinctive contributions. The architecture is essentially Gothic adapted to local conditions, the finest results of which are the Duomo and the Palazzo Communale, though the Renaissance, which came late to Siena, perhaps because of her success with the Gothic, is represented too. The Sienese school of painting flourished during the last part of the thirteenth century and first part of the fourteenth. First, Guido da Siena and then, notably, Duccio di Boninsegna (1260-1319) were its main exponents. Over the centuries others maintained the tradition: Simone Martini, Lippo Memmi, the Lorenzettis, Taddeo and Domenico di Bartolo, Matteo di Giovanni, Lorenzo di Pietro, Sassetta, then Sodoma and Beccafumi, among others. The walls are pretty well intact, with eight of the one-time 38 gates remaining. The three main streets are the Via Banchi di Sopra, the Via di Citta and the Via Banchi di Sotto.

Terzi, Contrade and the Palio

The city, only about one square mile in area, is divided into three medieval 'terzi' ('thirds') around the Campo, the main square – the oldest is the Terzo di Citta in the south-west; the Terzo di Camollia is in the north and the Terzo di San Martino in the south-east.

The 'terzi' are divided into 'contrade' or wards, the original political divisions from which the government representatives were taken. There are now only 17 contrade compared to the original 59, each with its own church, baptistry, museum (for hours see tourist offices), fountains (fed by a network of medieval underground pipes in the surrounding countryside), contrada offices, colours, flag, festivals and saint. In effect they remain independent communities, functioning much as they always have and genuinely chauvinistic. Each is named after and symbolised by an animal.

In the Terzo do Citta you will find Aquila (eagle), Chiocciola (snail), Onda (dolphin), Pantera (panther), Selva (rhinoceros), Tartuca (tortoise). The Terzo di San Martino has: Civetta (owl), Leocorno (unicorn), Nicchio (mussel), Torre (elephant),

Valdimontone (ram). The Terzo di Camollia has: Bruco (caterpillar), Drago (dragon), Giraffa (giraffe), Istrice (porcupine), Lupa (she-wolf), and Oca (goose).

The Palio is a horse race that takes place around the Campo, although it has become something of a tourist spectacle, in fact it is a passionately fought battle between the contrade, as powerful a symbol of rivalry as it was in the late thirteenth century when the first recorded race was run. Battles and games between various quarters of cities are not unique to Siena; there are similar contests all over Tuscany. None, however, are in the form of horse races and none are fought with the spectacular passion of the Siennese Palio.

The Palio is a silk banner embroidered with an image of the Virgin Mary offered to the winner of the race, which consists of three circuits around the Campo, taking place twice a year on 2 July (the Visitation) and 16 August (the day after the Assumption) and lasting about two minutes. Only ten contrade can be represented in each race; this is arranged by lottery. The horses are selected by lot too, but the jockeys (fantini) are selected by each contrada, a much sought-after honour. The brief race is merely the culmination of preparations that last for weeks; there are frequent rehearsals and a banquet for the jockey the night before. Each race is preceded by another rehearsal and pageantry in the form of processions and displays of flag-throwing skills, (the 'sbandierata') by the 'alfieri'. A great deal of money rests on the outcome of each race and on the morning of the race the horse of each contrada is escorted to the appropriate chapel to be blessed where it is considered a good omen if it defecates at the altar. The race is short, rough and with no holds barred; even a riderless horse may win and losers may suffer unpleasant recriminations. But the race is followed by extravagant celebrations, especially for the winning contrada. In order to see the Palio you can stand in the hot and crowded piazza centre or buy expensive stand tickets which need to be booked by April.

The Campo

In many Italian cities the Duomo is the fulcrum of the city. In Siena the hub is the Campo, the magnificent semi-circular plaza where the Palio is run and which is on the site of the Roman forum. It is a many-faceted celebration of patriotism and 'good government'. In its present form it is medieval and although only the Palazzo Pubblico and Palazzo Sansedoni date back to the fourteenth-century, the brick pavement, divided into nine sections representing the old Council of Nine, was originally laid in 1340. Designed before the symmetrical age that was the Renaissance it is an example of instinctive medieval urban design, full of character and variety, but not at the expense of harmony. It is said, in a city that has revered the Virgin for centuries, that the Campo is the protective cloak of the Madonna della Misericordia (Madonna of Mercy, who appeared before the Battle of Montaperti), under which the citizens may take refuge. Not belonging to a Contrada, it was always a neutral place for the citizens where arms were not to be used in anger and where love of city, as opposed to love of contrada, took precedence. It has been the site of many an exotic celebration - the visit of Frederick III and his bride, Eleanor of Portugal, in 1451 and the arrival of the new governess, Princess Violante of Bavaria in 1717. For centuries the campo was the site of the main market of the city.

In the thirteenth century, as Siena expanded, decisions were taken by the Nine to ensure that the Campo did not lose its integrity; regulations were made to prevent encroachment and to preserve a certain harmony of design without insisting on uniformity. Property in the area was purchased by the government and roads were built leading directly to the Campo, thus ensuring a geographical centralisation that coincidentally reflected it as the political centre. Furthermore, the use of brick was encouraged: it was cheaper and the material to produce it was in the fields around the city. If the Campo itself was a playground for the people, of course the palaces that define it belonged to the noble and powerful families of the city.

Clockwise from the Palazzo Pubblico the palazzos are: the Petroni, Piccolomini Salamoneschi, Piccolomini d' Aragona, Ragnoni, Mesxolombardi-Rinaldini, Tornaipuglia Sansedoni, Vincenti, Piccolomini, Rimbotti, the Mercanzia, Saracini, Scotti, Accarigi, Alessi, and Mattasala Lambertini.

The fountain, the Fonte Gaia, is a meagre nineteenth-century reproduction of the original created between 1408 and 1419 by the city's greatest sculpter, Jacopo della Quercia. The badly deteriorated remains of the original are preserved in the Palazzo Pubblico. Its name comes from the celebration of the construction of the water system reaching out into the countryside. Like much of the artistic work in the Palazzo Pubblico, it was a symbol of civic pride and a way of reminding citizens, through its sculpted imagery, where their duties lay.

The Palazzo Pubblico

Today's town hall is in the same Gothic building of 1297-1310 which housed the government of the Siennese Republic. With its 335-feet

One of the most elegant squares in the world – the Piazza del Campo, Siena with Palazzo Pubblico.

(102 metres) tall crenellated tower, it is a distictive symbol of the city. The **Torre di Mangia** is one of the highest medieval structures in Italy described as 'not a monument but a flight' by W. D. Howells in *Tuscan Cities* (Leipzig, 1911). At the top is a bell that used to be rung on occasions concerning the citizenry, the tower itself an assertion of republican authority, being higher than any noble's tower and as high as the Duomo. As a cockney is defined as one born within hearing of Bow Bells, a Sienese is one born in the shadow of the Mangia. The name of the tower comes from an early bell-ringer, one Giovanni di Balduccio or Mangiaguadagni ('earnings eater') whose statue is to be found in one of the palace courtyards. It is possible to climb to the top of the tower for the Tuscan view of your life, although you may have to wait your turn in a stuffy room and the steps are many. (Open 10.00-17.00 or 14.00 in winter.)

At the base of the tower is an open loggia, the Cappella della Piazza of 1352-76, built in gratitude for the end of the Black Death. When San Bernardino preached in front of the Palazzo in 1427, an altar was set up for the purpose with a pulpit before it, perhaps at the point between two upper windows where the round sun-like symbol containing Christ's monogram is placed.

The cost of building the Palace was enormous: it had been agreed that £2,000 would be spent every six months during its construction, a large sum then. Houses had to be purchased and destroyed to create a site and the slopes behind had to be raised and strengthened. The original 1310 building consisted of the stone ground floor and a single floor, with four windows, above. By 1342 another floor with merlons had been added, along with two wings consisting of only the stone ground floor. Additions were made over the years while the shields above each window and door commemorate Siena's republican period. The Medici arms date from 1560 when Siena lost its independence. Inside the palace is the Museo Civico.

Museo Civico

Open 09.30-18.30 in summer; or 09.30-13.30 in winter and on Sundays.

The ground floor of the palace is given over to municipal offices but the upper floor is well known, particularly for its series of frescoes in the former state rooms. The first is the Sala del Risorgimento with frescoes from 1878-90 commemorating the meeting of Garibaldi with King Vittorio Emanuele, and other events of the Risorgimento. Four rooms nearby display paintings from various schools from Italy and abroad. The staircase from the Sala del Risorgimento leads to the Loggia where are the remains of Jacopo della Quercia's Fonte Gaia that used to be in the Campo. The Sala della Signoria is decorated with sixteenth-century frescoed lunettes showing events in Siena's history.

The Sala di Balia is frescoed with scenes from the life of the Sienese Pope Alexander III by Spinello Aretino and his son (1407-08). Then, in the Sala del Concistoro, you will see three Gobelin tapestries representing Earth, Air, and Fire and some sixteenth-century Florentine ones. On the ceiling is one of the greatest examples of mannerist painting in Europe - frescoes from 1530 by the Sienese Beccafumi – illustrating the political virtues of the ancients. This was the last expression of Sienese independence before the Florentine conquest. In the Vestibule is what remains of a frescoed *Madonna* by A. Lorenzetti and a gilded she-wolf by G. di Turino (1429) which was originally on the exterior. The Anticappella is decorated with 1413 work by Taddeo di Bartolo, including portraits of illustrious Romans and Greeks, a panorama of ancient Rome and a wall devoted to St. Christopher representing the Commune's concern for the weak. This work aims to repeat the themes of Lorenzetti's Good and Bad Government but on this occasion the style is wholly different since Taddeo worked under the direction of two eminent Sienese Humanists, Pietro de' Pecci and Ser Cristoforo di Andrea, with the resulting emphasis on antiquity – hence the portraits of heroic figures representing different virtues. The Chapel itself (Cappella del Consiglio) is visible usually only through a gate by Jacopo della Quercia; within are more frescoes by Taddeo depicting the life of the Virgin and an altar by Sodoma. Most notable are the Gothic choir stalls by Domenico di Niccolo which took 13 years to complete in 1415-28.

The Sala del Mappamondo (room of the map of the world), the council room until 1342, is named after Lorenzetti's frescoed diagram of the world with Siena at its centre, now lost. There is, however the fresco of 1330 attributed to Simone Martini (1284-1344) of the condottiere Guidoriccio da Foligno setting out to besiege the rebellious town of Montemassi. This is considered to be the first example in Europe of a landscape and also the first full-sized painting of a historical figure. The depictions of saints Victor and Ansanus are by Sodoma. The work on the long wall is the *Victory of the Sienese at Poggio Imperiale* by Giovanni di Cristofori Ghini and Francesco d'Andrea from 1480 and *Victory at Val di Chiana* by Lippo Vanni.

Most beautiful of all in this room is the enthroned *Virgin* surrounded by saints ('Maesta') by Simone Martini; the depiction of the Virgin imbued with queenly dignity is a speciality of the early Sienese school, Siena having early on adopted Mary as their patron saint.

The most famous of the rooms is the Sala della Pace (room of peace). Here, in an attempt to remind the people's leaders of their duty, Ambrogio Lorenzetti frescoes of the early fourteenth century are allegories of good and bad government (buon governo and mal governo), considered one of the most important cycles of secular paintings from the Middle Ages. These depictions are extraordinary for their realism. There are two complementary themes: on the wall opposite the window Siena under good government, ruled by Justice with the help of Moderation, Courage, Wisdom and Generosity, a prosperous city of industrious, contented subjects (and in the background the harbour of Talamone which Siena hoped would be her base for maritime power); and Siena under bad government, ruled by Tyranny advised by Pride, Vanity, Avarice, Betrayal, War, Deception and Envy, a shabby city of misery and despair. Above 'Buon Governo' is a happy girl in summer; above 'Mal Governo' a man shivers in the snow. The cycle was commissioned by the Nine to decorate and to celebrate, functions considered as important at the time but detailed analysis reveals the subtlety of the allegory; these pictures were to be enjoyed but they were also to teach. There are mathematical correlations between the depictions here and the Bible: Siena is identified with the City of God and ordinary life in Siena is parallel to life in the ideal world. It aims to glorify Siena and illustrates a feeling of pride in its achievements. Nonetheless the allegory at its simplest is very clear; injustice engenders instability, good government does not. The Sala dei Pilastri contains a fine *Maesta* by Guido da Siena from the mid-thirteenth century.

Loggia della Mercanzia

The three main streets, the Via di Citta, Banchi di Sopra and Banchi di Sotto, meet behind the side of the Campo opposite the Palazzo Pubblico, at a point called Croce del Travaglio (cross of travail). Historically this was an important point since the Via Francigena, the main route between Rome and France, passed into the city along Via di Montanini and Via di Banchi di Sopra, leaving the city through the Porta Romana. At this point too is the Loggia della Mercanzia begun in 1417, the upper section added in the seventeenth-century. The statues of saints from 1456-63 are by A. Federighi and Vecchietta. This loggia was a centre for business transactions as well as the seat of the internationally famous commercial tribunal of Siena, where financial disputes were resolved. Its construction was not straightforwrd. The Sienese, having by then developed a strong Communal sense of image, argued over the design to the point where progress was slow in the extreme; an addition made one day was torn down the next. A committe was formed to resolve the question and several designs were displayed for all to see before a decision was made. In later centuries the Loggia became inactive but was favoured by the nobility as a meeting place.

On the corner of Banchi di Sotto and Via Rinaldini (Terzo di San Martino), on the left corner of the Campo as you look at the Palazzo Pubblico, is Siena's most impressive family palace, **Palazzo Piccolomini d' Aragona** by Rossellino in Florentine style from 1469. Now it houses the Siena State Archive, famous for the Tavolette della Biccherna, the treasury books. The Biccherna was originally in the Palazzo Pubblico. The books' covers are finely decorated with scenes of everyday life relating to financial matters. Here too is Boccaccio's will. Even by Italian standards, the Sienese archive is exceptionally detailed: records of expenditure date back to 1226 and General Council reports go back to 1249. (Open 09.00-13.00 or 12.30 on Saturdays; closed Sundays.)

On the other side of of Banchi di Sotto is the **University** founded in 1203 behind which is the church of **San Vigilio** and the medieval Via Sallustio Bandini. San Vigilio was one of several places to house the Biccherna before the construction of the Palazzo Pubblico. In the fourteenth-century a pulpit was frequently placed outside it from where readings from Dante's *Divine Comedy* were given.

Further down Banchi di Sotto, on the right, is the **Logge del Papa** ('Pope's Loggia'), a Renaissance loggia built for Pius II (Aeneas Silvius Piccolomini) in 1462 by Federighi. Nearby, on Via San Martino is the church of the same name with seventeenth-century façade and altarpiece with Beccafumi's *Nativity* and a *Circumcision* by Guido Reni. The Banchi di Sotto becomes the Via di Pantaneto, leading to **San Georgio** church whose campanile is of 1260.

Beyond is Via dei Pispini, left, leading to **Santo Spirito**, with 1519 entrance and tympanum by Perruzzi. The first chapel on the right inside has frescoes by Sodoma and the third chapel has a *Coronation of the Virgin* by Beccafumi. There are also works by Manetti, Sano di Pietro and Vanni.

Via Pispini ends at the **Porta Pispini**, the old exit to Perugia, above which is a faded *Nativity* by Sodoma. Here too, left of the Porta, is the one surviving bastion designed by Peruzzi. Via Pantaneto becomes Via Roma, leading to the **Porta Roma**, a well-preserved double wall gate. On the way you will see, at 71, the **Societa Esecutori di Pie Dispozizioni** (the Society of Executors of Benevolent Legacies) a descendent of a medieval lay brotherhood which has a small collection of paintings with works by Sano di Pietro, the school of Duccio and Sodoma, among others. (Open 09.00-12.00; closed on Sundays.)

Via Val di Montone, right from Via Roma, leads to the austere **Santa Maria dei Servi** (built 1471-1528) whose interior was designed by Peruzzi with a fine early Sienese *Nativity*, an altarpiece by Taddeo di Bartolo, a *Madonna* by Coppo di Marcovaldo of 1261 and another of 1317 by Lippo Memmi. In the chapel in the north transept is a *Madonna del Manto* ('Madonna of the Cloak'), of the type mentioned in relation to the Campo, by Giovanni di Paolo of 1436. There are two *Massacres of the Innocents* – one by Matteo di Giovanni from 1491 and another early fourteenth-century one by Pietro Lorenzetti.

The Terzo di Citta and the Duomo

The Terzo di Citta is the oldest part of Siena, reached by following the Via di Citta from the Campo. You will pass the **Palazzo Chigi-**

Saracini named after the Chigi, an important Sienese banking family. It contains a renowned music academy (concerts are given here) and a collection of thirteen to seventeenth-century art gathered by Galgano Saracini at the end of the eighteenth-century. It is open only for occasional exhibitions, or to scholars upon personal application at the head office of the Monte dei Paschi bank, who own it, on Piazza Salimbeni.

Nearby is the **Palazzo Piccolomini delle Papesse**, designed by Rossellino for Caterina Piccolomini, the sister of Pius II. The Piccolomini family, and particularly Pius II, left a large mark on Siena; the Piccolomini half-moon is to be seen everywhere. Note too, the **Palazzo Marsili** of 1459.

The Duomo

The Duomo is reached from Via di Citta by taking any right turn, as you go away from the Campo, in the vicinity of the above-mentioned palaces. The easiest route, however, is probably to continue until Via del Capitano, right, passing the sixteenth-century Palazzo Piccolomini Adami on the left corner and the thirteenth-century Palazzo del Capitano at number 15.

It was one of the first Gothic cathedrals in Tuscany, started at the end of the twelfth-century by the Commune as a fitting monument to the city's glory. The Pisan influence, with the green and white stripes reserved for ecclesiastical buildings, is strong although a variety of styles are evident; the campanile and lower façade are Romanesque. This variety reflects the fact that the Duomo project continued over the centuries. The body of the church was completed by 1215. Giovanni Pisano designed the lower façade in 1284, though the upper portion was only started in 1376. He also sculpted the Prophets, Philosophers and Patriarchs. Note the architrave over the main portal with stories from the life of the Virgin by Tino di Maiano; whilst the tondo over the south door is by Donatello. The mosaics are nineteenth-century. Some elements have been removed to the Opera del Duomo museum for safe-keeping and replaced with exact copies.

In 1316 it was decided to enlarge the Cathedral but by 1322 subsidence brought this to a halt. Instead a start was made on an ambitious plan to build a new nave to the south turning the first building into a transept, but abandonment came with political decline, construction problems and impoverishment following the plague. Thus it was decided to return to a more modest enlargement, almost completed to what we see today in 1377.

The Duomo does not, as in other cities, stand out strongly against the skyline but like the Campo it played an important role in the life of the Sienese, who every August 14, during the feast of the Assumption to which the Duomo is dedicated, flocked here to offer carved candles to the Board of Works of the Cathedral. This represented another of those moments in Sienese life where contrada and city allegiences met in the context of religious affection embodied in the Cathedral. During these celebrations special clothes were worn and all grudges were to be forgotten. Of course the Cathedral was the centre of several other festivals that involved the whole city – thanksgiving for the end of the Black Death and Corpus Christi, among others.

The responsibility for the construction of the Duomo rested with the lay authorities. It was financed mostly from communal income although extra taxes were levied from time to time when necessary. The project was the responsibility of the Operaio or Master of Works who controlled the finances and appointed architects. For many years this task fell to Cistercian monks from San Galgano who had a reputation for integrity; later the sculptor Jacopo della Quercia did the job which was well remunerated and powerful, spilling onto other areas of city life and other projects, like the Palazzo Pubblico. Although the power of the Operaio was considerable, his decisions often determining several aspects of the Duomo, the construction was a joint effort involving the Board of Works composed of citizens among whom usually were prominent artists; and a careful check on expenditure was kept by the General Council without whose permission certain fiscal decisions (like whether workmen should be provided with drink during working hours) could not be made. Communal involvement was a feature of the early Tuscan republics but Siena's obsession with its Duomo was unusually intense. Work would continue even during official holidays, crimes committed by artisans working on it might be overlooked, officials connected with it were confined to the city. Furthermore there was a general determination to stick to Sienese artistic tradition, ignoring the Florentine Renaissance if necessary. This is evident too in the themes of the decoration which deal often with aspects of the life of the Virgin, considered the city's protector, and with saints with Sienese connections. Its construction was a talking point, reflected today in the tendency of Italians to involve themselves verbally in events around them. It was the main economic investment of the time providing work for many people for many years.

The medieval architect was in fact more of a mason and the post of master mason was frequently held by an eminent artist who would have had a grounding in building skills. Among them were Giovanni Pisano, Tino di Camaino and Baldassare Peruzzi.

The interior embellishments reflect much more the taste of the powerful and the great who had their own chapels and altars and who made decisions concerning the layout of the Cathedral.

The interior

The interior is overwhelming. Perhaps the most striking thing, after the stripes, is the floor, decorated with a series of historical and Biblical designs, the most recent (sixteenth-century) in colour, the oldest (1369) in 'graffiti', black outline on white marble. Among the most interesting of these are: Beccafumi's *Sacrifice of Elias* and *Execution of the False Prophets of Baal*; Pinturicchio's *Fortune* in the fourth bay of the nave; *Life of Moses* by Beccafumi; *Massacre of the Innocents* by Matteo di Giovanni 1481, north transept; and *Ten Sibyls*, same artist 1481-83. Looking up it is worth noting the fifteenth and sixteenth-century stucco busts of popes beneath the cornice. The gilded statues on the dome are from the late fifteenth century.

In the south aisle the statue is of Pope Paul V by Signorini of 1605. Further along the south aisle towards the altar is the magnificent Gothic pulpit by Nicola Pisano, completed in 1268, six years after the more famous one in the Pisa Baptistry. Around the base of the main column are the figures of Philosophy and the Liberal Arts. At the top are the Christian Virtues, Prophets and Evangelists. The staircase is of 1543. The tomb of Bishop Tommaso Piccolomini above the connecting door to the campanile is by Neroccio (1484-85).

In the south transept is the Baroque Cappella Chigi designed by Bernini, containing the venerated *Madonna del Voto*; as recently as June 1944 the city keys have been placed before her and prayers made for deliverance.

In the choir the altar is by Peruzzi and the bronze ciborium by Vecchietta (1467-72). Some of the stalls date back to 1362. The eight candelabra in the form of angels are by Beccafumi. The round stained glass window in the apse is by Duccio from 1288; it is perhaps the oldest Italian-made stained glass in existence.

In the north transept is the 1310 tomb of Cardinal Riccardo Petroni by Tino di Maiano, an influential design. Before it is a bronze pavement tomb by Donatello of Bishop Giovanni Pecci. The lovely Renaissance Cappella di San Giovanni Battista is by Giovanni di Stefano of 1482. Within are Pinturichio frescoes of the life of John the Baptist and two kneeling portraits, one of whom is Aringhieri, the founder of the Order of St. John. The bronze statue of *St. John* is by Donatello.

The entrance to the Piccolomini Library, created in 1495 by Cardinal Francesco Piccolomini (Pius III) to hold the library of his uncle Pius II is in the north aisle. It is chiefly notable for the series of frescoes of the *Life of Pius II* by Pinturicchio among whose assistants was the young Raphael.

The scenes, clockwise from the window, are as follows: at the Council of Basle; at the Court of James II of Scotland; crowned as poet by Frederick III; as Emperor's envoy to Eugenius IV; as Bishop of Siena at meeting of Frederick III and Eleanora of Portugal at Porta Camollia; he is made a cardinal; he becomes Pope; he proclaims a crusade at Mantua; he canonises Catherine of Siena; and finally, he arrives, mortally ill, at Ancona.

The sculpted group in the middle of the room is *The Three Graces*, a Roman copy of the original by Praxiteles used as a model by many eminent painters and sculpters including Pinturicchio. Also on show are beautifully decorated cathedral choir books.

Near the library entrance is the Piccolomini Altar of 1485 by Andrea Bregno; the statues in the lower niches of four saints are by Michelangelo. The figure of of *St. Francis* above was started by Torrigiani, who later worked in London, and completed, it is thought, by Michelangelo. The *Madonna* at the top is an early work (1397-1400) of Jacopo della Quercia.

To the south of the Duomo, or on the right as you look at the altar, is Piazza Jacopo della Quercia and what remains of the projected 1330s cathedral. In here instead is the **Museo dell' Opera del Duomo** on three floors where (ground floor) many of the original statues from the façade may be seen, as well as (first floor) Duccio's magnificent *Maesta* and works by the Lorenzettis. On the second floor are church treasures and work by Vecchietta, Martini, Beccafumi and the influential *Madonna dagli Occhi Grossi* (wide-eyed Madonna), the original Duomo altarpiece by an anonymous painter of 1210. (Open 09.00-19.00 mid-March to the end of October; otherwise 09.00-13.30.)

The Baptistry

The Baptistry is behind the eastern end of the Duomo, on Piazza San Giovanni, down a set of steps on the south side between the Cathedral and the unfinished transept. Descending you will pass a delightful Gothic portal and the Cripta delle Statue with the earliest frescoes of the Siena school.

The incomplete Baptistry façade by Jacopo di Mino del Pellicciaio is of 1382. The gloomy interior is earlier, from about 1325 by Camaino di Crescentino. The frescoes in the vault are by Vecchietta. The font 1417-30 is one of the finest examples of Renaissance sculpture. The gilded panels illustrate the life of John the Baptist, with the annunciation of his birth by Jacopo della Quercia, his birth and him preaching by Giovanni di Turino, his imprisonment and the *Baptism of Christ* by Lorenzo Ghiberti and *Herod's Feast* by Donatello. Donatello sculpted the *Faith* and *Hope* statues in the corners, Neroccio sculpted *Fortitude* and G. di Turino *Justice*, *Charity* and *Prudence*. The marble tabernacle is by Jacopo della Quercia (the conservative Sienese dispensed with the Florentine Donatello's design for the tabernacle doors), the bronze angels by di Turino and Donatello.

Across the way from the Baptistry is the Palazzo del Magnifico by Cozzarelli 1504-08, which belonged to the Petrucci family who were powerful in fifteenth and sixteenth-century Siena. In front of the Duomo, on Piazza del Duomo, is the Ospedale di Santa Maria della Scala founded in the ninth century and important for pilgrims on the way to Rome. In the Pilgrim's Hall there are fine frescoes by Domenico di Bartolo and in the neighbouring thirteenth-century church a bronze Christ by Vecchietta and organ case by Peruzzi.

The building on the south side of the square, on the corner of Via del Capitano, is the Prefettura, formerly the Palazzo Reale, by Buontalenti.

Pinacoteca

Via del Capitano crosses Via di Citta at Piazza di Postierla and becomes Via San Pietro. Down here, left, is the fourteenth-century Palazzo Buonsignori, now the city **Pinacoteca** and housing the finest collection of Sienese art, all the city's artists being comprehensively represented. It includes work by Duccio, Guido da Siena, Segna di Bonaventura, Martini, the Lorenzettis, Taddeo di Bartolo, Spinello Aretino, Sano di Pietro, Cozzarelli, Daddi, di Paolo, Sassetta, Neroccio, Pinturicchio, Vecchietta, Beccafumi and Sodoma. There are also some works from elsewhere in Italy and from Flanders and Germany. The collection is arranged in chronological order. (Open 08.30-19.00 or 13.00 on Sunday; closed Mondays.)

Next door is the church of **San Pietro alle Scale** with the *Flight into Egypt* by Manetti, Siena's most eminent Baroque painter. Further down the Via San Pietro you will come to Via della Cerchia and the Prato di Sant' Agostino; number 4 is a geological and

zoological museum. Bearing left will bring you to the church of
Sant' Agostino of 1258 whose Rococo interior was designed by a
Dutchman whose Italiacised name was Vanvitelli. Within there is a
selection of fine art with work by Perugino (second altar south side),
Sodoma, A. Lorenzetti (Piccolomini chapel), Francesco di Giorgio
Martini, Signorelli (Cappella Bichi, south transept) and others. (If it
is closed, ring the bell at number 1 in the piazza four times.)

Via P. A. Mattioli leads south to Porta Tufi and passes near the
entrance to the **Orto Botanico** (botanical garden). Guided tours are
available at 08.00-13.00, and 15.00-17.00 Monday-Friday.

Returning to the Via della Cerchia and turning left will bring you
eventually to the fourteenth-century Santa Maria del Carmine,
redesigned by Peruzzi in the early sixteenth century. Within, a fine *St.
Michael* by Beccafumi and another Madonna and cloak theme
(*Madonna dei Mantellini*) by Francesco Vanni of 1240, at the east end.

Terzo di Camollia

If you are continuing from Santa Maria del Carmine, you enter this
quarter by walking along Pian dei Mantellini, Via del Fosso di San
Ansano, passing the church of San Sebastiano, taking Via di Valle
Piatta and, left, Via del Costone. This will bring you to the ancient
Fonte Branda, the beginning of Terzo di Camollia. Go uphill and bear
right into Vicolo dei Tiratori which will bring you to the Casa di
Santa Caterina, (discussed below.)

From near the Campo (at the Croce di Travaglio) the main
thoroughfare of this terzo is Via Banchi di Sopra which leads to
Piazza Tolomei and the Gothic **Palazzo Tolomei** (1208), the Tolomei
being a family of bankers, claiming descent from the Ptolomies of
Egypt and one of the five leading families in Siena's early republican
history. Before the construction of the Palazzo Pubblico the Sienese
government met here, sometimes in the piazza itself and occasionally
in the adjacent church of San Cristoforo which in the days when
certain families jostled for power, came to be regarded as the
Tolomei family chapel.

Further along Banchi di Sopra is, right, Piazza Salimbeni. It is
dominated by a block of three palaces, now the bank of the Monte dei
Paschi di Siena, founded in 1624. The **Palazzo Salimbeni** is in the
middle, the **Palazzo Spannocchi** (1473) right and **Palazzo Tantucci**
(1548) left. The Salimbeni were another of the five leading families,
important enough to play host to Emperor Charles IV in 1355 in an
earlier palace. This, perhaps the most beautiful palazzo in Siena, is

also of the fifteenth-century. The **Monte di Paschi** has another art collection here the other being the Chigi-Saracini. It is sometimes open to the public, or with special permission.

Further along Banchi di Sopra, left, is the Renaissance **Oratorio di Santa Maria delle Nevi** of 1471 by F. di Giorgio Martini. It contains a fine altarpiece, *St. Maria of the Snows*, (as in the name of the church), by Matteo di Giovanni (1477) but is often locked.

Beyond the church, right, is Via Vallerozzi which leads to Porta Ovile. On the way, right, a street leads to **San Donato** and its twelfth-century dome; and, left, is Via del Pian d'Ovile with the **Fonte Nuova** of 1293. Outside the Porta Ovile is the pretty **Fonte d' Ovile** of 1262.

Nearby, right from the Porta Ovile as you look at it from within, is the church of **San Francesco** (1326-1475), badly damaged by fire in 1655 and restored only at the beginning of the twentieth-century. Frescoes in the first and third chapels of the north transept are by Ambrogio and Pietro Lorenzetti (1331). In the first chapel of the south transept is a *Madonna* by A. Vanni. Next door is the fifteenth-century Oratorio San Bernardino built in honour of the great preacher. It boasts some fine frescoes by Beccafumi, Sodoma and G. del Pacchia in the upper chapel. If it is closed, ring the bell.

Take Via dei Rossi from opposite the Piazza San Francesco and then Via Provenzano Salvani, left, leading to the church of **Santa Maria di Provenzano** of 1594. Inside is the highly venerated fifteenth-century terracotta relief of Maria, believed to have been left by St. Catherine.

Continue along Via del Moro to Piazza Tolomei, cross it and turn right onto Via dei Termini. Take the first left until you meet Via delle Terme where you turn right. Turn left into Vicolo dei Tiratori until you come to the Santuario and Casa di Santa Caterina.

Casa di Santa Caterina

The entrance is in Costa Sant'Antonio. Open 09.00-12.00 and 15.00-18.00.

Caterina Benincasa or Catherine of Siena was born here on Annunciation Day in 1347, the last of 25 children. She saw visions at an early age, started to live the life of an ascetic and received the stigmata. Becoming a tertiary Dominican enabled her to remain outside convent life; she felt that complete isolation from the world was inappropriate and indeed part of her fame rests on a view of life

A medieval corner of Siena.

that was spiritually pure but also compassionate and filled with human understanding. Her fame spread far and wide, to pope and monarch, her advice was sought. She was influential in persuading the papal court from Avignon back to Rome and in promoting spiritual reform. She was the author of many a miracle, a popular subject for painters; and many a devotional treatise whose eloquent letters are preserved in Siena's library, the Biblioteca Comunale (see below). St. Catherine died in 1380, was canonised in 1460 and in 1939 became, with St. Francis, patron saint of Italy.

The loggia is thought to be by Peruzzi. Caterina's father was a wool dyer and part of the Benincasa house contains the old workshop downstairs, now the Oratorio della Contrada dell'Oca containing works by Sodoma, Neroccio and G. del Pacchia. Next to it is the Oratorio della Camera, Caterina's cell. Upstairs are the Oratorio del Crocifisso with a thirteenth-century Crucifix before which the saint received the stigmata in 1375 in Pisa. Opposite is the Oratorio della Cucina, in the family kitchen, with work by Riccio, Salimbeni and others.

Siena Library and the Etruscan Museum

Returning onto Vicolo dei Tiratori from St. Catherine's house turn left until you reach Fontebranda from where there is a fair climb to the church of San Domenico. North of Caterina's house, on Via della Sapienza, is the **Biblioteca Comunale** with illustrated books,

Caterina's letters, drawings by Peruzzi, and a Botticelli-illustrated work by Dante. (Open 09.00-20.00 Monday-Friday, Saturdays 09.00-14.00; closed on Sundays.) Next to it is the **Etruscan Museum** which includes a collection from Sarteano. (Open 09.00-13.30, 13.00 on Sunday; closed Wednesdays.)

San Domenico

This is a large, plain church begun in 1226, though much altered over the centuries. At the west end is a chapel with a contemporary portrait of Santa Caterina by Andrea Vanni and where some of her miracles took place. The Cappella di Santa Caterina is at the south end. There are works by Sodoma which include *SS Luke* and *Jerome* on the entrance arch, frescoes (on left and right of the altar) of *Santa Caterina in Ecstasy*, and on the left wall of her *Intercession for Life of a Youth*. The altar tabernacle contains a reliquary with Santa Caterina's head. The Tabernacle over the main altar is by Benedetto da Maiano (1475).

From here take the Via dei Mille past the municipal stadium to the **Forte Santa Barbara** (Fortezza Medicea) built in 1560 for Cosimo I de' Medici. As one would expect from a fortress, there are fine views from here over the city and countryside.

Turning right from Via dei Mille into Viale Venticinque Aprile leads to Viale C. Maccari and 'La Lizza', a pretty park. Heading back towards the centre, Viale C. Maccari brings you to Piazza Gramsci. Turn left to the church of San Stefano, right (1641). Bear right behind it and left into Via di Camollia. Continue until Vicolo Fontegiusta, left, which leads to the **Fontegiusta Church** (1482-84). The delightful portal is by Urbano da Cortona. Inside is a fine main altar Tabernacle by Marina and frescoes by Peruzzi on the north wall.

Via Camollia leads to the **Porta Camollia** with its famous inscription. Beyond is a column commemorating the meeting between Frederick III and Eleanora of Portugal in 1451, as illustrated by Pinturicchio in the Piccolomini Library. Then there is the Antiporto barbican of 1675; and the Palazzo dei Diavoli of 1460.

Siena is noted for its heavy but delicious cake (Torta di Siena), found in cake shops all over the city.

Environs of Siena

L'Osservanza, one mile west through Porta Ovile and Via San Martini, is a monastery of 1422 founded to restore the original

Franciscan discipline. There is a collection of early Sienese art and works by A. della Robbia in the church.

The **Lecceto** hermitage near Montecchio village has a twelfth-century cloister. **San Leonardo al Lago** has hermitage ruins with a standing church and fine 1360 frescoes by Vanni. The thirteenth-century **Torri Abbey** has a fine triple cloister, **Sovicille** boasts the interesting twelfth-century Romanesque church of Pieve di Ponte allo Spina and there is a Romanesque church at **Rosia**. Also in the area is the Villa di Monastero, the Castello di Belcaro and the Certosa di Pontgnano.

North of Siena to San Gimignano

Monteriggioni

This little fortified hill-top town once defended Siena against the Florentines. Its thirteenth-century walls and towers, mentioned by Dante, are still in excellent condition, concealing a sleepy piazza with pretty houses, a fourteenth-century church and a couple of interesting shops selling local produce and crafts. It sustains a population of about 200. A little way west is the twelfth-century Abbadia a Isola (abbey on the island) with a Taddeo di Bartolo fresco.

Most worthy of a visit is the town of **Colle di Val d'Elsa** which as the name suggests, runs along the crest of a hill. It is a handsome town, a major producer of glass and crystal today. It is the birthplace of the architect Arnolfo di Cambio who was responsible for Florence Cathedral and Santa Croce, among others. His family came here from Lombardy in about 1230, bringing northern Gothic masonry skills with them. Arnolfo moved to Florence in about 1270.

The new town is down below, the old town (Castello) above. It is possible to park outside and walk its length; it is hard to go wrong since the town is long and narrow. To be seen here are the Duomo, several palaces (including the Palazzo Campana by Baccio d' Agnolo), the church of of Sant' Agostino (with works by Ghirlandaio, Bronzino and Taddeo di Bartolo), the Museo Civico, the Museo d' arte Sacra in the former Bishop's Palace, the impressive Porta Volterrana and the house of Arnolfo di Cambio.

Near Colle (south-west) is the lonely Romanesque Badia a Coneo, which dates back to the early twelfth-century. Further south the town of Casole d' Elsa has a Collegiata with fourteenth-century Sienese frescoes.

Poggibonsi

Though now largely an industrial town and important crossroad, Poggibonsi was one of the largest and most important towns of Tuscany in the thirteenth-century. In the turmoil of that century, however, it was destroyed, leaving behind only a few items of antique interest – the Collegiata Church and the Palazzo Pretorio. Outside the town, just off the N2, is the Franciscan Basilica di San Lucchese with works by Bartolo di Fredi and Taddeo Gaddi. In the area you will notice several fortifications, a left-over from the years when Siena and Florence were constantly at war over this area.

San Gimignano

Tourist Information: Piazza del Duomo, 1 (Tel: 940008). The nearest railway station is seven miles north-east of the town.

One of the most distinctive towns in the whole of Italy, indeed in Europe, is San Gimignano, city of medieval towers. A view of the town from across the Tuscan hills is a most remarkable sight, described by E. M. Forster in his novel *Where Angels Fear to Tread* as 'like some fantastic ship city of a dream'. Yet, before the Renaissance, a great many Tuscan towns looked similar. The reason is that in the age of city states the great families withdrew into the cities but, wishing to preserve their status and identity, built these towers. In most towns the towers disappeared in the interests of civic harmony; but here they survived for reasons unknown. So the medieval streets have survived intact and so have 15 of the original 72 towers, built in the twelfth and thirteenth centuries.

San Gimignano has Etruscan origins and was an independent state between 1099 and 1353 after which it was ruled by Florence. For reasons that are obscure, the town takes its name from a martyred bishop of Modena who died in 387. Dante came here in 1299 as an ambassador of Florence to persuade the city to join the Guelf League. Its most famous citizen was the poet Folgore di San Gimignano (c. 1265-1332). Folgore (poet of 'lightening' qualities) was a nickname given by his fellow citizens. Not a lot is known about him, though he did military service in 1295, was sent to the Papal Court in the same year on a mission and in 1305 fought in the war against Pistoia. He was later involved in city politics and was 'knighted'. He is particularly remembered for his sonnets about days of the week and months of the year, a cycle of poems which celebrate the glories of earthly existence in the Tuscany of the era of communes, an almost hedonistic idea of conviviality day by day, month by month into eternity. The sonnet *Di Giugno* (In June) opens with a picture of unchanging Tuscany:

'Di Giugno dovvi una montagnetta
coverta di bellissimi arboscelli,
con trenta ville e dodici castelli,
che sian entorno ad una cittadetta'

('In June I present you with
a little mountain covered in
the loveliest of trees, with
thirty villas and a dozen
castles surrounding a little
city'.)

The area remains well known for its white wine, unappetisingly called 'Vernaccia'.

Unless you are staying in a hotel within, you will be forced to park in one of the car parks outside the city walls. No matter, for distances are short and you need only follow signs for the 'centro' or Piazza del Duomo. The **Duomo** is in fact the twelfth-century Collegiata di Santa Maria Assunta, with fifteenth-century additions. Although its exterior is unremarkable, inside there is much to see. The brickwork is Sienese and so are most of the frescoes. In the north aisle, left, is a 1360 series of Old Testament scenes by Bartolo di Fredi. In the south aisle, right, the 1380 frescoes by Barna da Siena are of New Testament scenes; according to Vasari the painter died after falling from a platform while painting the *Crucifixion*. On the entrance wall is a *St. Sebastian* by Gozzoli and a terrifying *Last Judgement* by Taddeo di Bartolo. The wooden *Annunciation* nearby is by Jacopo della Quercia.

On the right is the Chapel of **Santa Fina**. A local legend tells how Fina, mortified at having accepted a gift of fruit from a young man, prayed on a table without cease for five years until her soul was assumed into heaven by Sant' Antonio, whereupon all the towers of the city burst into flower. The story is illustrated with the 1475 frescoes of Domenico Ghirlandaio in this fine Renaissance chapel built by Giuliano da Maiano.

To the left of the Collegiata is a courtyard with the Etruscan Museum and the, museum of sacred art, **Museo di Arte Sacra**. (Open 09.30-12.30 and 15.00-18.00 or 14.30-17.30 in winter; closed Monday.) Also, on the outside wall of the Baptistry, is an *Annunciation* by Ghirlandaio.

The information office is in the old Palazzo del Popolo (1288-1323) in front and to the left of the Collegiata. Here is the **Museo Civico**; open 09.30-12.30, and 15.00-18.00 or 14.30-17.30 in winter, closed Mondays. In the little courtyard are fragments of fresco, some by Sodoma, and the entrance to the Museo Civico. Part of this is the famous Sala del Consiglio where Dante would have delivered his appeal and which is decorated with the 1317 fresco of the *Maesta*, a Madonna beneath a canopy surrounded by saints and a kneeling Podesta Mino de'Tolomei by Lippo Memmi. The chapel has a fresco of the Trinity by Pier Fr. Fiorentino. In the Pinacoteca upstairs are some interesting works including a fine thirteenth-century Crucifix by Coppo di Marcovaldo, a *Madonna and Child* by Guido da Siena, another by Gozzoli, an *Annunciation* by Filippino Lippi, a *Madonna with Saints Gregory and Benedict* by Pinturicchio, all in the main hall. In another room are some delightful fourteenth-century frescoes of domestic scenes by Memmo di Filippuccio and in others, works by Lorenzo di Niccolo Gerini, and notably scenes from the life of San Gimignano by Taddeo di Bartolo. There are fine views from the 178-feet (54 metres) **Torre Grossa**.

Adjacent to Piazza del Duomo is **Piazza della Cisterna** ('of the well', visible in the centre of the square), surrounded by a fine array of medieval houses, particularly the Palazzo Tortoli on the corner of Via D. Castello (which leads to the 1240 Church of San Lorenzo in Ponte with an exhibition (hours as museum) devoted to the medieval pharmacy that once functioned in the Hospital of Santa Fina.

Opposite the Collegiata is the thirteenth-century Palazzo del Podesta and the Torre Rognosa, 168 feet (51 metres), which represented the height limit for all the other towers of the city to prevent private rivalries developing to absurd lengths. Behind the Collegiata is the Rocca di Montestaffoli fortress of 1353 which offers good views of the city and surrounding countryside.

Van San Matteo, entered from Piazza del Duomo by passing the Salvucci Towers (named after the Salvucci, a Ghibelline family), is the most impressive street of the town. It passes, right, the church of San Bartolo, the Palazzo della Cancelleria and Palazzo Pesciolini, all grouped together. At the end of this street take Via Cellolese to the church of **San Pietro** (with early Sienese frescoes but rarely open) and, beyond, **Sant' Agostino**, famous for the frescoes behind the main altar illustrating the life of St. Augustine, by Gozzoli. The altarpiece is a *Coronation of the Virgin* by Piero Pollaiuolo of 1483. The *San Sebastiano* in the left aisle, is also by Gozzoli. There is also a fine 1465 cloister.

There are several other churches worth seeing including **San Jacopo**, by the east wall at the end of Via Folgore da San Gimignano, which was built by the Knights Templars in 1096 in Pisan

Romanesque style. **San Girolamo**, on the same street, has sixteenth-century works by Vincenzo Tamagni. South of here, still in the East wall, is the Porta delle Fonti which leads to the Fonti, an arcaded medieval public well-house.

About two and a half miles (four kilometres) from the Porta San Matteo in the west wall, is the charming thirteenth-century Pieve in the village of **Cellole**, the inspiration for Puccini's Suor Angelica.

Volterra

The nearest station is Saline di Volterra, seven miles (four kilometres) south-west, but services are infrequent. Tourist information Palazzo dei Priori, Via Turazza 2 (Tel: 86150). All museums are open 09.30-13.00, and 15.00-18.30, with winter amendments, and closed on Mondays.

The journey to Volterra, which is likely to be slow because of the winding road, takes you through some of the most extraordinary countryside in Tuscany, almost empty of the trees that characterise the rest of the region. This ancient Etruscan town sits imperiously atop a flat, steep hill which takes some time to climb even by car and continues after you seem to have arrived. Nevertheless it is a journey worth making.

One of the oldest of Italian towns, dating back to the Villanovan culture, it became an important and the northern-most member of the Etruscan Dodecapolis, when it was known as Velathri. Apart from strategic considerations, the importance of the site of the town may be accounted by the presence of alum, sulphur, salt, iron, lead, tin and, above all these days, alabaster. At the height of its Etruscan prosperity, in the fourth-century BC, the city was several times larger than today but declined with the growing power of Imperial Rome. It remained, nonetheless, important to the Romans as Volaterrae and subsequently to the Lombards, who made it their capital. It was then ruled by Bishops until it became an independent commune in the twelfth-century, falling to Florence in 1361. In 1472 Volterra was involved in a rather extraordinary debacle, involving alum (important in the dyeing of cloth) and money. The Vatican was heavily involved in the mining of alum and was not best pleased at attempts by Lorenzo il Magnifico to intrude on their monopoly. The Volterrans, feeling that they were being exploited by Florence, revolted. Lorenzo was excommunicated by the Pope and he hired the Duke of Urbino, Federico di Montefeltro, to suppress the rebellion, achieved with memorable brutality. There was one further rebellion against Florentine rule in 1530 but after that Volterra followed the destiny of the Duchy of Tuscany. Mining continued to play an important role here and the working of alabaster is the city's main industry, indeed many of the buildings here are made with the type of limestone which spawns the stuff. The town is filled with alabaster workshops; don't be afraid to wander in to have a look at the work but if you are interested in buying something more than a simple souvenir take time to see what is on offer. The town's most famous citizens were the Roman satirist Persius Flaccus, the successor to St. Peter as Pope, St. Linus, and the painter Daniele da Volterra (1509-66).

There are several car-parks at the various entrances to the city – perhaps the most convenient is the underground one near the south entrance at Porta all' Arco, from where it is but a stroll to the compact centre. But the first things to observe are the tremendous views from this 1,800-feet (545 metres) hill that forms a watershed between the rivers Era and Cecina. Near this car-park is the Parco Archeologico, an exceptionally pretty park with a few Roman and Etruscan remains.

The main square is Piazza dei Priori, surrounded by medieval palaces. Most important among these is, on the north-east side, the **Palazzo Pretorio** and **Torre del Porcellino** which takes its name from the pig at its base. On the south-west side are the **Bishop's Palace** and the thirteenth-century **Palazzo dei Priori**, the oldest municipal building in Tuscany with a tower that, if ever it were open, would offer the most stupendous views possible. The council chamber has a fourteenth-century Florentine fresco.

Behind the Palazzo dei Priori is the **Duomo** (twelfth to thirteenth century with sixteenth-century additions), with a 1493 campanile. The pulpit in the north aisle is thirteenth-century by the Pisanos. Above the main altar is a 1471 *Tabernacle* by Mino da Fiesole. The silver bust on the altar is of *San Ottaviano* by Antonio Pollaiolo. The thirteenth-century coloured wood *Deposition* by Raffaello Cioli in the chapel to the right is particularly fine. In the chapel to the left of the altar is the *Madonna dei Chierici* by Jacopo della Quercia. In the lady chapel (north, left aisle near the entrance) is a fresco of the *Magi* by Gozzoli. The 1283 Baptistry, possibly closed for restoration, faces the Duomo and contains a 1502 font by A. Sansovino. The arch around the altar was sculpted by Mino da Fiesole.

In the nearby **Museo Diocesano di Arte Sacra** there is a bust of *St. Linus* by Andrea della Robbia and a gilded Crucifix by Giambologna.

The roof of the world – houses in Volterra

Down Via Porta all'Arco (from near Piazza dei Priori) you will come to the **Arco Etrusco** (Etruscan arch), which is in fact part Etruscan and part Roman. In the arch, however, are three Etruscan heads which date back to 600 BC and which are believed to represent three Etruscan gods: Tinia (Jupiter), Uni (Juno) and Menvra (Minerva).

Via Ricciarelli leads from Piazza dei Priori (forming a picturesque junction with Via Buomparenti overlooked by medieval houses) to Via San Lino and the churches of **San Lino** and **San Francesco** which has a 1315 chapel frescoed with the story of the Holy Cross by Cenni di Francesco di Ser Cenni in 1410. This route passes the house of the painter Daniele da Volterra at Via San Lino 12. The Porta San Francesco leads out of the walls past the ruined San Stefano and brings you, after just over half a mile, to San Giusto and beyond, the well-preserved Etruscan walls with a fine view of the **Balze precipices**, chasms that continue to open up, revealing on one occasion the Etruscan necropolis which has provided many exhibits for the Museum. Visible too is a ruined eleventh-century **Badia**.

Outside the walls to the north is Viale Francesco Ferrucci which passes the old **Roman Theatre and Baths** from the first-century BC. From here you may re-enter the town through the Porta Fiorentina to Via Guarnacci.

At the junction of Via Guarnacci and Via dei Sarti is the Casa-Torre Toscano which includes the **Palazzo Viti** and its collection of porcelain and alabaster. In the church of nearby **San Michele** is a *Madonna* from the Della Robbia workshop. Further west along Via dei Sarti is the **Palazzo Solaini**, by A. da Sangallo, and the **Pinacoteca** which contains some fine Tuscan art notably a *Madonna and Saints* by Taddeo di Bartolo, and work by Benvenuto di Giovanni, Signorelli, Rosso Fiorentino (notably his extraordinary *Descent from the Cross*), Daniele da Volterra and Ghirlandaio.

To the right of San Michele as you look at it the road leads to Piazza XX Settembre, where the buses stop and start from, and then Via Don Minzoni. At 15 is the **Museo Etrusco Guarnacci**, named after its eighteenth-century founder, which has hundreds of alabaster and terracotta funeral urns from the third-century BC – these are decorated with sculptures of the dead and mythological subjects of Hellenic origin. The family of the deceased would commission a mason to sculpt a story or scene that seemed appropriate to the person in question. Some are marvellous, showing a sense of humanity and vulnerability without ever becoming undignified. All of them bear the upturned cup of life. The end of this street brings you to the **Fortezza Medicea**, begun in 1343, completed in 1472 by Lorenzo il Magnifico and used always as a prison.

About one kilometre down from Porta a Selci, which is at the east of the town, is the fifteenth-century **San Girolamo** church with a fine *Annunciation* by B. di Giovanni.

The vicinity of Volterra

South of Volterra the N439 crosses the Colline Metallifere ('metal hills') from which Volterra and the Etruscans gained their prosperity and which continue to be mined. **Pomarance**, the birthplace of two painters known as Pomarancio, is a walled town with some handsome palaces. **Larderello**, prickly with cooling towers, is the centre of Italian geothermal energy and a producer of boric acid. There is also a small museum devoted to the town's history and the interesting parish church designed by the man responsible for Florence's railway station. By following the 'itinerario dei soffioni' (steam route) around the area you will see the odd landscape, with bubbling and puffing geysers and swamps, and the soffioni (vapour-jets) from which the acid is evaporated. The countryside in the area of the pass known as Ala dei Diavoli (Devils' Wings) is very attractive.

The deep south

South-west of Siena on the N73, amid beautiful countryside, is the Cistercian Abbey of **San Galgano**. San Galgano, born nearby, was a wayward soldier who after seeing a vision of St. Michael gave up his evil ways and as a symbol of his change of heart thrust a sword into a stone and became a hermit. He performed many miracles, died in 1181 and was canonised not long after. He founded a Cistercian community here on Montesiepi where the monks became skilled architects and accountants, as noted on the Biccherna covers in the Siena archives. The Abbey was dissolved in 1600. The 1218 French Gothic church remains open to the skies, and the monastery is still in use. Above the Abbey is the **Cappella di Montesiepi**, built over Galgano's Sword in the Stone. It also contains frescoes about his life by A. Lorenzetti. The whole sits in beautiful countryside. Further to the south west is the hill-top town of **Chiusdino**, impressive for photographs either from within its walls or of the town from below.

Due east of Siena, amid the hills where the ochre 'burnt Siena' is mined, is the village of **Montaperti**, scene of the famous Sienese victory over Florence in 1260. **Rapolano Terme** is a medieval walled spa town. **Sinalunga** is a hill town where Victor Emmanuel arrested Garibaldi and also the scene of another Sienese victory in 1363; there are some interesting paintings in the Collegiata and in San Bernardino. **Gargonza** and **Monte San Savino** are both of considerable interest (see Arezzo area) as is the town of **Torrita di Siena** with its sixteenth-century towers. **Asciano's** walls date back to 1351 and its Museo di Arte Sacra has a noted collection of Sienese art. In the church of San Bernardino there is a small Etruscan Museum.

A pretty drive south of Siena on the N2 takes you through the delightful medieval town of **Lucignano** to Buonconvento. The old part of **Buonconvento**, where Emperor Henry VII died in 1313, has two imposing old gates and part of the old wall. The fourteenth-century church has an altar by Matteo di Giovanni while the nearby Museo di Arte Sacra has some fine Sienese paintings. (Open 10.00-12.00, Tuesday and Thursday. Saturday 10.00-12.00 plus 14.00-16.00. Sundays 09.00-13.00.)

Monte Oliveto

South of Asciano or east of Buonconvento on a densely-forested hill amid the 'crete' (areas of erosion) of the area, is the monastery of **Monte Oliveto Maggiore** founded in 1313 by the Siena merchant Giovanni Tolomei, who took the name Bernardo and was beatified. It is a masterpiece of Renaissance architecture. The entrance gate tower (1393) has terracottas by Della Robbia, but the monastery, at the end of the drive, is especially noted for its Great Cloister (1426-74) with its frescoes of the life of St. Benedict, the cycle beginning on the east side with nine by Signorelli and the rest by Sodoma who appears wearing white gloves on the left of 'Come Benedetto risaldo lo capistero che era rotto' (or how Benedict mended the tray). The church also contains works by Sodoma and others, as well as some of the finest choir-stalls, by Giovanni da Verona (1503), in the country.

The monks remain and it is possible to eat and to stay here in the guesthouse (as Pius II and Charles V did) but you are advised to ring in advance. (Open to daytime visitors 09.00-12.00 and 15.00-19.00.)

Montalcino – the Balcony of Tuscany

Due south of Buonconvento is the walled hill town of Montalcino, which became, for four years, capital of the Republic of Siena after the fall of Siena in 1555. The thirteenth-century Palazzo Comunale is on Piazza del Popolo. Sant' Agostino preserves some fourteenth-century frescoes whilst the Diocesan and Civic Museum has a good collection of Sienese art. (Open 10.00-12.00 and 15.00-17.00; closed Mondays.)

At the east end of Via Ricasoli is the fourteenth-century fortress (open 10.00-12.00) that enabled the Republicans to hold out for four years – the last act of medieval republicanism in Italy. There are good views to be had and wines to be tasted in the Enoteca (such as the famous Brunello di Montalcino, considered by many to be the finest Italian wine). The Duomo is on Via Spagni at the end of which are fine views.

Sant' Antimo

A few miles further south is the very fine Romanesque monastery church of Sant' Antimo. (Open Sundays 09.00-12.00 and 14.00-17.00; on other days ask the custodian in nearby Castelnuovo dell' Abate.) The ruined monastery is supposed to have been founded by Charlemagne and the remaining church of 1118 retains some of the ninth-century masonry. Its limpid, light interior is accounted for by the use of alabaster: note the campanile dome, the frescoes in the sacristy and, upstairs, the Matroneum.

San Quirico d' Orcia

Back on the N2 and east of Montalcino is the fine Romanesque Collegiata of San Quirico d' Orcia, started in 1080, notable for its thirteenth-century south portal and original west door. Further south is the tiny spa town of **Bagno Vignoni** with Medici-built pool and pretty piazza, and the attractive medieval town of **Castiglione d' Orcia**.

Pienza

Seven miles east of San Quirico on the N146 is Pienza, one of the most interesting little Renaissance towns in Tuscany. It is also famous for its sheep's cheese. It has a singular history. Aeneas Silvius Piccolomini, later Pius II, was born here during his family's exile from Siena. When he became Pope he decided to transform what was then called Corsignano into a city and art centre to be called Pienza. It was designed mostly by Bernardo Rossellino and may be seen as a model of town planning which never got further than the main square with palace and cathedral, all of which were built from 1459-62.

Piazza Pio II

This is an exceptional example of the Florentine style. The Duomo of 1462 boasts an elegant travertine façade and was one of the earliest Tuscan Renaissance churches. The interior is Gothic in style and has not been altered since the day it was built. There are some fine altarpieces by Vecchietta, Sano di Pietro, Matteo di Giovanni and Giovanni di Paolo. The Baptistry font is by Rossellino. Unfortunately subsidence is a problem, perhaps an insuperable one.

On the south side of the square is Rossellino's masterpiece, the Palazzo Piccolomini, inspired by the Palazzo Ruccellai in Florence, open to the public every day except Monday (hours 10.00-13.00 and 15.00-18.00 or 14.00-16.00 in winter). It has a lovely garden.

Behind the Palace, in Via del Corso, is the church of San Francesco from the original town. On the east side of the square is the Palazzo Ammannati (Palazzo Newton), built by a cardinal of the same name, the Bishop's Palace and the Canonical Palace which is a museum of painting, tapestry and embroidery. The Palazzo Communale is on the north side. The well near the Duomo is also by Rossellino.

Near the town, about one kilometre, is the twelfth-century Romanesque **Pieve di Corsignano**, where Pius II was baptised; note the exotic carvings over the entrance and the fourteenth-century wooden Crucifix.

Montepulciano

This is not very convenient by train. You are advised to disembark at Chiusi-Chianciano Terme and take the bus. Tourist Information is at Via Ricci, 9, (Tel. 716935) or, more likely, a new office in the car-park below and to the right of Porta al Prato. By road, proceeding further east from Pienza on the N146 and branching left onto the N326 brings you to the town.

Montepulciano is another hill town famous for its wine the Vino Nobile di Montepulciano, and its palatial works of art. It was an Etruscan settlement and later a sort of Florentine stronghold in the endless rivalry between the two major powers of the area. Nothing testifies to this more than the fact that the town's most famous son made his name at the court of the Medici. Angelo Poliziano or Politian (an inhabitant of the town is a 'poliziano') but whose real name was Ambrogini, was one of the great Humanist poets, famous particularly for 'Le Stanze per la Giostra' and 'La favola d'Orfeo'. The annual Bruscello festival in August maintains the literary tradition.

The main entrance is the Porta al Prato. The main street is Via di Gracciano: at 82, left, is the **Palazzo Tarugi** bu Vignola (he of the Villa Giulio in Rome) and at 91, right, the **Palazzo Avignonesi** by the same architect. **Palazzo Bucelli** at 73 is, unusually, built on Etruscan urns and decorated with Etruscan designs. Further on, right, where the road rises steeply, is **Sant' Agostino** with a façade by

Michelozzo and inside in the second south chapel a *San Bernadino* by Giovanni di Paolo and in the third north chapel a *Crucifixion* by Lorenzo di Credi. Opposite the church is the **Torre del Pulcinella**, Pulcinella being the Commedia dell'Arte – a form of traditional theatre from Naples – figure who rings the bell, apparantly left as a gift from a Neopolitan bishop in exile. Where Via di Gracciano meets Via di Voltaia nel Corso there is, left, the ancient hospital of **Santa Maria della Cavina** and, opposite, the old **Grain Market**. Bear left: on the left of Via di Voltaia is the large **Palazzo Cervini** by Sangallo, then at 55 the **Palazzo Grugni**. Next to it is the Collegio della Compagnia di Gesu and beyond it, the **Gesu** church, a fine example of Italian Baroque by Andrea Pozzo. Take Via dell'Opio ahead of you and cross Via delle Farine into **Via Poliziano** where the author was born in the fourteenth-century house at number 5.

The street becomes lined with trees and leads to the thirteenth-century **Santa Maria dei Servi**, with Tuscan-Gothic façade, and inside a *Madonna and Child* by Duccio. The road splits here: the left leads down to the **Tempio di San Biagio**, the right, Via San Donato, leading up to the oldest part of the town, with the **Fortress** to the right.

Re-entering the town on Via della Fortezza brings you to the beautiful Piazza Grande and the seventeenth-century **Duomo**, at the highest part of the city. The Duomo is on your right as you enter the square. Within is a fine triptych at the main altar by Taddeo di Bartolo, one of the finest examples of fourteenth-century Sienese art. In the first north chapel is a Della Robbian tabernacle around a bas-relief by Benedetto da Maiano. In the north aisle is a *Madonna* by Sano di Pietro. By the west door is the statue from the tomb of Aragazzi, secretary to Pope Martin V, by Michelozzo; other fragments are to be found on the first two pillars of the nave, a frieze on the main altar and statues on either side of it.

On the left of the square as you enter is the fourteenth-century **Palazzo Communale**, by Michelozzo, in Florentine style. Ascend the tower for tremendous views even of Siena on a clear day. Continuing clockwise around the square is, across the street and behind the well, the Gothic **Palazzo del Capitano del Popolo**. Next to it is the **Palazzo Tarugi,** by Sangallo and then the **Palazzo Contucci**, by the same architect.

Continue along Via Ricci with, almost immediately right, the **Palazzo Neri-Orselli**, the **Museo Civico**, (closed Mondays) in Sienese Gothic style, with works from the Umbrian and Tuscan Schools), with opposite, the **Palazzo Ricci**, by Peruzzi. At the end of Via Ricci is the church of **San Francesco** and a beautiful view from the adjacent square. Via Santa Lucia, right of San Francesco, leads down to the Church of **Santa Lucia**, with a *Madonna* by Signorelli in a chapel on the right. Bear right to bring you down on to the main street.

Outside the walls is the Renaissance church of the **Madonna di San Biagio**, the masterpiece of Antonio da Sangallo with lovely interior (including an eighteenth-century organ), based on a central square and Greek cross. It is constructed in travertine. Nearby is a delightful Canon's house, with five main arches and a gallery of delicate, upper arches, by the same architect.

As for the wine, there are any number of cantine where you may taste and buy. The **Cantine Cantucci** on Piazza Grande also has a room with frescoes by Andrea Pozzo.

Cne kilometre outside the town, along the Viale Calamandrei towards the Val di Chiana, is the sixteenth-century church of **Santa Maria delle Grazie**, by Ippolito Scalza. Within is a beautiful and precious organ, its pipes made entirely from cypress wood, said to have been donated by one Vincenzo Salimbeni at Christmas in 1600.

South-west of Montepulciano is the town of **Monticchiello** with a thirteenth-century church and altarpiece by P. Lorenzetti. In July it hosts an open-air theatre festival.

Chianciano Vecchia and Chianciano Terme

The nearest train station is Chiusi-Chianciano Terme, from where you may take a bus. Tourist information Via G. Sabatini, 7 (Tel: 63538).

The N146 going south-east brings you to the pleasant town of **Chianciano Vecchia** and its Museo d'Arte Sacra with a collection of Florentine and Sienese art. Modern **Chianciano Terme** nearby, known to the Etruscans and Romans, is noted for its warm saline and chalybeate waters; there are a large number of pleasant bathhouses where you can bathe and be massaged, drained and generally cosseted. Some of the water may be taken for liver complaints. The main season lasts from April to October.

Chiusi

The railway station is in the lower, newer part of the town. Tourist information: Via Porsena, 67 (Tel: 227667).

A few miles east of Chianciano is this ancient town divided into modern on the plain and old on the hill. Originally the Etruscan

Even the unsung Tuscan towns have their own beauty – Chiusdino.

'Camars', it has long been associated with Lars Porsena, the leader of the Etruscan Confederation in their fight against the Romans in 508 BC and a hero of Macaulay's *Horatio*. The Romans finally conquered it in 295 BC. Then came decline, partly because of the invincible marshiness of the Valdichiana area which once, in prehistory, was the bed of the Arno. When Cosimo de' Medici finally drained the area, the town regained something of its prosperity. It is a town that retains much of its illustrious Etruscan past to this day.

Etruscan tombs and tunnels and the Etruscan Museum

Guides for the tombs may be obtained at the Museo Nazionale Etrusco, well worth a visit in itself. It has many Etruscan sarcophogi among which is the alabaster one for Lars Sentinates, and cinerary urns, some of which have sculpted figures of the dead on top. (Open 09.00-13.30 or 09.00-12.00 on Saturday. Closed Monday.)

The tombs form a huge necropolis on the outskirts of the town (and mostly approachable by car), many of which are fine examples of painted tombs. If they are locked, custodians who live nearby will open them. On the road to Chianciano, Via delle Tombe Etrusche leads, right, to Tomba della Pellegrina (Pilgrim Lady's Tomb), Tomba della Scimmia (Ape's Tomb) which has the best paintings, and Tomba del Granduca (Grand Duke's Tomb) complete with cinerary urns. Leaving the city by the Cimitero Nuovo (New Cemetery) will bring you to the Tomba Casuccini with paintings of sports and games.

North of the city is the Poggio Gaiella, a hill of passages and galleries, the legendary mausoleum of Lars Porsena. There are many Etruscan tunnels of mysterious purpose beneath the town itself, some of which were later to become Christian catacombs. It is sometimes possible to enter them by asking at the Museum ('e possible vedere le gallerie sotterranee, per favore?'). The first-century BC Roman cistern beneath the Duomo may usually be visited.

The Romanesque **Duomo**, built out of Etruscan and Roman remains for the most part, is the oldest in Tuscany. The present building is twelfth-century, though parts of it date back to the original sixth-century building. The Chapter House has a fine collection of illuminated antiphonaries or choir books. The mosaic-like paintings on the walls are recent – 1915. The Fortezza is twelfth-century.

South-west of Chiusi

The N478 going south west to Radicofani takes you near very pretty **Cetona** and its castle and Etruscan museum, through **Sarteano** with palaces and works by Beccafumi and Giacomo di Mino in the San Martino and San Francesco churches and through rugged countryside.

Radicofani lies atop a basalt hill amid some splendid countryside. Here the English Pope Hadrian IV built a castle of which the remains are visible and in which the Abbot of Cluny was imprisoned by the bandit Ghino di Tacco, as related in the *Decamaron*. The church of San Pietro has work by Della Robbia. The seventeenth-century Palazzo La Posta was used as a hotel by many nineteenth-century men of letters including Charles Dickens who said of it:

'there is a windy, creaking, wormy, rustling, door-opening, foot-on-staircase-falling character about this Radicofani Hotel, such as I never saw, anywhere else.'

Abbadia San Salvatore

Tourist information (for the Monte Amiata area): Via Mentana 95 (Tel: 0577 778608).

A few miles west of Radicofani is the ancient Cistercian abbey of San Salvatore, formerly the most powerful one in Tuscany. The town has an unspoilt medieval centre and the old abbey church on Via del Monastero was founded in 743 after a vision seen by a Lombard king. It was rebuilt in 1036 in Romanesque style, by which time the abbey had become extremely influential. The story of the vision is told in frescoes by Nasini. There is a twelfth-century Crucifix and the Byzantine crypt dates back to the original church. The town is now a popular resort.

Monte Amiata

This is an extinct volcano a few miles to the west of the Abbadia San Salvatore. At 5,735 feet (1,738 metres) it is the highest point in south Tuscany. Covered in beech and chestnut forest, it has become a popular skiing and walking resort, as well as being an important mercury mining centre. It is possible to take a road to the summit where there are magnificent views.

Castel del Piano, Arcidosso, Santa Fiora and Piancastagnaio

A few miles north-west of Monte Amiata is **Castel del Piano**, a well preserved medieval town. South of it is **Arcidosso** with its tenth-century church of Pieve di Lamulas and well known for its associations with the nineteenth-century prophet and socialist, Davide Lazzaretti, who built a communal church, still standing, on Monte Labbro to the south. To the south too is **Santa Fiora** with churches containing Della Robbia terracotta work. East of here is the mountain resort of **Piancastagnaio**, a town of chestnut groves and an imposing Aldobrandeschi palace, the Palazzo Bourbon del Monte, with museum.

TWENTY

The East and South-east

East Tuscany

Arezzo

Thirty-one miles (50 kilometres) north-east of Siena and 37 south-east of Florence, Arezzo, an ancient Etruscan town, is located on a hill at the meeting point of the Valdarno, the Casentino Valley and the Valdichiana. The most scenic route from Florence would be along the N67, N70 and N71.

Tourist Information can be found in front of the station which is on the south-west edge of the town. The main one, on Piazza Risorgimento 116 (Tel: 0575 23952) seems to direct you to the one at the station. You are advised to park in this general area and walk up to the attractive old town.

Arezzo was a free commune with Ghibelline sympathies in the Middle Ages, its golden age coming in the early fourteenth-century when it was ruled by warrior bishops. It lost its independence to Florence in 1384. Louis d'Anjou, who was besieging the city, demanded a ransom, duly paid by Florence, who assumed rule. Arezzo has been the birthplace of some eminent citizens: Guido d'Arezzo in the eleventh-century is accredited with the invention of musical notation, and Petrarch, born in the fourteenth-century, was one of Europe's greatest poets. In the late Renaissance Arezzo produced the painter and biographer Giorgio Vasari and the writer Pietro Aretino (an 'Aretino' is a native of the city).

It suffered somewhat in World War II but recovered to become a small town of considerable charm, with an important gold and jewellery industry, furniture and antiques, all of which are still widely sold in the shops. The old quarter lies in the general area of the three main streets of the Corso Italia, Via Cesalpino and Via

Guido Monaco, all of which follow a gradual ascent in the direction of the Cathedral from where there are some good views.

San Francesco

Open 07.00-12.30 and 15.00-19.00. (Check that restoration work has been completed.)

Via Guido Monaco leads up from the station and ends at Piazza San Francesco with its famous church of 1322, built by Fra Giovanni da Pistoia. The church is celebrated for one of the greatest of all fresco cycles, *The Legend of the True Cross* by Piero della Francesca, painted between 1454-66. They form a work of intense spirituality coupled with a virtuoso mastery of the techniques of perspective and realism. The cycle is as follows: on the right hand wall, top, as you look at the window is the death of Adam; below is the Queen of Sheba received by Solomon and the sacred wood being buried by order of Solomon; below again is Constantine's victory over Maxentius; on the left wall, top, is the exaltation of the Cross; below is the discovery of the three crosses and the verification of the true cross; below again is the victory of Heraclius over Chosroes. On the window wall are two prophets the below, left, the supplication of the Jew and, right, the transportation of the cross; below again, left, the Annunciation and then the dream of Constantine.

In the chapel left of the altar is another *Annunciation* attributed to Luca Signorelli; the nave walls are decorated with frescoes by local artists including an *Annunciation* by Spinello Aretino towards end of the right wall.

Piazza Grande

From San Francesco take Via Cavour to the right until you meet the Corso Italia. Turn left into it as it becomes Via dei Pileati until you meet the twelfth-century Pieve di Santa Maria church on your right. The impressive façade uses pillars with human figures and is decorated with with medieval reliefs depicting the months of the year. The interior, especially the arches, hints at the transition to Gothic; and the raised presbytery has a polyptych by Pietro Lorenzetti.

From Piazza Grande, behind the church, you have a good view of its lovely arcaded Romanesque apse and of the 1330 campanile. The square is eccentrically picturesque, an 'architectural anthology'. Two sides of the square are lined with medieval houses and towers. Next to the church is the Gothic-Renaissance Palazzetto della Fraternita (fourteenth to sixteenth-century), the palace of a lay fraternity of monks founded in thirteenth-century, with a lunette by Rossellino. The fourth side is the Loggiato del Vasari (Vasari's Loggia) of 1573, intended to provide shade for shops and offices. The square is the site of an antiques fair the first weekend of every month and a festival, the Giostra del Saracino, the first Sunday of September. This is a celebration of the battles against the Saracens, dating back to the thirteenth-century. Revived in 1932, representatives of the four town quarters battle for a golden lance. Seats are bookable in advance.

The arcade extends out onto Via dei Pileati as it ascends towards the Duomo. As you follow it you will pass, left, the sixteenth-century **Palazzo Camaini**, containing Provincial Archives, with fourteenth-century tower; the fourteenth-century **Palazzo Pretorio**, now the public library, with the coats of arms of various Podesta; and then, at Via dell'Orto, is **Casa Petrarca**, Petrarch's house, (closed on Saturdays), now an academy for Petrarchan studies. It was rebuilt in 1948 following war damage and contains manuscripts and an autographed letter.

Beyond, at the top of the road, is the Duomo. To its right is the **Passeggio del Prato**, a park with fine views and modern statue of Petrarch; and to its right is the sixteenth-century **Medici Fortress**, dismantled in 1800.

The Duomo

The Cathedral was begun in the late thirteenth century but finished only in 1510. The Gothic style campanile was added in 1859, the façade completed in 1914.

The interior is rather gloomy but has some fine works of art. In the south aisle near the entrance, notice the monument to Gregory X who died here in 1276. Beyond is the canopied Tarlati chapel with fourth-century sarcophagus and a *Crucifixion* by the local 'Maestro del Vescovado'. There are several terracottas by the Della Robbias in the Lady Chapel on the north aisle as well as the remains of Gregory X. Also on the north aisle is the tomb of Bishop Guido Tarlati who died in 1327 by Di Giovanni and Angiolo da Siena with panels illustrating his life, emphasising his role as Ghibelline (note Ghibelline eagle) ruler of Arezzo when the city's territory was greatly expanded. Nearby is a lovely 1466 fresco of St. Mary Magdalen by Piero della Francesca.

The marvellous High Altar contains the body of the patron saint of the city, San Donato, martyred in 361. The magnificent stained glass windows were created by the sixteenth-century French master,

Guillaume de Marcillat. The sacristy gives on to the Museo Diocesano (diocese museum) with church silver and works by Rossellino, Vasari, Spinello Aretino and others.

The façade of the Cathedral overlooks Piazza della Liberta. On the town side of the square, at the top of Via Cesalpina, is the old **Palazzo del Commune** of 1333. Beyond, right, is Via Sassoverde leading to **San Domenico**, founded in 1275, with Romanesque portal and Gothic campanile. Inside there is a Crucifix by Cimabue of 1265 in the apse. Beyond the church is Via San Domenico off which Via Venti Settembre will take you to **Vasari's House** at 55. It contains paintings and letters from Michelangelo.

At the bottom of this street, where it meets Piaggia del Murello, is the **Galleria e Museo Mediovale e Moderno** housed in the fifteenth-century Palazzo Bruni, with works arranged chronologically from the school of Guido da Siena, by Spinello Aretino, Signorelli, Andrea della Robbia, Carracci, Salimbeni, Vasari and others. There is also a fine collection of majolica from Faenza and a collection of glass. (Open 09.00-14.00 or 13.00 on Sundays; closed Mondays.) Further along Piaggia del Murello, left, is **Santa Maria in Gradi** of 1592 with an altarpiece by Andrea della Robbia.

On Via Garibaldi, which leads down towards the town is the Renaissance **Santissima Annunziata**, right. There is an *Annunciation* by S. Aretino outside and a fine interior with stained glass by Guillaume de Marcillat and a painting by Pietro da Cortona.

Further down, left, is a street to Piazza D. Badia and the thirteenth-century abbey of **Santissima Flora e Lucilla** remodelled by Vasari (the high altar was intended to be his tomb) with a fresco of San Lorenzo by Bartolomeo della Gatta in 1476. Also a beautiful ciborium by Benedetto da Maiano (left aisle) and *Crucifixion* by Segna di Bonaventura (1320, right aisle). There is a lovely fifteenth-century cloister entered at number 2.

Via Garibaldi continues across Via Guido Monaco and then the Corso Italia. By turning left into the Corso you will come to the above-mentioned Museum of Modern Art, right. Via Garibaldi continues to **Piazza Sant' Agostino** with thirteenth-century campanile. Turning right into Via Margaritone brings you to the **San Bernardo Convent**, the remains of the **Roman amphitheatre** and the **Museo Archeologico Mecenate** which contains examples of Etruscan art, jewellery and bronzes, Roman mosaics and corallino vases, Palaeolithic and neolithic finds, scent boxes from Egypt and Asia. (Open 09.00-14.00 or 13.00 on Sunday, closed Mondays.)

A 15-minute walk along Viale Mecenate leads from the south corner of the city, just beyond the archeological museum, to the pretty Renaissance church of **Santa Maria delle Grazie** of 1449. The beautiful loggia is by Benedetto da Maiano and altar by Andrea della Robbia.

Near Arezzo

North of Arezzo is the Casentino, a peaceful area of hills and valleys around the lower reaches of the Arno.

Bibbiena

In this, the capital of the Casentino seek out the fine Renaissance Palazzo Dovizi, the church of San Lorenzo with terracottas by Andrea della Robbia, and the twelfth-century Church of SS Ippolito e Donato.

La Verna

This magnificent working Franciscan monastery sits up on a high rock at 3,726 feet (1,129 metres) amid the Alpi di Catenaia between the Arno and Tiber valleys to the east of Bibbiena. The site was given to St. Francis in 1213 upon which he proceeded to build for his followers. He visited the site several times himself for meditation and received the stigmata in the Cappella della Stimmate. Note the particularly fine terracottas by the Della Robbias in all of the churches - the Chiesa Maggiore of 1450-70, Santa Maria degli Angeli (1216-18), and the other, oldest, church which also has Renaissance stalls. A path takes you a little higher to La Penna, offering excellent views.

Poppi

A short way north of Bibbiena is Poppi, the home of the Guidi Counts who gave shelter to Dante during his exile and who ruled the Casentino between the eleventh and fifteenth centuries. It was also the birthplace of the artist Mino da Fiesole (1431-84). The well-preserved medieval Guidi castle (Palazzo Pretorio) is worth seeing with its frescoed Great Hall and chapel, the tower and its fine views and a marvellous courtyard.

The town has a pretty, arcaded medieval centre and the Romanesque church of San Fedele. Local shops specialise in copperware.

A corner of the delightful town of Poppi, the seat of the Guidi Counts

Camaldoli

A few scenic miles to the north-east of Poppi is the town of Camaldoli and its Monastery of an order founded in 1012 by the Benedictine San Romualdo for monks to lead hermetic lives. The original hospice with cloister and chapel is there, built to discourage pilgrims from disturbing the monks, though the main buildings date from the seventeenth and eighteenth centuries apart from the interesting sixteenth-century Pharmacy. Further up (one hour's walk) are the monastic cells, with their chapels and plots (the monks are vegetarian) and Baroque church on the site of the original hermitage; this is called the Eremo and only men are allowed beyond the gate.

Romena

A little way north of Poppi, not far from Pratovecchio (the birthplace of the artist Paolo Uccello) is the Pieve di San Pietro di Romena, a beautiful Romanesque church founded in 1152 with early frescoes and striking pillar capitals in the form of a variety of exotic creatures. (Entrance may have to be obtained from the house across the road). Nearby is the Castello di Romena, a Guidi castle that was one of the most formidable in the Casentino. On the road just south of Pratovecchio you may notice a column commemorating the Battle of Campaldino (1289) in which Dante fought and which consolidated Florentine power.

North of Pratovecchio is the wool town of **Stia** with its Romanesque Santa Maria Assunta containing works by Andrea della Robbia; nearby is the Porciano Guidi castle with agricultural implement museum. Not far from Stia is the source of the Arno (Capo d'Arno) and the trail to the summit of Monte Falterona, 5,458 feet (1,654 metres).

Near Poppi

West of Poppi are the cool mountain resorts of Vallombrosa and **Saltino**, very pleasant for walking on their shaded slopes. **Vallombrosa** is also famous for its monastery, founded by St. John Gualberto in 1040, the first for the Vallombrosan order. The church is mainly seventeenth-century. Milton stayed here in 1638 – there is a tablet commemorating the fact.

North of Vallombrosa is the Passo della Consuma at 3,375 feet (1,023 metres) linking the Casentino and Val d'Arno.

South of Vallombrosa is **Regello**, a pretty country town with charming arcaded square. The road from here to Arezzo via Castelfranco di Sopra, Loro Ciuffena, **Gropina** (with a beautiful thirteenth-century Romanesque church), and **Castiglion Fibocchi** is very picturesque.

North-east of Arezzo – the Valtiberina (the Tiber Valley)

The SS73 from Arezzo leads scenically for 25 miles (40 kilometres) to the town of Sansepolcro. It bypasses **Monterchi**, a little frontier town of medieval streets with interesting parish church but more famous for a unique work of art. In the cemetery chapel, just below the village which was the birthplace of the artist's mother, is a fresco showing the Virgin close to giving birth, the *Madonna del Parto*, (1445) by Piero della Francesca.

The road also passes close to **Anghiari**, a delightful medieval town known for furniture making and the scene of an important Florentine victory in 1440 over Milan, the subject of a lost Da Vinci work in the Palazzo Vecchio in Florence. Worth seeing are the churches of the Abbey and San Giovanni, the Collegiata, and the Palazzo Taglieschi which contains a museum of traditional crafts of the area.

Borgo Sansepolcro

This is the birthplace of the painter Piero della Francesca and where he spent most of his life. Its well-preserved walls amid tobacco fields enclose the Piazza Torre di Berta, the scene of an annual archery contest, the Palio della Balestra, against Gubbio on the second Sunday in September. Also here are the palaces on Via Matteotti including the Museo Civico, in the Palazzo Communale, which houses Piero della Francesca's *Resurrection* and his Misericordia Polyptych, works by Signorelli, Pontormo and others. (Open 10.00-13.00 and 15.00-18.00, 17.00 in winter.) The Duomo, also on Via Matteotti, has a work by Santi di Tito (1538-1603), another native; the churches of San Francesco and San Lorenzo are also worth investigation.

Sansepolcro has also been the home since 1827 of the Buitoni pasta factory.

North-west of Sansepolcro is **Pieve Santo Stefano** with an interesting Collegiata, and Caprese Michelangelo, birthplace of the artist. His father, Leonardo Buonarroti, was podesta here and Michelangelo was born in the fourteenth-century town hall (Casa del Podesta), now a museum, and christened in the thirteenth-century San Giovanni Battista chapel.

North-west of Arezzo – the Valdarno

The route that basically follows the A1/N69 has some interesting possibilities. **Montevarchi** is noted for the Collegiata di San Lorenzo in the town centre where there is a tempietto covered with work by Andrea della Robbia and its Paleontological Museum; (open 09.00-12.00, and 16.00-19.00, or Sunday 10.00-12.00; closed Mondays). **Cavriglia** has a nature reserve.

San Giovanni Valdarno, in an area of lignite mining, despite its gloomy aspect, has an impressive centre. The street plan was designed by Arnolfo di Cambio (as was the Duomo in Florence) in the thirteenth-century. The arcaded central square boasts the Palazzo Comunale/Pretorio with coloured decoration by the Della Robbia workshop. The church of Santa Maria delle Grazie, with seventeenth-century interior, has a *Madonna and Saints* attributed to Masaccio, who was born here. This was also the birthplace of the painter Giovanni da San Giovanni (1592-1636). Just south of here is the Renaissance Convento di Montecarlo, with a fine *Annunciation* by Fra Angelico.

Figline Valdarno, the birthplace of the Humanist Marsilio Ficino (1433-99), is a busy town with a Pretorian Palace, the old hospital Serristori and the Collegiata di Santa Maria with a fine fourteenth-century *Madonna* by the Maestro di Figline. Ficino was a protege of Cosimo de' Medici and a pillar of the Platonic Academy. Incisa di Valdarno, named after the chalk cliffs washed by the river, was home to Petrarch in his youth and the site of much fighting in 1944.

North-east of here is the town of **Sanmezzano**, with a Medici Villa altered in nineteenth-century Moorish style. In **Rignano sull' Arno**, in the Church of San Clemente, are works by Mino da Fiesole and Bernardino Rossellino.

South of Arezzo

The Valdichiana towards Cortona is the broad valley running due south of Arezzo, much favoured by the Etruscans for agriculture. By the middle ages, however, it had become something of a swamp until the nineteenth-century when it was reclaimed. In the area are a number of of delightful villages and towns.

Following the SS73 south-west will bring you to **Monte San Savino**, the birthplace of the architect Andrea Sansovino (1486-1570), a medieval town west of the valley with many fine Renaissance palaces. Sansovino was a favourite architect of Lorenzo de' Medici. His pupil Jacopo took the same name and went on to make his name in Venice.

The city walls were built by the Sienese and the Palazzo Pretorio by the Perugians. Sansovino designed the lovely Loggia del Mercato and was responsible for some of the sculptural works in Santa Chiara. It is thought that Sant' Agostino was perhaps rebuilt by Sansovino; it also contains a Vasari altarpiece. The Palazzo Comunale was the work of Sangallo the Elder.

Further west is **Gargonza**, a walled village perched on a hill and dominated by a huge tower. The entire village has become a rather unusual hotel.

South of Monte San Savino is **Lucignano**, a charming hill town built as four circles with four little piazze. On these squares are the fourteenth-century Palazzo Communale with the Museo Civico containing Sienese art of the thirteenth to the fifteenth centuries, the beautiful fourteenth-century reliquary 'Albero di Lucignano' by the goldsmiths of Arezzo and a *Madonna* by Signorelli. There is also the Collegiata, the church of San Francesco, a Medici fortress and a temple called the Madonna delle Querce (Madonna of the oaks) attributed to Vasari.

North-east of Lucignano is **Marciano della Chiana**, an imposing fortress town. South-west is **Foianao della Chiana** with a Collegiata containing a *Coronation of the Virgin* by Signorelli.

Castiglion Fiorentino

Across the valley, due east of Monte San Savino, is this medieval market town with the Gothic San Francesco containing a thirteenth-century painting by Margaritone d' Arezzo. There are plenty of Renaissance elements too such as the Palazzo Comunale and museum with a *Stimmata di San Francesco* by Bartolomeo della Gatta and silver reliquaries. The Collegiata also has work by Gatta. Outside the walls there is an octagonal sixteenth-century Renaissance temple, the Madonna della Consolazione with a fresco attributed to Signorelli.

A few miles south is the castle of **Montecchio Vesponi**, once the lair of the English condottiere in the pay of the Florentines in the fourteenth century, Sir John Hawkwood.

Cortona

Tourist Information, Via Nazionale 72 (Tel: (0575) 630352/630353/603190). Parking facilities are to be found near San Domenico on Piazzale Garibaldi or outside the Porta Sant' Agostino from which the steep and attractive Via Guelfa leads up to the centre. One railway station (Camucia-Cortona) is 3 miles (5 kilometres) west of Cortona; the other (Cortona-Terontola) is 7 miles (11 kilometres) south.

South of Castiglion Fiorentino, just off the SS71, Cortona is one of the loveliest and most ancient of hill towns, set on terraced slopes dominated by a fortress, its ancient streets ascending steeply to produce fine views across the Valdichiana and towards Lake Trasimeno. Its history is long, long enough to have generated myths about its origins. Legend has it that it was founded by one Corythus, father of Dardanus who eventually founded Troy and after whom the Dardanelles were named. In corroboration it is believed by some that the mysterious Etruscans originated in Asia Minor.

It is certain that Cortona was an important Etruscan city, the foundations of which are still visible in the city walls. In the fourth-century it was taken over by the Romans and then ignored. It was later a medieval commune with Ghibelline sympathies and in the fourteenth century ruled by the Casali family. In 1409 the city fell under the rule of Florence.

It has produced its fair share of artists. Luca Signorelli was born here, as was Pietro da Cortona (1596-1669) and latterly the Futurist Gino Severini (1883-1966). Fra Angelico worked here for much of his life, and the principal architect of the Maltese capital Valletta, Laparelli (1521-70), was born here.

Note, as you walk past the older houses, the **Porte dei Morti** (doors of the dead), a feature unique to Tuscany and Umbria. These are small, raised doorways, used supposedly for the passage of coffins, or as an alternative entrance and exit in difficult times.

The fifteenth-century **San Domenico** at the entrance to the town, by Piazzale Garibaldi, has an elegant interior with altarpiece by Gerini, a present to the Dominican order by Lorenzo de'Medici; and, in the chapel to the right of the apse, an early *Madonna* by Signorelli. On the left wall is a *Madonna* in a lunette by Fra Angelico. From here is a **Passeggiata Pubblica** or parterre leading prettily through gardens and parks with fine views.

From Piazzale Garibaldi, Via Nazionale, the main street (with information office), leads to the main square, **Piazza della Repubblica**. Here the thirteenth-century **Palazzo Comunale** has a sixteenth-century tower. Behind it, on Piazza Signorelli, is the thirteenth-century Palazzo Pretorio Casali, restored after the war and now the Museo Civico or **Museo dell' Accademia** Etrusca. (Open 10.00-13.00 and 16.00-19.00 April 1-September 30 and 09.00-13.00 and 15.00-17.00 October-March, closed Mondays.) It has a delightful courtyard and a collection which includes Greek and Egyptian antiquities, Etruscan bronzes (including the extraordinary fifth-century BC chandelier with lamps in the form of squatting human figures, dolphins and a gorgon – probably the finest piece of Etruscan bronzework in existence), Roman painting, works by Gerini,

The ruined Gothic abbey of San Galgano.

Pinturrichio, Bicci di Lorenzo, Signorelli, and more recent art by Cigoli and Severini.

Via Casali takes you to the **Duomo**, originally eleventh-century but much changed in the sixteenth by Giuliano da Sangallo. The campanile is by Laparelli. Behind the high altar are works by Cigoli (a *Madonna and Saints*), Alessandro Allori (also *Madonna and Saints*) and school of Signorelli (*Crucifixion*). There is also a mosaic by Severini and ciborium by Cuiccio di Nuccio.

Opposite the Duomo, in the former Gesu church with its fine wooden ceiling, is the **Museo Diocesano** with works by Signorelli, among them his marvellous *Deposition*, a beautiful Fra Angelico *Annunciation*, works by P. Lorenzetti, Duccio and Sassetta, and a Roman sarcophagus much admired by Donatello and Brunelleschi. (Open 09.00-13.00, 15.00-18.30 April 1-September 30 or 09.00-13.00, 15.00-17.00 October-March; closed Mondays.) In the area of the museum are some picturesque medieval streets, notably Via del Gesu, with its canopies and wooden supports.

From Piazza Signorelli Via Dardano will take you to the **Porta Colonia** where the Etruscan wall remains, and the Roman and medieval walls above, are clearly visible. Beyond, up, is the **Medici Fortress** built by Laparelli in 1549. It is a ten-minute walk to the lovely Renaissance church of **Santa Maria Nuova** below.

Via Santucci leads up from Piazza della Repubblica to the old hospital, the palatial Via Maffei and, next to the hospital, the Church of **San Francesco** founded in 1245 by the saint's disciple Elias of Cortona. The artist Signorelli is buried here; there is a Byzantine ivory reliquary of the Holy Cross which belonged to the Emperor Nicephoras Phocas; it is sometimes locked away – ask the Sacristan. On the wall, left, is an *Annunciation* by Pietro da Cortona.

Via Berrettini leads steeply up from San Francesco to Piazza del Pozzo, Piazza Pescaia, Via San Nicolo, where you turn left to find the Romanesque **San Nicolo**, favoured by San Bernardino da Siena's Company of San Nicolo, for whom Signorelli painted a fine *Deposition*, and a *Madonna and Child*, on the standard inside.

Still higher up from here (turn right out of San Niccolo back onto Via San Nicolo and then right at San Cristoforo church) is the nineteenth-century church of **Santa Margherita di Laviano**, replacing the original thirteenth-century church founded by the saint whose remains are on the high altar in a fine, locally-made tomb of 1362. The fortress is close to here. You can return to Piazzale Garibaldi by way of Via Santa Margherita and Via Crucis, the latter built in gratitude after the war and lined with mosaic Stations of the Cross by Severini.

Outside the town, below Piazzale Garibaldi, is **Santa Maria del Calcinaio**, the 1485 masterpiece by the Sienese Francesco di Giorgio Martini, with stained glass by Guillaume de Marcillat.

Also outside the town, to the south-west, near Camucia, is the so-called **Tanella di Pitagora**, a fourth-century BC Etruscan hypogeum. Pythagoras did not live here but in the south Italian town of Croton, hence the confusion.

Two miles east of Cortona, still on Monte Egidio, is the **Eremo di San Egidio**, the hermitage founded and used by St. Francis in 1211. His stone bed is still in his cell.

Appendix

Common Italian words and phrases

A basic knowledge of Italian can be grasped quite easily. It is pronounced as it is written – once you know the rules governing the pronunciation of each letter – but needs to be enunciated with more vigour and more openly than usually is the case with English. Obviously the following is not exhaustive – many terms and words are listed elsewhere, e.g. food, artistic terms – but it may help from time to time. Above all don't be afraid to make mistakes and don't worry about grammar. Use of key words should be sufficient for your purposes and therefore the number of phrases have been kept to a minimum.

Pronunciation and dictionary

a – as in car
b – as in bus
c – before i or e as in chair, otherwise as in kettle
d – as in dog
e – as in egg
f – as in fact
g – before i or e as in register, otherwise as in go
h – silent
i – as in peek
j – as in jewel
k – as in kart
l – as in lamb
m – as in moment
o – pontif
p – as in palace
qu – as in quilt
r – as in rant (but rolled)
s – as in Saturday
t – as in tassle
u – as in loom
v – as in vantage
w – not in ordinary use
x – not in ordinary use
y – found only in foreign words
z – two ways: as in maids and cats

gn – as in onion
gl – as in halliard

Generally speaking the accent falls on the penultimate syllable. Note that the polite form of 'you', used with strangers, is the third person; as a foreigner you are not expected to have mastered this.

Words

accident – incidente
after – dopo
afternoon – pomeriggio
airport – aeroporto
American – Americano
and – e
art gallery – pinacoteca (art – arte)
Australian – Australiano
bad – cattivo
be – essere   (I am, etc. – sono, sei, e, siamo, siete, sono)
bed – letto   (double bed – letto matrimoniale)
before – prima
big – grande
boy – ragazzo
change (money) – il resto, small change – spiccioli, change (verb) –
   cambiare
bridge – ponte
British – Britannico
can – potere   (I can, etc.– posso, puoi, puo, possiamo, potete,
   possono)
Canadian – Canadese
cheap – buon mercato
chemist – farmacia
church – chiesa
closed – fermato
clothes – vestiti
cold – freddo   (I am cold – ho freddo)
crossroads – bivio
dangerous – pericoloso
daughter – figlia
doctor – medico
down – giu   (up – su)
entrance – ingresso, entrata

excuse me – (apology) scusi,   (please move out of the way –
   permesso)
English – inglese
exit – uscita
expensive – caro
far – lontano
fast – veloce
father – padre
ferry – traghetto
friend – amico
girl – ragazza
go – andare   (I go, etc. – vado, vai, va, andiamo, andate,
   vanno)
go away – vatene (brisk); lasciami in pace, per favore (polite
   plea to be left in peace)
good – buono
have – avere (I have, etc. – ho, hai, ha, abbiamo, avete,
   hanno). Do you have? – ce l'avete per caso?
he – lui
hello/cheerio (informal) – ciao. (To people you do not know it
   is better to say Buongiorno (Good Day) and Arrivederci
   (Goodbye). Use Buonasera (good evening) after the middle of
   the afternoon)
help – aiuto
here – qua
hot – caldo (I am hot – Ho caldo)
how – come (how much? – quanto? how are you? – come va, come
   sta? how long does it take? – quanto tempo ci vuole)
hunger – fame (I am hungry – ho fame)
husband – marito
I – io
ill – malato (headache – mal di testa stomach ache – mal di
   stomaco)
inside – dentro
Irish – Irlandese
lavatory – bagno/toilette
left – sinistra
lift – ascensore
like – come (comparison)   (I like – mi piace, I don't like – non
   mi piace)
lose – perdere   (I have lost – ho perso)
money –soldi

morning – mattina
mother – madre
museum – museo
near – vicino
newspaper – giornale
New Zealander – Nuova Zelandese
night – notte
no – no
not at all, you're welcome (used invariably as a response to
    'thankyou') – prego
now – adesso, ora
O.K. – va bene
open – aperto
outside – fuori
please – per favore
reserve – prenotare
right – (oppposite of left) destra; just – giusto
road – strada
rob – rubare (I've been robbed – mi hanno rubato)
Scottish – Scozzeze
seat (in train etc.) – posto
she – lei
shop – negozio
slow – lento (slow down – rallentare)
small – piccolo
son – figlio
sorry – scusi
speak – parlare (I don't speak Italian – non parlo Italiano)
station – stazione
straight – dritto
street – via
thankyou – grazie
the – il (masculine, plural 'i') la (feminine, plural 'le')
there – la
they – loro
thirst – sete (I am thirsty – ho sete)
this – questo
that – quello
ticket – biglietto
today – oggi
toll – pedaggio
tomorrow – domani

too much/many – troppo
understand – capire   (I don't understand – non capisco)
up – su, down – giu
want – volere   (I would like – vorrei)
water – acqua   (acqua potabile – drinking water)
Welsh – Gallese
who – chi
what – che   (What is the time? – Che ora e?   What is your
    name? – lei, come si chiama?)
where – dove
wife – moglie
why – perche because – perche
work – lavorare, funzionare   (It doesn't work – non funziona)
yesterday – ieri
you – tu (sing.), voi (pl.).

Points of the compass
North – nord; south – sud; east – est; west – ovest.

Numbers
1 – uno, 2 – due, 3 – tre, 4 – quattro, 5 – cinque, 6 – sei, 7 – sette, 8 –
otto, 9 – nove, 10 – dieci, 11 – undieci, 12 – dodici, 13 – tredici, 14 –
quattordici, 15 – quindici, 16 – sedici, 17 – diciasette, 18 – diciotto,
19 – diciannove, 20 – venti, 21 – ventuno, 22 – ventidue, 30 – trenta,
40 – quaranta, 50 – cinquanta, 60 – sessanta, 70 – settanta, 80 –
ottanta, 90 – novanta, 100 – cento. 200 – duecento. 1000 – mille.

Days
Monday – Lunedi; then Martedi, Mercoledi, Giovedi, Venerdi,
Sabato, Domenica.

Months
January – Gennaio; then Febbraio, Marzo, Aprile, Maggio, Giugno,
Luglio, Agosto, Settembre, Ottobre, Novembre, Dicembre.

INDEX

All services for Florence (e.g. hotels, restaurants, medical services) are listed in the main body of the index. See under **Florence** for buildings, streets, squares

Map of Siena – Principal Monuments

11	Chiesa di S. Francesco	57	Casa e Santuario di S. Caterina
13	Oratorio di S. Bernardino		
14	Chiesa di S. Giovanni Staffa	58	Teatro
17	Casa dello Studente	59	Palazzo del Magnifico
19	Fonte Ovile	60	Battistero di S. Giovanni
20	Porta Ovile	61	Duomo
21	Chiesa di S. Donato	62	Cortile Cap, di Giustizia
22	Chiesa di S. Pietro Ovile	63	Palazzo Granducale
23	Monte dei Paschi di Siena	64	Questura
24	Chiesa di S. Maria di Provenzano	65	Museo dell'opera Metropolitana
25	Chiesa di S. Cristoforo	66	Palazzo Piccolomini
26	Chiesa di S. Vigilio	67	Accademia Degli Intronati
27	Università	68	Ente Prov. Turismo
28	Palazzo Sansedoni	69	Palazzo Chigi-Saracini
30	Il Campo	70	Accad. Mus. Chigiana
31	Palazzo Pubblico	71	Palazzo Buonsignori
32	Palazzo Piccolomini (Archivio di Stato)	72	Chiesa di S. Pietro alle Scale
34	Chiesa di S. Martino	73	Museo di Storia Naturale
35	Chiesa della Misericordia	74	Instituto S. Anna
36	Chiesa di S. Giuseppe	76	Instituto per Sordomuti T. Pendola
37	Chiesa di S. Agostino		
38	Convitto Naz. Tolomei	77	Chiesa di S. Lucia
42	Villa Rubini	80	Chiesa di Fonte Giusta
43	Instituto Duca degli Abruzzi	81	Chiesa di S. Bartolomeo
44	Chiesa Inglese	82	Chiesa di S. Stefano
45	Chiesa della Compagnia di S. Sebastiano	83	La Lizza
		84	Stadio Comunale
46	Chiesa di S. Andrea	85	Chiesa di S. Domenico
47	Fonte Nuova	86	Fontebranda
48	Palazzo Constantini	87	Porta Fontebranda
49	Oratorio di S. M. d. Nevi	88	Ospedale di S. Maria della Scala
50	Palazzo Tantucci		
51	Azienda Aut. Turismo	89	Chiesa di S. Sebastiano in Valle Piatta
52	Palazzo Spannocchi		
53	Palazzo Tolomei	90	Instituto S. Teresa
54	Loggia della Mercanzia	91	Palazzo Pollini
55	Biblioteca Com. Intronati e Museu Archeologico	92	Chiesa di S. Maria del Carmine
		95	Fortezza S. Barbara
56	Portico dei Comuni d'Italia	96	Porta Laterina

Map reproduced from the City Map of Siena, courtesy of Litografia Artistica Cartografica (L.A.C.), Florence.